"Megan DeFranza has done the church a tremendous service in producing this fine contribution on an important but neglected aspect of theological anthropology."

— Roy E. Ciampa
Nida Institute for Biblical Scholarship

"This book will take your breath away. Some will find it jarring, but good theological reflection ought to make us feel uncomfortable. Megan DeFranza takes us on a journey into the complex and sometimes harrowing domain of sexuality and anthropology and how Christians engage sex difference.... Reading DeFranza's book, I was entranced, intrigued, delighted, forced out of my comfort zone, and above all humbled."

— Frank A. James III
Biblical Theological Seminary, Philadelphia

"DeFranza claims it is time for Christians, particularly those from more conservative traditions, to reflect on their theologies and communal practices from the perspective of intersex people, and she is right. The National Institutes of Health and the American Psychological Association have recently modified their treatment protocols in response to the testimony of intersex clients and what we are learning about sex and gender development from neurobiology. Here DeFranza lays the groundwork for similarly transforming our ecclesial institutions, but in a manner that holds fast to Scripture and the good contained in the traditions of the church."

— Teri Merrick
Azusa Pacific University

Sex Difference in Christian Theology

Male, Female, and Intersex in the Image of God

Megan K. DeFranza

William B. Eerdmans Publishing Company
Grand Rapids, Michigan / Cambridge, U.K.

Published 2015 by
Wm. B. Eerdmans Publishing Co.
2140 Oak Industrial Drive N.E., Grand Rapids, Michigan 49505 /
P.O. Box 163, Cambridge CB3 9PU U.K.

Printed in the United States of America

Library of Congress Cataloging-in-Publication Data

DeFranza, Megan K., 1975-
Sex difference in Christian theology: male, female, and intersex in the image of God /
Megan K. DeFranza.
pages cm
Includes bibliographical references.
ISBN 978-0-8028-6982-1 (pbk.: alk. paper)
1. Sex differences — Religious aspects — Christianity. I. Title.

BT708.D457 2015
233′.5 — dc23

2014045539

www.eerdmans.com

To Lianne Simon and all our intersex siblings,
for your generosity, wisdom, and faith
despite exclusion and distrust
in the hope of welcome
and embrace

Contents

Acknowledgments xi

Preface xiii

How I Got Here xiii

Another Conversion xv

Introduction: Male, Female, and Intersex in the Image of God 1

Images of the Image of God 2

Intersex and the Current Culture War 7

Methodology 9

Extant Theological Work on Intersex 10

The Intersexed Have Faces 13

A Preview 17

PART I: MORE THAN TWO: CHALLENGES TO THE BINARY SEX MODEL

1. Intersex: Medical and Sociological Challenges to the Two-Sex Model 23

What Is Intersex? 23

How Many Intersex Persons Are There? 44

History of Intersex: From the Margins to Medicalization 46

What Is in a Name? From Hermaphrodite to Intersex to Disorders of Sex Development (DSDs) 56

From Medical Management to Social Change: Questioning the Binary Sex Model 57

Is Christianity to Blame? 65

2. Biblical Resources beyond Adam and Eve: The Case of Eunuchs 68

Jesus' Eunuchs: Biblical and Historical Context 70

The Transformation of Eunuchs in the History of Interpretation: West and East 84

Intersex as Eunuch: Problems and Possibilities 102

3. How We Got Here: Historical Shifts in Theological Anthropology 107

The Classical Period: Substance Dualism and a Single Sex 108

The Modern Period: Substance and Sex Dualism 125

Postmodern Shifts: From Substance and Sex Dualism to Relational Ontology and the Multiplication of the Sexes 137

PART II: CRITIQUE AND CONSTRUCTION: THEOLOGICAL ANTHROPOLOGY IN THE POSTMODERN PERIOD

4. Sex, Gender, and the Image of God: From Other to Others 153

The Common Witness of Roman Catholic and Evangelical Theologies of the Body 154

Sex Difference in Roman Catholic and Evangelical Theological Anthropologies 158

A Theology of Intersex Bodies: Ontological Sameness and Real Difference 173

From Other to Others: Properly Extending the Evangelical and Roman Catholic Traditions 175

Conclusion 184

5. Sexuality and the Image of God: The Relational Turn 186

The Image of God and Spousal Sexuality in Stanley J. Grenz and John Paul II 187

Uncovering Hidden Dangers 195

Clarifying Conflations 216

Restoring the Social Trinity to the Social Imago 230

Conclusion 237

6. Jesus the True Image: Sex, Gender, and Sexuality in the Postmodern Already/Not Yet 239

Jesus as the True Image: Christological and Eschatological Tensions 239

Christology, Identity, and Imago 273

Conclusion: Male, Female, and Intersex in the Image of God: Theological Anthropology in the Already/Not Yet 285

Bibliography 290

Index of Subjects and Names 309

Acknowledgments

It takes a village to raise a theologian . . . and help her write a book. This book, and my life, testify to the power of communities formed in the image of God.

To my beloved husband, Andrew, for two decades of faithful love, patience, perseverance, help, wisdom, and laughter, without whom I would be a lesser person and none of this would have been possible; to my daughters, Lórien and Eden, for loving me, teaching me, and keeping my feet firmly planted in the real world; to my parents, Jack and Pat Shannon, for giving me life, introducing me to Jesus, and supporting me even when you wondered where these ideas came from and where they were going; to my brother, Mark Shannon, friend and editor extraordinaire; to Rebecca Cheney, my recreational therapist; to Angela McManus, for loving me and my children; to Barbara DeFranza, for moving away from husband and home to care for grandchildren and daughter-in-law, and to Angelo for letting her go; to Edie and Dave, Greg and Christine, Abi and John, Cheryl, Jennifer, Erika, Anita, Kellie and Jeff, and all of 3A — I am who I am because of you; to all who have believed in me, counseled me, cheered me on, prayed for me, been patient with me, forgiven me, and journeyed with me . . .

. . . words cannot express my gratitude and love.

This book began as a dissertation in the Department of Theology at Marquette University and would not have gotten off the ground without the support of that department — especially D. Lyle Dabney, Wanda Zemler-Cizewski, M. Therese Lysaught, Joseph Mueller, Gale Prusinski — as well as mentors from other institutions: Hessell Bouma, Alice Mathews, Roy

Ciampa, Mimi Haddad, Beth Maynard, William and Aída Besançon Spencer. Special thanks (and possible complaints for not redirecting me toward an easier career path) go to Doug Matthews and Tim and Julie Tennent, the first to suggest that graduate school might be in my future.

Theologians never work alone. I am especially grateful to Susannah Cornwall for her generous collaboration, careful scholarship, and editorial genius, as well as for her work with the Lincoln Theological Institute in organizing the first global conference on intersex, theology, and the Bible at Manchester University. A number of my thoughtful colleagues and I were invited to come together there to learn from one another. I am also grateful to Patrick S. Cheng, whose gracious generosity and critically constructive feedback made this a better book and me a better scholar.

Thanks to Wesley Wildman and the Boston University School of Theology and the Institute for the Bio-Cultural Study of Religion for welcoming me as a colleague.

I am particularly indebted to John Franke, friend and mentor. Thank you for believing in me and my work, for opening doors, leading with courage, and living out the postcolonial values you preach . . . and for introducing me to Michael Thomson at Eerdmans.

Thank you, Michael Thomson, for believing in this project. Thank you, Tom Raabe, for making me sound more eloquent than I am. And thanks to Linda Bieze, Mary Hietbrink, Ahna Ziegler, Rachel Bomberger, and others working tirelessly behind the scenes. I am honored to join the Eerdmans community.

Lastly, I would be remiss not to thank those theologians whose work made possible the pages that follow. Charles Colton wisely quipped that "imitation is the sincerest [form] of flattery," but so is critique. For a theological system to warrant careful review and criticism, it must be worthy of the attention. Thank you, Stan Grenz, for lighting my early theological path, modeling a humble and irenic spirit, and showing me how to be a critically loyal evangelical. Thanks also, John Paul II, for bringing Roman Catholics and evangelicals closer together and for allowing me to stand on your shoulders (and pick a little lint out of your mitre).

To the God who made even me in the image of the loving and holy Trinity, who redeemed me from my sin and continues to forgive me for my failings, who perseveres in remaking me in *imago Dei,* conforming me to Christ, reconciling me in the community, and renewing me by the Spirit . . . to this God be glory now and forever, amen.

Preface

For love and sex and faith and fear
All the things that keep us here
In the mysterious distance
Between a man and a woman

From "A Man and a Woman," U2

How do we measure the mysterious distance between a man and a woman? How different *are* men and women, *really*? What about those whose bodies and lives tend to bridge and blur the very distance of difference? How much does it all matter at the end of the day? These are just some of the questions that have dogged me for almost two decades now, despite my many attempts to outrun them.

How I Got Here

Difference certainly mattered in the church of my youth. In the conservative corner of the evangelical Midwest in which I grew up, questions of sex difference were rarely raised but rules of sex difference were regularly enforced. Under our quaint white country steeple, women could sing and serve as Sunday school teachers, but preaching and passing the communion plate were out of the question. Come to think of it, I don't think I ever saw a woman take the offering in all my years there. I didn't care much at the time. Petite, inquisitive, Goody Two-Shoes that I was, I was content to serve as a pillar of the youth group and president of Fellowship of Christian Athletes at my local high school. No one seemed to mind female leadership in those contexts. At least *someone* was bringing prayer into a public school!

Of course, all that changed when I attended a little Christian college in the foothills of the Smoky Mountains. As a female undergraduate student in the Bible and Theology Department, I received mixed messages. My revered (and feared) Greek professor warned that I would be sinning, violating God's instructions in 1 Timothy 2, were I to pursue a career teaching theology at the college level — unless, of course, it was at a girls' school, or a very liberal university. According to his logic, it was better to have a woman teaching orthodox theology at a liberal school than a man teaching heterodoxy. Apparently the best I could hope for was a career of lesser evil. On the other hand, my theology and homiletics professor painted visions of me returning to the college as its first female faculty appointment in the department. With such conflicting messages, I could do little else but apply myself more diligently to my studies of the Bible, biblical languages, theology, philosophy, history, hermeneutics, gender, sex difference, and eventually (unwittingly) sexuality.

First at my evangelical seminary and then in doctoral studies at a Roman Catholic university, I began to study differences in sex and gender — two words often confused in common discussions. I learned that sex difference is rooted in the body — chromosomes, hormone levels, internal and external reproductive organs, as well as secondary sex characteristics (developing with puberty), such as the Adam's apple, skeletal shape, hair growth, voice pitch, etc. On the other hand, gender is influenced by physiology but is lived (some say performed) according to cultural patterns. For instance, while men in the American West and Italy may both cherish manliness, one culture will value the silent Marlboro man who conceals his emotions while the other embraces effusive, passionate conversation — each culture drawing gendered conclusions accordingly. For the record, I married an Italian American, grateful that at least one of us was unafraid to communicate and express emotions! I wanted to get behind the stereotypes to understand what differences *really* exist between men and women and then ask how much these mattered — practically, theologically, personally.

Along the way I discovered transsexuals — persons who feel a sense of disjunction between their bodily sex and their gender identity — and intersex — persons whose bodies do not line up clearly with the medical norms for biological maleness or femaleness (e.g., chromosomes other than XX or XY, ambiguous genitalia, internal reproductive structures of one sex with external sex features of the other sex, just to name a few possibilities). I learned that sex reassignment technologies for transsexual surgeries were first developed to treat intersex persons (including children) and that intersex was much more common than I had imagined (on average 1 in every 2,500-4,500 live births). While I had heard of transsexuality and homosexuality and was being initiated into Christian debates over nature or nurture and how to respond, I had never heard a word about intersex, and found almost no resources from Christians for beginning the conversation.

An*other* Conversion

As a white, middle-class, evangelical, heterosexual, virgin-until-married, cisgender female, I began my exploration, as all of us do, driven by my own questions, my own concerns, my own frustrations — for example, confusion over whether I should accept invitations to preach, frustrations at sometimes being treated as an equal to male colleagues and other times feeling like a second-class citizen in my own church, at my own school. But somewhere along the way, I experienced a conversion of sorts from researching sex and gender so I could understand what they meant for me, and women like me (and the few men who cared), to genuinely caring about other persons in their own right. I discovered that some intersex people ask questions similar to mine, but they also have concerns I had never considered — concerns about medical intervention and legal recognition. In short, I encountered an *other* — one I could not put into a box, one I needed to listen to and learn from. Eventually, as I overcame my own fears and confusion, I was converted.

I became intent on raising awareness about intersex, particularly among conservative Christians (evangelicals, Catholics, Anglicans, and others) who have been so embroiled in debates over sexual ethics that they have ignored and sometimes suppressed information about intersex out of fear that it would undermine what they believe to be God's design for marriage. I wanted to try to quell some of these fears so that Christians were no longer ignorant or afraid of intersex, so that intersex persons didn't have to hide in their own churches, and so all of us could work together to understand ourselves a little better, and begin to navigate the mysterious distance between each and every *other* as we spur one another on toward love and the good (Heb. 10:24).

Two decades later — decades that included my marriage to the best of men and the gift of two daughters, my best educators — I offer this book as a resource for others who contemplate the mysteries of sex and gender difference and their relationship to Christian perspectives on God, self, marriage, sexuality, theology, church, and who folds the laundry.

INTRODUCTION

Male, Female, and Intersex in the Image of God

In the Beginning God created the heavens and the earth. . . .
Then God said, "Let us make human[kind][1] *in our image, according*
to our likeness,
and let them rule over the fish of the sea, and over the birds of the air,
and over the cattle, and over all the wild animals of the earth,
and over every creeping thing that creeps upon the earth."
So God created the human in his image, in the image of God he
created [the human],[2]
male and female he created them.
And God blessed them and said to them,
"Be fruitful and increase in number, fill the earth and subdue it.

1. This passage is my translation. The term that I have translated as "humankind" here is *adam* in the original Hebrew. Where it appears without the article, *adam* can be translated as "human," "man," "a man," or "humankind." I chose the inclusive "humankind" in order to match the plural verb, "let them rule."

2. I have chosen to substitute the noun to which the pronoun is referring in order to avoid the confusion between natural and grammatical gender to which English-language readers are often prone. The Hebrew pronoun here is masculine because it must correspond to the masculine noun *adam.* We know that *adam* is an inclusive noun not only from this passage where it is then described as male and female but also from Gen. 5:2, "God created them male and female, and God blessed them and named them *adam* in the day when they were created" (translation mine). Some translators change the Hebrew singular to an English plural in order to bring out the inclusive: "He created *them.*" I have chosen to retain the singular by substituting the noun to which the pronoun refers. For similar reasons, I should also replace every pronoun for God. However, given the limited acceptance of a common gender-neutral personal pronoun in the communities for whom this book is written, and the focus of this study on anthropology, I'll leave that for another book.

Rule over the fish of the sea and the birds of the air
and over every living creature that moves on the ground."

Genesis 1:1, 26-28

Every Christian account of humanity begins here, in Genesis chapter 1. From this passage we learn that human beings are made in God's image and likeness, that humans were created male and female and given the charge to "fill the earth and subdue it." And yet, the questions, "What is the human?" and "What is the image?" have been answered very differently by theologians throughout history.

Images of the Image of God

For centuries theologians have connected the image of God with "subduing" or "ruling" the earth — what has come to be called the "functional view" of *imago Dei.* Others have searched behind function to substance: identifying rationality as that which made ruling possible, locating reason in the soul. Because the soul was believed to be made out of the same substance as the divine, this came to be known as the "substantive" or "structural view" of the *imago Dei.*[3] It was also believed that the substance or structure of the soul was the seat of other human capacities such as the ability to love or to pursue virtue or holiness — attributes associated with the image of God by different theologians in history.[4] Much less often have theologians linked "filling the earth" or "being fruitful" to the image. Even less often have they considered being created "male" or "female" relevant to the discussion; although a number of them thought males more closely reflected the image of God because they believed males were more rational and therefore more natural, or rightful, rulers.[5] Nevertheless, most theologians separated the image of God from being male or female or from human sexuality and procreation because they believed the testimony of John that "God is spirit" (John 4:24 NRSV). God does not have a body. Even when God did take on a body in

3. Gregory A. Boyd and Paul R. Eddy, *Across the Spectrum: Understanding Issues in Evangelical Theology* (Grand Rapids: Baker Academic, 2002), 76.

4. Stanley J. Grenz, *Theology for the Community of God,* 2nd ed. (Grand Rapids: Eerdmans, 2000), 168.

5. Frederick G. McLeod, S.J., *The Image of God in the Antiochene Tradition* (Washington, D.C.: Catholic University of America Press, 1999), esp. chap. 6, "Are Women Images of God?"

the person of Jesus of Nazareth, God did not engage in sexual activity by marrying or physically fathering children.

Despite historical ambivalence to sex, gender, and sexuality in the Christian tradition, contemporary theologians are beginning to reconsider what connections may exist between human sex, gender, sexuality, and God. Instead of viewing sex and sexuality as ways that humans mirror the animals, or associating sexuality with concupiscence as the primary illustration of sinful (disordered) desires, Christians are exploring the theological significance of bodily sex difference, gendered identity and behavior, and sexual desire and practice. In their attempts to answer these questions, many theologians are returning to the image of God.

Although he was not the first to do so, Karl Barth (1886-1968) is often credited for challenging the traditional interpretations of the *imago Dei.*[6] Rather than understanding the image as the soul's ability to reason, or human responsibility to rule over creation, Barth looked to the creation of Adam and Eve as a symbolic picture, an image of the Trinity. In Genesis 1:26, God said, "Let us make humankind in our image," and then what does God make? Not one but two, a man and a woman, who are to "become one flesh" (Gen. 2:24 NRSV). Just as God is a plurality and unity, three in one, so humankind, created in God's image, exists as two who are called to become one.[7] Thus,

6. Barth pulled together the contributions of Martin Buber, Wilhelm Vischer, Dietrich Bonhoeffer, Emil Brunner, Charlotte von Kirschbaum, and Friedrich Schleiermacher to argue that the way in which humans image God is in their existence as relational beings. Barth wrote, "Could anything be more obvious than to conclude from this clear indication that the image and likeness of being created by God signifies existence in confrontation, i.e., in this confrontation, in the juxtaposition and conjunction of man which is that of male and female . . . ?" Karl Barth, *Church Dogmatics* III/1, trans. J. W. Edwards, O. Bussey, and Harold Knight, ed. G. W. Bromiley and T. F. Torrance (Edinburgh: T. & T. Clark, 1958), 195. Cited in Stanley J. Grenz, *The Social God and the Relational Self: A Trinitarian Theology of the* Imago Dei (Louisville: Westminster John Knox, 2001), 271. Cf. F. LeRon Shults, *Reforming Theological Anthropology: After the Philosophical Turn to Relationality* (Grand Rapids: Eerdmans, 2003), 124; Rosemary Radford Ruether, "*Imago Dei:* Christian Tradition and Feminist Hermeneutics," in *Image of God and Gender Models in Judaeo-Christian Tradition,* ed. Kari Elisabeth Børresen (Oslo: Solum Forlag, 1991); Suzanne Selinger, *Charlotte von Kirschbaum and Karl Barth: A Study in Biography and the History of Theology* (University Park: Pennsylvania State University Press, 1998); Janet Martin Soskice, *The Kindness of God: Metaphor, Gender, and Religious Language* (Oxford: Oxford University Press, 2007), 50.

7. Some theologians have even gone so far as to include procreation as a functional view of the *imago* — procreation as analogous to divine creation of the universe. Grenz cites Henri Blocher and Meredith Kline as representatives of this view in Grenz, *Theology for the Community of God,* 175.

after Barth, we find that human sex difference and human sexuality (the means by which these two become one) are being taken up into theological accounts of what it means to be made in the image of God. This view has come to be labeled the "relational" or "social view" of the *imago Dei.*[8]

The social view of the *imago Dei* has much to recommend it. First and foremost, as Barth pointed out, it provides a more thorough exegesis of the biblical text. While in 1:26 the author of Genesis connects the image to ruling and subduing, in verses 27-28 the image immediately precedes the distinction of humankind as male and female, followed by the commands to increase in number and fill the earth, and subdue the earth. A comprehensive theology of the *imago* should account for all that is within the text.

A second strength of the social view is the full inclusion of women as equal participants in the image of God. Theologians who stress the social view insist that the man as male is not, nor can he be, the complete or perfect image of God to which woman is an afterthought, deviation, or lesser image — interpretations that have long histories in Roman Catholic and Protestant theological traditions. Theologians who attend to the social view of the *imago* insist that male and female must partner, not only in the filling of the earth but also in its rule and care. It is a theological vision arising from and issuing in praxis. The idea that God is a community of love and created humans to image the community of love in (human) sameness and (sex) difference has theological weight as well as practical power to change the ways in which we live in the world.

Lastly, the social view of the *imago Dei,* with its attention to human embodiment and sex difference, is also being connected to human sexuality. Although Barth was careful not to construe the I-Thou relationship between Adam and Eve as sexual, many who have built on his model have extended the social *imago* to include sexual desire and sexual union, as the following chapters will show. Just as contemporary theologians are working to overcome histories of interpretation that have devalued female embodiment, so many theologians are laboring to address centuries of Christian traditions that have devalued sexual bodies, sexual desire, and sexual acts within and outside of marriage. The social view of the *imago* has much to recommend it.

At the same time, the social view need not eclipse other interpretations

8. This position appears under various names: relational, communal, social, etc. Grenz speaks of the "social God" and "relational self" in his theological anthropology by the same title, while in his *Theology for the Community of God* he discusses the social or relational view under the heading "The Divine Image as Special Community" (178). I find that using the term "social" for both Trinity and *imago Dei* clarifies the connection.

of the image of God. Most theologians continue to highlight the significance of human reason and human responsibility to care for creation. Nevertheless, history has taught us that an overemphasis on rationality and rule has been the demise of the West. The rule of reason has been used to oppress and subjugate many who were believed to be less reasonable — women, ethnic minorities, cultural and religious "others." Postmodern thinkers recognize that reason is not enough. Love, community, mutuality, and the goodness of bodies and of sex, gender, and sexuality are goods too often lost when reason and rule are the center of our vision of God and God's image in humanity. The social *imago* has been the means by which theologians are recovering the value of human community, and the value of sex, gender, and sexuality. It has been added to structural and functional views of the *imago,* not to eclipse the former but to present a more complete picture of humanity created in God's image.

While the social view of the image of God has recovered essential components of what it means to be human created in the image of God, it is not without its weaknesses. First and foremost is the omission of anyone who does not fit into the sex/gender binary paradigm of Adam or Eve, male or female — human persons once labeled androgynes or hermaphrodites whom we now call intersex or persons with disorders of sex development.[9] Physicians estimate that 1 in every 2,500-4,500 children is born intersex — a startlingly high number given how little recognition has been given to these persons in contemporary Western society.[10] Indeed, many modern Westerners do not even know what intersex is, much less the statistical probability that they know intersex persons at work, in their families, or within their religious communities.

The rediscovery of intersex in our day is significant for theological reflection on humankind as image of God. John Calvin opened his systematic theology insisting that "true and solid wisdom consists almost entirely of two parts: the knowledge of God and of ourselves. But as these are connected together by many ties, it is not easy to determine which of the two precedes and gives birth to the other."[11] Calvin recognized that theological anthropology and theology proper are mutually conditioning. How we conceive of God affects how we conceive of the human and how we interpret

9. The debates surrounding the naming of intersex will be addressed in chapter 1.

10. Sharon E. Preves, *Intersex and Identity: The Contested Self* (New Brunswick, N.J.: Rutgers University Press, 2003), 3. I. A. Hughes et al., "Consensus Statement on Management of Intersex Disorders," *Archives of Disease in Childhood* 2 (May 4, 2006): 1. See chapter 1 for a more detailed discussion of the frequency of intersex.

11. John Calvin, *Institutes of the Christian Religion* 1.1.1, trans. Henry Beveridge (Grand Rapids: Eerdmans, 1989, 1997), 37.

the image of God. Likewise, how we conceive of humans affects how we conceive of the image of God and also impacts our understanding of God. The challenge for theologians today is that our knowledge of ourselves is changing.[12] The (re)discovery of intersex is one of the ways in which our knowledge of humankind is changing.

Ignorance of intersex may be pardonable. Willful marginalization is not. Changes in contemporary Western society brought on by philosophical and cultural shifts often grouped under the label "postmodern" have made us more aware of and concerned to celebrate the genuine diversity that exists in the human family and extend human rights to all persons. Thus, theological work in the postmodern period is much more attentive to differences of sex, gender, ethnicity, age, class, language, sexuality, and able and disabled bodies. It is within this milieu that intersex is resurfacing into public discourse. Churches and theologians are beginning to ask questions about intersex — questions that have not been asked for centuries by Christians in the West.

Now that theologians are rediscovering that intersex persons have been members of the human family in each generation, it is necessary that we take their humanity seriously, listen to their concerns, respond to their criticisms, and consider what they have to teach us about the ways in which we think about biological sex, gender, and sexuality. This reconsideration necessarily returns us to the image of God.

Mary McClintock Fulkerson reminds us that the image of God is a weighty doctrine because "the image is a symbolic condensation of what in the Christian tradition it means to be fully human. . . . In important respects the *imago Dei* can serve as an index of *whom* the tradition has seen as fully human."[13] Fulkerson recounts the fact that women (and ethnic minorities) have rarely been viewed (or treated) as true images of God, but we must extend the inquiry further. For, if women were not always recognized as fully human or fully created in the image of God (especially under the functional or structural views of the *imago*), how are the intersexed to be included in discussions of the social *imago,* which pays attention to sexed bodies, but only the sexed bodies of males and females? Are the intersexed fully human? Are the intersexed true images of God? Can intersex persons image God if they are unable to embody heterosexual "male-and-female-in-relation,"

12. John R. Franke, *The Character of Theology* (Grand Rapids: Baker Academic, 2005), 14.

13. Mary McClintock Fulkerson, "The *Imago Dei* and a Reformed Logic for Feminist/Womanist Critique," in *Feminist and Womanist Essays in Reformed Dogmatics,* ed. Amy Plantinga Pauw and Serene Jones (Louisville: Westminster John Knox, 2006), 95.

imaging divine relationality through human sexual relations? These are just a few of the questions that intersex raises for Christian theology.

Intersex and the Current Culture War

Already some churches have begun to include intersex as one more color within the rainbow of options that includes persons who identify as lesbian, gay, bisexual, transgender, queer, or questioning (LGBTQI). More conservative Christians, those who hold to heterosexual monogamous ethics, have yet to attend to the challenges intersex persons bring to their theologies and communities. Many are unaware of the phenomena, while others have dismissed intersex because of its association with LGBTQ.[14] As a theologian raised, educated, and teaching in evangelical and Roman Catholic institutions, I am particularly aware of the challenge of addressing intersex within these traditions. At the same time, I am convinced that the gospel calls us to overcome fear and misunderstanding in order to acknowledge the complexity of sex development, to learn from the intersexed, and to recover the good news for the intersexed.

Some theologians have approached their study of intersex looking for help to disrupt the heteronormative binary framework. I came to the study of intersex in hopes of unraveling the theological significance of sex difference as it relates to gender rules, performance, and enculturation. But it is essential to state at the outset that while intersex does contribute to conversations concerning sex, gender, and sexuality, intersex persons and their experiences are significantly diverse so as not to align neatly with one particular party. Some intersex persons live happily within the binary sex/gender framework. Others do not. Some intersex persons want to challenge heteronormative sexual ethics, others do not. Some intersex persons identify with LGBTQ perspectives, others do not.[15] While intersex activists have learned much from LGBT advocacy, they also ask that their concerns not be confused with the former. Emi Koyama and Lisa Weasel explain: "While LGBT communities can certainly provide forums for addressing intersex

14. Cf. Charles Colson, "Blurred Biology: How Many Sexes Are There?" *BreakPoint,* October 16, 1996, http://www.colsoncenter.org/commentaries/5213-blurred-biology.

15. Suzanne Kessler reports that two devout Christians who showed some interest in the Intersex Society of North America stopped participating in online discussions due to conflicting opinions. They were never heard from again. Suzanne J. Kessler, *Lessons from the Intersexed* (New Brunswick, N.J.: Rutgers University Press, 1998), 87.

issues, conflating or collapsing intersexuality into LGBT agendas fails to acknowledge the specific and urgent issues facing intersex people."[16]

The "specific and urgent issues facing intersex people" include education about intersex, legal recognition of intersex, and advocacy for better medical care. Intersex advocates are working to end "shame, secrecy, and unwanted genital surgeries" — challenging medical paternalism that, until recently, kept patients (and sometimes parents) ignorant of their (or their child's) medical conditions and made access to records difficult or impossible. Many intersex advocates are working to influence the medical community as well as parents of the next generation of intersex children to postpone irreversible technological attempts to "correct" intersex (genital surgery and hormone therapies) until children are of the age of consent and pubertal changes (if any) have been allowed to manifest.

As will be discussed in more detail in chapter 1, most intersex surgeries are not medically necessary. Many are performed to help the child appear less ambiguous, in the hope that parents will be better able to bond with their infants if they are not affronted at every diaper change, and so that their children can avoid other potentially difficult societal interactions (e.g., in locker rooms or at urinals). Despite the good intentions of parents and doctors, many intersex persons recount harrowing stories of surgeries gone badly, of sex assignments rejected, and of medical treatment experienced as sexual abuse. These cries are leading to changes in medical standards of treatment. However, when conservative Christians insist that male and female are the only human options, theological weight is cast in favor of (early) medical intervention, and stories of suffering and pleas for better care from the intersexed are ignored. Conservative Christians must give ear to these marginalized voices in our families, communities, and churches. As I will argue, Christian theological anthropologies, even the conservative anthropologies of evangelicals and Roman Catholics, do not necessarily stand in the way of these goals.

I write as a theologian raised, educated, and teaching in the evangelical world, having completed doctoral studies at a Roman Catholic university, and worshiping in the halfway house between these two, more commonly known as the Anglican/Episcopal Communion. These are the traditions that have formed my life of faith and within which I wish to speak as we continue

16. Emi Koyama and Lisa Weasel, "From Social Construction to Social Justice: Transforming How We Teach about Intersexuality," in *Teaching Intersex Issues: A Guide for Teachers in Women's, Gender, and Queer Studies,* ed. Emi Koyama, 2nd ed. (Portland, Ore.: Intersex Initiative Portland, 2003), 5.

to wrestle with the theological significance of sex, gender, and sexuality in the postmodern context. I do not presume to offer a universal theological anthropology in the modernist sense. Rather, as a postmodern theologian who recognizes the situatedness of all interpretation, I offer my arguments as one voice in the ongoing conversation on the meaning of sex, gender, and sexuality for theological anthropology in the postmodern context.

Many evangelicals, conservative Anglicans, and Roman Catholics continue to defend traditional Christian (hetero)sexual ethics, even in the face of serious cultural and theological challenges. But in holding to the significance of sex complementarity for marriage (one man and one woman), theologians within these traditions have, at times, overemphasized the significance of sex "difference," using sex complementarity to justify theological notions of gender complementarity (e.g., the church as the bride of Christ). In their attempts to provide theological justification for heterosexual ethics, some have turned a blind eye to the presence of intersexed persons in the Scriptures, in Christian history, and among us today, while others have argued that intersex can and should be fixed through medical technology in order to approximate what they believe to be "creational givens."

It is my hope that by (re)educating ourselves on the phenomena of intersex we will be better able to read the Scriptures afresh, recover the full humanity of intersex persons and their place in the community of faith, and attend to the lessons they can teach us about the complexity of sex difference so that we can advance our exploration of the theological significance of sex, gender, and sexuality. Intersex raises questions for theologians on two fronts: (1) What are the implications of Christian theology for understanding, care, and ministry to/with/by the intersexed? (2) What are the implications of intersex for theological anthropologies built upon a binary model of human sex differentiation? In this book I begin to address the latter set of questions in the hopes that they will remove theological stumbling blocks to the former.

Methodology

Given that a growing number of works have already been written by intersex persons themselves[17] or have been drawn from interviews with intersex per-

17. E.g., Kailana Sidrandi Alaniz, Cheryl Chase [Bo Laurent], Sally Gross, Thea Hillman, Morgan Holmes, Emi Koyama, Jane Spalding, Lisa Weasel.

sons by the nonintersexed,[18] this work was accomplished through text-based research of available materials. At the same time, as I was working on this project, I was privileged to talk with several persons with intersex conditions, who were willing to identify themselves and discuss their experiences with me. I thank them for their courage, trust, and contributions to my own thinking.

Extant Theological Work on Intersex

Medical, historical, anthropological, legal, and sociological works on intersex are becoming increasingly available.[19] Only a few theological explorations have been proffered, most of modest length.

Independent scholar J. David Hester begins his study of intersex by connecting it to the ancient category of the eunuch and moving from the gender transgression of eunuchs to advocating "transgressive sexualities."[20] Ordained in the United Church of Christ and now serving on the faculty at the Pacific School of Religion, Karen Lebacqz works from an ethic of the alleviation of suffering but does not engage with Scripture.[21] Virginia Ramey Mollenkott identifies herself as a former fundamentalist who continues to identify as evangelical in her approach to the Bible but left the evangelical subculture when she came out as a lesbian in the 1970s.[22] Her work *Omnigender: A Trans-religious Approach*[23] focuses on the experiences of trans-

18. E.g., Gerald N. Callahan, Alice Domurat Dreger, John Money, Sharon E. Preves, Elizabeth Reis.

19. These have been written by, e.g., Accord Alliance, Alice Domurat Dreger, Julia Epstein, Anne Fausto-Sterling, Julie A. Greenberg, Gilbert Herdt, Melissa Hines, Ieuan Hughes et al., Intersex Society of North America, Intersex Support Group International, Katrina Karkazis, Suzanne Kessler, Thomas Laqueur, Wendy McKenna, Sharon E. Preves, Elizabeth Reis, Leonard Sax, Sharon E. Sytsma, Claudia Wiesemann et al., Andrew Zinn, Kenneth J. Zucker.

20. J. David Hester, "Eunuchs and the Postgender Jesus: Matthew 19.12 and Transgressive Sexualities," *Journal for the Study of the New Testament* 28, no. 1 (2005): 13-40; and "Intersexes and the End of Gender: Corporeal Ethics and Postgender Bodies," *Journal of Gender Studies* 13, no. 3 (November 2004): 215-25.

21. Karen Lebacqz, "Difference or Defect? Intersexuality and the Politics of Difference," *Annual for the Society of Christian Ethics* 17 (1997): 213-29.

22. Virginia Ramey Mollenkott and Richard Mouw, with Krista Tippett, "Gay Marriage: Broken or Blessed? Two Evangelical Views," on *Speaking of Faith,* August 3, 2006, http://being.publicradio.org/programs/gaymarriage/index.shtml.

23. Virginia Ramey Mollenkott, *Omnigender: A Trans-religious Approach* (Cleveland: Pilgrim Press, 2001).

gender, to which she believes intersex is related, as a biological justification for disrupting the binary sex/gender system. Oliver O'Donovan (ordained as a priest in the Church of England, currently teaching at the University of Edinburgh) looks upon intersex through the lens of transsexualism as an exception to the dimorphic norm and suggests a pastoral approach aimed at the alleviation of suffering.[24]

Susannah Cornwall, an Anglican, offers the most helpful and comprehensive theological explorations of intersex to date, evaluating the contributions of many of the above authors and comparing/contrasting intersex to transgender, disability, and queer theologies.[25] These writers attend to "the specific and urgent issues facing intersex people" at the same time that they move away from traditional heterosexual ethics in the direction of queer theology/sexuality.[26] It is the dearth of substantial reflection from evangelicals and Roman Catholics that motivated the present study.

A few evangelicals have written briefly on the phenomena of intersex. Chuck Colson's treatment in "Blurred Biology: How Many Sexes Are There?" represents the knee-jerk evangelical response that views intersex as a product of the Fall — punishment for the original sin of Adam and Eve. "The Bible teaches that the Fall into sin affected biology itself — that nature is now marred and distorted from its original perfection. This truth gives us a basis for fighting evil, for working to alleviate disease and deformity — including helping those unfortunate children born with genital deformities."[27] Colson's theological conviction that intersex is a product of the Fall leads directly to an

24. Oliver O'Donovan, "Transsexualism and Christian Marriage," *Journal of Religious Ethics* 11 (Spring 1983): 143.

25. Susannah Cornwall, "British Intersex Christians' Accounts of Intersex Identity, Christian Identity and Church Experience," *Practical Theology* 6, no. 2 (2013): 220-36; "The Kenosis of Unambiguous Sex in the Body of Christ: Intersex, Theology, and Existing 'for the Other,'" *Theology and Sexuality* 14, no. 2 (January 2008): 181-200; "No Longer Male and Female: The Challenge of Intersex Conditions for Theology" (Ph.D. diss., University of Exeter, 2007); "Running to Catch Up with Intersex," *Church Times* 7644 (September 18, 2009): 13; "'State of Mind' versus 'Concrete Set of Facts': The Contrasting of Transgender and Intersex in Church Documents on Sexuality," *Theology and Sexuality* 15, no. 1 (2009): 7-28; *Sex and Uncertainty in the Body of Christ: Intersex Conditions and Christian Theology* (London and Oakville, Conn.: Equinox, 2010); ed., *Intersex, Theology, and the Bible: Troubling Bodies in Church, Text, and Society* (New York: Palgrave Macmillan, 2015).

26. See Elisabeth Stuart, ed., *Religion Is a Queer Thing: A Guide to the Christian Faith for Lesbian, Gay, Bisexual, and Transgendered People* (London and Washington, D.C.: Cassell, 1997), and Patrick S. Cheng, *Radical Love: An Introduction to Queer Theology* (New York: Seabury Books, 2011), for an introduction to queer theology.

27. Colson, "Blurred Biology."

argument for medical intervention — a logical move paralleled in evangelical ethicist Dennis Hollinger's *Meaning of Sex: Christian Ethics and the Moral Life.*[28] Colson's dismissal of intersex seems motivated by his fear of what he calls "the homosexual lobby."[29] He does not attend to intersex in its own right.

Other evangelicals have provided more helpful treatments. Amanda Riley Smith opens the door to the possibility of welcoming the intersexed *as* intersexed in her article "What Child Is This? Making Room for Intersexuality."[30] Heather Looy and Hessel Bouma III, psychologist and biologist respectively, argue for the consideration of the full humanity of intersex, their inclusion in the community of faith, and better medical, psychological, and pastoral care.[31] Their articles begin to wrestle with the theological issues attending intersex, but they write to ask theologians to contribute to the task. They confess, "We must acknowledge that our expertise is as a psychologist and biologist, drawing on science and experience. Our search of the theological literature to understand creation norms for human sexuality and gender has uncovered little in-depth or well-developed material. It is our hope that this article may stimulate conversations and promote the theological scholarship needed to help address these issues further."[32]

Fewer than a handful of Roman Catholics have written on intersex. Patricia Beattie Jung of Loyola University Chicago evaluates Scripture and tradition to argue that biblical texts do not require sexual dimorphism, thus the tradition need not continue to defend it.[33] Christine Gudorf of Florida International University argues similarly, that traditional interpretations of sacred

28. Dennis P. Hollinger, *The Meaning of Sex: Christian Ethics and the Moral Life* (Grand Rapids: Baker Academic, 2009), 74, 84.

29. Colson, "Blurred Biology."

30. Amanda Riley Smith, "What Child Is This? Making Room for Intersexuality," *Regeneration Quarterly* 8, no. 2 (Winter 2002): 27-30.

31. Heather Looy, "Male and Female God Created Them: The Challenge of Intersexuality," *Journal of Psychology and Christianity* 21 (2002): 10-20; Heather Looy, "Sex Differences: Evolved, Constructed and Designed," *Journal of Psychology and Theology* 29, no. 4 (Winter 2001): 301-13; and Heather Looy and Hessel Bouma III, "The Nature of Gender: Gender Identity in Persons Who Are Intersexed or Transgendered," *Journal of Psychology and Theology* 33, no. 3 (2005): 166-78.

32. Looy and Bouma, "The Nature of Gender," 176.

33. "In fact, [the creation accounts in Genesis] can be shown to be congruent with sexual polymorphism, just as the scriptures are now readily seen to be compatible with a number of scientific concepts, such as the notions of a heliocentric solar system, polygenism and the ongoing, evolutionary development of the universe, etc." Sharon E. Sytsma, introduction to *Ethics and Intersex,* ed. Sharon E. Sytsma (Dordrecht: Springer, 2006), xxv. Sytsma is writing in summary of Jung's contribution to the volume.

texts cannot stand up to scientific recognition of polymorphous sexuality, thus Christians, Jews, and Muslims should "resist defining sexuality," "decenter sexuality," and focus on "lifelong, age-appropriate sexual education" that includes "access to supportive information about sexual orientation, its varieties and development."[34] She connects the realities of intersex to the undoing of the dimorphous model that undergirds gendered constructions of virtue (men as gracious leaders, women as submissive followers), sex roles (the education and ordination of women), and sexual ethics. Her conclusion is worth quoting at length for it illustrates the potential future conservatives fear and the reason they believe so much is at stake.

> It is difficult to avoid the conclusion that the multiplication in sexual possibilities in the shift from dimorphous to polymorphous sexuality, combined with decreased conceptual clarity about sexuality, will continue to encourage a greater reliance on experience and experimentation. For example, open polymorphous sexuality makes us question whether perhaps human sexual identity is a never settled question, task, option. Is the future to be filled with parents and grandparents, as well as children and young adults, who change their genitalia, their sexual roles, or their sexual orientation as frequently as people today change their clothing or hair color? Regardless of how much religious communities are troubled by such a turn, if they are to have a chance at preventing it, they must offer an alternative means for interpreting and coping with the complexities of polymorphous sexuality and not merely close their eyes to the reality of the shift from dimorphism to polymorphism.[35]

Her analysis may provide some of the reasons why the Roman Catholic Church reacted so strongly to one particular intersex person within its own ranks.

The Intersexed Have Faces

One of the most interesting theological perspectives on our topic comes from an intersex person and former Dominican priest.[36] The story of Sel-

34. Christine E. Gudorf, "The Erosion of Sexual Dimorphism: Challenges to Religion and Religious Ethics," *Journal of the American Academy of Religion* 69, no. 4 (December 2001): 885-86.

35. Gudorf, "Erosion of Sexual Dimorphism," 887.

36. Sally Gross, "Intersexuality and Scripture," *Theology and Sexuality* 11 (1999): 65-74.

wyn/Sally Gross is worth recounting at length for it places the theological arguments made by Gross, myself, and others in their proper context — the lives of real people.

Gross was born in South Africa to Jewish parents in August 1953. The birth heralded not joy but distress as the mother was told that her infant "was likely to die of dehydration." Looking back on the moment, Sally considers, "Now a new born infant doesn't die of dehydration unless you don't feed it. . . . My suspicion is that back then in 1953 the reaction was: 'Oh my God! What do we do, let's let nature take its course.' But then someone relented."[37]

Although born intersexed with ambiguous genitals, Gross was given the sex assignment of male and named Selwyn.[38] Selwyn knew that he was different, especially when he hit puberty and his sexual drive never developed. Gross simply assumed that he was "one of nature's celibates," but he found little room for celibacy within Judaism where "[o]ne is expected to produce grandchildren."[39] Although a committed Orthodox Jew, Gross began to look elsewhere to make sense of his experiences. "I did not believe at the time that Orthodox Judaism had religious symbols which could make sense of the way in which I was different, whatever it was." The place that Roman Catholicism carved out for celibates led him to consider Christianity. "The image of the Cross seemed to be an icon of all manner of confusion and suffering. The Holocaust was there, the horror of apartheid was there, and my own personal confusion and pain — which I could never publicly admit — was there as well. And in the resurrection was a symbol that this was transcended. And at the back of my mind, there would have been an awareness that in Christianity there are strands of tradition in which celibacy is valued and turned to positive use."

Selwyn was baptized in 1976. After working against apartheid in South Africa and engaging in political activism in Israel for several years, he moved to Oxford in 1981 and was accepted as a novitiate in the Dominican Order. Selwyn was ordained to the priesthood in 1987, whereupon he taught moral

37. Sally Gross, "The Journey from Selwyn to Sally," *The Natal Witness Features* (South Africa), February 21, 2000, http://www.intersex.org.za/publications/witness1.pdf. In fact, the intersex condition congenital adrenal hyperplasia (CAH) does bring the risk of dehydration to newborns (see chap. 1). But as Gross does not name her intersex condition, it is not clear whether this diagnosis applies to her case. See p. 31.

38. Intersex Society of South Africa, "Biographies: Sally Gross," http://www.intersex.org/za/biography.html.

39. Gross, "The Journey from Selwyn to Sally." The information, including quotations, in the remainder of this paragraph and the next two is from this article.

theology, ethics, and philosophy at Blackfriars, Oxford, and other Oxford University colleges. Later he became subprior at the priory at Cambridge.

In the early 1990s Selwyn was invited by the Dominicans to return to South Africa to teach. The struggle against apartheid, in which Gross had been deeply involved, had been won. Looking back, Sally reflects that there was finally space to consider the tensions in her own life. " 'There were two areas of tension: there was the issue of my Jewish/Christian identity and the issue of bodiliness and gender, although I thought that was secondary. . . . At that stage I rather naively thought I'd see someone with some expertise in this area and after a couple of sessions I could get on with the rest of my priestly life, full stop.' Gross laughs. 'It wasn't as simple as that.' "

Selwyn's counselor was more experienced with transsexuality than with intersex, but the counselor still encouraged Gross to submit to medical testing. "These tests showed that Gross's testosterone levels were in the middle of the normal female range and less than an eighth of the bottom of the male range. 'The counselor was absolutely spot on but nevertheless sought to regiment this in terms of transsexuality and a change of gender.' "[40]

Gross was granted a one-year leave from the Dominicans to explore the possibility of a gender change but was forbidden to contact fellow brothers, parents, and most friends, and "denied moral and material support as a matter of principle." However, one senior Dominican priest encouraged Gross to look upon this exploration as "something which was priestly — maybe that in my bodiliness, God was working out a preaching of that passage in Paul: 'In Christ there is neither Jew nor Gentile, slave nor free, male nor female.' But all of them, all assimilated here." Unfortunately, this latter view was not taken up by her religious superiors. When they learned of the congenital nature of Gross's condition — indicating the possibility of being raised as female instead of as male — she was greeted with suspicion, as a threat that needed to be removed.

> [A] Papal Rescript stripped Gross of clerical status and annulled her religious vows, [but] not without an element of subterfuge. Rumors had been circulating in Catholic circles that Gross had reverted to ultra-orthodox Judaism. This seemed to suggest that a dismissal was being prepared on the grounds that she had "notoriously defected from the faith" — a cause

40. Sally Gross, "Shunned by the Church," *The Natal Witness Features* (South Africa), February 22, 2000, http://www.intersex.org.za/images/articles/witness2.pdf. The information in the following paragraph comes from this article.

> for immediate dismissal and excommunication without right of appeal. Gross pre-empted such a hostile dismissal on such false grounds by agreeing to co-operate in a laicisation process. . . . Gross was laicised on the basis of a notional petition for dispensation from priestly celibacy but celibacy had never been the issue. "I am one of nature's celibates. It was not my petition, it was contrary to what I had said."
>
> Even with lay status, further prohibitions were placed on Gross, although without any canonical justification. "They effectively made it impossible for me to remain in communion."

Gross had hoped to remain not only within the Catholic Church but also within her religious community, since in the Dominican Order "there are congregations of women and some mixed communities as well. Had there been a willingness to find a way of accommodating my religious vocation, a way could have been found without too great a difficulty, although it would have taken a lot of courage."

Employing her Jewish and Christian education, Gross responds to the assertion, "put to me by a conspicuously pious, intelligent, theologically sophisticated but fundamentalistic Christian of my acquaintance," that, on the basis of Genesis 1:27, "an intersexed person such as me does not satisfy the biblical criterion of humanity, and indeed even that it follows that I am congenitally unbaptizable."[41] She finds this "rather comical" given that the rabbinical tradition suggests that the original human may have been a hermaphrodite before God removed the woman from the side of the man (70). She also notes traditions that state that Abraham and Sarah were each intersexed (71-73). Although Gross admits that the commentaries on Abraham and Sarah, "like many rabbinical exegetical glosses of an anecdotal rather than legal character, are perhaps a trifle far-fetched and quaint," nevertheless, "They do make it abundantly clear that those who, more than any others, cherished and preserved the Hebrew text of Scripture and sought faithfully to ensure that no scriptural 'jot and tittle' was changed, did not see intersex conditions as falling under the condemnation of the canon of Hebrew Scripture. Quite the contrary, they contemplated with equanimity the possibility that leading and revered scriptural characters were intersexed" (73).

Given the possibility of defending hermaphroditism/intersex from the Scriptures, and the additional prohibition of the removal of gonads (when

41. Gross, "Intersexuality and Scripture," 70. Page numbers to this work have been placed in the following text.

they do not constitute a health risk) suggested by Deuteronomy 23:1, Gross concludes, "[b]iblical literalists are indeed arguably bound by Scripture to respect the sense of many people who are intersexed that violence was done to them in infancy by the imposition of what was in effect cosmetic surgery, and to accept that it is right and proper that those who are born intersexed be enabled to remain physically as they are and to identify as intersexed" (74). Elsewhere she testifies, "I am a creature of God, and . . . I'm created, and intersexed people are created, no less than anyone else, in the image and likeness of God."[42]

A Preview

I offer the following pages as a means to help Roman Catholics, evangelicals, and other conservative Christians begin to open up space for the intersexed among us who are, truly, created in the image of God, so that together we may all become more fully human. We must respond to Gudorf's challenge and "offer an alternative means for interpreting and coping with the complexities of polymorphous sexuality and not merely close [our] eyes."[43] To do this, I will present several challenges to the binary sex model in part I, arguing that Christian theological anthropology can no longer assume that all humans fit into the category of either "Adam" or "Eve."

Chapter 1 will explain the phenomena of intersex and the medical and sociological challenges intersex brings to the idea that humans exist, or should exist, only as male or female. I will document the growing evidence that medical technology cannot "fix" all intersex conditions and that some persons are justified in their desire to be recognized as intersex, rather than as male or female, and should be granted the right to such recognition, outside and inside the church.

Chapter 2 will detail the existence of intersex persons in history, especially as recorded in the Bible and Christian history. The Christian tradition has more to offer than simplistic appeals to Adam and Eve. The ancients had many names for intersex — hermaphrodites, androgynes, barren women, and eunuchs. I will show how Jesus' recognition of those who are eunuchs from birth in Matthew 19:12 changed the course of intersex and discussions

42. Sally Gross, speaking in J. Wentzel van Huyssteen, *The Third Sex,* broadcast SABC (South Africa), November 2003; cited in Cornwall, *Sex and Uncertainty,* 1.

43. Gudorf, "Erosion of Sexual Dimorphism," 887.

of the theological significance of sex, gender, and sexuality in ways that have been lost to contemporary students of the Bible.

Chapter 3 will review the history of theological anthropology, paying close attention to how answers to the questions "What is the human?" and "What is the image?" relate to biological sex differentiation. I will recount how different historical figures have wrestled with how many sexes *are* or *should be* recognized by society as well as how theologians have thought about the sexes as equally human and, thus, as equally valid images of God. To do this, I will trace the development of Western theology in three movements: from its inception in the classical period, through the Protestant and Victorian Reformations in the modern period, into current, postmodern reconstructions of the human and the *imago Dei.*[44]

Part I establishes medical, sociological, biblical, historical, and philosophical challenges to the binary sex model. Part II of the book will explore how we must reconstruct theological anthropology today as it relates to sex, gender, and sexuality. I focus in particular on evangelical and Roman Catholic theological anthropologies, for these are some of the most vocal conservative voices in contemporary discussions of sexuality in the American context. These will be brought into conversation with other conservatives, and with liberal and queer theological traditions.

Chapter 4 will analyze how sex and gender have been treated in evangelical and Roman Catholic theological literature and argue that these traditions must move from thinking about women as the paradigmatic "other" to the recognition of other "others."

Chapter 5 will show how the binary sex model has been used to read sexuality into certain visions of the *imago Dei* such that the social *imago* is being transformed into the sexual/spousal *imago.* I will illustrate the dangers of these trajectories for both evangelical and Roman Catholic anthropologies, and will suggest alternative readings of the creation narratives in Genesis and a return to the social *imago* as a way to avoid the sexualization of the *imago Dei.*

Chapter 6 will conclude this project by exploring the tensions that Christology and eschatology bring to discussions of sex, gender, and sexuality. I will argue that, rather than dismantling the categories of male and

44. I am a theologian writing in the United States of America, and thus recount the history of Western Christianity. It is my hope that my Western reflection will join in conversation with other non-Western voices as we work to learn from and care for those in our respective contexts.

female, space can and should be opened up for the addition and inclusion of intersex, whose humanity was also taken up by Jesus Christ in the incarnation. I will conclude by suggesting that Christology does not lead to the erasure of sex/gender identities "in Christ" even while it does call for a decentering of personal identity, which makes space for the healing of the self and reconciliation in the community of God. Thus do we begin to explore mysteries of sex difference in Christian theology — male, female, intersex in the image of God.

PART I

More Than Two: Challenges to the Binary Sex Model

CHAPTER 1

Intersex: Medical and Sociological Challenges to the Two-Sex Model

I begin this chapter by exploring contemporary medical descriptions of intersex. I will trace the history of intersex from the time before medical technology — when intersex existed at the margins of society — to the virtual erasure of intersex by the medical establishment. We will then hear objections to the medicalization of intersex, paying particular attention to the voices of intersex persons themselves. Lastly, we will hear from those who lay the blame for the abuse of the intersexed at the feet of the two-sex model and ask whether Christianity is to blame for the binary.

What Is Intersex?

Typical Sex Development

"Intersex" is a term used to describe persons who do not fit into standard medical descriptions of male or female. It is important at the outset to establish what is considered normal or typical by the medical community so that variations from the norm can be understood. In this book "normal" is employed according to the classical sense of "norm," "standard," or "type." Thus, "abnormal" does not indicate "freakishness" but atypical development.

Brown University biologist Anne Fausto-Sterling describes what is considered "typical" or "normal" by medical practitioners today:

> We define the typical male as someone with an XY chromosomal composition, and testes located within the scrotal sac. The testes produce sperm which, via the vas deferens, may be transported to the urethra and

ejaculated outside the body. Penis length at birth ranges from 2.5 to 4.5 cm; an idealized penis has a completely enclosed urethra which opens at the tip of the glans. During fetal development, the testes produce the Müllerian inhibiting factor, testosterone, and dihydrotestosterone, which juvenile testicular activity ensures a masculinizing puberty. The typical female has two X chromosomes, functional ovaries which ensure a feminizing puberty, oviducts connecting to a uterus, cervix and vaginal canal, inner and outer vaginal lips, and a clitoris, which at birth ranges in size from 0.20 to 0.85 cm.[1]

Intersex as an Umbrella Concept

The term "intersex" is not a diagnosis but an umbrella concept used to cover a wide range of variations in sex development. Many intersex conditions result in ambiguous genitalia, either at birth or throughout the life course of the individual; however, not all intersex conditions are indicated by genital inspection. The Consortium on the Management of Disorders of Sex Development lists the following as intersex-related conditions: "congenital development of ambiguous genitalia, congenital disjunction of internal and external sex anatomy, incomplete development of sex anatomy, sex chromosome anomalies and disorders of gonadal development."[2] Each of these will be described in what follows.

"Intersex is not a discrete or natural category."[3] While most people believe they know what makes a person male or female — chromosomes, gonads, genitals, secondary sex characteristics — it is not clear what type and how many variations to these norms it takes to classify a person as intersex. Should a person with external female genitalia who has XY chromosomes

1. Melanie Blackless et al., "How Sexually Dimorphic Are We? Review and Synthesis," *American Journal of Human Biology* 12 (2000): 152. Although this article is cited as Blackless et al., Fausto-Sterling explains in her larger work (*Sexing the Body: Gender Politics and the Construction of Sexuality* [New York: Basic Books, 2000], 51) that she researched the literature "together with a group of Brown University undergraduates." Given this admission, and so that the reader can more easily connect the threads of her arguments, I will list Fausto-Sterling as the author in my text.

2. Consortium on the Management of Disorders of Sex Development, *Clinical Guidelines for the Management of Disorders of Sex Development in Childhood* (Rohnert Park, Calif.: Intersex Society of North America, 2006), 2.

3. Intersex Society of North America (hereafter ISNA), "What Is Intersex?" http://www.isna.org/faq/printable, 1.

and testes be considered male, female, or intersex? How large does a clitoris need to be before it is considered a micropenis? These decisions are made by humans, typically by doctors. What doctors believe about physical norms and variations, the usefulness of the intersex designation, and gender value all factor into decisions about sex assignment. These beliefs also contribute to debates over which conditions "count" for estimates of frequency rates.

It will be helpful for the reader to become familiar with certain intersex conditions before entering the debate over which variations "count." An exhaustive list of intersex conditions is not possible or necessary here. Instead, I will describe some of the more common variations and their implications for what follows.

Types of Intersex Conditions

Androgen Insensitivity Syndrome (AIS) AIS is an intersex condition that occurs roughly once in every 13,000 births.[4] Androgen insensitivity comes in two types: complete (CAIS) and partial (PAIS). Persons with AIS are born with XY chromosomes (i.e., as in a typical male). XY chromosomes set into motion the normal development of testes, which begin to secrete higher levels of testosterone in XY individuals as early as the eighth week of gestation.[5] But people with AIS are unable to process male hormones (androgens). Because their cells lack the proper receptors, persons with CAIS develop female external genitals. They retain undescended or partially descended testes. They usually have a short vagina and no cervix, though some lack a vagina altogether. Because genitals appear normal (for females) at birth, CAIS is not usually discovered until puberty when menstruation does not occur.

Given this description of androgen insensitivity, the reader may not find it surprising that these "girls" do not menstruate. What is surprising, however, is that these individuals do develop secondary sex characteristics typical of pubescent females. The Intersex Society of North America (ISNA) explains how feminizing puberty is possible. "At puberty, the testes are stimulated by the pituitary gland, and produce testosterone. Because testoster-

4. ISNA, "How Common Is Intersex?" http://www.isna.org/faq/frequency, 1. Blackless et al., "How Sexually Dimorphic Are We?" list the frequency as .076/1,000 on p. 153. This translates as 1:13,153 (according to my calculations), which the ISNA has rounded to 1:13,000. I prefer to cite frequency rates as "1 person per" so that one does not need to think of percentages of persons.

5. Melissa Hines, *Brain Gender* (Oxford: Oxford University Press, 2004), 23.

one is chemically very similar to estrogen, some of the testosterone converts back to estrogen ('aromatizes') in the bloodstream. This estrogen produces breast growth, though it may be late."[6] Thus, higher levels of testosterone during puberty result not in the typical masculinization of those with androgen receptivity (i.e., growth of underarm and pubic hair, Adam's apple, voice descent, increased muscle mass); rather, higher levels of testosterone have the opposite effect — increased feminization of XY individuals. CAIS has been called "classical testicular feminization" in recognition of this process. It has also been labeled "male pseudohermaphroditism."

The designation "male pseudohermaphroditism" gained parlance in the Victorian era. During the nineteenth century, doctors looked to gonads to determine sex assignment when genitals were "unclear" or, in CAIS individuals, when normal sex development — such as menstruation — did not occur.[7] Gonads were seen as primary for two reasons. First, reproduction was viewed as the principal marker for sex identification. Second, scientific knowledge of gonadal hormone production and gonadal influence on sex development was growing. Within the Victorian schema, the CAIS patient, with male gonads and female genitalia, would be considered a "male" on account of "his" testes, but a "pseudohermaphrodite" on account of "her" genitals and secondary sex traits. On the flip side, a person with male external genitals and ovaries would have been labeled a "female pseudohermaphrodite." The only persons labeled "true hermaphrodites" were those who possessed both an ovary and a testis, a rare condition now called "ovo-testes."[8] More recent scholars reject the term "pseudohermaphrodite" because it is considered offensive, confusing, and imprecise.[9]

While in the Victorian era persons with AIS would have been consid-

6. ISNA, "Androgen Insensitivity Syndrome (AIS)," http://www.isna.org/faq/printable, 3-4.

7. "Sex assignment" is the phrase used to denote what sex the child is labeled at birth, that is, what is recorded on the birth certificate. Sex assignment is irreversible in some societies.

8. Alice Domurat Dreger, "Doubtful Sex: The Fate of the Hermaphrodite in Victorian Medicine," *Victorian Studies* (Spring 1995): 335-70. See also Anne Fausto-Sterling, "The Five Sexes: Why Male and Female Are Not Enough," *Sciences,* March/April 1993, 20-24; reprinted in *Sexuality and Gender,* ed. Christine L. Williams and Arlene Stein (Malden, Mass.: Blackwell, 2002), 468-73.

9. Alice D. Dreger et al., "Changing the Nomenclature/Taxonomy for Intersex: A Scientific and Clinical Rationale," *Journal of Pediatric Endocrinology and Metabolism* 18, no. 8 (2005): 729-33. See also Consortium, *Clinical Guidelines,* 16. The ISNA explains that the term "hermaphrodite" is a "mythological term" implying "that a person is both fully male

ered "men" by the medical establishment, today these individuals are overwhelmingly declared to be women. They look like girls at birth. They look like women after puberty. Paradoxically, CAIS women develop along the lines of the contemporary, Western ideal of womanhood: they are tall and lean, with little to no body hair.[10] Additionally, these individuals typically have unquestioned female gender identities and roles until confronted with their diagnosis, either at puberty or as adults.[11]

Partial androgen insensitivity is less common than the complete form, occurring approximately in only 1 in 130,000 births.[12] Whereas individuals with CAIS appear "unambiguously" female, persons with partial androgen insensitivity syndrome (PAIS) have bodies that fall anywhere along the spectrum. Charmian Quigley and Frank French, doctors at the Laboratories for Reproductive Biology, University of North Carolina at Chapel Hill, "proposed a grading system for the phenotypic features (external appearance) in AIS. The scale runs from AIS Grade 1 to Grade 7 with increasing severity of androgen resistance — and hence decreasing masculinization with increasing feminization."[13] The following chart and explanatory paragraph may be found at www.AISSG.org, the Web site of one of the largest and most trusted support groups for persons with AIS:

Grade 1	PAIS	Male genitals, infertility
Grade 2	PAIS	Male genitals but mildly "undermasculinized," isolated hypospadias[14]

and fully female. This is a physiologic impossibility." ISNA, "Is a Person Who Is Intersex a Hermaphrodite?" http://www.isna.org/faq/printable, 16.

10. Sharon E. Preves, *Intersex and Identity: The Contested Self* (New Brunswick, N.J.: Rutgers University Press, 2003), 28.

11. Hines, *Brain Gender*, 32. See also the Androgen Insensitivity Syndrome Support Group (AISSG), UK, "Terminology Problems," http://www.aissg.org/21_OVERVIEW.HTM.

12. ISNA, "How Common Is Intersex?" 1. Blackless et al., "How Sexually Dimorphic Are We?" list the frequency as .0076/1,000 on p. 153. This translates as 1:131,530 (according to my calculations), which the ISNA has rounded to 1:130,000.

13. Androgen Insensitivity Syndrome Support Group (AISSG), UK, "What Is AIS? Forms of AIS (Complete and Partial)," http://www.aissg.org/21_OVERVIEW.HTM. Charmian A. Quigley et al., "Androgen Receptor Defects: Historical, Clinical and Molecular Perspectives," *Endocrine Reviews* 16, no. 3 (June 1995): 271-321; see p. 281 for chart and explanations. The scale is modeled on the Prader classification for congenital adrenal hyperplasia (CAH).

14. Hypospadias is a condition of the penis where the urinary opening (meatus) is located off-center on the glans (mild), along the penile shaft (medium), or under the pe-

Grade 3	PAIS	Predominantly male genitals but more severely "undermasculinized" (perineal hypospadias; small penis; cryptorchidism, i.e., undescended testes; and/or bifid scrotum)
Grade 4	PAIS	Ambiguous genitals, severely "undermasculinized" (phallic structure that is indeterminate between a penis and a clitoris)
Grade 5	PAIS	Essentially female genitals (including separate urethral and vaginal orifices; mild clitoromegaly, i.e., enlarged clitoris)
Grade 6	PAIS	Female genitals with pubic/underarm hair
Grade 7	CAIS	Female genitals with little or no pubic/underarm hair

> At the CAIS end of the spectrum the outward appearance is completely female (AIS grades 6/7) and the sex of rearing is invariably female. In PAIS the outward genital appearance can lie anywhere from being almost completely female (grade 5), through mixed male/female, to completely male (grade 1); it has been suggested that slight androgen insensitivity might contribute to infertility in some otherwise normal men. Some babies with PAIS may be raised as males but many are re-assigned as female. . . . Before puberty, individuals with Grade 6 or 7 are indistinguishable.[15]

Some individuals with complete androgen insensitivity reject the label intersex. They consider themselves females and resent association with those whose sex or gender identities are less certain. On the other hand, individuals with partial androgen insensitivity, especially those resulting in ambiguous genitals, are more likely to resonate with intersex terminology and the efforts of intersex advocacy groups. Despite recent efforts by some AIS support groups to distance themselves from intersex concerns, the question of intersex remains. What should determine sex assignment: external genitalia or internal gonads, reproductive structures or personal gender identity?

The shifting opinion of the medical community over the years illustrates

---

nis (severe). Suzanne J. Kessler, *Lessons from the Intersexed* (New Brunswick, N.J.: Rutgers University Press, 1998), 166-67.

15. Androgen Insensitivity Syndrome Support Group (AISSG), UK, "What Is AIS? Forms of AIS (Complete and Partial)."

how scientific categories as basic as sex difference are nevertheless subject to social construction. When society (e.g., the medical establishment) considers gonads or chromosomes as the primary markers of sex, persons with CAIS are identified as "really" men. When the medical or psychological establishment considers external genitalia and personal gender identity as primary, persons with CAIS are labeled as "really" women.[16]

Given the reality of social construction for sex among the intersexed, it is valid to question the entire schema within which such construction currently takes place. Should persons with CAIS or PAIS be forced to choose between two options for sex assignment? Should they be given a third option, intersex, along with the traditional categories, male and female? Some have proposed an even more nuanced scheme, wherein one would combine labels. Thus, a person with CAIS who identifies as a woman would be considered an "intersex woman."[17] Such a designation recognizes that XY individuals with CAIS can appear more feminine than XX women and more accurately reflects the complexity of the issues for sex and gender identification.

Fausto-Sterling once suggested public recognition of the five sex categories used by medical doctors since the Victorian period: male, female, male pseudohermaphrodite, female pseudohermaphrodite, and true hermaphrodite.[18] Sociologists Suzanne Kessler and Wendy McKenna argue that the entire system should be tossed. If people want to identify as a particular sex, or as intersex, let them. Some may want to identify as male or female during their reproductive years, so as to find a suitable partner, and then change designation at other (nonreproductive) seasons of life. They ask: What's the harm?[19] We will return to their proposals toward the end of this chapter, but now we turn to one condition formerly known as "female pseudohermaphroditism."

16. When, in 1968, the International Olympic Committee moved from genital and breast inspection to buccal smears to verify the sex of athletes, AIS women were rejected from competitions and some medals were revoked. Ironically, because CAIS women cannot respond to any androgens, even the normal level of androgens circulating in XX women, they are at a greater disadvantage than their XX female competitors. Fausto-Sterling, *Sexing the Body,* 1-5.

17. Kessler, *Lessons from the Intersexed,* 88-89.

18. Fausto-Sterling, "The Five Sexes."

19. Suzanne J. Kessler and Wendy McKenna, *Gender: An Ethnomethodological Approach* (Chicago: University of Chicago Press, 1978, 1985), 166.

Congenital Adrenal Hyperplasia (CAH) CAH is an intersex condition that occurs anywhere between 1 in 13,000 and 1 in 36,000 births.[20] It is an "inherited enzyme deficiency condition, causing a malfunction of the fetus's adrenal gland, which results in the overproduction of fetal androgen."[21] Thus XX individuals can have androgen levels that are similar to those of typical males, and XY individuals can have higher than average levels.[22] Higher levels of androgens "can make XX embryos have larger than average clitorises, or even a clitoris that looks rather like a penis, or labia that look like a scrotum."[23]

"Virilization in girls with CAH is highly variable," Melissa Hines writes. At the same time, "in a small number of cases, virilization is so extensive that genetic females are misidentified as males at birth and assigned and reared as boys until other consequences of the CAH syndrome result in a correct diagnosis. Usually, this occurs sufficiently early to allow reassignment to the female sex. However, in some cases it does not. XX individuals with CAH do not have testes or Müllerian Inhibiting Factor, and so they retain female internal reproductive organs and are capable of reproducing."[24] Virilization does not stop after the birth of the child. CAH can trigger other secondary sex characteristics typical of male puberty: "dense body hair, a receding hairline, deep voice, prominent muscles, etc."[25]

In 1954 Andrea Prader created what has come to be called the Prader Scale to classify degrees of virilization caused by CAH:[26]

20. ISNA, "How Common Is Intersex?" 1. Blackless et al., "How Sexually Dimorphic Are We?" list the frequency as .0770/1,000 on p. 156. This translates as 1:12,987 (according to my calculations), which the ISNA has rounded to 1:13,000. Blackless et al. list this rate for classic CAH caused by 21-hydroxylase deficiency — the most common enzyme deficiency associated with CAH. Other enzyme deficiencies are also listed with additional frequency rates. They do not provide a combined estimate.

21. Kessler, *Lessons from the Intersexed,* 165-66.

22. Hines, *Brain Gender,* 29.

23. ISNA, "Congenital Adrenal Hyperplasia (CAH)," http://www.isna.org/faq/printable, 5.

24. Hines, *Brain Gender,* 30.

25. ISNA, "Congenital Adrenal Hyperplasia (CAH)," 5.

26. The image on p. 31 is republished with permission from Melissa Hines, *Brain Gender* (Oxford: Oxford University Press, 2004), Fig. 2-5, 30; permission conveyed through Copyright Clearance Center, Inc. Description of scale from CARES Foundation (Congenital Adrenal Hyperplasia Research Education Support), "What Is the Prader Scale?" http://www.caresfoundation.org. Adapted from diagrams published by Phyllis W. Speiser and Perrin C. White, "Congenital Adrenal Hyperplasia Due to 21-Hydroxylase Deficiency," *Endocrine Reviews* 21, no. 3 (2000): 251.

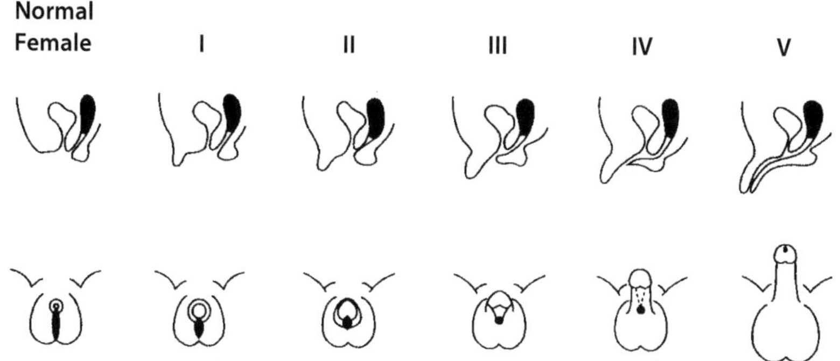

Prader Scale

Normal Female	normal female genitals
I	slight enlargement of the clitoris (cliteromegaly)
II	enlarged clitoris and partial fusion of the labia producing a "funnel-shaped" cavity for the urethra and vaginal openings
III	enlargement of the clitoris such that it is often described as a "phallus." At this stage the labia are so fused that they are indistinguishable from a scrotum, and there is only one "urogenital" opening
IV	complete fusion of the scrotum with urogenital opening at the base or shaft of the "phallus," what is often labeled hypospadias on a genetic male
V	mild to medium hypospadias

"Among the many causes of intersex, only CAH represents a real medical emergency in the newborn period."[27] CAH can cause severe dehydration leading to death within the first weeks of the infant's life. At puberty, additional medical intervention is needed to create a vaginal opening separate from the urethra for menstruation and so that urine does not pool in an internalized vagina.[28]

CAH can also occur in XY males, who may be in need of medical care and counseling. "[U]ntreated CAH can cause boys to have their puberty earlier than other boys. This can be a problem because it will stop them from

27. ISNA, "Congenital Adrenal Hyperplasia (CAH)," 5.
28. Consortium, *Clinical Guidelines,* 6.

growing taller . . . and because it can cause them to be very sexual well before other children their age are having such strong sexual thoughts and desires."[29]

CAH is considered an intersex condition only when it occurs in XX individuals. The Intersex Society of North America notes that while "1 in 10,000 to 18,000 children are born with congenital adrenal hyperplasia . . . the prevalence of CAH-related intersex is about 1 in 20,000 to 1 in 36,000."[30] But these numbers only represent classic CAH conditions that begin in utero. CAH can also start later in life, something that has been coined late-onset CAH, or LOCAH.

Late-onset congenital adrenal hyperplasia is an enzyme deficiency that occurs anytime after age five. If a child shows premature signs of puberty, clitoral growth, or male pattern hair growth (hirsutism), doctors may check for LOCAH. After puberty, signs of the condition "include hirsutism, menstrual disorders, and clitoral enlargement."[31]

Late-onset CAH is the single most common intersex condition. Fausto-Sterling explains that "[w]hile the incidence of late-onset 21-hydroxylase varies widely among different ethnic groups, its overall frequency is extremely high." Because of the degree of variation, it is helpful to see the distribution among groups:[32]

Ashkenazi	37/1,000
Hispanics	19/1,000
Yugoslavs	16/1,000
Italians	3/1,000
Mixed Caucasians	.01/1,000
Average by my calculations	15.002/1,000, or 1:67

The possibility that 1 in every 67 persons could have an intersex condition may come as a shock. However, while the ISNA and others list LOCAH as an intersex condition, others have contested its inclusion.[33] Fausto-Sterling calculates frequency rates for all intersex conditions with and without LOCAH.[34] Leonard Sax and Ieuan Hughes have argued, to the contrary,

29. ISNA, "Congenital Adrenal Hyperplasia (CAH)," 5.

30. ISNA, "Congenital Adrenal Hyperplasia (CAH)," 5.

31. Blackless et al., "How Sexually Dimorphic Are We?" 156.

32. Blackless et al., "How Sexually Dimorphic Are We?" 156.

33. ISNA, "How Common Is Intersex?" 1.

34. "If [LOCAH] is deleted, the frequency estimates obtained from population surveys would come to 0.228%, the same order of magnitude found after combining the incidences

that LOCAH is not an intersex condition and should not be counted in relevant estimates.[35] Sax bases his argument on the fact that these children are born with genitals that match their chromosomal patterns (i.e., XX babies have female genitals, XY babies have male genitals). He insists that the symptoms of LOCAH in adult women — "oligomenorrhea" (infrequent menstrual cycles), "hirsutism" (male-pattern hair growth), "infertility," "acne," "mild clitoromegaly," and a complete lack of symptoms in others — disqualify LOCAH patients from classification as intersex.[36]

I would agree with Sax that persons who do not present symptoms and yet inflate the numbers for intersex should lead researchers to show caution when calculating frequency rates. Still, I wonder what Sax would say to the young woman who begins to grow a beard, learns she is infertile, and, as a result, begins to question her femininity. According to John Money, an early leader in the field of sexology and the medical management of intersex, "a girl with excessive hair growth . . . will generally need special counseling to help prevent serious social disturbance of social and personality development." But he also writes, "Androgen-induced hirsutism in girls is not accompanied by a corresponding masculinization of the gender identity or the body image. Therefore the woman with hirsutism is mortified and intent on ridding herself of the unwanted hairiness."[37] In a culture where gender is considered foundational to one's identity, such experiences can lead to severe personal disorientation. While the term "pseudohermaphrodite" may

---

of severe and medium hypospadias and cryptorchidism (0.05 + 0.4 = 0.45%). Alternatively, if mild hypospadias and late-onset CAH are included in the final calculations the combined figure is 2.27% for hypospadias and cryptorchidism, compared with 1.728% obtained from summing the incidence of all known causes for which available data exist. . . . Which number one chooses to use depends on the specific population under study, and the assumption as to what should count as true dimorphism. It would appear, however, that earlier estimates that intersexual births might run as high as 4% are unwarranted, except in populations in which a particular genetic condition occurs with high frequency (Fausto-Sterling, 1993; Money, 1993)." Blackless et al., "How Sexually Dimorphic Are We?" 161.

35. Leonard Sax, "How Common Is Intersex? A Response to Anne Fausto-Sterling," *Journal of Sex Research* 39, no. 3 (August 2002): 176. Ieuan Hughes, in personal correspondence via e-mail (November 4, 2008), in which I asked him how he and his colleagues arrived at the figure of intersex rates as 1:4,500 cited in I. A. Hughes et al., "Consensus Statement on Management of Intersex Disorders," *Archives of Disease in Childhood* 2 (May 4, 2006): 1-10.

36. Sax, "How Common Is Intersex?" 176.

37. John Money, *Sex Errors of the Body and Related Syndromes: A Guide to Counseling Children, Adolescents, and Their Families*, 2nd ed. (Baltimore: Paul H. Brookes Publishing Co., 1994), 79-80.

be rejected as politically incorrect in current parlance, such language may more accurately reflect the feelings of affected parties.[38]

In the West, if a child born with ambiguous or masculinized genitals is discovered to have CAH, doctors typically recommend that parents raise the child as a girl. Medical management includes the preservation of female internal reproductive organs, genital surgery (e.g., vaginoplasty, clitoral reduction), and hormone therapy to ensure that masculine secondary sex characteristics do not develop naturally. Doctors in Saudi Arabia, trained in Western medical traditions, typically follow the same procedures; however, some Saudi parents have rejected their recommendations. Fausto-Sterling recounts how these parents rejected the suggestion that they begin raising their "son" as their daughter. "Nor would they accept feminizing surgery for their child. As the reporting physicians write, 'female upbringing was resisted on social grounds. . . . This was essentially an expression of local community attitudes with . . . the preference for male offspring.' "[39] About this same example, another commentator writes: "It has to be accepted that attitudes toward sex of rearing and in particular toward feminizing genitoplasties in late-diagnosed patients with CAH in the Middle East [are] going to be very different from those in Europe."[40]

Westerners are keen to critique the sexism so apparent in the example above, but feminist scholars are eager to point out that sexism pervades Western medical practices. In addition to the preservation of female reproductive organs, surgeons explain that feminizing genital surgeries are believed to be easier to perform than masculinizing procedures given the present state of technological development. Simply put, it is difficult to construct a well-functioning penis that can both urinate and stand erect. A vagina, on the other hand, is not considered as difficult to construct. Fausto-Sterling reports one surgeon remarking: "you can make a hole but you can't build a pole."[41] Kessler describes the frustrations of many that though

38. In fact, many intersex persons have found relief in finding a name for their condition, be it hermaphrodite, pseudohermaphrodite, intersex, or a more medical description. See discussion below, about true hermaphrodites, for evidence that these "politically incorrect" terms have become a rallying point for many.

39. Fausto-Sterling, *Sexing the Body,* 58-59, quoting V. Sripathi S. Ahmed et al., "Gender Reversal in 47,XX Congenital Virilizing Adrenal Hyperplasia," *British Journal of Urology* 79 (1997): 786-87.

40. J. D. Frank, "Editorial Comment," *British Journal of Urology* 79 (1997): 789, quoted in Fausto-Sterling, *Sexing the Body,* 281-82.

41. Fausto-Sterling, *Sexing the Body,* 59.

a well-functioning penis is often the criterion for male sex assignment, a well-functioning vagina (self-lubricating, sensitive, able to change size and shape) is not required for female sex assignment. A vaginal opening with the potential of receiving a penis (even if painful) is all that is required.[42]

These illustrations serve to remind us that sex, at least for the intersexed, is socially (and medically) constructed. Societies have presuppositions about gender that influence how they construct sex for the intersexed. When (Western) society gives preference to chromosomes and internal reproductive organs over external genitals and makes gendered assumptions about the relative difficulty of genital surgeries, CAH patients are assigned as female and medically "managed" along the female pathway. When (Middle Eastern) societies give priority to external genitalia and social preference for male children, CAH patients are reared and medically "managed" along the masculine pathway.

Cultural differences, like those described above, shed light on the socially constructed nature of sex assignment for the intersex debate. Though some may think that Sax and Fausto-Sterling are being overly pedantic when they debate the inclusion of LOCAH in intersex tallies, given the information presented above, we can at least grant that debate is warranted. Presuppositions must be excavated and put on the table.

Ovo-Testes Ovo-testes is one of the rarer intersex conditions. Though frequency rates vary significantly among populations, Fausto-Sterling proposes an average of 1 in 100,000 live births.[43] With ovo-testes, an individual is born with one ovary and one testis or a combination of gonads that contains both ovarian and testicular tissue. Ovo-testes sometimes produces ambiguous external genitals but not always. Ovo-testes accounts for "fewer than 5 percent of all cases of ambiguous genitals."[44]

In the Victorian era, when gonads were seen as primary indicators of sex, this condition was labeled "true hermaphroditism."[45] Today, physicians and some intersex persons reject the label "hermaphrodite" because, unlike the mythological creature, persons with ovo-testes cannot impregnate themselves.

42. Kessler, *Lessons from the Intersexed,* 26-28.

43. Blackless et al., "How Sexually Dimorphic Are We?" 159.

44. Kessler, *Lessons from the Intersexed,* 13-14, quoting Mariano Castro-Magana, Moris Angulo, and Planton J. Collipp, "Management of the Child with Ambiguous Genitalia," *Medical Aspects of Human Sexuality* 18, no. 4 (April 1984): 172-88.

45. Dreger, "Doubtful Sex," 335-70.

Other Variations of Gonadal Development Like ovo-testes, Swyer syndrome is a variation on typical gonadal development. Persons with Swyer syndrome are born with "streak gonads," "minimally developed gonad tissue present in place of testes or in place of ovaries." An XY baby born with Swyer will look like a typical female at birth. Unlike persons with AIS, persons with Swyer will not develop secondary sex characteristics at puberty because the gonads cannot produce androgens or estrogens. Where medical treatment is available, children are typically reared as girls and given hormone replacement therapy to bring about feminizing puberty.[46] Swyer syndrome confirms the thesis that without higher levels of androgens (typical of male development), genitals will develop along the female pathway whether or not the individual has a Y chromosome.[47]

Gonadal dysgenesis is a "form of intersexuality characterized by undifferentiated gonads, sometimes resulting in atypical external genitals. It represents about one-third of all cases of intersexuality."[48] Swyer is a type of gonadal dysgenesis for XY individuals.[49] Turner syndrome can also be seen as a type of gonadal dysgenesis, but because it is caused by a variation of the chromosomes, it will be discussed below.

Alternative Chromosome Combinations There are a number of variations from the normal patterns of XX female and XY male. Fausto-Sterling lists the most common variations as "XXY, XO [one X chromosome], XYY, XXYY, XX males, and 47XXX females."[50] Some individuals are "mosaics," having different genetic combinations in different cells. We need not investigate all these variations in detail. Rather, I will select a few of the more common syndromes associated with genetic anomalies as examples.

In Turner syndrome, a genetic abnormality affecting 1 in 2,000 to 3,000 female births, all or part of one sex chromosome is missing.[51] Therefore, its karyotype is listed as XO or 45,X, although it can also occur in XY individu-

46. ISNA, http://www.isna.org/faq/printable, 9.

47. Hines, *Brain Gender*, 24-27.

48. Kessler, *Lessons from the Intersexed*, 166.

49. http://en.wikipedia.org/wiki/Swyer_syndrome.

50. Blackless et al., "How Sexually Dimorphic Are We?" 152.

51. Blackless et al. list the frequency rate as 0.369/1,000, which translates as 1:2,710 (by my calculations). Blackless et al., "How Sexually Dimorphic Are We?" 152. The Turner Syndrome Society of the United States lists 1:2,000 on their Web site. Andrew Zinn, "Turner Syndrome — the Basics, Genetic Overview," http://www.turnersyndrome.org/index.php?option=com_content&task=view&id=40&Itemid=57.

als. In addition to causing ovarian failure, Turner syndrome may cause other physiological abnormalities.[52]

Because most Turner syndrome babies lack a Y chromosome, their bodies do not make typical male levels of testosterone necessary for male reproductive and genital development. Most Turner patients, therefore, present as female. This is why Leonard Sax has argued against the inclusion of this syndrome in intersex estimates.[53] On the other hand, many individuals with Turner syndrome have a mosaic karyotype. Some cells have 45,X, others 46,XX. Some can even have cells with a Y chromosome.

While Andrew Zinn claims that the presence of some cells with a Y chromosome is "not enough to cause male sexual features,"[54] others present evidence to the contrary. Jane Spalding, an intersex woman writing under a pseudonym, explains her condition as XY–Turner Mosaic. Mosaicism indicates that while some cells carry one karyotype, other cells carry a different pattern. Jane's karyotype (45X and 46XY) produced "masculine-seeming genitals," but even these never caused her to question her sense of female gender identity. After puberty she didn't develop the secondary sex characteristics of either sex.

> At 22 I looked like an underdeveloped girl with the genitals of a 14-year old boy. I had reached 5'6" but weighed less than 120 pounds. My arms and legs were disproportionately long from delayed epiphyseal closure. I had neither the broad shoulders of a man nor the full hips of a woman. I had no Adam's apple, no muscle mass, no breast development, and no beard. Not even those masculine-looking genitals had completed their journey to manhood.
>
> I wasn't homosexual. I didn't want to be effeminate or a transvestite. I didn't understand why my heart insisted that I was female when my genitals were clearly male. And if they were male then why wasn't the rest of me? Even with short hair, people said that I looked like a girl.[55]

52. E.g., extra neck skin, cardiac abnormalities, mild hearing loss, greater risk of nonverbal learning disabilities. If they are not treated with growth hormones, they are typically "16 centimeters shorter than their predicted adult height based on parental heights." Zinn, "Turner Syndrome"; Sax, "How Common Is Intersex?" 176; Consortium, *Clinical Guidelines,* 7.

53. Sax, "How Common Is Intersex?" 176.

54. Zinn, "Turner Syndrome."

55. Clara Jane Spalding, "What Do Children Know?" http://www.obgyn.net/young-woman/young-woman.asp?page=/young-woman/articles/xyturner. Originally published at http://www.sonoworld.com/Client/Fetus/page.aspx?id=389 (August 6, 1999).

Turner syndrome is included by Fausto-Sterling because it does not fall into either traditional karyotype: 46,XX (female) or 46,XY (male).

Klinefelter's syndrome is also included as an intersex condition because of its atypical chromosome patterns: XXY, XXYY. "XXY individuals diagnosed with Klinefelter syndrome have external male genitalia, small testes, impaired spermatogenesis" (most are infertile), and "frequent gynecomastia" (breast growth).[56] Sax writes against the inclusion of Klinefelter's syndrome as an intersex condition because it can go unnoticed by many men. Some discover their diagnosis during fertility evaluations. Still, for others, Klinefelter's syndrome leads to profound ambiguity. One man with the syndrome explains how he appreciates the label "intersexed" because it fits with his experience.

> It is only fairly recently that I have discovered the term "intersexed" and how it relates to my body. I like the term because I prefer more choices than male or female. . . . It wasn't until I was 29 years old that a label was put on my physical differences, differences I never quite understood. I had large nipples on smallish breasts, peanut-size testicles, and cellulite-type hairless fatty tissue over most of my body. I was told at an infertility clinic that I had an extra X chromosome and a karyotype of XXY-47. This is commonly known as Klinefelter's syndrome. I was informed that I was genetically sterile and that my "sex glands" produced only 10 percent of what was considered normal testosterone levels for a male. I was advised to immediately start testosterone replacement therapy. . . . The medical journals called my condition "feminized male." I had always felt caught between the sexes without knowing why.[57]

Despite arguments to the contrary, Klinefelter's syndrome does at times blur the lines of clear demarcation between the two traditional sexes. It occurs in roughly 1 in 1,000 births.[58]

Other non-XX, non-XY chromosome combinations such as 47,XXY

56. Blackless et al., "How Sexually Dimorphic Are We?" 152.

57. D. Cameron, "Caught Between: An Essay on Intersexuality," in *Intersex in the Age of Ethics,* ed. Alice Domurat Dreger (Hagerstown, Md.: University Publishing Group, 1999), 90-96.

58. ISNA, "How Common Is Intersex?" 1, http://www.isna.org/faq/frequency (accessed online July 2, 2008). Blackless et al., "How Sexually Dimorphic Are We?" list the frequency as .922/1,000 on p. 152. This translates as 1:1,085 (according to my calculations), which the ISNA has rounded to 1:1,000.

males, 47,XYY males, 46,XX males, and 47,XXX females occur in roughly 1 in 1,500 births.[59] Whether these variations should be considered intersex is open for debate. Fausto-Sterling includes them on the basis of their chromosome pattern alone. Sax argues against their inclusion because their genes do not result in genital ambiguity or questions of gender identity. He notes that men with an extra Y chromosome have lower than average intelligence, though their fertility is usually unaffected. Similarly, "women with an extra X chromosome . . . are fertile" but may also have lower than average intelligence.[60]

Other Genital Anomalies Fausto-Sterling notes that "XY babies born with testes, but complete absence of a penis, are extremely rare, probably occurring only 1:1,000,000 births. In contrast, complete or partial vaginal agenesis is fairly common."[61]

Vaginal agenesis (also called Müllerian agenesis, congenital absence of the vagina or aplasia of the vagina) can be attributed to androgen insensitivity and also to Mayer-Rokitansky-Küster-Hauser Syndrome (MRKH).[62] MRKH affects as many as 1 in 6,000 females.[63] In addition to the absence of a vagina, MRKH can also cause the uterus to be underdeveloped or missing. Nevertheless, these women have functional ovaries that stimulate feminizing puberty, though they do not menstruate.[64]

While vaginal agenesis is included by Fausto-Sterling as a deviation from the ideal male or female and is listed by the ISNA, some question its inclusion as an intersex condition. An American medical Web site insists: "It is important to understand that young women with this syndrome are

59. Blackless et al., "How Sexually Dimorphic Are We?" 152.

60. Sax, "How Common Is Intersex?" 176.

61. Blackless et al., "How Sexually Dimorphic Are We?" 156.

62. "The earliest references to vaginal agenesis and proposed therapy can be found in Hippocrates' work, 'The Nature of Women.' Other references can also be found in the Roman and Greek eras. The first contemporary description was in 1781. The description of congenital absence of the vagina with incompletely developed uterine remnants or a completely absent uterus as a specific syndrome can be traced to the work of 4 individuals. They were Mayer (1829), Rokitansky (1838), Küster (1910) and Hauser (1961-1973)." MRKH UK Support Group, http://www.mrkh.org.uk/mrkh.html (accessed October 27, 2008).

63. ISNA, "How Common Is Intersex?" 1. Blackless et al., "How Sexually Dimorphic Are We?" list the frequency as 0.1694/1,000 on p. 157 but note that this may be an underestimate. Their figure translates as 1:5,903 (according to my calculations).

64. "Vaginal Agenesis: A Guide for Parents and Guardians," http://www.youngwomenshealth.org/mrkh_parent.html (accessed October 27, 2008).

genetic females."[65] Leonard Sax also argues against its inclusion in intersex calculations. "Surgical correction for vaginal agenesis is conceptually no different from surgical correction for cleft palate."[66] I would concede that vaginal agenesis does not represent the same kind of intersex condition as ambiguous genitalia, but Sax's comparison with cleft palate is overstated. It is because genitals have been granted such power to convey meaning and personal identity that vaginal agenesis differs from cleft palate not only in kind, but also in degree. The comparison between a technological "fix" for cleft palate and vaginoplasty is also poor. A few years before Sax's article, Diamond and Sigmundson made the comparison with cleft palate and concluded that "unlike persons who have had neonatal surgery for cleft palate or meningomyelocele, many of those who have had genital surgery or been sex reassigned neonatally have complained bitterly of the treatment."[67]

Surgical "success" for reconstruction of the vagina has been severely criticized by the intersex community. The results of a "successful" surgery will be lost if the patient does not keep up with regular maintenance of the neo-vagina, which includes daily insertion of a dilator to keep the opening from permanently reducing in size. Adults choosing the procedure acknowledge the psychological difficulty of the practice, but rarely is the psychological well-being of the child considered. Suzanne Kessler intimates that such procedures could be considered a form of child abuse and argues from this basis that vaginoplasties — and all other forms of intersex surgeries to "correct" non-life-threatening conditions — should be delayed until after puberty, when the adolescent or adult can supply informed consent.[68]

Given the limited success of vaginoplasties and recommendations that they be delayed or rejected altogether, it seems reasonable to at least consider vaginal agenesis under the rubric of intersex. Without serious medical intervention, these (intersex) women are cut off from typical heterosexual relations and from the possibility of delivering children — both traditional markers of femininity.[69]

65. "Vaginal Agenesis."

66. Sax, "How Common Is Intersex?" 177.

67. Milton Diamond and H. Keith Sigmundson, "Management of Intersexuality: Guidelines for Dealing with Individuals with Ambiguous Genitalia," *Archives of Pediatrics and Adolescent Medicine* 151 (June 10, 1997): 1050.

68. Kessler, *Lessons from the Intersexed,* 58-64.

69. Sax has argued that that these women "can and do go on to have successful term pregnancies," but it must be granted that these cannot occur without serious technological intervention. Sax, "How Common Is Intersex?" 177.

Hypospadias is a condition of the penis where the urinary opening (meatus) is located off-center on the glans (mild), along the penile shaft (medium), or under the penis (severe).[70] A severe hypospadias is one way of naming an ambiguous genital when the presumed sex of the individual is male. Thus an XY individual with testes who has a urogenital opening underneath a phallus is considered a male with severe hypospadias. An XX individual with ovaries and the same external genitals would be considered a female with an enlarged clitoris (clitoromegaly). John Money refers to severe hypospadias as an "open gutter" in the "female position."[71] Severe cases can present with the complete absence of the urethra.[72] Kessler explains that although hypospadias is estimated as occurring in 1 in every 200 male births, it is much more rarely (1 in 10,000 births) a sign of an underlying intersex condition.[73] Fausto-Sterling and her colleagues list intersex rates that both include and omit hypospadias.

Kessler argues that, aside from an absent urethra, surgeries for hypospadias are rarely medically necessary but are performed so that parents are not affronted by the shape of the boy's penis and so that the boy may urinate "like a man" (i.e., in the standing position). She counters that urinary positions are cultural tests for masculinity and should not be granted such weight when deciding whether to seek surgical correction.

Howard Devore recounts the physical and psychological trauma of surgeries for hypospadias. He suffered sixteen surgeries in all, ten before the age of ten. He explains that he could have avoided at least twelve surgeries had his physicians and parents been content to allow him to urinate in a sitting position.

> I regularly get bladder infections. And I still have to sit to pee. I have never been without fistulae [holes in the penis where the surgery has broken down], and I've had the entire tube replaced twice, with large skin grafts. If they had just let me pee sitting down, neither I nor my family would have had to suffer all of that — the expense, the pain, the repeated surgeries, the drugs, the repeated tissue breakdowns and urine leaks. It would have been just fine to have a penis that peed out of the bottom instead of

70. Kessler, *Lessons from the Intersexed,* 42.

71. Money, *Sex Errors,* 49, 17.

72. Kessler, *Lessons from the Intersexed,* 42, quoting Steven Y. C. Tong, Karen Donaldson, and John M. Hutson, "When Is Hypospadias Not Hypospadias?" *Medical Journal of Australia* 164 (February 5, 1996): 153-54.

73. Kessler, *Lessons from the Intersexed,* 42.

> the top, and didn't have the feeling damaged. . . . Such a large skin graft can't heal with the blood supply that is available in the genitals. I believe they know that, but it seems that genital appearance and the promise of normalcy are more important to young parents than a clear-headed acceptance of reality.[74]

Kessler asks, given the limited results of genital surgeries, why infant intersex surgeries still continue. She suggests two reasons: "commitment to the concept of medical advancement and dimorphic genitals."[75] The binary sex system, combined with a belief in technological correction, has fueled current approaches to the management of intersex conditions.

It is curious that many of these writers criticize social standards for masculinity (peeing like a man) yet fail to admit the challenge severe hypospadias presents for male fertility — an older form of validation of masculinity. As chapter 2 will show, the ability to produce offspring was the primary test of masculinity in the ancient world and remains such in a number of non-Western cultures.

Naturally Occurring Sex Change: 5-Alpha Reductase Deficiency Syndrome (5-ARDs) One intersex condition varies from most of those discussed above in the level of change between the phenotype (physical appearance) of the child at birth and as an adult. 5-alpha reductase deficiency syndrome (5-ARDs) produces a baby with female or ambiguous genitals at birth whose body is transformed at puberty into that of a male. "5-alpha-reductase is an enzyme that converts the weaker testosterone into the more potent dihydrotestosterone (DHT)."[76] Lower levels of this enzyme allow genitalia in an XY individual to develop along the female pathway (as it would in an XY individual with Swyer syndrome or streak gonads). Unlike Swyer, where testosterone levels never reach sufficient levels to masculinize the child, persons with 5-ARDs do experience masculinizing puberty.[77] At puberty, the testes descend and virilization causes "enlargement of the phallus, erection and ejaculation, deepening of the voice, development of masculine body structure and a male psychosex-

74. Howard Devore, "Growing Up in the Surgical Maelstrom," in *Intersex in the Age of Ethics,* 80-81.

75. Kessler, *Lessons from the Intersexed,* 74.

76. Androgen Insensitivity Syndrome Support Group (AISSG), "Related Conditions: 5-alpha-reductase Deficiency," http://www.aissg.org/24_RELATED.HTM#Reductase.

77. AISSG, "Related Conditions."

ual orientation."[78] As adults, persons with 5-ARDs resemble other men in most ways except that facial hair is sparse, hairlines on the forehead do not recede, they do not have acne, and their prostates remain small.[79]

This rare condition has been documented in larger numbers in ethnic groups in locations "ranging from Central America to Vietnam. Indeed, more than 50 families with over 100 affected individuals have been reported. However, no population or gene frequencies are available."[80] Extensive study of the condition has been documented by anthropologists working in the Dominican Republic and among the Sambia of Papua New Guinea. Because these communities do not possess advanced medical technology, persons with 5-ARDs are integrated into the culture.

In the Dominican Republic, the colloquial term "Guevedoche" or "Guevedoces" (literally, "eggs at twelve") indicates the transformation of what were believed to be labia into descended testes.[81] "Such persons have a folk classification which permits them the flexibility to change dress and tasks, names and decorative motif, with alterations in sexual partners, albeit those of the 'appropriate' sex object at that stage of their lives."[82]

Among the Sambia, a baby with 5-ARDs, whose genitals appear ambiguous, is assigned not as male or female but as *kwolu-aatmwol* — "a person of transformation, a 'female thing changing into a male thing.' "[83] Gilbert Herdt, the anthropologist responsible for documenting this phenomenon in Papua New Guinea, has argued that the *kwolu-aatmwol* constitutes a third sex within Sambian culture, complete with peculiar social and ethical attitudes and responsibilities.[84] Those not identified at birth are raised as females and only discovered to be *kwolu-aatmwol* at puberty. Upon discovery, they are identified as *kwolu-aatmwol* and required to transition out of female roles and into male roles within the culture.

Because the phenomenon is known, there is social space for a girl to tran-

78. Urology Science Research Foundation, "The Guevedoces of the Dominican Republic," http://www.usrf.org/news/010308-guevedoces.html.

79. Urology Science Research Foundation, "The Guevedoces of the Dominican Republic."

80. Blackless et al., "How Sexually Dimorphic Are We?" 153.

81. Urology Science Research Foundation, "The Guevedoces of the Dominican Republic."

82. Gilbert Herdt, introduction to *Third Sex, Third Gender: Beyond Sexual Dimorphism in Culture and History,* ed. Gilbert Herdt (New York: Zone Books, 1994), 68. "Sambia" is a fictional name created by Herdt to protect the identity of the people. See Gilbert H. Herdt, *Guardians of the Flutes: Idioms of Masculinity* (New York: McGraw-Hill, 1981), xx.

83. Herdt, *Third Sex,* 16-17.

84. Herdt, introduction to *Third Sex,* 69.

sition to a boy. Sambian mythology includes a hermaphroditic ancestor — a religious help for those who undergo transition. Still, the change is not easy for those raised as females. Some girls have confessed that if they were able to remain as women, they would have chosen to do so.[85] Herdt explains that despite the mythology, *kwolu-aatmwol* are not admired within Sambian culture, and he speculates that this may add to the difficulty for cultural females to accept their new status at puberty, not only as males but as *kwolu-aatmwol.*[86]

In Western culture, where gender identity is considered less flexible, and only two sexes are recognized in society, individuals with 5-ARDs who strongly identify as females are encouraged to pursue gonadectomies before puberty, and begin hormone replacement therapy so that they can acquire bodies consonant with their female gender identities. On the other hand, in some cases the child "naturally migrates to a male role," but this is not an easy task within Western culture at this time.[87]

How Many Intersex Persons Are There?

The reader will be able to recognize by now that the answer to this question depends upon one's definition. Should intersex be defined as any deviation from the medical ideals of male and female, as Fausto-Sterling has argued? Or should a condition only be recognized as intersex if, as Leonard Sax insists, "chromosomal sex is inconsistent with phenotypic sex, or in which the phenotype is not classifiable as either male or female"?[88]

Sax's definition excludes late-onset congenital adrenal hyperplasia, vaginal agenesis, Turner syndrome, Klinefelter's syndrome, and other non-XX and non-XY chromosome patterns. True intersex conditions, he writes, only occur in 0.018 percent of the population (or 1:55,556).[89] Fausto-Sterling's definition produces a frequency of 1.7 percent of all live births, or 1 to 2 per 100.[90] This frequency rate may appear high, but it is significantly reduced from the 4 percent figure she cited in earlier research.[91]

85. Herdt, introduction to *Third Sex,* 68-69.

86. Herdt, introduction to *Third Sex,* 68.

87. AISSG, "Related Conditions."

88. Sax, "How Common Is Intersex?" 174.

89. Sax, "How Common Is Intersex?" 177.

90. Blackless et al., "How Sexually Dimorphic Are We?" 151, 161.

91. Julia Epstein attributes the 4 percent rate to John Money in "Either/Or — Neither/Both: Sexual Ambiguity and the Ideology of Gender," *Genders* 7 (1990): 131 n. 6; but Money

A consensus statement, by an international team of almost fifty medical practitioners specializing in intersex, records a frequency rate of 1 in 4,500 (approximately 0.22 percent of live births).[92] They do not list which conditions they include or exclude, but their estimate (0.22 percent) is very close to the figure Fausto-Sterling supplies for intersex conditions excluding LOCAH or intersex conditions excluding hypospadias.[93] She does not give a figure that subtracts both groups.

It may be best to represent the figure as a range, such as .02 percent to 1.7 percent. For the argument of this book, it is enough to note that even with the most conservative of numbers, given by Sax, there are at least "about 50,000 true intersexuals living in the United States" at this time.[94]

Sax argues: "These individuals are of course entitled to the same expert care and consideration that all patients deserve. Nothing is gained, however, by pretending that there are 5,000,000 such individuals."[95] But, in truth, there is much to be gained by greater numbers. One intersex advocate expressed frustration over the difficulty of wading through debates over frequency rates and questioned the point: "Just because organizations/donors/governments tend to give money/recognition to larger numbers doesn't mean that numbers should legitimize conditions or feelings."[96]

A woman with androgen insensitivity responded to her comments, saying, "Over and over and over again I hear from women with AIS and similar conditions such as Swyer, Turner, MGD, PGD, MRKH, 5ARDS, etc. that they have been told by physicians who should know better that 'you will never meet another person like yourself as long as you live.' . . . Rarity Feeds Freakishness. The knowledge that 1 in 1500 people have an intersex condition is EMPOWERING. . . . Would it offer some comfort or consolation that this is the case with thousands of people and that it is,

---

denies publishing this rate in his "Letter to the Editor," *Sciences,* June/July 1993, 4. What Money *does* say is that these conditions "are not exceptionally rare." Thus, "[t]he reader who is engaged professionally in sex education and counseling, whether he be school teacher, doctor, pastor, social worker, psychologist, marriage counselor, or whatever, . . . sooner or later he will come across some of them in real life." Money, *Sex Errors,* xvi. Fausto-Sterling cited the 4 percent rate in her 1993 article, "The Five Sexes," though she has abandoned this figure for 1.7 percent in her 2000 book *Sexing the Body.*

92. Hughes et al., "Consensus Statement," 1.

93. Blackless et al., "How Sexually Dimorphic Are We?" give the figure 0.228 percent (1:4,386 by my calculations) on p. 161.

94. Sax, "How Common Is Intersex?" 177.

95. Sax, "How Common Is Intersex?"

96. ISNA, "Do Frequency Rates Matter?" http://www.isna.org/notde/972, 1.

after all, a naturally occurring element of nature?"[97] Another writer with the ISNA summarizes the debate: "Should a person's rights depend on the frequency of his or her condition? No! But does frequency matter to individuals' experiences of group identity (thus leading to an end of shame and secrecy)? Yes!"[98]

The truth is: frequency rates do matter. The less frequently intersex conditions occur, the easier it is to dismiss them as "accidents" or "freaks of nature" or "anomalies." One can more easily argue that intersex is "not normal" or "not natural" when it is rare. Some of the questions we are exploring are: What happens when we take intersex seriously, rather than dismissing it as an anomaly? What can we learn from the intersexed — about sex, gender, and sexuality, and about human nature? Intersex is rare, but it may not be as rare as we thought.

Given even the conservative rates of intersex mentioned above, one must ask why the average person is unfamiliar with these phenomena. Intersex may be as common as schizophrenia, which occurs in 1 percent of births. It is at least as common as Down syndrome (0.125 percent), and more common than albinism (1 in 20,000).[99] These other conditions are typically accepted as rare but regularly occurring phenomena, while intersex is not. Why are people more likely to be familiar with albinism, Down syndrome, and schizophrenia than with intersex? The following brief history lesson will show that a decrease in cultural space for intersex, combined with increasingly sophisticated medical technologies, has contributed to the virtual erasure of intersex from the consciousness of Western culture.

History of Intersex: From the Margins to Medicalization

Classical Myths and Medical Models

The idea of persons of mixed sex goes back as far as cultures can remember. In the West, the term "hermaphrodite" comes from the Greek and has its

97. ISNA, "Do Frequency Rates Matter?" 2.

98. ISNA, "Do Frequency Rates Matter?" 1.

99. For rates on albinism, see Fausto-Sterling, *Sexing the Body,* 53. Rates for schizophrenia and Down syndrome were drawn from Heather Looy, "Male and Female God Created Them: The Challenge of Intersexuality," *Journal of Psychology and Christianity* 21 (2002): 12. Looy cites M. W. Thompson and J. S. Thompson, *Genetics in Medicine,* 5th ed. (Toronto: W. B. Saunders Co., 1991).

roots in two different myths.[100] In the first, Hermes (the son of Zeus; patron god of music, dreams, and livestock) and Aphrodite (goddess of sexual love and beauty) conceive a child of mixed sex whom they name after themselves, Hermaphroditos. In the second legend, their beautiful male child falls desperately in love with a water nymph who becomes joined to him in an eternal embrace. Plato transposed these myths into a theory of origins, suggesting that there were originally three sexes: male, female, and hermaphrodite. He speculated that the third had been lost over the generations.[101] Early Jewish commentators on the creation of Eve out of the rib of Adam proposed that the first human was a hermaphrodite, and only in the separation of the woman from *the adam* (the human) did sexual differentiation come into being.[102]

But hermaphrodites in the ancient world were not confined to the realm of myth or legend. Both Greek and Jewish societies developed theories to understand and laws to regulate persons of mixed sex in their communities. Aristotle speculated that a hermaphrodite developed in the womb when the mother contributed more matter than was necessary for one child but not quite enough for twins. In this scheme, a hermaphrodite was a malformed twin who "really" belonged to one of two sexes, not a third. Aristotle did not look to genitals or gonads to determine true sex; rather he followed Hippocrates' theory of temperature, believing the "heat of the heart" revealed the difference. Men were warm. Women were cool. Galen (the second century C.E. Greek physician whose medical influence reigned until the modern era) further developed Aristotle's theory of heat but took issue with the two-sex model.[103] Galen proposed a sliding scale of sex that combined the theory of male heat and dominance with the right side of the uterus and female coolness and passivity with the left side of the uterus. "Depending upon where on the grid an embryo fell, it could range from entirely male, through various intermediate states, to entirely female."[104]

Sharon Preves details how Galen's theory of bodily heat and gender in-

100. I will use the term "hermaphrodite" when discussing the history of intersex, as is standard practice among historians in this field.

101. Fausto-Sterling, *Sexing the Body,* 32-33.

102. *Genesis Rabbah* 8.1 and *Leviticus Rabbah* 14.1; cited in Kristen E. Kvam, Linda S. Schearing, and Valarie H. Ziegler, eds., *Eve and Adam: Jewish, Christian, and Muslim Readings on Genesis and Gender* (Bloomington and Indianapolis: Indiana University Press, 1999), 77-78.

103. Preves, *Intersex and Identity,* 34. Fausto-Sterling, *Sexing the Body,* 33-34.

104. Fausto-Sterling, *Sexing the Body,* 34.

fluenced medical theory as late as the seventeenth century. The seventeenth-century surgeon Ambroise Paré explained the development of male secondary sex characteristics in pubescent girls (perhaps a sign of late-onset congenital adrenal hyperplasia?) as the result of excessive heat brought about by physical exertion. Girls who jumped or played roughly raised their body temperature enough to "push out" their female organs (conceived as inversions of male genitals) in masculine form.[105] These medical explanations coexisted with folk beliefs that blamed the conception of a hermaphrodite on the imagination of the mother during pregnancy.[106]

Classical and Medieval Law

Physicians in the classical and medieval periods were familiar with hermaphroditic bodies, and while they theorized about their origins, they did not usually attempt to alter them. The management of intersex was more often handled on the familial, legal, and religious levels. Jewish scribes pulled from laws pertaining to men and women to regulate religious and domestic behaviors of hermaphrodites. "The Tosefta, for example, forbids hermaphrodites from inheriting their fathers' estates (like daughters), from secluding themselves with women (like sons), and from shaving (like men). When they menstruate they must be isolated from men (like women); they are disqualified from serving as witnesses or as priests (like women); but the laws of pederasty apply to them."[107] Jewish and Christian religious perspectives on the hermaphrodite will be explored at greater length in the next chapter.

Roman and European laws varied. Under Romulus, hermaphrodites were in danger of capital punishment.[108] In the first century C.E., Pliny reports that such "monsters" were often put to death by drowning but that "at the present day they are employed for sensual purposes."[109] European laws varied by country and depended upon which medical theory of origins pre-

105. Preves, *Intersex and Identity,* 34.

106. Epstein, "Either/Or — Neither/Both," 117.

107. Fausto-Sterling, *Sexing the Body,* 33. See also Julie A. Greenberg, "Defining Male and Female: Intersexuality and the Collision between Law and Biology," *Arizona Law Review* 41, no. 2 (1999): 277.

108. Fausto-Sterling, *Sexing the Body,* 34.

109. Epstein, "Either/Or — Neither/Both," 107, 133-34, citing *The Natural History of Pliny,* trans. and ed. John Bostock and H. T. Riley, 6 vols. (London: Henry G. Bohn, 1855-1857), 2:136.

vailed in the region.[110] Punishments brought upon hermaphrodites seemed primarily to arise when they moved from one gender role to another, usually discovered through sexual activity or "cross-dressing." Thus, men who married women only later to give birth to a child of their own, or women who donned men's clothing and sought the right to marry other women, found themselves before civil and ecclesiastical authorities. Hermaphrodites who successfully "passed" as one of two prevailing genders and comported themselves appropriately were left relatively alone.[111] Fausto-Sterling recounts the works of Sir Edward Coke, a legal expert in early modern England who wrote " 'an Hermaphrodite may purchase according to that sexe which prevaileth.' Similarly, in the first half of the seventeenth century, French hermaphrodites could serve as witnesses in the court and even marry, providing they did so in the role assigned to them by 'the sex that dominates their personality.' "[112] She summarizes European legal history by stating that before the nineteenth century, "the individual him/herself shared with medical and legal experts the right to decide which sex prevailed, but once having made the choice, was expected to stick with it. The penalty for reneging could be severe. At stake was the maintenance of the social order and the rights of man (meant literally). Thus, although it was clear that some people straddled the male-female divide, the social and legal structures remained fixed around a two-sex system."[113]

The Victorian Era and Modern Medicalization

While hermaphrodites had been known to exist in the hidden corners of society for millennia, medical doctors in the nineteenth century began documenting larger and larger numbers of hermaphroditic patients. Alice Dreger explains how advances in gynecological science, greater willingness by individuals to submit to medical examination, and growing concern about sex, gender, and sexual politics all collided to bring about a turning point in the history of hermaphroditism. Early feminist movements and public concern over growing numbers of homosexuals made "physicians sensitive to their patients' sexual identities, anatomies, and practices."[114]

110. Fausto-Sterling, *Sexing the Body,* 34.
111. Fausto-Sterling, *Sexing the Body,* 34-36.
112. Fausto-Sterling, *Sexing the Body,* 36.
113. Fausto-Sterling, *Sexing the Body,* 36.
114. Alice Domurat Dreger, "A History of Intersex: From the Age of Gonads to the

In the face of rapidly increasing knowledge of bodily variations, scientists attempted to bring order out of chaos. Biologist Isidore Geoffroy Saint-Hilaire laid the foundation for the study of unusual births (a science he dubbed "teratology") in the hopes that it would also illuminate "normal" sex differences.

> Saint-Hilaire divided the body into "sex segments," three on the left and three on the right. He named these zones the "profound portion," which contained ovaries, testicles, or related structures; the "middle portion," which contained internal sex structures such as the uterus and seminal vesicles; and the "external portion," which included the external genitalia. If all six segments were wholly male, he decreed, so too was the body. If all six were female, the body was clearly female. But when a mixture of male and female appeared in any of the six zones, a hermaphrodite resulted.[115]

Priority was eventually given to the "profound portion" — the gonads for determining sex, due to their part in reproduction and the initiation of secondary sex characteristics at puberty.[116] Theodore Klebs combined Saint-Hilaire's classification system with the priority of gonads to coin new terminology in 1876: the pseudohermaphrodite versus the true hermaphrodite.[117]

> No matter how womanly a patient looked, no matter if she had a vagina, fine and round breasts, a smooth face, and a husband she loved, if she had testes, she would be labeled a male — in this case a "male pseudohermaphrodite." . . . [S]o strong was doctors' belief in the Gonadal Definition of Sex and the primacy of the gonads that in Britain the "problem" of "women" with testes was sometimes "solved" by removing the testes from these women and in France by imploring these patients to stop their "homosexual" alliances with men. (As you might guess, incredulous hermaphroditic patients sometimes thought their doctors daft or cruel.) Commenting on [a French fashion model] labeled by her doctors

---

Age of Consent," in *Intersex in the Age of Ethics,* 6. Dreger argues that "it cannot be a coincidence that at the same time Michel Foucault and other historians find the emergence of the homosexual, I find the virtual extinction of the true hermaphrodite." "Doubtful Sex," 364.

115. Fausto-Sterling, *Sexing the Body,* 37.

116. Dreger, "Doubtful Sex."

117. Preves, *Intersex and Identity,* 26. Fausto-Sterling, *Sexing the Body,* 38. Alice Domurat Dreger, *Hermaphrodites and the Medical Invention of Sex* (Cambridge: Harvard University Press, 1998).

> as "frankly homosexual" because she passionately loved only men, a pair of French experts observed, "The possession of a [single] sex [as male or female] is a necessity of our social order, for hermaphrodites as well as for normal subjects."[118]

Elsewhere, Dreger explains how the redefinition of hermaphroditism (as true or false) worked to keep chaos at bay. "By equating sex identity simply with gonadal tissue, almost every body could be shown really to be a 'true male' or a 'true female' in spite of mounting numbers of doubtful cases. Additionally, given that biopsies of gonads were not done until the 1910s and that Victorian medical men insisted upon histological proof of ovarian and testicular tissue for claims of 'true hermaphroditism,' the only 'true hermaphrodites' tended to be dead and autopsied hermaphrodites."[119]

In the face of social and ethical confusion over sex and gender and sexuality, physicians attempted to bolster the traditional dichotomy by restricting and virtually eliminating the numbers of true hermaphrodites on medical record. The irony of the project should not go unnoticed. At the very time medical men were documenting larger numbers of persons with mixed sex characteristics, by redefining their terms, they were able to virtually eliminate that same number. Again, we are confronted with the reality of the social construction of sex for the intersexed.

Twentieth Century: From Medical Management to the Disappearance of Hermaphrodites

The sex classification system offered by Theodore Klebs did not go uncontested. Doctors and patients alike found it difficult to continue to label persons who looked female on the outside, albeit with testes on the inside, as "men." By the 1920s this disjunction led to the development of another philosophical category: gender as separate from sex. As medical technologies advanced, surgeons began offering "surgical 'corrections' to bring the biological sex into line with assigned gender."[120] By the 1950s Johns Hopkins University

118. Dreger, "A History of Intersex," 9.

119. Alice Domurat Dreger, "'Ambiguous Sex' — or Ambivalent Medicine? Ethical Issues in the Treatment of Intersexuality," *Hastings Center Report* 28, no. 3 (1998): 26.

120. Intersex Society of North America, "What's the History behind the Intersex Rights Movement?" 28. http://www.isna.org/faq/printable. Milton Diamond credits Freud with the distinction between sex and gender in "Sex, Gender, and Identity over the

created the first multidisciplinary team of specialists to address intersex. The team was headed by psychologist John Money, and its goal became the elimination of intersex through medical intervention in early childhood.[121]

John Money led the charge for early medical correction of intersex based on the belief that gender identity was malleable in early childhood given the right conditions. He supported this claim on the basis of the now highly publicized case of David Reimer (a.k.a. "John/Joan"), in which a nonintersexed, male child's penis was ablated (i.e., removed) at eight months of age during a botched circumcision.[122] The family was eventually referred to Johns Hopkins Hospital, where they received counsel to surgically feminize the child and raise him as a girl. What made this case a perfect experiment was that the boy had an identical twin.[123]

Money followed up with the family during childhood and published the success of the experiment in his widely acclaimed book, cowritten with Anke A. Ehrhardt: *Man and Woman, Boy and Girl.*[124] They reportedly found a happy little girl who preferred stereotypical feminine clothing and behavior. The case seemed closed, at least for Money and Ehrhardt.[125]

Milton Diamond, a younger sex researcher skeptical of Money's theory of gender plasticity, followed up with "John/Joan" in later years. After years of trying to find and convince Reimer's doctors to come forward with follow-up information, he was finally able to rally H. Keith Sigmundson — one of Reimer's therapists — to join him in challenging Money's dominant interpretive position.[126] At last, the truth came out that "Joan's" sex reassignment had never taken. Though she tried to comply with the wishes of her parents, "Joan" knew she was different. Reimer explains that his realization

---

Years: A Changing Perspective," *Child and Adolescent Psychiatric Clinics of North America* 13 (2004): 591.

121. Money, *Sex Errors,* 6.

122. The Intersex Society of North America explains that David was born in 1965 and, while not intersex, did have a "medical problem involving his penis" for which circumcision was recommended at eight months as "treatment." ISNA, "Who Was David Reimer (Also, Sadly, Known as 'John/Joan')?" http://www.isna.org/faq/printable, 26.

123. Milton Diamond and H. Keith Sigmundson, "Sex Reassignment at Birth: A Long Term Review and Clinical Implications," *Archives of Pediatrics and Adolescent Medicine* 151 (March 1997): 298-304.

124. John Money and Anke A. Ehrhardt, *Man and Woman, Boy and Girl* (Baltimore: Johns Hopkins University Press, 1972).

125. Kessler, *Lessons from the Intersexed,* 7.

126. See Fausto-Sterling for a lively narrative of the decades-long battle waged between Money and Diamond over their differing philosophies of gender; *Sexing the Body,* 66-71.

that he was a boy seemed to solidify between the ages of nine and eleven. At age twelve she rebelled against feminizing hormone therapy, and at age fourteen she succeeded in convincing her therapists and parents to assist her in transitioning to life as a male. He received a mastectomy at age fourteen and began phallic construction between fifteen and sixteen. He had his first sexual encounter at age eighteen, and at twenty-five married a woman a few years older and adopted her children.[127]

Diamond and Sigmundson relayed David Reimer's story under the pseudonyms "John/Joan," but David later came forward himself to work with Diamond in disabusing the medical establishment (and public at large) of the success of his case. He did not want others to suffer the "psychic trauma" he had to endure.[128] Despite years fighting to overcome the challenges of his life, David ended his own life at the age of thirty-eight, on May 5, 2004.[129]

Money used the alleged success of Reimer's case to argue that intersex persons should be given early genital surgery and that surgery, accompanied by unambiguous gender rearing, would result in a well-adjusted, heterosexual male or female. But his efforts rebounded to undo the intended result. Some intersexed persons who had been treated according to Money's philosophy rejected their sex assignment and resented (to put it mildly) the medical treatment they had received. Still, most persons suffered in silence, believing what they had been told by doctors, that their conditions were so rare that they would never meet anyone in the world like themselves. Trained by parents, physicians, and psychologists to keep quiet about their abnormalities (out of genuine concern for the well-being of the patient), the intersexed did not find a voice until the 1990s.

1990s: Intersex Emerges from the Closet

The 1993 publication of Anne Fausto-Sterling's article "The Five Sexes: Why Male and Female Are Not Enough" in *The Sciences* and the *New York*

127. Diamond and Sigmundson, "Sex Reassignment at Birth," 299-300.

128. Diamond and Sigmundson, "Sex Reassignment at Birth," 299. See also Preves, *Intersex and Identity,* 96-97. Kessler explains that the popularity of Money's theory has made it difficult for the truth of Reimer's story to alter the way sex and gender are still taught in many social science and medical textbooks. Feminists in particular were eager to apply the insights of Money's theory to their own causes. Kessler, *Lessons from the Intersexed,* 7.

129. John Colapinto, "Gender Gap: What Were the Real Reasons behind David Reimer's Suicide?" *Slate.com* (Thursday, June 3, 2004, at 3:58 P.M. Eastern time).

Times motivated an intersex woman Cheryl Chase (Bo Laurent)[130] to do something.

> In response [to Fausto-Sterling's article], Cheryl Chase wrote a letter to *The Sciences* announcing the founding of the Intersex Society of North America (ISNA). She founded the group because of her own attempts to recover her history of sex-reassignment in infancy and medically-induced shame, and because of the disinterest of most of her former care providers in what had happened to her. Soon Chase had brought together dozens of people with intersex. Though ISNA began as a support group, it quickly turned into an advocacy group because its members realized that they had suffered from similar problems. Like many of the early ISNA members, Chase drew on her political consciousness as a lesbian woman to recognize the degree to which intersex had been unnecessarily socially and medically pathologized. With the successes of the women's health movement and the queer rights movement as a backdrop, people with intersex began agitating for openness and reform.[131]

Similar movements sprang up all over the globe.[132] Kessler explains, "Although there are some differences among the intersex advocacy groups, most members criticize the way their intersexuality was and is handled and argue that there needs to be a break in 'the vicious cycle in which shame [about variant genitals] produces silence, silence condones surgery, and surgery produces more shame (which produces more silence).' "[133]

130. "When Cheryl founded ISNA, in 1993, she knew that she planned to change her legal name, but had not yet decided for herself just what name to adopt. In 1995, she changed her legal name from Bonnie Sullivan to Bo Laurent. However, by that time 'Cheryl' was beginning to be known. She worked on intersex issues using the name Cheryl Chase until 2008, when she began to use Bo Laurent in all aspects of her life." ISNA, "Cheryl Chase (Bo Laurent)," http://www.isna.org/about/chase.

131. ISNA, "What's the History behind the Intersex Rights Movement?" http://www.isna.org/faq/printable, 29.

132. Simultaneous groups have sprung up in Canada, Europe, Asia, Australia, Japan, and New Zealand. "In Germany, a group of intersexuals, using some of the same strategies as ISNA, established a peer support and advocacy group. The initial name of the group, Intersex Support Network Central Europe, was later changed to Genital Mutilation Survivor's Support Network and Workgroup on Violence in Pediatrics and Gynecology, reflecting the fury of its political evolution." Kessler, *Lessons from the Intersexed,* 79.

133. Kessler, *Lessons from the Intersexed,* 79-80, quoting *Hermaphrodites with Attitude* 1, no. 1 (Winter 1994).

With the goal of ending "shame, secrecy, and unwanted genital surgeries for people born with an anatomy that someone has decided is not standard for male or female," ISNA now focuses their work on influencing the medical profession to change standard treatment for intersex.[134]

Despite resistance, their efforts are beginning to produce positive results.[135] Diamond and Sigmundson published their guidelines for the "management of intersexuality" in 1997, emphasizing "the key belief that the patients themselves must be involved in any decision as to something so crucial to their lives."[136] Since 1997 Diamond has repeatedly called for a moratorium on infant surgeries among the American Academy of Pediatrics. His efforts were aided by the publication of Kessler's *Lessons from the Intersexed* in 1998 and Dreger's *Intersex in the Age of Ethics* in 1999, with the result that in 2000 and 2001 the American Academy of Pediatrics and the British Association of Pediatric Surgeons did update their standards of care to reflect some of their recommendations. Still, Diamond laments that neither the British nor the American pediatric society has called for a complete halt to infant surgeries.[137]

In October of 2005, fifty experts from ten countries met in Chicago to produce a consensus statement for the treatment of intersex to be published in medical journals worldwide. ISNA distributed its own *Clinical Guidelines* and *Handbook for Parents* to participants at the conference.[138] The consensus statement was published in the *Archives of Disease in Childhood* in May of 2006.[139] While the statement does not argue that all non-life-saving surgical interventions should be delayed until the child reaches the age of consent, it does advise greater caution and tout the benefits of delaying surgery when possible.[140] In addition to summarizing the current medical definitions and

134. ISNA, "What Is ISNA's Mission?" http://www.isna.org/faq/printable, 15.

135. Kessler explains how some physicians at Johns Hopkins Medical Center had tried to dismiss intersex advocates arguing that those who participate in ISNA are a "self-selected group brought together through their negative experiences," thus not representative of many who may be satisfied with treatment. Kessler, *Lessons from the Intersexed,* 87.

136. Diamond and Sigmundson, "Management of Intersexuality," 1046.

137. Diamond, "Sex, Gender and Identity," 600. While European and North American physicians have yet to end surgery on intersex infants, the South American country of Colombia outlawed the procedure in 1998. According to Diamond, the "Constitution guarantees free development of one's own personality, which implies a right to define one's own sexual identity" (601).

138. Barbara Thomas, "Report on Chicago Consensus Conference October 2005," www.AISSG.org, 2-3.

139. Hughes et al., "Consensus Statement," 1-10.

140. Hughes et al., "Consensus Statement," 4.

the most up-to-date management strategies, the consensus statement also recommends substituting the umbrella term "disorders of sex development" (DSDs) for "intersex"; the new term offers more precise terminology for individual conditions, and avoids sex and gender labels.[141]

What Is in a Name? From Hermaphrodite to Intersex to Disorders of Sex Development (DSDs)

While the moves away from hermaphroditic terminology and gendered labels for intersex conditions (e.g., from "testicular feminization" to androgen insensitivity syndrome) were met with little resistance, the shift from intersex to DSDs has not gone uncontested. Diamond and others have argued that "Variation in Sex Development (VSD) [is] a term that is without judgment and neither prohibits or ordains medical intervention."[142]

Nevertheless, the shift to DSDs is gaining ground. Even the Intersex Society of North America employed the new terminology in its *Clinical Guidelines* and *Handbook for Parents* (with a disclaimer noting objections by certain contributors).[143] Barbara Thomas, a German woman with AIS who participated in the Chicago conference, concedes the pragmatic value of the new nomenclature but expresses frustration as well: "given the reluctance of health insurance firms to deliver goods to intersex customers, the more PC [term] 'variation' is not helpful when campaigning for better care."[144]

Given the shift in language approved by so many within the medical community, it is fair to ask why I continue to use the label "intersex" instead of "DSD." One of the reasons "intersex" was rejected by physicians is that it carries with it associations of "identity politics and sexual connotations."[145] "Disorders of sex development" does not automatically flag the same concerns. Nevertheless, as the rest of this text will show, sex, gender, and sexuality, while distinct, cannot easily be disentangled from one another. Theologians must acknowledge and attend to the interconnectedness of these

141. Hughes et al., "Consensus Statement," 1.

142. Hazel Glenn Beh, William S. Richardson, and Milton Diamond, "Letter to the Editor: Variations of Sex Development Instead of Disorders of Sex Development," *Archives of Disease in Childhood* 91 (July 27, 2006).

143. Consortium, *Clinical Guidelines,* acknowledgments.

144. Thomas, "Report on Chicago Consensus Conference," 3.

145. Elizabeth Reis, "Divergence or Disorder? The Politics of Naming Intersex," *Perspectives in Biology and Medicine* 50, no. 4 (Autumn 2007): 535-43.

ideas. Theologian Susannah Cornwall makes a similar argument and offers the compound "intersex/DSD" as a "visual reminder of the uncertainty of the term and its resonances. . . . Much more than either/or, intersex/DSD is at once both and neither, a perpetually-debatable term for a perpetually-debated group of phenomena."[146]

What the shift in nomenclature does illustrate is the climax of the narrative of the medicalization of intersex. This short history shows how the hermaphrodite began as a legendary creation of the gods, was tolerated at the margins of societies for millennia, only to be surgically eliminated in the last hundred years. But the sexual revolution is overcoming the medical establishment. Through lessons learned from LGBTQ activists, intersex persons are coming out of the closet and demanding better medical treatment and the end of secrecy and shame. Their voices are beginning to be heard in the medical arena, and they are working hard to raise awareness in society at large.

From Medical Management to Social Change: Questioning the Binary Sex Model

Multiple Sexes

Anne Fausto-Sterling's article "The Five Sexes: Why Male and Female Are Not Enough" was the catalyst that emboldened Cheryl Chase (Bo Laurent) to launch the Intersex Society of North America. Fausto-Sterling shares the concern of ISNA to end unwanted genital surgeries, but her goals call for even greater reform — reform of our very concepts of sex and gender. Fausto-Sterling calls us to abandon the notion of two sexes and fling the gate wide for the multiplication of sexes. While she has abandoned the language she used in 1993 (Klebs's five-sex schema, including true hermaphrodites and pseudohermaphrodites), her critique of the binary sex model remains.

Fausto-Sterling lays the blame for the abuse of intersex persons on the belief in a two-sex system. Rather than calling for better care within the two-sex model, she posits an alternative solution:

> But what if things were altogether different? Imagine a world in which the same knowledge that has enabled medicine to intervene in the med-

146. Susannah Cornwall, *Sex and Uncertainty in the Body of Christ: Intersex Conditions and Christian Theology* (London: Equinox, 2010), 19.

> ical management of intersexual patients has been placed at the service of multiple sexualities. Imagine that the sexes have multiplied beyond currently imaginable limits. It would be a world of shared powers. Patient and physician, parent and child, male and female — all those oppositions and others would have to be dissolved as sources of division. A new ethic of medical treatment would arise, one that would permit ambiguity in a culture that had overcome sexual division. The central mission of medical treatment would be to preserve life. Thus hermaphrodites would be concerned primarily not about whether they can conform to society but about whether they might develop potentially life-threatening conditions . . . that sometimes accompany hermaphroditic development. In my ideal world medical intervention for intersexuality would take place only rarely before the age of reason; subsequent treatment would be a cooperative venture between physician, patient, and other advisers trained in issues of gender multiplicity.[147]

Historians of intersex are quick to concede that physicians and parents advocating for early medical correction of intersex have done so out of genuine concern for the well-being of children/patients. Nevertheless, Fausto-Sterling claims that these same physicians failed to do their homework. She insists, "modern investigators tend to overlook a substantial body of case histories . . . before surgical intervention became rampant. Almost without exception, those reports describe children who grew up knowing they were intersexual (though they did not advertise it) and adjusted to their unusual status. . . . [I]n any event, there is not a psychotic or a suicide in the lot."[148]

Her description of intersexed persons and that of John Money could not be more different. He calls Fausto-Sterling's proposal "extreme," and argues the following:

> Without medical intervention, the fate of many hermaphroditic babies is to die. Before contemporary medical interventions, many children with a birth defect of the sex organs were condemned to grow up as they were born, stigmatized and traumatized. It simply does not make sense to talk of a third sex, or a fourth or fifth, when the phylogenetic scheme of things is two sexes. Those who are genitally neither male nor female but incomplete are not a third sex. They are a mixed sex or an in-between

147. Fausto-Sterling, "The Five Sexes," in *Sexuality and Gender,* 472.
148. Fausto-Sterling, "The Five Sexes," in *Sexuality and Gender,* 472.

> sex. To advocate medical nonintervention is irresponsible. It runs counter to everything that this book stands for, which is to enhance health and well-being to the greatest extent possible.[149]

The question, of course, remains: Who gets to determine what enhances "health and well-being to the greatest extent"? Some intersex persons may be content with their medical treatment. Diamond and Sigmundson concede that "humans can be immensely strong and adaptable." Some have adjusted to medical treatment because they cannot recover what they lost. Some are "living in silent despair but coping." But others "have complained bitterly of the treatment."[150] Those who are not content and have found voices to complain have argued that intersex, as naturally occurring phenomena, is not the problem. The problem is the two-sex system, which leaves no room for naturally occurring variations from the dominant categories of male and female.

In place of the binary sex model, Fausto-Sterling argues that we should view sex as a continuum. "The implications of my argument for a sexual continuum are profound. If nature really offers us more than two sexes, then it follows that our current notions of masculinity and femininity are cultural conceits."[151] However, it would be more accurate to say that if nature offers us more than two sexes, we may be justified in adding to our current cultural constructs more sexes than male and female and more genders than masculine and feminine. In some ways Western culture has already done this at the level of gender. We have language and conceptual space for "tomboys" and "sissies," though the latter is more often a category of derision than the former.[152] The problem, of course, that Fausto-Sterling and others have outlined, is where to draw the lines? Three sexes? Four? Five? Twenty? David Hester suggests there are "literally hundreds of possible sexes that humans can inhabit."[153] We are left with the challenge of who defines male, female, in-between, and other.

149. Money, *Sex Errors,* 6.

150. Diamond and Sigmundson, "Management of Intersexuality," 1050.

151. Fausto-Sterling, *Sexing the Body,* 31.

152. There is an ironic inversion of assumptions when one considers the history of these terms. "Tomboy" comes from "tommy," the eighteenth-century term for female lesbian transvestites, but most tomboys today are not always assumed to be lesbians. The same is not true for the effeminate male. Randolph Trumbach, "London's Sapphists: From Three Sexes to Four Genders in the Making of Modern Culture," in *Third Sex, Third Gender,* 112.

153. J. David Hester, "Intersexes and the End of Gender: Corporeal Ethics and Postgender Bodies," *Journal of Gender Studies* 13, no. 3 (November 2004): 219.

Gilbert Herdt, in his work *Third Sex, Third Gender,* shows how alternative sexes/genders have been documented in a number of societies at different times throughout history. But he explains that his use of "third" is not to be taken literally; rather, the notion of the third serves to undermine the absolute contrast that arises within a binary system.[154]

The Elimination of Gender

Suzanne Kessler is even more radical in her proposal. She recommends we do away with the categories of sex and gender altogether.[155] In her earlier work with Wendy McKenna, Kessler argued that gender, not sex, is the more salient force in contemporary culture. In everyday interactions, humans do not respond to persons' genitals but to their display of gender through clothing, hairstyles, shaving, and verbal and nonverbal communication. How we "do" gender is much more important for everyday life than what exists underneath our clothing.[156] Kessler's work reveals the circular logic at the root of the two-sex system: human bodies come as one of two sexes. Two sexes imply two genders. When bodies do not fit clearly into either sex category, the belief in two genders is used to advocate a medical fix in order to bring bodies back in line with the belief in two sexes. But what if we refuse to "fix" intersex? According to Kessler, both our categories of sex and gender will begin to unravel. "The consequences of refusing to alter the body in accordance with gender ideals are obvious. A world populated with flat-chested, hairy women with penis-sized clitorises and large-breasted, hairless men with micro-penises would be a world of blended gender, and eventually, blended gender is no gender."[157]

She explains how gender ideals, once impossible for most, are descending from the realm of the forms into everyday lives thanks to the ever-increasing skills of cosmetic surgeons. Perfect bodies can be purchased by intersexed and nonintersexed alike, provided the price is right.[158] But she

154. Herdt, preface to *Third Sex, Third Gender,* 19-20.

155. Virginia Ramey Mollenkott makes a similar proposal in *Omnigender: A Trans-religious Approach* (Cleveland: Pilgrim Press, 2001), esp. 164-85. Regarding intersex, she writes, "In short, intersexual people are the best biological evidence we have that the binary gender construct is totally inadequate and is causing terrific injustice and unnecessary suffering" (51).

156. Kessler and McKenna, *Gender.*

157. Kessler, *Lessons from the Intersexed,* 117.

158. Kessler, *Lessons from the Intersexed,* 111.

warns that making cosmetic genital surgery available could lead to greater intolerance for variations from the norm.[159] "Surgical solutions for variant genitals need to be seen in the context of a cultural tide that is shrinking rather than expanding the range of what is considered normal for all parts of the body. Endocrinologists are prescribing a regimen of growth hormone for children who are deemed too short. Orthodontists are diagnosing denture abnormalities and providing 'necessary' corrections for virtually every middle-class child's teeth. 'Imperfections [are] remediable today with the early help of a skilled surgeon.'"[160] Kessler insists that "[i]f we want people to respect particular bodies, they need to be taught to lose respect for ideal ones."[161] But losing respect for the ideals of gender may carry consequences for which we are not prepared.

Kessler finds the eradication of gender liberating, not only for the intersexed but also for anyone who finds gender rules oppressive. Rather than trying to change the rules of the gender system, as many feminists have done, she argues that we simply dispense with the idea that sex is tied to genitals and allow gender to evolve or dissolve altogether.

> By subverting genital primacy, gender will be removed from the biological body and placed in the social-interactional one. Even if there are still two genders, male and female, how you "do" male and female, including how you "do" genitals, would be open to interpretation. Physicians teach parents of intersexed infants that the fetus is bipotential, but they talk about gender as being "finished" at sixteen or twenty weeks, just because the genitals are. Gender need not be thought of as finished, not for people who identify as intersexed, nor for any of us. Once we dispense with "sex"

159. "The analogy to noses is obvious. People electing to alter theirs choose the small upturned one, characteristic of the privileged class, rather than a variety of 'ethnic' ones. Given that pattern, what will happen if it becomes fashionable to alter one's genitals? Will this mean that everyone — female and male — will want large phalluses like the privileged gender, or will it mean that males, evoking their privilege, will restrict large phalluses to males and demand that more females have their clitorises reduced? Will women start to feel inadequate about yet another body part, in this case a body part that had been off limits, by virtue of our culture's puritanical silence about things 'down there'? All of this is worth pondering as we play with the idea of usurping control of genital surgery to undercut gender." Kessler, *Lessons from the Intersexed,* 119.

160. Kessler, *Lessons from the Intersexed,* 157-58. For a similar critique of medical fixes for "normal" deviations from the norm, see Carl Elliott, *Better Than Well: American Medicine Meets the American Dream* (New York: Norton, 2003).

161. Kessler, *Lessons from the Intersexed,* 118.

> and acknowledge gender as located in the social-interactional body, it will be easier to treat it as a work-in-progress.
>
> This is assuming, though, that gender is something worth working on. It may not be. If intersexuality imparts any lesson, it is that gender is a responsibility and a burden — for those being categorized and those doing the categorizing. We rightfully complain about gender oppression in all its social and political manifestations, but we have not seriously grappled with the fact that we afflict ourselves with a need to locate a bodily basis for assertions about gender. We must use whatever means we have to give up on gender. The problems of intersexuality will vanish and we will, in this way, compensate intersexuals for all the lessons they have provided.[162]

Intersexuality (as well as hetero- and homo- and bisexuality) only makes sense when sex is tied to genitals.[163]

Third Sex: For Adults Only

It may come as a surprise to the reader that the Intersex Society of North America does not advocate for a third sex category, nor the elimination of gender — at least when it comes to the raising of children. Whereas Fausto-Sterling calls for a few good parents to brave social disapproval in raising their children as unabashed intersexuals, the ISNA is more cautious in its proposals.[164] Those at ISNA give two reasons why they do not recommend raising children in a third gender or no gender. First, they recognize that someone has to decide where to draw the boundary lines and that this venture, attempted in the past, is fraught with difficulty. "Second, and much more importantly, we are trying to make the world a safe place for intersex

162. Kessler, *Lessons from the Intersexed,* 132.

163. "One can imagine that just as a heterosexual woman today can legitimately claim not to be attracted to men with excessive body hair, in a newly configured system she could claim not to be attracted to men with breasts and a vagina. What then would heterosexual mean? In what sense could a woman with a vagina who is sexually gratified by being penetrated by a 'woman' with a large clitoris (that looks and functions like a penis) be said to be a lesbian? If gendered bodies fall into disarray, sexual orientation will follow. Defining sexual orientation according to attraction to people with the same or different genitals, as is done now, will no longer make sense, nor will intersexuality." Kessler, *Lessons from the Intersexed,* 124.

164. Fausto-Sterling, "The Five Sexes," in *Sexuality and Gender,* 472.

kids, and we don't think labeling them with a gender category that doesn't exist would help them."[165]

Diamond and Sigmundson concur and urge physicians to advise parents in similar fashion with one exception: as children grow, they should be given the option to choose whether or not to identify themselves as intersex.[166] While some intersex persons are perfectly content within a two-sex/gender system, others are not.[167] "In our society intersex is a designation of medical fact but not yet a commonly accepted social designation. With age and experience, however, an increasing number of hermaphroditic and pseudohermaphroditic persons are adopting this identification. . . . With increasing maturity, the designation of intersex may be acceptable to some and not to others. It should be offered as an optional identity along with male and female."[168]

Questions remain whether intersex should become an option in our current society — at the legal, religious, and practical levels.[169] Julia Epstein summarizes: "The law assumes a precise contrariety between two sexes, whereas medical science has for several centuries understood sex determination to involve a complex and indefinite mechanism that results in a spectrum of human sexual types rather than in a set of mutually exclusive categories."[170]

165. ISNA, "Does ISNA Think Children with Intersex Should Be Raised without a Gender, or in a Third Gender?" http:/www.isna.org/faq/printable.

166. Kessler sees a connection between self-identification as intersex and medicalization. She quotes Morgan Holmes, an intersexed member of ISNA Canada. "'Was I intersexed before I was medicalized?' [She] compares herself to a woman friend with a three-and-a-half-inch clitoris that escaped 'correction.' Holmes's friend refuses the intersex label for herself, claiming that this would be an additional burden, making her even more of an outsider than her lesbianism already does. I suspect that her rejection of the label has more to do with an identity fit. She was not diagnosed; she was not 'surgicalized;' she does not feel like an intersexual. Holmes's own argument confirms this: 'It is partly in the naming that bodies become intersexed.'" Kessler, *Lessons from the Intersexed,* 89, quoting Morgan Holmes, "Homophobia in Health Care: Abjection and the Treatment of Intersexuality" (paper presented at the Learned Societies CSAA meetings, Montreal, June 1995). Kessler also notes the irony that the intersexual identity is connected to surgical experience despite physicians' assertions that early surgical intervention will allow the child to grow up without questions of gender identity (86).

167. Cornwall, *Sex and Uncertainty,* 18.

168. Diamond and Sigmundson, "Management of Intersexuality," 1047-48.

169. Greenberg, "Defining Male and Female," 265-328.

170. Epstein, "Either/Or — Neither/Both," 101.

Third Sex and Alternative Sexualities

One of the biggest obstacles to the creation of a third sex category in American culture is the link between a biological third sex and alternative sexualities. In his cross-cultural and historical account of third sexes, Gilbert Herdt illustrates how, in Western society, the figure of the hermaphrodite became conflated with the "sexual deviant" so that in the modern period the homosexual was labeled a "hermaphrodite of the soul."[171] His anthology is entitled *Third Sex, Third Gender,* but it would have been more true to the materials to add one more phrase, *Third Sexuality,* to accurately describe the contents. Of course, Herdt's inclusion of alternative sexualities is intentional, as he believes "cross-cultural variations in sexual and gender patterns have been downplayed when it comes to discussions of 'normal' reproductive sexuality and kinship." He lays the blame for this neglect upon "intellectual, social and morally defined strictures of sexual dimorphism."[172] Thus, according to Herdt, the binary sex model is dependent as much upon a heterosexual ethic as it is upon scientific observance of sex differences. His work echoes the arguments of Judith Butler, who insists that "gender identity" and the binary model upon which it is built are a "regulatory ideal" resulting from "compulsory heterosexuality."[173]

Fausto-Sterling's longer treatise, *Sexing the Body,* documents how the "specter of homosexuality" has haunted sex and gender studies from the beginning.[174] Despite her caveat that "each person experiences [intersex] differently," Dreger still makes the sweeping generalization that "intersex is, and always will be, about sex, that is, sexual relations."[175] Dreger does overstate her case, as the testimony of intersex woman Sally Gross illustrates. Gross has described her own experience of intersex, and her lack of sexual desire, as indicating that she was one of "nature's celibates."[176] The sexual experiences of intersex persons are as varied as the sexualities of every human being. One cannot claim a unified "intersex sexuality." Even

171. Herdt, introduction to *Third Sex, Third Gender,* 23.

172. Herdt, preface to *Third Sex, Third Gender,* 12.

173. Judith Butler, *Gender Trouble: Feminism and the Subversion of Identity,* 2nd ed. (New York: Routledge, 1990), 24.

174. Fausto-Sterling, *Sexing the Body,* esp. 71-73. See also Epstein, "Either/Or — Neither/Both," 100-101.

175. Dreger, "Introduction to Part 2," in *Intersex in the Age of Ethics,* 69.

176. Sally Gross, "Shunned by the Church," *The Natal Witness Features* (South Africa), February 22, 2000.

so, the connection between sexual politics and sex differentiation is a close one.

It cannot be disputed that a new openness toward homosexuality in the last decade has led to a greater willingness by physicians to improve the standard medical treatment of intersex. Diamond and Sigmundson argued for greater openness to alternative sexual expression for the intersexed in 1997, and their recommendations were heeded by the international consensus group in 2005.[177] Thus, the consensus group concluded, "homosexual orientation (relative to sex of rearing) or strong cross-sex interest in an individual with DSD is *not* an indication of incorrect gender assignment."[178] It seems that social acceptance of variations of sex development is more closely intertwined with social acceptance of variations of sexual orientation than many would like to admit.

Is Christianity to Blame?

Fausto-Sterling and others have argued that the abuse of intersex by the medical establishment over the last two hundred years has resulted from the oppressive binary sex model dominant within Western culture, and that this binary sex model is the result of a heterosexual ethic. She does not lay the blame on the Judeo-Christian tradition directly, but comes very close when she indicts Western religious sensibilities and Victorian sexual mores.[179] Gordene MacKenzie is less subtle. In her book *Transgender Nation,* she lays the blame for the binary model squarely at the feet of the Judeo-Christian tradition.[180]

177. "Certainly the full gamut of heterosexual, homosexual, bisexual, and even celibate options — however these are interpreted by the patient — must be offered and candidly discussed." Diamond and Sigmundson, "Management of Intersexuality," 1047-48.

178. Hughes et al., "Consensus Statement," 1.

179. "I do not pretend that the transition to my utopia would be smooth. Sex, even the supposedly 'normal,' heterosexual kind, continues to cause untold anxieties in Western society. And certainly a culture that has yet to come to grips — religiously and, in some states, legally — with the ancient and relatively uncomplicated reality of homosexual love will not readily embrace intersexuality. No doubt the most troublesome area by far would be the rearing of children. Parents, at least since the Victorian era, have fretted, sometimes to the point of outright denial, over the fact that their children are sexual beings." Fausto-Sterling, "The Five Sexes," in *Sexuality and Gender,* 472.

180. Gordene Olga MacKenzie, *Transgender Nation* (Bowling Green, Ohio: Bowling Green State University Popular Press, 1994), 14.

Is this a fair critique? Does Christianity require a two-sex system? Most Christian theologians certainly function under the assumption that there are but two sexes, male and female, and two genders that follow, naturally, one from each sex. This belief is grounded in the accounts of the creation of Adam and Eve found in the book of Genesis and reinforced throughout the Scriptures through simple description (heterosexual marriages and genealogies), ethical legislation to protect the boundaries of heterosexual marriages (do not covet your neighbor's wife, punishment for adultery), and theological analogies based on the image of heterosexual marriage (Zion as the daughter/bride of YHWH, the church as the bride of Christ).

Mainstream Christian tradition has reinforced this binary sex/gender paradigm through its value of heterosexual marriage and the alternative pathway of male or female celibate religious life. And yet, there is evidence of a third option in corners of the Christian tradition. As the next chapter will show, Christian language about eunuchs, grounded in Jesus' recognition of three types of eunuchs, created space for those who did not fit neatly into the sex categories of male or female. Monasteries were founded for eunuchs in the Middle Ages, and eunuchs emerged as a recognized third gender in the Byzantine Christian Empire. Marginal though the eunuch has always been, it at least existed within Christian culture and thought. But this is no longer true. From myth to margin, to medical erasure, intersex is believed to be a thing of legend, not persons among us. As a result, the eunuch no longer exists in contemporary theology and church life.

Alice Domurat Dreger believes it is no coincidence that when traditional sexual mores are being challenged by alternative sexualities, the "true" hermaphrodite disappears in Western culture.[181] She documents how medical doctors attempted to create clarity out of ambiguity by refusing to acknowledge intersex in the public sector.

Western Christians stand at a similar crossroads today. While some "welcoming and affirming" churches readily employ arguments from the existence of intersex persons to justify accepting transsexualities, homosexualities, and bisexualities, conservative Christians may be tempted to follow in the footsteps of Victorian physicians by attempting to shore up traditional categories of sex and gender, further marginalizing the intersexed in response.[182] I will argue that these are not the only options. The Scriptures offer a third way for recognizing a third gender.

181. Dreger, "Doubtful Sex," 364.

182. See Ann Thompson Cook, *Made in God's Image: A Resource for Dialogue about the*

In the next chapter we will explore the category of the eunuch, its place within the biblical canon, Christian history, and theology. I will argue that by recovering the concept of the eunuch, theologians will find fresh avenues for rethinking the meanings of sex and gender for theological anthropology and a starting place to address the challenges and incorporate the insights learned from intersex.

Recovering the concept of the eunuch and acknowledging the presence of the intersexed in our communities do not necessarily lead to a thoroughgoing evacuation of the entire narrative of sex, gender, and sexuality found within the Christian tradition; but they do challenge and complicate the ways conservative Christians typically discuss the sex difference. As this chapter has shown, the simplistic binary model is no longer sufficient. It is dishonest to the diversity of persons created in the image of God.

Acknowledging the complexity of sex difference behooves theologians to reconsider theological edifices they have constructed upon the simplistic binary model. Chapters 2 and 3 will supply the biblical, historical, and philosophical resources for evaluating a few of these edifices. Then the edifices themselves will be examined — the value of sex difference for theological notions of personhood and *imago Dei* (chap. 4) and current constructions of relationality that have been built upon the model of heterosexual marital relations (chap. 5). Finally, chapter 6 will explore the relationship between Jesus as the true image and the eschatological consummation of that image for those who are "in Christ." In all these ways, I hope to provide a more nuanced and balanced model for theological reflection on sex difference.

Church and Gender Differences (Washington, D.C.: Dumbarton United Methodist Church, 2003). Cf. Charles Colson, "Blurred Biology: How Many Sexes Are There?" *BreakPoint,* October 16, 1996.

CHAPTER 2

Biblical Resources beyond Adam and Eve: The Case of Eunuchs

In this chapter we turn away from contemporary medical, political, and sociological explorations of sex difference and roll back the clock several millennia. In many ways the ancient world was much more rigid in defining and protecting the borders between men and women than is the contemporary West. And yet, despite this great fear of gender blending, the ancients were more open to recognizing that their binary model of sex difference needed supplementation in order to address the full range of human bodies as they occur in the real world.

One such supplement was the concept of the eunuch. Much like the term "intersex," "eunuch" was an umbrella concept — a word to cover a range of phenomena wherein humans did not measure up to the male ideal. Additional ancient terms were employed to describe other sex differences. Barren women are mentioned in numerous places in the Bible, and the designator is sufficiently broad to describe infertile women as well as intersex women (for example, women with androgen insensitivity syndrome, Swyer syndrome, Turner syndrome, etc.). Hermaphrodites or androgynes are not mentioned in the Scriptures but appear in Jewish commentaries and early Christian literature. What is clear is that the ancients were quite familiar with variations of sex development and found ways to expand their binary model to include others.

And yet the category of eunuch differed from the hermaphrodite or the barren woman in that it remained a term of "in-between-ness," as the following chapter will show. Barren women remained women — although they suffered shame from their inability to perform the duties of their sex.[1]

1. Cf. Isa. 54:1-8; 1 Sam. 1:1–2:10.

Surprisingly, hermaphrodites and androgynes were sometimes classified as men. Augustine explains, "Although androgynes, whom men also call hermaphrodites, are very rare, yet it is difficult to find periods when they do not occur. In them the marks of both sexes appear together in such a way that it is uncertain from which they should properly receive their name. However, our established manner of speaking has given them the gender of the better sex, calling them masculine."[2]

On the other hand, Augustine claims that a castrated eunuch is "neither changed into a woman nor allowed to remain a man."[3] For Augustine, the eunuch stood outside of the binary system while hermaphrodites could be folded within. Augustine cites grammatical gender as the reason for this classification,[4] but others may provide more complete explanation. From their mythological conception, androgynes or hermaphrodites were believed to have the sexual characteristics of both sexes — not deficient genitals of one sex. Within the androcentric economy of the ancient world, only the male genitals really mattered.[5] Unlike eunuchs, some hermaphrodites were capable of begetting children — an act that (according to standards of the day) proved they were more manly than some eunuchs could ever be.[6] In a move analogous to the Victorian creation of pseudohermaphrodites that Alice Dreger has documented, the classification of some intersex persons as barren women and others as androgynous men allowed the ancients to reduce the number that could not be hidden within a two-sex system.[7]

The eunuch is also of particular importance to Christians, not only because it provided an alternative sex/gender category in the ancient world, but especially because of its association with Jesus. Jesus not only acknowl-

2. Augustine, *The City of God against the Pagans,* trans. Eva Matthews Sanford and William McAllen Green, Loeb Classical Library, vol. 5 (Cambridge: Harvard University Press, 1965), 16.8, p. 47.

3. Matthew Kuefler, *The Manly Eunuch: Masculinity, Gender Ambiguity, and Christian Ideology in Late Antiquity* (Chicago: University of Chicago Press, 2001), 249; citing Augustine, *City of God* 7.24.

4. Augustine, *City of God* 16.8

5. Kuefler, *The Manly Eunuch,* 22-24. On the other hand, if the phallus was less pronounced or failed to work properly, or if the individual preferred the female role in sex and society, the rights of the male could be withdrawn from the hermaphrodite and "he" would be assigned as a "she."

6. Kuefler, *The Manly Eunuch,* 31.

7. Alice Domurat Dreger, "Doubtful Sex: The Fate of the Hermaphrodite in Victorian Medicine," *Victorian Studies* (Spring 1995): 335-70. See chapter 1 for a short history of this erasure.

edged the existence of eunuchs but went so far as to commend those who modeled their lives after these mysterious figures. "For there are eunuchs who have been so from birth, and there are eunuchs who have been made eunuchs by others, and there are eunuchs who have made themselves eunuchs for the sake of the kingdom of heaven. Let anyone accept this who can" (Matt. 19:12 NRSV).

In the history of Christian thought in the West, Jesus' statements about eunuchs have not been fully appreciated. Roman ideals of masculinity prevented many early Christians from accepting the radical challenge that the eunuch posed to their cultural assumptions about sex difference. Over time Jesus' language was tamed so that the eunuch came to represent nonmarried men: a partial but much less radical challenge to social structures and personal identity based on sex, gender, and sexuality.

Jesus' first type of eunuch — who has "been so from birth" — provides a biblical door through which theologians may pass to explore the contributions provided by intersex to current concepts of human personhood, identity, image of God, sex, gender, and sexuality. The eunuch may also function as a window through which intersex persons can see themselves already recognized as members of the Christian community. Indeed, a number of intersex Christians do find themselves in the faces of biblical eunuchs.[8] This chapter will show that already in the midst of the Christian story, the grand narrative beginning with Adam and Eve, there has been room for others.

Jesus' Eunuchs: Biblical and Historical Context

Biblical Context

Jesus' comments in Matthew 19 are not the first appearance of eunuchs in the Bible; nevertheless, his words provide a helpful starting point for the discussion. In verse 12 Jesus identifies three types of eunuchs as he answers a question about the legality of divorcing one's wife "for any and every reason" (v. 3 NIV). To the immediate question Jesus responds with a scriptural quotation. "'Haven't you read,' he replied, 'that at the beginning the Creator "made them male and female," and said, "For this reason a man will leave his

8. The Intersex Support Group International, a Christian intersex support group, begins reflection on intersex with eunuchs. "Director's Page" (1999-2002), http://www.xyxo.org/isgi/director.html.

father and mother and be united to his wife, and the two will become one flesh"? So they are no longer two, but one. Therefore what God has joined together, let man not separate'" (vv. 4-6 NIV).

Some Pharisees challenge Jesus' interpretation of Genesis by arguing that Moses made provisions for certificates of divorce. But Jesus is unmoved. He replies, "Moses permitted you to divorce your wives because your hearts were hard. But it was not this way from the beginning. I tell you that anyone who divorces his wife, except for marital unfaithfulness, and marries another woman commits adultery" (vv. 8-9 NIV). But his disciples surmise that marriage, without the option of divorce (especially in a culture where one's spouse was often chosen by others), is not a good option.[9] In light of Jesus' strict rule, they conclude, "it is better not to marry" (v. 10 NIV).

Jesus does not applaud their deduction; rather, he admits, "Not everyone can accept this teaching, but only those to whom it is given. For there are eunuchs who have been so from birth, and there are eunuchs who have been made eunuchs by others, and there are eunuchs who have made themselves eunuchs for the sake of the kingdom of heaven. Let anyone accept this who can" (vv. 11-12 NRSV).

Jesus mentions three types of eunuchs, repeating a pattern familiar to rabbinic scholars. First-century Jews called naturally born eunuchs "eunuchs of the sun" *(saris khama)* — indicating that they were discovered to be eunuchs at the moment the sun shone upon them.[10] Babies born with ambiguous or poorly formed genitals were considered eunuchs from the day of their birth.[11] The second type of eunuch was a castrated male, while the third invited interpretive debate.

Scholars dispute the meaning of "this teaching." Does it refer back to Jesus' teaching on the indissolubility of marriage in verses 3-6, the exception clause for adultery in verse 9, or his statement on eunuchs in verse 12? Modern commentators tend to soften this word about divorce, and late antique and medieval Christians tended to agree with the disciples that it was better

9. Craig S. Keener, *A Commentary on the Gospel of Matthew* (Grand Rapids: Eerdmans, 1999), 471.

10. W. D. Davies and Dale C. Allison Jr., *A Critical and Exegetical Commentary on the Gospel according to Saint Matthew,* vol. 3 (Edinburgh: T. & T. Clark, 1988), 22; Ulrich Luz, *Matthew 8–20: A Commentary,* trans. James E. Crouch, ed. Helmut Koester (Minneapolis: Fortress, 2001), 501. See also Alfred Cohen, "*Tumtum* and Androgynous," *Journal of Halacha and Contemporary Society* 38 (1999): 74.

11. Kathryn M. Ringrose, *The Perfect Servant: Eunuchs and the Social Construction of Gender in Byzantium* (Chicago: University of Chicago Press, 2004), 15.

not to marry; however, the natural flow of the text suggests that Jesus is correcting the conclusion of his disciples.[12]

Given the wider context, it is understandable why some modern translations have abandoned the language of the eunuch altogether, opting for dynamic equivalents such as those "incapable of marriage" or who have "renounced marriage."[13] In this context, the eunuch does represent the nonmarried. But we must ask why, if this was his intent, Jesus did not say what the apostle Paul said in 1 Corinthians 7: that the unmarried should follow his example (vv. 7-8) in order to avoid trouble (v. 28), so that they may devote themselves entirely to the Lord (vv. 32-35), and for their own personal happiness (v. 40)?

Many early Christians did not interpret these passages this way. According to Eusebius, Origen, compelled by his desire to follow Jesus' instructions perfectly, presented himself to a physician for castration. Some speculate that Origen was concerned about his reputation and wanted to protect himself from scandal given his willingness to educate both men and women. But Peter Brown argues that Origen was after something much more profound.[14] "What Origen may have sought, at that time, was something more deeply unsettling. The eunuch was notorious (and repulsive to many) because he had dared to shift the massive boundary between the sexes. . . . This body did not have to be defined by its sexual components, still less by the social roles that were conventionally derived from those components. Rather, the body should act as a blazon of the freedom of the spirit."[15]

Origen may have been the most famous early Christian eunuch, but he was hardly unique. There were enough Christians taking Jesus' words literally that the Church Fathers, as early as the Council of Nicaea (325), saw the need to address the issue. They declared that self-castration would henceforth disqualify an individual from ordination to the priesthood, while involuntary castration would not, of itself, bar a man from holy orders.[16] The

12. Davies and Allison draw attention to the number of qualifications in the text: "not all," "those to whom it is given," "he who is able." "In other words, Matthew uses the saying on eunuchs to confirm celibacy as a calling, but [Jesus'] emphasis — in contradiction to his disciples — is upon its special character." Davies and Allison, *Gospel according to Saint Matthew,* 20-21, 499.

13. New American Bible.

14. Peter Brown, *The Body and Society: Men, Women, and Sexual Renunciation in Early Christianity* (New York: Columbia University Press, 1988), 168-69.

15. Brown, *The Body and Society,* 169.

16. Council of Nicaea, canon 1; quoted in J. David Hester, "Eunuchs and the Postgen-

language of the eunuch, while not opposed to the simple translation "remain unmarried," is far more complex and rich when understood in the context of the ancient world.

Historical Context

The Greek term *eunoukhos* is believed to stem from *ho tēn eunēn ekhōn* — literally, "the one holding/guarding/keeping watch over the bed," typically the bedchamber of the king.[17] Eunuchs were guardians of *haram* — "a sacred place, a sanctuary, or a royal palace, a place that one is generally forbidden to enter."[18] Piotr Scholz explains how "for historical reasons *haram* has come to be applied mostly to the apartments in oriental palaces allotted to females," but eunuchs had wider responsibilities in the ancient world.[19]

Greek etymology emphasizes the duties of eunuchs, rather than their physical nature. The corresponding Hebrew term is *saris,* from *sar* in Babylonian (an older Semitic language), which means "king."[20] *Saris* is translated as "eunuch" or "official" depending on the context. For example, Genesis 37 recounts Joseph being sold to Potiphar, who is identified as a *saris* (*eunoukhos* in the Septuagint) but "official" or "officer" in most English translations. We know that Potiphar had a wife; so, he was certainly not prohibited by his office or by his physical state from marriage. In this way, the context usually determines which English translation is preferred.

In the sixth century B.C.E., Babylon fell to the Persians, who are the oldest and most useful source for information on eunuchs in the Middle East.[21] It is said that at the height of the Achaemenid dynasty, which lasted

---

der Jesus: Matthew 19.12 and Transgressive Sexualities," *Journal for the Study of the New Testament* 28, no. 1 (2005): 33-34 n. 80. See also Ringrose, *The Perfect Servant,* 13; Piotr O. Scholz, *Eunuchs and Castrati: A Cultural History,* trans. John A. Broadwin and Shelley L. Frisch (Princeton: Markus Weiner Publishers, 2001), 170-71.

17. Ringrose, *The Perfect Servant,* 16.

18. Scholz, *Eunuchs and Castrati,* 23.

19. Scholz, *Eunuchs and Castrati,* 23.

20. Scholz, *Eunuchs and Castrati,* 76.

21. China also has a long history of castrated eunuchs in the service of the emperor, but Persian practices seem to have had the greatest impact on our area of study. See Scholz, *Eunuchs and Castrati,* chap. 5, "The Emperor of China and His Eunuchs." Even though the Chinese practiced "full" or "double" castration (the removal of both the penis and testes), China had only a 2 percent mortality rate for castration, while other regions lost three out of four victims to death (Scholz, 16). Ringrose finds evidence of the "doubly castrated" in tenth-

from the rule of Cyrus II ("the Great") in 550 until the conquest of Alexander the Great in 330 B.C.E., more than 3,000 eunuchs could be found at court.[22] Scholz explains that "the question whether eunuchs in the ancient Middle East were always castrated has never been resolved."[23] What we do know is that by the time Persia passed through Greek control into the hands of the Romans, even though Romans despised castration, many Roman emperors and elite householders depended upon castrated eunuchs.[24] Scholz writes, "Even in Judaea, where the practice of castration was frowned upon and outlawed, Herod the Great (37 B.C.–A.D. 4) found it impossible, as Josephus Flavius (A.D. 37-95) relates, to manage his affairs without eunuchs."[25]

Eunuchs handled everything from powerful administrative functions and military command to cup-bearing and guarding the intimate spaces of their masters and mistresses. Cut off from their families of origin, raised to see the family of their master as their own family, and prevented from fathering children of their own, eunuchs owed their entire identity, complete loyalty, to their masters. Their inability to procreate barred them from claiming power in their own name, and also from producing heirs who might challenge the dynastic authority of the sacred king or emperor.[26] Their gender ambiguity also enabled them to mediate between men and women, elite and public, sacred and secular.[27] Thus, Kathryn Ringrose has aptly labeled eunuchs "perfect servants."[28]

Eunuchs were elite slaves, entrusted with any number of important duties, but they were also considered luxury items and status symbols in the Roman Empire.[29] The price for a castrato was many times more than that of an ordinary slave. Pliny the Elder, a historian writing during the first century C.E. (around the same time the Gospel of Matthew was written), complains of the exorbitant price paid for one particularly beautiful castrato. "When Lutorius Priscus bought of Sejanus, the eunuch, Pæzon, for fifty million

century Byzantine literature. These were called *curzinasus,* "from the name Khwarizm, which refers to a region in Central Asia where physicians knew how to perform this complex and risky surgery." Doubly castrated eunuchs were scarce in Constantinople, fetching a very high price (Ringrose, *The Perfect Servant,* 15).

22. Scholz, *Eunuchs and Castrati,* 81.

23. Scholz, *Eunuchs and Castrati,* 76.

24. Scholz, *Eunuchs and Castrati,* 112-23. See also Kuefler, *The Manly Eunuch,* 61.

25. Scholz, *Eunuchs and Castrati,* 83.

26. Ringrose, *The Perfect Servant,* 5; Scholz, *Eunuchs and Castrati,* 115.

27. Ringrose, *The Perfect Servant,* 82-85.

28. Ringrose, *The Perfect Servant,* 202.

29. Scholz, *Eunuchs and Castrati,* 113-14.

sesterces, the price was given by Hercules! rather to gratify the passion of the purchaser than in commendation of the beauty of the slave."[30]

The association of eunuchs with the bedchamber may have begun with the responsibilities of guard or attendant, but it did not stop there. Castrati were also valued for their beauty and sexual allure. It was believed that by castrating a boy before he was twenty, one could preserve his youthful beauty. Scholz explains that this beauty "was more highly esteemed in antiquity than that of women . . . ideals of beauty derived from the exaltation of the androgyne and the hermaphrodite. We can trace them back to the influence of the oriental aesthetic, which also helped to shape the Hellenistic idea of the beautiful."[31]

Nero was infamous for becoming enamored of one such boy. He met Sporus when the latter was a child and was struck by Sporus's resemblance to the emperor's late wife, Poppaea Sabina. Nero had Sporus castrated to preserve this beauty, married him, assigned him a dowry, dressed him in the clothes of an empress, and did not hesitate to kiss him amorously in public.[32] The second-century historian Cassius Dio recounts that crowds at the wedding shouted "all the customary good wishes, even to the extent of praying that legitimate children might be born to them."[33] Suetonius, a writer who lived from 70 to 120 C.E., lamented: "the world would have been a happier place had Nero's father Domitius married that sort of wife."[34] It was not until 342 C.E., when Christianity had spread through the ranks of Roman authority, that marriages of men to eunuchs were outlawed.[35]

The sexuality of eunuchs was highly debated in the ancient world. They were trusted to care for women of elite households because they were believed to lack sexual desire, yet there is evidence that some of these women preferred eunuchs for their own sexual pleasure, because they could engage them without fear of pregnancy.[36] Although such activities were considered scandalous and did result in severe penalties when discovered, nonprocre-

30. Scholz, *Eunuchs and Castrati,* 114, citing *The Natural History of Pliny,* trans. John Bostock and H. T. Riley (London: George Bell and Sons, 1890), 7:128f.

31. Scholz, *Eunuchs and Castrati,* 117.

32. Scholz, *Eunuchs and Castrati,* 117-18.

33. Kuefler, *The Manly Eunuch,* 100-101.

34. Scholz, *Eunuchs and Castrati,* 118; Tranquillius Gaius Suetonius, "Nero," in *The Twelve Caesars,* trans. Robert Graves, rev. Michael Grant (London: Penguin Press, 1989), 28.1f.

35. Kuefler, *The Manly Eunuch,* 101-2.

36. Scholz, *Eunuchs and Castrati,* 120; Kuefler, *The Manly Eunuch,* 96-102.

ative sexuality was considered less a peril to the empire than offspring who might threaten those in power.[37]

Roman men were anxious about the affairs to which their eunuchs were attending. They worried whether they could trust eunuchs with their money, their women, their reputation, their power, their food. But they were also anxious about what eunuchs said about them as men.[38] Peter Brown explains: "In the Roman world, the physical appearance and the reputed character of eunuchs acted as constant reminders that the male body was a fearsomely plastic thing."[39] Galen, the medical authority of the second century C.E., argued that "lack of heat from childhood on could cause the male body to collapse back into a state of primary undifferentiation. No normal man might actually become a woman; but each man trembled forever on the brink of becoming 'womanish.' "[40] Brown goes on,

> It was never enough to be male: a man had to strive to become "virile." He had to learn to exclude from his character and from the poise and temper of his body all telltale traces of "softness" that might betray, in him, the half-formed state of a woman . . . a man's walk . . . the rhythms of his speech . . . the telltale resonance of his voice. Any of these might betray the ominous loss of a hot, high-spirited momentum, a flagging of the clear-cut self-restraint, and a relaxing of the taut elegance of voice and gesture that made a man a man, the unruffled master of a subject world.[41]

Eunuchs represented what happened when men lost their masculinity. The master became the servant. The man became womanish. The ambiguity of a eunuch's body did not merely symbolize the loss of virtue and power, it explained it.[42]

Eunuchs were entrusted with the most intimate and powerful responsibilities and yet suffered the reputation of being untrustworthy on account of their physical condition. They were simultaneously considered asexual and unable to restrain themselves from sexual passions. The physical ambiguity

37. Kuefler, *The Manly Eunuch,* 98; Shaun F. Tougher, "Byzantine Eunuchs: An Overview, with Special Reference to Their Creation and Origin," in *Women, Men, and Eunuchs: Gender in Byzantium,* ed. Liz James (London and New York: Routledge, 1997), 170.

38. Kuefler, *The Manly Eunuch,* 96.

39. Brown, *The Body and Society,* 10.

40. Brown, *The Body and Society,* 11.

41. Brown, *The Body and Society,* 11.

42. Ringrose, *The Perfect Servant,* 51.

of eunuchs was translated into the moral realm in areas well beyond sexuality. Eunuchs suffered the same aspersions of character as did women in the ancient world. They were "carnal, irrational, voluptuous, fickle, manipulative and deceitful."[43] Women and eunuchs "were assumed to lack the ability to control their physical, emotional and sexual appetites."[44] Self-control was believed to be a masculine virtue, visible in the hardness of men's bodies. The etymological link between *virtus* (virtue) and *vir* (man, male) is debated; nevertheless, the linguistic association remained strong among Latin speakers. Lactantius, a fourth-century writer and tutor of Constantine I (who ruled from 306 to 337), preserved "a well-known, if invented, etymology": "Thus man [*vir*] was so named because strength [*vis*] is greater in him than in woman; and from this, virtue [*virtus*] has received its name. Likewise, woman [*mulier*] . . . is from softness [*mollitia*], changed and shortened by a letter, as though it were softly [*mollier*]."[45] To be soft or effeminate was to be weak, not only physically but morally.[46] Virtuous eunuchs were considered anomalies; they were against nature.[47]

From the perspectives of ancient Jewish and Christian writers, the impossibility of virtuous eunuchs was corroborated by their presence in certain religious contexts. In the Roman era, ritual castration was a part of the cult of Cybele, which was derived from prehistoric fertility religions, worship of the *Magna Mater* (Great Mother), and was integrated into the Roman pantheon as the *Mater Deum* (Mother of the Gods).[48] These castrated priests were known in the ancient world as the *galli*. We do not know to what extent (if at all) sacred prostitution (involving female priestesses and eunuch priests) was a part of the cult. Evidence is unclear, but accusations of their sexual activities abounded, especially in Christian sources.[49] Augustine complains not only about the paganism and sexual sins of the *galli* but also about their gender transgressions. They are "effeminates [*molles*] consecrated to the Great Mother, who violate every canon of decency in men and women," visible "in the streets and squares of Carthage with their pomaded hair and

43. Kuefler, *The Manly Eunuch,* 35.

44. Ringrose, *The Perfect Servant,* 36.

45. Kuefler, *The Manly Eunuch,* 21, citing Lactantius, *De opificio Dei* 12.16-17.

46. Kuefler, *The Manly Eunuch,* 24-25.

47. Kuefler, *The Manly Eunuch,* 35. Virtuous females we also consider against nature. See also Gillian Cloke, *"This Female Man of God": Women and Spiritual Power in the Patristic Age,* AD *350-450* (New York: Routledge, 1995), 214-15.

48. Scholz, *Eunuchs and Castrati,* 93-94.

49. Kuefler, *The Manly Eunuch,* 250-52.

powdered faces, gliding along with womanish languor."[50] According to Augustine, a eunuch priest was "neither changed into a woman nor allowed to remain a man."[51]

From the ancient Hebrew perspective, castrated eunuchs were quintessential foreigners, the epitome of "other." Castration was forbidden within Judaism. Animals that had been castrated could not be offered on the altar (Lev. 22:24). Castrated humans were excluded from the assembly of Israel (Deut. 23:1) and banned from the Israelite priesthood (Lev. 21:20). At best, they could not fulfill Jewish obligations to marry and have children; at worst, they were associated with the power structures of oppressive regimes, pagan religious cults, and illicit sexual activities.[52] It is probably their association with ancient fertility religions that stands behind their exclusion from the assembly of the Lord in Deuteronomy 23:1.[53]

And yet, in spite of all the marks against eunuchs, the prophet Isaiah predicted a time when they would be included with God's people and receive a blessing beyond what Jewish men and women could hope for.

> Do not let the foreigner joined to the LORD say,
>   "The LORD will surely separate me from his people";
> and do not let the eunuch say,
>   "I am just a dry tree."
> For thus says the LORD:
> To the eunuchs who keep my sabbaths,
>   who choose the things that please me
>   and hold fast my covenant,
> I will give, in my house and within my walls,
>   a monument and a name
>   better than sons and daughters;
> I will give them an everlasting name

50. Kuefler, *The Manly Eunuch,* 253, citing Augustine, *De civitate Dei* 7.26.

51. Kuefler, *The Manly Eunuch,* 249, citing Augustine, *De civitate Dei* 7.24.

52. R. T. France, *The Gospel of Matthew* (Grand Rapids: Eerdmans, 2007), 722. See also Cohen, "*Tumtum* and Androgynous," 70, for contemporary Jewish commentary on the obligation to marry.

53. Gordon McConville, "Deuteronomy," in *New Bible Commentary, 21st Century Edition,* ed. D. A. Carson et al. (Downers Grove, Ill.: InterVarsity, 1994), 221. This passage specifies both types of emasculation (crushing the testicles and cutting off the penis) but goes on to speak of forbidden marriages and foreign peoples: Ammonites, Moabites, Edomites, Egyptians, and their descendants (Deut. 23:2-8).

that shall not be cut off.
And the foreigners who join themselves to the LORD,
to minister to him, to love the name of the LORD,
and to be his servants,
all who keep the sabbath, and do not profane it,
and hold fast my covenant —
these I will bring to my holy mountain,
and make them joyful in my house of prayer;
their burnt offerings and their sacrifices
will be accepted on my altar;
for my house shall be called a house of prayer
for all peoples. (Isa. 56:3-7 NRSV)

Even with the prediction of Isaiah, its fulfillment in Acts 8, and Jesus' positive mention of eunuchs, Christians continued Jewish prejudices against eunuchs. On the whole, the eunuch continued to be understood as the quintessential foreigner — pagan and sexually immoral.[54] These associations may explain why Christians reacted so strongly against castration in the Latin West.[55]

But Jews and Christians were mistrustful of eunuchs for another reason, which may be of particular relevance for discussions of intersex. In addition to being ethnically other, religiously other, sexually other, and morally other, eunuchs did not fit into traditional Roman, Jewish, or Christian ideals regarding gender. In the Talmud, eunuchs are derided for unmanly characteristics. They are "crudely and pejoratively described as having no beard, smooth skin, and lanky hair."[56] Boys who were castrated before puberty developed unique physical traits, distinct from men and women. "Those who are young might be mistaken for adolescent boys, albeit slightly unusual adolescent boys, with fine, fair skin, faces that are just a bit broad, and tall thin bodies with narrow shoulders and graceful carriage. Older eunuchs often show signs of poor health. Their faces are prematurely lined, and youthful fairness has become pallor. Their bodies are stooped from osteoporosis. Even so, they sport a thick, luxuriant head of hair."[57]

54. Kuefler shows how such prejudices were extended, not only to the products of the East imported to the West — castrated slaves — but also to Easterners in general who were slandered for being effeminate, that is, morally weak. Kuefler, *The Manly Eunuch,* 47.

55. Kuefler, *The Manly Eunuch,* 254.

56. Davies and Allison, *Gospel according to Saint Matthew,* 25, citing *b. Yebamot* 80b.

57. Ringrose, *The Perfect Servant,* 1.

Castrated eunuchs were excluded from Jewish religious assemblies, but *saris khama* were not. To integrate naturally born eunuchs into society, Jews pulled from laws for men and laws for women to make sure they had all their bases covered. In the Tosefta, they are alternatively forbidden "from inheriting their fathers' estates (like daughters), from secluding themselves with women (like sons), and from shaving (like men)." On the other hand, "[w]hen they menstruate they must be isolated from men (like women); they are disqualified from serving as witnesses or as priests (like women); but the laws of pederasty apply to them."[58] Contemporary Jewish scholars continue this rationale. Alfred Cohen describes the majority opinion that stricter rules be applied to make sure that nothing is left undone.[59] Within Judaism, their place between male and female either excluded eunuchs from religious assemblies or imposed a double burden of religious duty.

The very existence of eunuchs threatened legal, religious, and ethical systems built upon the separation of the sexes. Romans debated the legal status of eunuchs and whose rights were granted or withheld, depending upon who was in power.[60] While such debates may be difficult to understand from a modern point of view, one should not forget that legal processes, such as *testifying* in court and creating a last will and *testament,* are etymologically dependent on *testis,* the male organ. Genesis 24:9 and 47:29 recount the practice of placing one hand on the male genitals (euphemistically translated "under the thigh") when taking an oath.[61] Eunuchs and women simply did not have the anatomical equipment to make promises, bear witness, or issue bequests.

Legally other, morally other, sexually other, socially other, religiously other, and ethnically other, eunuchs were "exiles from the society of the human race, belonging neither to one sex nor the other,"[62] as fourth-century Roman poet Claudius Mamertinus eloquently portrayed them.

58. Anne Fausto-Sterling, *Sexing the Body: Gender Politics and the Construction of Sexuality* (New York: Basic Books, 2000), 33. Greenberg cites *Encyclopedia Judaica* — CD Rom edition (1997) — for the same material. (The Mishnah is the compilation of Jewish oral law documented around the year 200 C.E. The Tosefta is the commentary upon and supplement to this oral law.)

59. Cohen, "*Tumtum* and Androgynous," 62-85.

60. Kuefler, *The Manly Eunuch,* 33.

61. Scholz, *Eunuchs and Castrati,* 78-79.

62. Kuefler, *The Manly Eunuch,* 36. A few decades after him, Claudian disparaged eunuchs as those "whom the male sex has discarded and the female will not adopt" (Kuefler, 36). In the third century, Severus Alexander went so far as to call them "a third sex of the human race." Shaun Tougher, "Social Transformation, Gender Transformation? The Court

Returning to the Matthean Context: Childlikeness, Christian Perfection, and Angels

Given such a background, it is a wonder that Jesus was willing to use the term "eunuch" at all! But what would Jesus' Jewish audiences have heard? Would they have envisioned officials in elite, pagan households, whether Persian, Greek, or Roman? Sexual consorts of the upper echelons of Roman society? Gender transgressors? Participants in cultic castration? Matthew records Jesus' words in the context of divorce, marriage, and sacrifices for the sake of the kingdom of heaven. His setting does not emphasize the political or cultic contexts of eunuchism but speaks of the relation of the eunuch to social bonds created by sex, gender, and sexuality and places these ideas near other parables of the kingdom.

Matthew 19:14 declares that the kingdom of God will be inherited by those who are childlike. In this literary context, one wonders at the significance of the child. Did children represent those unfettered by the concerns of marriage and the pain of divorce? Did those who had not yet reached puberty represent those without gender or the innocence associated with a lack of sexual desire?[63]

The verses that follow shift attention from this life to the next and raise the bar for ideas of Christian perfection. When asked which good works are necessary for gaining eternal life, Jesus answers that one must obey the commandments and love one's neighbor as oneself. But when pressed for more, Jesus adds in verse 21: "If you want to be perfect, go, sell your possessions and give to the poor, and you will have treasure in heaven. Then come, follow me" (NIV). Apparently, the disciples wanted to know what kind of treasure Messiah was promising. "Peter answered him, 'We have left everything to follow you! What then will there be for us?' Jesus said to them, 'I tell you the truth, at the renewal of all things, when the Son of Man sits on his glorious

---

Eunuchs, 300-900," in *Gender in the Early Medieval World: East and West, 300-900,* ed. Leslie Brubaker and Julia M. H. Smith (Cambridge: Cambridge University Press, 2004), 71; citing Severus Alexander, *Historia Augusta* 23.4-8.

63. "Before reaching puberty and becoming an adult male or female, a child is sometimes referred to as a 'neuter' in terms of the development of secondary sex characteristics." Scholz, *Eunuchs and Castrati,* 6. In Greek, the word for child *(teknon)* is neuter. Tertullian connects the childlikeness that inherits the kingdom of heaven to the virginal state in *On Monogamy* 8, trans. S. Thelwall, in *Fathers of the Third Century: Tertullian, Part Fourth; Minucius Felix; Commodian; Origen, Parts First and Second,* ed. Alexander Roberts and James Donaldson, rev. A. Cleveland Coxe, American ed. (Peabody, Mass.: Hendrickson, 1999), 65.

throne, you who have followed me will also sit on twelve thrones, judging the twelve tribes of Israel. And everyone who has left houses or brothers or sisters or father or mother or children or fields for my sake will receive a hundred times as much and will inherit eternal life' " (vv. 27-29 NIV).

Peter's concern recalls the worry of eunuchs in Isaiah 56, who are told not to complain, "I am just a dry tree" (v. 3), because "the eunuchs who keep my sabbaths, who choose the things that please me" (v. 4), will be given "a monument and a name better than sons and daughters; . . . an everlasting name that shall not be cut off" (v. 5). There are a number of significant poetic contrasts in Isaiah's passage. First, the Lord promises to those who have been "cut" a name that "shall not be cut off." Second, those who "keep" or "guard" the bedchamber and sacred spaces of the king are contrasted with eunuchs who "keep" or "guard" the Sabbath, the sacred time of the divine King. These pious eunuchs will no longer be excluded from God's people. In other words, eunuchs would no longer be judged by their physicality; they would be judged by their moral practice — their faith that binds them to YHWH and their obedience to God's Law. Disciples who make themselves eunuchs for the sake of the kingdom, like the virtuous eunuchs of Isaiah, need not fear renunciations in this life because God will richly reward them.[64] Matthew's inclusion of Jesus' provocative saying about eunuchs may have served as one more proof of Jesus' identification with the messianic visions of Isaiah.[65]

Admittedly, it is difficult to know how Jesus' audience interpreted his words about three types of eunuchs only a few verses earlier, but we do know that the Gospel writer either preserved this original context or set these sayings alongside one another because he believed they were related. The broad themes of this passage — the question of what one could do above and beyond the standard commandments, in order to be "perfect," and the eschatological order of things — found fertile soil in the ascetic minds of early Christians. In the early church, "eunuchs for the sake of the kingdom" came to be understood as those who were willing to leave behind the burdens and earthly joys of family, in the hopes of everlasting reward. While most manuscripts of this Gospel list only siblings, parents, and children, early Christians soon added "wife" as the most pivotal renunciation of all. The associations and responsibilities of family life (marriage, sexuality, children,

64. Such teaching certainly fits with other passages in which Jesus pushes his hearers to place discipleship above the duties of family life; cf. Luke 11:27-28.

65. The Gospel writer quotes Isaiah explicitly in Matt. 3:3; 4:14-16; 8:17; 12:17-21; 13:14-15; 15:7-9. Isaiah is mentioned by name in the First Gospel more than in any other New Testament book.

inheritance, ownership of property) came to be viewed as the evil powers of this "present age."[66] And Jesus had taught that these would be left behind in the age to come. A few chapters later, in Matthew 22:30, the Gospel writer records Jesus' teaching that "At the resurrection people will neither marry nor be given in marriage; they will be like the angels in heaven" (NIV).

Whether intended by Jesus or not, eunuchs came to be associated with angels on account of their (assumed) sexual continence, their freedom from the obligations of marriage (especially its ties to the economic structures of the day), and their alternative gender and gender status.[67] In the Byzantine context, iconography would soon depict angels as beardless and genderless.[68] Hagiographical accounts describe eunuchs and angels being confused for one another on account of similar physical features and dress. Both acted as mediators and messengers for the sacred king, bridging the divide between the sacred and the profane.[69]

Eunuchs were angelic, not only in appearance but also in voice. Because women were prohibited from singing in church, boys were castrated to ensure soprano singers in Eastern and Western Christendom — a practice that can be dated at least as far back as the fourth century C.E. and was not abandoned by the Roman Church until the last century.[70] In fact, the voice of the "last angel of Rome," Alessandro Moreschi (1858-1922), was preserved by one of the earliest sound recordings of the twentieth century.[71]

Jesus' teaching on eunuchs — read through the lenses of children, angels, and sacrifices for the sake of the kingdom — radically altered the way eunuchs have been understood in the West. Rather than elite slaves or castrated (but sexually active) priests of Cybele, eunuchs came to signify non-castrated but sexually continent priests and the castrato singers of the church — perfect servants of the King of kings. Free from the fetters and distractions of family, innocent and asexual as children and angels, with angelic voices that raised audiences to the heavens — eunuchs were transformed from the immoral other into a new model of Christian perfection.

66. Brown, *The Body and Society,* 99-100.

67. Ulrich Luz, *Matthew 21–28: A Commentary,* trans. James E. Crouch, ed. Helmut Koester (Minneapolis: Fortress, 2005), 73. See also, Shaun Tougher, "Holy Eunuchs! Masculinity and Eunuch Saints in Byzantium," in *Holiness and Masculinity in the Middle Ages,* ed. P. H. Cullum and Katherine J. Lewis (Cardiff: University of Wales Press, 2004).

68. Scholz, *Eunuchs and Castrati,* 190.

69. Ringrose, *The Perfect Servant,* 161.

70. Scholz, *Eunuchs and Castrati,* 273.

71. Scholz, *Eunuchs and Castrati,* 287.

The Transformation of Eunuchs in the History of Interpretation: West and East

In his detailed study *The Body and Society: Men, Women, and Sexual Renunciation in Early Christianity,* Peter Brown warns that sex, gender, and sexuality carried "profoundly different" meanings in the early centuries compared to the meanings given in the Middle Ages and modern period (with which we are more familiar).[72] Meanings also varied from region to region.[73] Thus, one must take care not to move too quickly from biblical material to contemporary interpretations. Because it will be impossible to cover every nuance in this volume, we will trace the development of certain themes as they relate to our own study of sex difference as it was understood by many ancient Christians.

Eunuchs and the Renunciation of Sex, Gender, and Sexuality in Early Christianity

Brown explains how Jesus' words about becoming eunuchs for the sake of the kingdom of heaven were interpreted through the lens of Paul's first letter to the Corinthian church, wherein he presents married sexuality as a concession for those who cannot control their burning passion (1 Cor. 7:5-9). Brown highlights Paul's concern that married persons are divided in their loyalties (7:32-34) and provides evidence that the "undivided heart" was a traditional Jewish and early Christian metaphor for holiness.[74] Brown writes, "Ascetic readers of Paul in late antiquity did not mis-hear his tone of voice."[75] Despite Paul's affirmation of the sacramental value of marriage in Ephesians 5, the early Christian belief that perfection depended upon a rejection of marriage was rooted in Paul's epistles and the saying of Jesus in Matthew 19:12.

But the Pauline legacy included another radical text, a baptismal formula recorded in Galatians 3:28 that declares: "There is no longer Jew or Greek, there is no longer slave or free, there is no longer male and female; for all of you are one in Christ Jesus" (NRSV). Along with the symbol of the

72. Brown, *The Body and Society,* xv.
73. Brown, *The Body and Society,* xiv.
74. Brown, *The Body and Society,* 36.
75. Brown, *The Body and Society,* 56.

eunuch in Matthew 19 and the devaluation of married sexuality in 1 Corinthians 7, this text also brought into question the significance of sex and gender for Christians. What remained to be debated in the centuries that followed were the ramifications of such notions. Did baptism and the rejection of marriage undo all societal roles based on gender? Some Christians believed that they did.

Brown believes that these notions stood at the root of some of the concerns Paul was attempting to address in the Corinthian church. Women were removing their veils — symbols of female sex difference and gendered subordination, and coverings for sexual allure — in order to prophesy in the Spirit (1 Cor. 11). Similar practices have been documented in the church of Carthage toward the end of the second century C.E. These Christians encouraged their continent women to stand in church without veils as living symbols of Christian hope. Their conquest of sexuality stood as icons of sanctification for all believers. "I am not veiled because the veil of corruption is taken from me; . . . I am not ashamed, because the deed of shame has been removed far from me."[76] Virgins were not only lifted above the shame associated with sexual activity; they were lifted above the shame of sex difference.

Tertullian (160?–220) would have none of it. In his treatise *On the Veiling of Virgins,* he demanded that after puberty, women, even virgins, remain covered. Hope for the redemption of human sexuality was for the next life, not this one. In this life, "A girl above shame was, quite bluntly a 'sport of nature, a third sex.' "[77] Brown quips that Tertullian was the first, but hardly the last, to argue that humans, even Christians, could never overcome the "facts of sex."[78]

On the other hand, Tertullian did believe that humans would shed sex distinctions in the life to come, becoming like the angels. He wrote, "I have to return after death to the place where there is no giving in marriage, where I have to be clothed upon rather than to be despoiled — where, even if I am despoiled of my sex, I am classed with angels — not a male angel, nor a female one. There will be no one to do aught against me, nor will they find any male energy in me."[79]

It is difficult to untangle Tertullian's legacy given that he changed opinions over the course of his life. He both affirms and denies the significance

76. Brown, *The Body and Society,* 81, quoting *Acts of Judas Thomas* 10.

77. Brown, *The Body and Society,* 81, quoting Tertullian, *On the Veiling of Virgins* 7.6.

78. Brown, *The Body and Society,* 81.

79. Kuefler, *The Manly Eunuch,* 229; Tertullian, *Adversus Valentinianos* 32.5, "non angelus, non angela."

of sex differences. He provides examples of the worst of Christian misogyny and yet, at the end of his life, after joining the Montanists, he concedes female participation in ritual leadership.[80] This ambivalence can also be found in his comments on eunuchs.[81]

Tertullian ridiculed his opponent, Marcion, for being "no better than a eunuch," and yet he is one of the few writers willing to speak of Jesus as a eunuch. Tertullian exhorted his followers by saying that Jesus " 'stands before you, if you are willing to copy Him, as a voluntary eunuch in the flesh.' Christ in fact 'opens the kingdoms of the heavens to eunuchs, as being Himself, withal, a eunuch.' "[82] Kuefler notes that Tertullian's words about Jesus as a "eunuch in the flesh" are ambiguous, leaving open the possibility of Jesus as a physical, not merely spiritual, eunuch.[83]

Tertullian's legacy is mixed, and his authority for later Christian teachers was also undermined by his association with the Montanist sect. Nevertheless, although Kuefler claims that later Latin writers "never . . . referred to Jesus as a eunuch,"[84] many of Tertullian's ideas lived on in later writers. Unfortunately for the history of Christianity, it was his misogyny, rather than his emphasis on the sexless eschatological life, that is most often remembered. Kuefler speculates that Roman ideals about gender persuaded Western Christians to preserve the former and ignore the latter. "Notions of male superiority and female inferiority were too deeply embedded in Roman cultural values for a religious philosophy arguing for their eradication to have succeeded in the West, even if that eradication had roots in earliest Christianity. Admitting the possibility of gender ambiguity in the soul while condemning it in the body was a means of rendering the genderless ideal of earliest Christianity quaint but harmless."[85] This focus on the life to come can be found most profoundly in the works of Origen, whose "towering

80. Kuefler, *The Manly Eunuch,* 228-30.

81. Kuefler, *The Manly Eunuch,* 266-67.

82. Kuefler, *The Manly Eunuch,* 266. Tertullian, *De monogamia* 5.3. Kuefler has changed some of the traditional translations for *spadones* from "virgins" to "eunuchs" in order to reflect the literal meaning of *spado* rather than its metaphorical application. Kuefler, 387 n. 95. S. Thelwall's translation reads: "Christ . . . stands before you, if you are willing (to copy Him), as a voluntary celibate of the flesh" (chap. 5). And "the Lord Himself opens 'the kingdom of the heavens' to 'eunuchs' as being Himself, withal, a virgin; to whom looking, the apostle also — himself too for this reason abstinent — gives the preference to continence" (chap. 3). Tertullian, *On Monogamy,* trans. Thelwall, 60, 62.

83. Kuefler, *The Manly Eunuch,* 266.

84. Kuefler, *The Manly Eunuch,* 267.

85. Kuefler, *The Manly Eunuch,* 230.

genius . . . dominates all accounts of the further development of notions on sexuality and the human person in the Greek world."[86]

Origen (185-254) was keenly aware of the passing nature of the present form of human life. He learned as a teenager, at age sixteen or seventeen, to give priority to spiritual family, rather than the fleeting ties of blood, when his father was martyred. This perspective is crucial for understanding Origen's teaching on human persons, sex and gender distinctions, as well as his own (alleged) castration. Matthew Kuefler explains,

> In an age that idealized the willingness to shed one's own blood for the sake of religion in the glorification of martyrs, self-castration may not have seemed either too strange or too demanding. . . . Moreover, in the same way that martyrdom was admired by Christians because it showed courage greater than most were capable of and lent to those willing to suffer it a charismatic authority unequalled by others, men willing to castrate themselves might have been respected and obeyed precisely because their behavior was atypical.[87]

Most historians explain Origen's castration as an attempt to protect himself from slander because he was willing to include women among his disciples.[88] But Peter Brown believes that Origen would have known that castration performed after puberty did not necessarily relieve him of sexual desire or sexual ability. He writes,

> What Origen may have sought, at that time, was something more deeply unsettling. The eunuch was notorious (and repulsive to many) because he had dared to shift the massive boundary between the sexes. He had opted out of being male. By losing the sexual "head" that was held to cause his facial hair to grow, the eunuch was no longer recognizable as a man. . . . Deprived of the standard professional credential of a philosopher in late antique circles — a flowing beard — Origen would have appeared in public with a smooth face, like a woman or like a boy frozen into a state of prepubertal innocence. He was a walking lesson in the basic indeterminacy of the body.[89]

86. Brown, *The Body and Society,* xiv.

87. Kuefler, *The Manly Eunuch,* 263-64.

88. Eusebius criticized Origen for believing he could shield himself from such scandal by the act. Ringrose, *The Perfect Servant,* 113; Eusebius of Caesarea, *Historia ecclesiastica* 1.2. Brown, *The Body and Society,* 168.

89. Brown, *The Body and Society,* 169.

For Origen, the loss of male sexual identity in this life was no bother, considering his belief that human souls were sexless before being placed in bodies, and that bodies and souls would be transformed in the future so that the limitations of sex differentiation were shed once again.[90] "This body did not have to be defined by its sexual components, still less by the social (gendered) roles that were conventionally derived from those components. Rather, the body should act as a blazon of the freedom of the spirit."[91]

Chastity was a sign of human freedom, resisting the pressures of the world. "To reject sexuality, therefore, did not mean, for Origen, simply to suppress the sexual drives. It meant the assertion of a basic freedom so intense, a sense of identity so deeply rooted, as to cause to evaporate the normal social and physical constraints that tied the Christian to his or her gender."[92] Virginity was the state of souls before their relocation in bodies. Therefore, to remain a virgin was to recall this past and speed up its future.[93]

Origen challenged his students to believe in the possibility of their sanctification, a sanctification rooted in future glory but capable of powerful work in the present life. "Resolve to know that in you there is a capacity to be transformed."[94] Sadly, among early Christian writers, Origen's optimism is exceptional. As we look forward, and westward, we will find that others were much less confident that the heavenly future could make a difference in this life.

Sexual Renunciation in the West

Ambrose (337?–397) followed Origen's dualism, reading Pauline language about the war between flesh and spirit through the lens of mind and body.[95] Sexuality was central to Ambrose's notion of the flesh that was "put off" in baptism. The Christian was clothed with Christ in baptism, Christ who was born of a virgin and lived a continent life. According to Ambrose, baptism and the virginal life enabled those born from the taint of the sexual act to be remade in the image of Christ, a foretaste of heavenly glory.[96]

90. Brown, *The Body and Society*, 167.
91. Brown, *The Body and Society*, 169.
92. Brown, *The Body and Society*, 170-71.
93. Brown, *The Body and Society*, 169.
94. Brown, *The Body and Society*, 162, quoting Origen, *Dialogue with Heraclides* 150.
95. Brown, *The Body and Society*, 348.
96. Brown, *The Body and Society*, 350-51.

For Ambrose, the eunuch represented the virginal man or woman. He wrote to convince Christians of his day that physical castration was not the proper application of Jesus' words in Matthew 19:12.

> And there are eunuchs who have castrated themselves. . . . I touch upon this point advisedly, for there are some who look upon it as a state of virtue to restrain guilt with a knife . . . but then consider whether this tends not rather to a declaration of weakness than to a reputation for strength. . . . No one, then, ought, as many suppose, to mutilate himself, but rather gain the victory: for the Church gathers in those who conquer, not those who are defeated. . . . For why should the means of gaining the crown and of the practice of virtue be lost to a man who is born to honor, equipped for victory? How can he through courage of soul castrate himself?[97]

Ambrose's words provide more evidence that Christian self-castration was still practiced and honored even after the ruling of Nicaea.[98] Given his emphasis on the sexual as representative of sinful flesh, it may not be so surprising that Christians were willing to castrate themselves to ensure their participation in the kingdom of God. An inability to control their sexual drive any other way may have led some to desperate measures. Others prayed for God to deliver them from their sexual organs. "[H]oly men dreamt of being castrated by angels."[99]

Like Ambrose, Jerome (347-420) was indebted to Origen. Jerome's earlier writings (from the 380s) were modeled on Origen's view of human persons (i.e., sex and gender were passing phases, inconsequential to the sexless spirit). Consequently, Jerome allowed himself the companionship of educated women who were committed to sexual continence and the study of the Scriptures. Nevertheless, he did not think that many men could live as he lived — in close, chaste association with women. Unlike Origen and the Desert Fathers (whose seclusion the fourth-century scholar had abandoned after only two years), he was not convinced that the sexual urge could be conquered in this life.[100]

Like Origen, Jerome associated the life of virginity with the life of angels,[101] and even suggested that the virginal state removed the distinctions

97. Kuefler, *The Manly Eunuch,* 268-69 n. 104. Ambrose, *De viduis* 13.75-77.

98. Kuefler, *The Manly Eunuch,* 269.

99. Tougher, "Holy Eunuchs!" 94.

100. Brown, *The Body and Society,* 266, 373.

101. "I want you to be what the angels are. It is this angelic purity which secures to vir-

of sex: "Observe what the happiness of that state must be in which even the distinction of sex is lost. The virgin is no longer called a woman."[102] But in 393, his hero was condemned of heresy. Origen's works came under attack. His views of the sexless eschatological life were believed to undermine Christian claims of the resurrection of the body. Brown explains that "Jerome was forced to choose. He could no longer base his *persona* as a spiritual guide to noble ladies on so unpopular a figure. After 395, he came down firmly on the side of views that stressed the lasting differences between men and women."[103] In 398 Jerome defended his belief in the resurrection and sex distinctions, saying,

> I will openly confess the faith of the Church. The reality of a resurrection without flesh and bones, without blood and members, is unintelligible. Where there are flesh and bones, where there are blood and members, there must of necessity be diversity of sex. Where there is diversity of sex, there John is John, Mary is Mary. You need not fear the marriage of those who, even before death, lived in their own sex without discharging the functions of sex. When it is said, "In that day they shall neither marry, nor be given in marriage," the words refer to those who can marry, and yet will not do so . . . but where there is sex, there you have man and woman. . . . Who can have any glory from a life of chastity if we have no sex which would make unchastity possible? . . . Likeness to the angels is promised us, that is, the blessedness of their angelic existence without flesh and sex will be bestowed on us in our flesh and with our sex. . . . Moreover, likeness to the angels does not imply a changing of men into angels, but their growth in immortality and glory.[104]

---

ginity its highest reward." Jerome, *The Perpetual Virginity of Blessed Mary, against Helvidius* 23, translated by W. H. Fremantle, Christian Classics Ethereal Library, http://www.ccel.org/ccel/schaff/npnf206.vi.v.html.

102. Jerome, *Against Helvidius* 22. In the same section of this treatise Jerome writes: "She who is not subject to the anxiety and pain of child-bearing and having passed the change of life has ceased to perform the functions of a woman, is freed from the curse of God: nor is her desire to her husband, but on the contrary her husband becomes subject to her, and the voice of the Lord commands him, 'In all that Sarah saith unto thee, hearken unto her voice.' Thus they begin to have time for prayer. For so long as the debt of marriage is paid, earnest prayer is neglected."

103. Brown, *The Body and Society,* 379.

104. Jerome, *To Pammachius against John of Jerusalem* 31, trans. W. H. Fremantle, Christian Classics Ethereal Library, http://www.ccel.org/ccel/schaff/npnf206.vi.viii.html.

While Jerome maintains that there will be no sexual activity in heaven, despite the ability of men and women to marry and engage in sexual functions, he says nothing in this treatise about gender distinctions such as the hierarchy of male over female. It may be that this hierarchy was also to be left behind, given that Jerome understood marriage as one of the primary agents of female servitude.[105] The eunuch, understood as exemplar of the virginal life, continued to represent a freedom, if not from sex distinctions, at least from some of the gender distinctions associated with marital life in that day.[106]

After the condemnation of Origen, Western Christian writers were much more careful to distinguish between "eunuchs for the sake of the kingdom" and real, physical eunuchs. Matthew Kuefler, in his study of masculinity, gender ambiguity, and Christian ideology in late antiquity, explains how Latin Church Fathers employed the rhetoric of manliness and unmanliness to defend their view of a true eunuch. "[U]nmanly eunuchs [were those] who castrated their bodies and manly eunuchs [were those] who castrated their spirits but left their bodies intact."[107] Jerome could speak of the eunuch as a sort of "shorthand" for Christian perfection. " 'When you make yourself a eunuch for the kingdom of Heaven's sake,' Jerome wrote to one man, 'what else did you seek to achieve than the perfect life?' "[108]

Augustine sat under the teaching of Ambrose and was baptized by the latter when he finally converted to Christianity. Like Ambrose and Jerome, he associated true Christianity with the virginal life. As a good Roman, he understood the virtue of marriage as consisting of a hierarchically ordered household within a hierarchically ordered city overseen by a hierarchically ordered church. Differences between the sexes and class distinctions formed the basis for these hierarchies.

Within his massive corpus, Augustine does not elaborate on Jesus' teach-

105. In his letter to Pammachius, written between 393 and 394, Jerome quotes Ambrose *(On Widows),* who spoke of good marriages as still enjoining servitude of the wife to her husband, but Jerome argues, " 'Ye are bought' says the apostle [Paul], 'with a price; be not therefore the servants of men.' You see how clearly he defines the servitude which attends the married state." Jerome, Letter 48, *To Pammachius* 14.

106. Kuefler is wise to point out the unequal application of this ideal in the Roman world. "It must be admitted that for early Christians, 'no more male or female' often meant 'no more female.' But if the genderless ideal in earliest Christianity was understood mostly as a call for women to become men, the idea that women might choose to abandon their gender identity and all its limitations and restrictions was still a challenge to the sexual hierarchy." Kuefler, *The Manly Eunuch,* 226.

107. Kuefler, *The Manly Eunuch,* 267-68.

108. Kuefler, *The Manly Eunuch,* 268; Jerome, *Epistula* 14.6.

ing about eunuchs in Matthew 19:12. When he did speak about eunuchs, Augustine was almost always railing against the *galli,* castrated priests of the cult of Cybele prominent in the city of Carthage where he had spent more than ten years of his life. He despised the *galli* not only for their religious beliefs and their sexual exploits, but also for their transgression of gender boundaries. And gender transgression was something that Augustine would not tolerate. When confronted with Christian ascetics who called themselves "eunuchs for the sake of the kingdom" and wore their hair long to display their disregard for gendered comportment, Augustine responded with rhetorical force:

> How lamentably ridiculous is that other argument, if it can be called such, which they have brought forward in defense of their long hair. They say that the Apostle forbade men to wear their hair long, but, they argue, those who have castrated themselves for the sake of the kingdom of Heaven are no longer men. O astonishing madness! . . . They have heard, or at least have read, what was written: "For all you who have been baptized into Christ, have put on Christ. There is neither Jew nor Greek, there is neither slave nor freeman, there is neither male nor female." Yet they do not know that this was said according to the concupiscence of carnal sex, because in the interior man, where we are renewed in the newness of our minds, there is no sex of this sort. There, let them not deny that holy people are men because they do nothing of a sexual nature.[109]

These monks knew of Paul's words that long hair was a "disgrace" to men. They knew that anything conceived as gender transgression would be considered a disgrace for men, but they assumed disgrace willingly: "We assume this disgrace, because of our sins."[110]

Augustine was more than ready to make use of feminine metaphors (i.e., the bride of Christ) for the spiritual life of priests, bishops, and monks; nevertheless, he was careful to uphold gender distinctions in hierarchy and comportment in the public sphere. The feminine spirituality of bishops before God only worked to bolster their masculine authority in the church and over the city.[111]

109. Kuefler, *The Manly Eunuch,* 274 n. 131; Augustine, *De opere monachorum* 32. Kuefler comments on this passage: "We should not miss the fact that Augustine was opposing what was apparently a developed exegetical tradition. He complained that these long-haired monks also compared themselves to the men called Nazirites among the ancient Hebrews" (274).

110. Kuefler, *The Manly Eunuch,* 275 n. 132; Augustine, *De opere monachorum* 31.

111. Kuefler, *The Manly Eunuch,* 139-42.

Gender distinctions were an important part of the ordered fabric of society, and yet Augustine was willing to look ahead to a time when the ways of this world would give way to the order of the world to come. Augustine attempts to explain Jesus' teaching in Luke 14:26 ("If any man come to me, and hate not his father, and mother, and wife, and children, and brethren, and sisters, yea, and his own life also, he cannot be my disciple" [KJV]) by an appeal to Matthew 22:30 ("For in the resurrection they neither marry nor are given in marriage" [NRSV]) and Galatians 3:28 and Colossians 3:11 ("there is neither Jew nor Greek, there is neither bond nor free, there is neither male nor female" [KJV]; "but Christ is all, and in all" [KJV]). "Hence it is necessary that whoever wishes here and now to aim after the life of that kingdom, should hate not the persons themselves, but those temporal relationships by which this life of ours, which is transitory and is comprised in being born and dying, is upheld; because he who does not hate them, does not yet love that life where there is no condition of being born and dying, which unites parties in earthly wedlock."[112]

Marriage was seen as part of the earthly system, providing birth as a remedy to death. But in the next life, marriage, sexual activity, and the birth of children would be abandoned. Augustine explains that a good husband will look forward to sharing the heavenly life with his wife but not as respects her being his wife: "to love the creature of God, whom he desires to be transformed and renewed; but to hate the corruptible and mortal conjugal connection and sexual intercourse: i.e. to love in her what is characteristic of a human being, to hate what belongs to her as a wife."[113]

In this passage, Augustine highlights the fundamental humanity of women, a humanity that is revealed in the next life, when gender distinctions, marriage, and sexuality fall by the wayside. Unlike Tertullian, he does not suggest that men might actually lose "what belongs to them as husbands." But even while Augustine was willing to speak about gender distinctions losing their value in the life to come, he was far from willing to allow a blurring of the sexes in the present time.

Along with others in the West, Augustine argued that the only positive value of the eunuch was as an exemplar of the virtue of virginity. Gender distinctions were an essential part of life in the present order of things, even

112. Augustine, *Sermon on the Mount* 1.15.40, translated by William Findlay, revised and annotated by D. S. Schaff, Christian Classics Ethereal Library, http://www.ccel.org/ccel/schaff/npnf106.v.ii.xv.html?scrBook=Matt&scrCh=22&scrV=30#v.ii.xv-p7.1.

113. Augustine, *Sermon on the Mount* 1.15.41.

if, in the eschaton, a common humanity would be all that mattered. Similar to Tertullian's affirmation of a sexless soul, Augustine's presentation of a sexless resurrection — or an eschatological life that focused on a shared humanity and downplayed sex distinctions — while at the same time affirming sex distinctions in the present aeon, protected the power structures of the present age, "rendering the genderless ideal of earliest Christianity quaint but harmless."[114]

Kuefler summarizes the Western tradition, saying that Latin Church Fathers "offered a host of alternative meanings for the 'eunuchs who have made themselves that way for the kingdom of Heaven.' "[115]

> Spiritual eunuchs might be virgins, continent persons, men or women in sexless marriages, or widows. The variety of interpretations, all related to sexual renunciation, and the willingness of the Church fathers to refer to women as well as men as spiritual eunuchs, merely highlights the real exegetical imperative behind the statements: *eunuch must mean anything but a castrated man.* (We must assume that the extension of the image of castration to women, according them an identity as eunuchs, was a much less dangerous gender ambiguity than the gender ambiguity of physically castrated men.)[116]

Augustine's views dominated the exegetical tradition to follow in the Western part of the Christian Empire. However, in the East, physical eunuchs remained a part of public life in Byzantine Christianity. Though in the early days of the Byzantine Empire, Eastern Church Fathers tended to display the same sort of disdain for eunuchs as those in the West, over the course of several centuries opinions about eunuchs changed significantly for the better.

Eunuchs in the Early East

Although Christians in the East and West both understood the eunuch as the exemplar of the ascetic, virginal life, the theological tradition of the East did not view sexuality as the centerpiece of human sinfulness. Desert monastics,

114. Kuefler, *The Manly Eunuch,* 230.
115. Kuefler, *The Manly Eunuch,* 268.
116. Kuefler, *The Manly Eunuch,* 268, italics mine.

formative of spirituality in the Eastern Christian Empire, viewed sex not as an evil in itself but as that which tied the believer to the power structures of the world.[117]

John Cassian (360-435), a Roman Christian who receives the credit for bringing much of the wisdom of the Eastern desert monastics to the West, attempted to refute Augustine's views on concupiscence and the bondage of the will. Whereas Augustine "had placed sexuality irremovably at the center of the human person," Cassian — drawing from Eastern monastic wisdom — believed that sexual fantasies and temptations actually revealed more dangerous vices lodged within the soul, such as anger, greed, or pride.[118] In his view, the sexual drive was to be received as a gift of God, natural because it is universal and a good gift because it aids Christians on the road to holiness.

Despite differences of opinion on the nature of sexuality and human sin, Cassian and other Western Christian Fathers agreed that Jesus' words about eunuchs were not to be taken literally. We do not cut off "our hands or feet or our genitals," but the "body of sin."[119] Cassian's relatively neutral view of physical eunuchism must be contrasted with the standard Eastern opinion exemplified by Basil of Caesarea (330-379), whose letter to Simplicia illustrates "a standard part of the repertoire used by authors critical of eunuchs."[120] Kathryn Ringrose, who has written extensively on eunuchs in the Christian East, explains.

> The tone of the letter is angry and negative, . . . and was aimed at a group that he clearly dismissed as less than human. St. Basil says that the eunuch is damned by the knife and that although he is chaste, his chastity will go unrewarded. He claims that eunuchs cannot make moral judgments because their "feet are twisted." Backward feet were a sign of being in league with the forces of evil, particularly the Devil. Finally, St. Basil claims that

117. Brown argues that for the desert monastics, it was the belly, the drive for food, that was seen as more dangerous than the sexual drive. The symbols of the new humanity were those who could build a city in the desert, deprived of food. Brown, *The Body and Society,* 217-18. Given this perspective, the Desert Fathers did not interpret the sin of Adam and Eve in a sexual light. Rather, they interpreted it as "ravenous greed." "[G]reed, and in a famine-ridden world, greed's blatant social overtones — avarice and dominance — quite overshadowed sexuality" (Brown, 220). The Desert Fathers also learned through their practical experience of famine that the sexual drive was diminished when the belly was not fed. Thus, they found that through fasting, sexual desire could be overcome, even in this life (224-25).

118. Brown, *The Body and Society,* 421-22.

119. Kuefler, *The Manly Eunuch,* 269 n. 106; John Cassian, *Conlationes* 12.1; cf. 1.20.

120. Ringrose, *The Perfect Servant,* 116.

eunuchs did experience sexual passion and that they raved with intemperate passion in general, but this passion could not achieve fruition. St. Basil's writings were widely cited by later commentators as the definitive "word" on eunuchs.[121]

Because of the desire of the early Fathers to associate eunuchs with the life of continence, away from more literal interpretations, they read these values back into their interpretations of Matthew 19:12. Gregory of Nazianzus (329-389) models this exegesis in his commentary on the passage. He argues that the first type of eunuchs are "born without sexual desire. The second group, those who are 'castrated by others,' refers to men who have been taught celibacy by others. The third group, those who choose celibacy on their own, have the spiritual power to teach it to themselves."[122] While castration does not appear in his analysis of Matthew 19, elsewhere he criticizes eunuchs as "womanlike and, among men, are not manly, of dubious sex."[123]

John Chrysostom (347-407) shared Basil's negative assessment of eunuchs. He is remembered for having a lengthy political battle with Eutropios, a powerful court eunuch (when the former was patriarch of Constantinople), and for having preached a sermon against the latter from his pulpit in the Hagia Sophia.[124] Chrysostom argued that physical eunuchs would gain no reward for their celibacy. Only those who castrate themselves metaphorically, exerting effort to live the continent life, would be rewarded. He may have believed that "virginity made plain that 'the things of the resurrection stand at the door,'"[125] but literal castration was the "Devil's work." Castration "injures God's creation and allows men to fall into sin." In this context, Chrysostom probably means sexual sin.[126]

Chrysostom distanced Jesus' statement from literal eunuchs and also asserted strongly that Daniel and his friends should not be understood as

121. Ringrose, *The Perfect Servant,* 116. The interior quotation comes from St. Basil, *The Letters* 115, l.24.

122. Ringrose, *The Perfect Servant,* 116; Gregory of Nazianzus, *Discours* 16.305.

123. Kathryn M. Ringrose, "Living in the Shadows: Eunuchs and Gender in Byzantium," in *Third Sex, Third Gender: Beyond Sexual Dimorphism in Culture and History,* ed. Gilbert Herdt (New York: Zone Books, 1994), 89; citing Gregory of Nazianzus, *In Praise of Athanasius,* in Patrologia graeca, 35:1106.

124. Ringrose, *The Perfect Servant,* 25, 90.

125. Brown, *The Body and Society,* 442; John Chrysostom, *On Virginity* 73.1.6.

126. Ringrose, *The Perfect Servant,* 115; Chrysostom, *Homily XXXV on Chapter XIV of Genesis.*

eunuchs of the Babylonian court, even though they were chosen for their beauty and given responsibilities that paralleled those given to eunuchs in the Byzantine Empire.[127] For Chrysostom, physical eunuchs could not be representatives of holiness.

Kathryn Ringrose explains that "The low esteem in which eunuchs were held in Late Antiquity and early Byzantium is reflected in the near absence of eunuchs from church offices in the early centuries of the Byzantine Empire."[128] Monasteries also regularly set down rules that boys, eunuchs, and beardless men were not to be admitted. It was believed that the androgynous beauty of eunuchs and boys would tempt other monks into sexual sin.[129]

Nevertheless, despite this predominantly negative picture of eunuchs — as those outside the means of holiness — they were not represented in such negative light in late antique hagiography. "These texts present eunuchs as sexually continent and scholarly . . . [they] have noble character, are kind to colleagues and servants, are good-tempered, and exhibit personal integrity. They are characterized as sincere, brotherly, pious, without malice, careful of what they say, abstemious of food and drink, unwilling to take bribes or play favorites, and generous in their philanthropy. In many cases these eunuch saints are fictional characters, but the characterization remains useful."[130]

Changing Attitudes toward Eunuchs: Eunuchs in Middle and Late Byzantium

Historians of Byzantine literature have found that, during the next few centuries, there occurred a change in attitudes toward eunuchs. Ringrose dates it to about the eighth century, "when eunuchs begin to appear in prominent religious positions."[131] In the eighth and ninth centuries, eunuchs were found even among the patriarchs of the Byzantine Church. Religious historians praised eunuchs who were church leaders as well as holy eunuchs in imperial

127. Ringrose, *The Perfect Servant,* 90-91; Chrysostom, *Commentary on the Book of Daniel.*

128. Ringrose, *The Perfect Servant,* 117.

129. Ringrose, *The Perfect Servant,* 112-13. See also Shaun F. Tougher, "'The Angelic Life': Monasteries for Eunuchs," in *Byzantine Style, Religion, and Civilization,* ed. Elizabeth Jeffreys (Cambridge: Cambridge University Press, 2006), 238-52.

130. Ringrose, *The Perfect Servant,* 117.

131. Ringrose, *The Perfect Servant,* 118. Page numbers in the following text refer to Ringrose's book. See also Tougher, "Social Transformation, Gender Transformation?" 79.

service. Saints Nikephoros and Niketas Patrikios were two such eunuchs of the tenth century. They are of particular interest because their parents castrated them as young children and brought them to be trained as servants of the imperial household. Both eunuchs eventually left the court to serve the church. Niketas had a successful political career and served as a military commander. He eventually left these posts to become a monk, and is remembered for his ability to heal men "tormented by sexual desires" (86).

Ringrose suggests that such men represent the "normality of castration" during this period (86). It was not unusual for parents to castrate their own boys as infants or young children with the hopes that they would be able to make a career as a eunuch of the court or the church. Such children were then not only trained in particular tasks associated with their duties, but they were also acculturated "into patterns of behavior considered to be 'normal' for [eunuchs]" (5). Ringrose argues that these patterns of behavior (e.g., expectations regarding their dress, manner of walking, speed of talking, and facial expressions), accompanied by physical features distinctive of eunuchs, explain how eunuchs came to be understood as a third gender, if not a third sex, within Byzantine culture (3-4, 75).

Parents who castrated their children were not prosecuted by the state, even though castration ran counter to Byzantine law (3). Castrating an adult was considered an offense; it was believed to change his nature. But castrating a child was simply understood to be a method for retaining the values natural to children: "his beauty, his lack of sexuality, his lack of aggressive behavior, his willingness to serve" (59). As in the West, boys were also made into eunuchs to preserve their "angelic voices." A monastery was founded near the Hagia Sophia to train young castrati singers for service there and at other churches (74). Children were not looked upon as "'unripened' men and women but . . . unformed, malleable beings. . . . [T]he idea that society molds a male child into a model of perfect masculinity is very well established in Greek society" (122).

The growing acceptance of eunuchs at court, in monasteries,[132] and in churches brought about a change in the way some Byzantine exegetes read the Bible. Unlike Chrysostom, who was careful never to suggest that Daniel and his companions were "cut men," the tenth-century hagiographer

132. Ringrose notes a shift in monastic practice. Despite the fact that boys, beardless men, and eunuchs were not permitted on Mount Athos, one tenth-century monastic document includes an exception clause, provided the "superiors of the Mountain give their consent." Ringrose, *The Perfect Servant,* 112. See also Tougher, "The Angelic Life."

Symeon Metaphrastes saw no difficulty in Daniel and his friends living as both court eunuchs and holy men. Throughout his commentary on the book of Daniel, Metaphrastes reworks the material to show the similarities between Daniel and court eunuchs of his own day. A ninth-century Byzantine icon of Daniel presents him as "beardless, reclining on a couch and wearing Persian court dress. To Byzantine eyes the iconography would clearly identify him as a court eunuch."[133] Ringrose highlights the contrasts between Metaphrastes' and Chrysostom's commentaries on the book of Daniel to illustrate the significant shifts in attitudes toward eunuchs in the intervening centuries.[134] Still, this shift was not universal.

Eunuchs continued to be treated harshly, especially when their behavior accorded with negative assumptions about their character. In the ninth century, the patriarch Photius I (ca. 820-891) accused the head of the imperial department of finances, a eunuch, of laughing in church. His letter employed standard critiques of eunuchs to denounce his behavior.

> To John the patrician descended from Angourioi. Those who are wise among the Greeks liken you to Attis, calling you one of the *galli.* Our wise men confine you in the women's quarters and consider and call you androgynous. Whence [from the women's quarters] you have overstepped the rules on either side and intruded yourself upon the mysteries of God's church, turning everything upside down and through your corrupt nature, making the most fertile and prolific church of Christ fruitless and useless.[135]

Photius employs the standard comparison between physical and spiritual fruitfulness as well as the comparison of eunuchs to women. Later in this letter he likens the eunuch to the "Devil's gateway," a phrase Tertullian employed against women.[136]

Ringrose shows how, over the course of centuries, the Byzantine perspective on eunuchs changed considerably. While in late antiquity eunuchs were almost universally judged as morally bankrupt, between the eighth and the eleventh century eunuchs could also be described as the holiest of God's servants.[137]

133. Ringrose, *The Perfect Servant,* 99.

134. Ringrose, *The Perfect Servant,* 92-100.

135. Photios I, *Epistolae,* vol. 1, p. 95, letter 50; quoted in Ringrose, *The Perfect Servant,* 76-77.

136. Tertullian, *On the Apparel of Women* 1.1.

137. Shaun Tougher notes changes in the number of eunuchs employed at court and

By far, one of the most interesting works on eunuchs appears from the pen of a twelfth-century bishop, Theophylaktos of Ohrid (1050-1126), who devoted to the issue an entire treatise, *Defense of Eunuchs.* Theophylaktos's gloss on Matthew 19:12 reflects the commentary of Gregory of Nazianzus. The first type of eunuch lacks "sexual desire or [is] without functioning genitalia. Those who are made eunuchs by men are those who have learned celibacy from others. Those who are 'eunuchs for the sake of the kingdom of heaven' are those who have been able to teach themselves celibacy."[138]

Noticeably absent is any mention of castration. Elsewhere in his *Defense* he notes that there are good and bad eunuchs; thus, castration has no bearing on chastity. The castrated man, though it may be easier for him than others, must learn celibacy, either from others or directly from the Spirit.[139] Given this exegesis, even a eunuch must learn to become a eunuch.

Like others of his day, Theophylaktos believed castration done to an adult man was wrong. He likened it to murder and argued that it was "against nature." Ringrose suspects that his "real objection" may have been that "it represents a voluntary change in a man's gender assignment after he has passed puberty. Given prevailing ideas about acculturation and gender hierarchies, Theophylaktos probably found this culturally unacceptable" (122). On the other hand, castration done at a young age, to help a child "fulfill God's plan for his life," is "praiseworthy" and likened to the pruning of the gardener. This kind of castration, rather than being "against nature," allows a person to live "beyond nature" (122). Ringrose explains that "in the Late Antique and Byzantine contexts, men who gave up their reproductive powers were thought to acquire expanded spiritual and intellectual powers as a kind of compensation. Consequently, eunuchs, and especially those castrated in childhood, were often thought to have access to realms outside mundane space and time. . . . [T]hey were sometimes depicted as able to penetrate heavenly realms" (67-68).

---

the shift toward castrating citizens of the empire rather than foreigners, but he is less certain of a drastic shift in opinions about eunuchs throughout the empire. He argues that positive and negative pictures of eunuchs can be found in early, middle, and late Byzantium, and that multiple gender stereotypes and gender identities continued to exist side by side, even "in the writings of a single individual." Tougher, "Social Transformation, Gender Transformation?" 82.

138. Ringrose, *The Perfect Servant,* 121; Theophylaktos of Ohrid, *Enarratio en evangelium Matthaei* 19.12; Patrologia graeca, 125:352.

139. Ringrose, *The Perfect Servant,* 121. Page numbers in the following text refer to Ringrose's book.

Theophylaktos turns a number of assumptions about eunuchs on their head, even going so far as to create a new etymology. Instead of "the guardian of the bedchamber" *(ho tēn eunēn ekhōn),* he proposes that "eunuch" comes from *eunoos,* "well-minded" or "high-minded" (16, 198). Similarly, he refutes those who argue that castration ruins the moral character of a man. Instead of suggesting that eunuchs are tarnished by association with women — thus acculturated into the weaknesses of women — he states the contrary. By close association with godly empresses, "they might draw themselves in the glory of the divine image and become a likeness of the Divine word and propriety" (70). The assumption here is that eunuchs are influenced by whomever they serve, for good or for ill. At the core of the bishop's defense of eunuchs is the argument that there is more than one type of eunuch. There are good eunuchs and there are bad eunuchs. Each must be judged for his own merit rather than the state of his body (195).

Summary of Eunuchs in the Ancient World

Before Jesus' words about eunuchs in Matthew 19:12, eunuchs were considered the epitome of "other" — to Greeks, Romans, and especially Jews. They were foreigners, pagans, morally suspect, sexually illicit, neither male nor female, "exiles from the society of the human race." But Jesus' positive evaluation of eunuchs in the context of his teaching on marriage transformed the discussion of eunuchs into a declaration of the virtues of the virginal life. The metaphorical eunuch became the new icon of Christian perfection. East and West shared this theological assumption, but while the East eventually permitted physical eunuchs in prominent places in politics and the church, Western Christendom tended to employ literal eunuchs only as castrati singers in the churches. There is no Western treatise comparable to Theophylaktos of Ohrid's *Defense of Eunuchs.*

Christian writers in both the East and the West attempted to distance Jesus' statement about eunuchs from the practice of castration and gender ambiguity. Both traditions drew from ancient wells of gendered prejudice that associated manliness with perfection. Therefore, if the eunuch was to represent Christian perfection, the eunuch had to be transformed from a symbol of gender ambiguity and effeminacy to an alternative version of manliness. In the West, this manliness was defended as metaphorical eunuchism — the virtuous virginal life — described in masculine language of warfare against the devil and the devil's agents: women, physical eunuchs, prepubescent boys, and vices lodged deep within the soul. Eastern Church Fathers shared many of these assumptions; however, as eunuchs became more prominent in Byzantine life and proved themselves as "perfect servants," Byzantine writers became increasingly willing to ascribe virtue and holiness to literal eunuchs. By the twelfth century, Theophylaktos of Ohrid was able to argue for two alternative paths to masculine virtue. As Ringrose puts it: "two different ladders, each leading to a different conception of full masculine perfection. It is clear that the older pattern of classical Graeco-Roman society, in which young aristocratic males were acculturated with great care to ensure that they would become proper men, has now been adapted to an ecclesiastical context that emphasizes early childhood rearing and may include physical mutilation to ensure celibacy."[140] Rather than using the category of the eunuch to overturn the importance of manliness for ecclesiastical privilege, Theophylaktos and others expanded the category of manliness to include eunuchs. Whereas Origen could make himself a eunuch in order to display his sexless spirit, Theophylaktos presented castration as an alternative path to spiritual (i.e., masculine) perfection.[141] Thus, both East and West distanced the eunuch from its origins as a representative of androgyny, reconstructing the eunuch as a model of manliness. Perfection, even Christian perfection, continued to be construed as a ladder of ascent toward manliness (a connection we will explore in greater detail in the next chapter).

Intersex as Eunuch: Problems and Possibilities

Given the diverse history of the eunuch, it is fair to ask whether it is even helpful to recover such a concept when beginning to think about intersex in our own day. Susannah Cornwall downplays the connection between eunuchs and intersex.[142] Meanwhile, some intersex Christians look to Matthew 19:12 as the starting point for exploring their intersexuality from a biblical framework.[143] Is the eunuch a valid lens for intersex? The answer must be yes and no.

140. Ringrose, "Living in the Shadows," 105-6.

141. Ringrose, *The Perfect Servant,* 105.

142. Susannah Cornwall, *Sex and Uncertainty in the Body of Christ: Intersex Conditions and Christian Theology* (London: Equinox, 2010), 10.

143. Intersex Support Group International, "Director's Page," http://www.xyxo.org/isgi/director.html. Personal correspondence with Jane Spalding, January 12, 2011.

"Intersex" and "natural eunuch" are not univocal terms. As ancient writers did not give descriptions of the genitals of those they classified as "natural eunuchs" — and had little to no knowledge of internal reproductive organs, chromosomes, or hormone levels — it is difficult to assess where they would have drawn the boundary lines.[144] Nevertheless, from their discussions of eunuchs we are able to conclude that people in the ancient world were more familiar with variations of sex development than many contemporary Christians are, and that they supplemented their binary model of human sex/gender with the marginal category of the eunuch.

Some intersex conditions, like Klinefelter's syndrome, bring about physical characteristics almost identical to those described of castrated eunuchs in the ancient world. Mr. Cameron, an intersex man with Klinefelter's syndrome, describes himself as tall and explains how testosterone stops the growth of long bones in arms and legs, so that those with lower levels of testosterone grow taller than the average man.[145] He goes on to detail his bodily features: "large nipples on smallish breasts, peanut-size testicles, and cellulite-type hairless fatty tissue over most of my body . . . genetically sterile. . . . The medical journals called my condition 'feminized male.' I had always felt caught between the sexes without knowing why."[146] Mr. Cameron's description is strikingly similar to ancient descriptions of eunuchs, as is his experience of feeling caught between the sexes.

While a barren woman remained a woman and an androgyne could be classified as a man, "eunuch" remained a term of "in-between-ness." Over time, particularly in the Byzantine East, eunuchs moved out of the shadows into prominent public positions and began to transform their shameful differences into a valuable third gender.[147] Their own liminal status and unique gendered behaviors enabled them to contribute as "perfect servants" of the imperial household or "perfect servants" of God — mediating divided realms.[148]

The ability of eunuchs to stand as a public challenge to the two-sex, two-gender paradigm of the ancient world certainly illuminates the possibility of

144. Kathryn Ringrose, personal correspondence via e-mail, July 19, 2009.

145. D. Cameron, "Caught Between: An Essay on Intersexuality," in *Intersex in the Age of Ethics*, ed. Alice Domurat Dreger (Hagerstown, Md.: University Publishing Group, 1999), 93.

146. Cameron, "Caught Between," 90-96.

147. At the same time, one could argue that the ability of eunuchs to function publicly may have been a result of the transformation of the eunuch from a symbol of gender ambiguity to an alternative "manliness." Ringrose, "Living in the Shadows," 105-7.

148. Ringrose, *The Perfect Servant*.

carving out public recognition of intersex even within the most conservative of Christian cultures that continue to defend heterosexual complementarity. On the other hand, contemporary Christians must be careful not to emulate the ways in which this third category was employed in the Byzantine East; despite its leaders' willingness to make public and private space for eunuchs, they continued to accuse eunuchs of moral inferiority. Nevertheless, we can learn from those willing to supplement the sex/gender binary model in our own efforts to make space for all human beings today.

The history of the interpretation of the eunuch also stands as a warning. The power structures of the ancient world were built upon a hierarchical chain of gendered being. Elite men were at the top. Women were at the bottom. Eunuchs, effeminate men, and virile women were somewhere in between. Early Christian (male) leaders reinterpreted the eunuch as the manly Christian, trading in ancient Roman versions of masculinity such as sexuality and violence for the new Christian virtues of continence and martyrdom. Nevertheless, these virtues continued to be presented as manly. The subject had changed but the rhetoric — the hierarchical gendered power structure — did not. Given these interpretive shifts, it is essential to understand Jesus' language about eunuchs in its original context.

By analyzing Jesus' statement about natural eunuchs through the lens of intersex, one can draw several conclusions. First, Jesus was not afraid of eunuchs. He was not disgusted by them. He did not ridicule them, as did Jews, Romans, and Greeks; nor did he speak of them as "proof of the Fall." David Hester notes an important contrast. "Jesus heals the blind, the paralyzed, the possessed, the fevered, the leprous, the hemorrhaging, even the dead, in every case restoring them to full societal membership. In the case of the eunuch, however, there is no implication whatsoever of 'illness' or social 'deformity' in need of restoration. Instead, the eunuch is held up as the model to follow."[149]

Out of his great compassion for outcasts, Jesus took up the shameful identity of the eunuch and turned it upside down into an identity for his disciples — a personal identity that did not conform to the gender ideals of the ancient world. Just as Jesus transformed the cross from a symbol of defeat into a symbol of victory, he brought eunuchs in from outside and raised them up from shame and suspicion to become icons of radical discipleship.

In the metaphor of the eunuch, Jesus presented the possibility of renouncing marriage for the sake of the kingdom, but he did not do so within

149. Hester, "Eunuchs and the Postgender Jesus," 38.

a patriarchal framework. He did not call for the "manly men," the men who did not need women, to come follow him. Rather, he challenged their most valued identity, the identity of masculinity within a patriarchal world. He called them to leave the power of the *paterfamilias,* to reject the honor associated with the husband, father, grandfather, and to take up shame instead — the ambiguous, scandalous reputation of the eunuch.

Those who renounced marriage for the sake of the kingdom would no longer be defined by traditional gender markers. They would not be fathers or mothers, husbands or wives. Nor would they be potential spouses and parents, as young virgins were assumed to be. Their primary identity would not be a gendered identity. Or, if it was, it was to be a confused gender identity. They would embrace service, an unmanly trait. They would leave behind power, prestige, wealth — prerogatives of the male — in order to embrace another kind of life — "a life hidden with Christ in God." They would become "exiles from the human race," "strangers and aliens in a foreign land."

In calling his disciples to learn from eunuchs, Jesus was calling them to learn from those whose gender identity was not secure, to learn that gender identity is not the central value in the kingdom of heaven. Jesus was undermining the power structures of the day: family ties, inheritance of wealth and property, gender privilege. Many early Christians found that some of these were easier to renounce than others. The history of the church reveals that many found it easier to abandon sexual pleasure than masculine power and privilege. Christians today may find the reverse to be true. That the eunuch was reworked into a masculine metaphor is a tragedy yet to be corrected.

It is true that contemporary readers may find Jesus' words about eunuchs difficult to understand. But Jesus' teaching should certainly be read as "good news" for the intersexed. Many intersex persons have testified to feeling like "exiles from the human race" — the very phrase Claudius Mamertinus used to describe the social condition of eunuchs in the Roman Empire.[150] An intersex woman with androgen insensitivity syndrome (AIS) described her experience by saying: "The world has tried to make us feel like freaks. We have felt like freaks. I felt like a freak most of my life, but look at me. I'm just a human being just like everybody else. . . . I really have a place in the world. I really am a human being, a very valid human being. It's just wonderful. I am very proud to come out as an AIS person."[151]

150. Kuefler, *The Manly Eunuch,* 36.

151. Sharon E. Preves, "For the Sake of the Children: Destigmatizing Intersexuality," in *Intersex in the Age of Ethics,* 62, 61.

Kathryn Ringrose explains that "[b]iological and medical lore treated eunuchs as neither fully male nor fully female. . . . In his ambiguity, the eunuch challenged the church's definition of humanity."[152] The physicality of eunuchs, naturally born and castrated, forced ancient Christians to apply the nature and significance of sex, gender, and sexuality to what it means to be human and what it means to be Christian. Today, intersex is calling for contemporary Christians to do the same.

Before its reconfiguration into an alternative symbol of masculine perfection, the eunuch provided an important supplement to the binary model of human sex and gender. The eunuch emerged as a symbol of the sexless spirit, Christian perfection, the angelic life, and life in the resurrection — when distinctions of gender would be shed and men and women would relate to one another according to a common humanity, an identity hidden in Christ. Additionally, as an icon of the continent life, the eunuch also stood as a corrective to the exaltation of sexuality — whether for procreation or pleasure — challenging the centrality of sexuality for human personhood and human fulfillment. We will explore these contributions in the next few chapters, particularly in light of current constructions of human persons with regard to sex and gender in chapter 4 and sexuality in chapter 5. Chapter 6 will return to develop the notion of identities hidden in Christ in light of christological and eschatological contributions. But before we move on to theological critique and construction, we must recover one more piece to the puzzle — the relation of various historical constructions of sex difference in the West to Christian notions of the image of God.

152. Ringrose, *The Perfect Servant*, 67-68.

CHAPTER 3

How We Got Here: Historical Shifts in Theological Anthropology

After the last chapter you, persevering reader, may be more than ready to cut to the chase — or at least to the present, to theological anthropology today. I promise you: this chapter will get us there. But, once again, we must excavate a few more pieces of philosophical and theological framework that shape the ways we think about human persons and sex difference today. As the last chapter has shown, Christian understandings of sex difference have varied throughout history and across cultures. These various perspectives altered the ways Christians interpreted the Bible and its contributions to discussions of sex difference. This chapter will trace three significant shifts in Western thought that have influenced the development of theological anthropology; this will frame the contemporary debate.

Male, female, and intersex persons have been a part of the human family from ancient times to the present; and yet, the diversity of human bodies has been set against particular ideals in different historical periods. Many of these ideals shaped the ways in which Christians answered questions about human nature in general and the image of God in particular. We will trace Western developments of human being, sex difference, and the image of God through three movements: from their inception in the classical period, through Protestant and Victorian reformations in the modern period, into current, postmodern reconstructions.[1] In each era we will see how the ques-

1. As a theologian writing in the United States of America, I recount the history of Western Christianity (knowing that even this nomenclature is not unproblematic [i.e., First Nations cultures of the Americas]). It is only in the postmodern period that Western theologians are learning to appreciate non-Western (nonwhite, non-middle-class and non-upper-class, nonmale) contributions and critiques of Western theological construction. I offer this as one voice in that larger conversation.

tion, *What* is the human with its sex? (ontology), is connected to the questions, *How many* sexes are there, and *whence* do they come? (cosmology). Each contributes to theological reflection on the image of God.

The Classical Period: Substance Dualism and a Single Sex

Classical Greek Ontology

When asked, "What is the human?" classical Greek philosophers volunteered various answers. Plato argued that the human was a rational, immortal, sexless soul that had fallen from the realm of the forms, was imprisoned in a (sexed) body, and must strive for release from the (sexed) body through the cultivation of reason and the rule of reason over bodily passions (including the sexual passions). Aristotle, on the other hand, argued that the soul was the "form" of the body such that the two were not so easily separable.[2] Nevertheless, Aristotle also identified three types of soul that make up the human: the vegetable (nutritive) soul, the animal (sensitive) soul, and the human (rational) soul.[3] Thus, while these philosophers disagreed about the relation of body and soul, they located reason in the soul as the primary difference between humans and animals. While Aristotle conceded that animals have the first two types of soul, and that humans and animals both have bodies, humans were ultimately differentiated from animals by the possession of a *rational* soul. Their contributions laid the foundation for the Western conversations about human sex differentiation for the last two millennia.

Plato's Cosmologies Plato gives several accounts of the origin of the sexes. In the *Timaeus,* he argues that women came into existence after men failed to cultivate reason and virtue. These lesser men — souls that had failed to develop the mind in order to control the passions of the body — were reincarnated as women.[4]

Alternatively, in the *Symposium* Plato places a long discourse in the

2. F. LeRon Shults, *Reforming Theological Anthropology: After the Philosophical Turn to Relationality* (Grand Rapids: Eerdmans, 2003), 166-67.

3. Shults, *Reforming Theological Anthropology,* 170.

4. Plato, *Timaeus* 42c, 90e; in *Plato: Complete Works,* ed. John M. Cooper (Indianapolis and Cambridge: Hackett, 1997), 1245, 1289.

mouth of the poet Aristophanes, a colleague of Socrates, to explain the creation of the sexes. According to Plato's Aristophanes,

> the original human nature was not like the present, but different. The sexes were not two as they are now, but originally three in number; there was man, woman, and the union of the two, having a name corresponding to this double nature, which had once a real existence, but is now lost, and the word "Androgynous" is only preserved as a term of reproach. In the second place, the primeval man was round, his back and sides forming a circle; and he had four hands and four feet, one head with two faces, looking opposite ways, set on a round neck and precisely alike. . . .
>
> . . . Now the sexes were three, and such as I have described them; because the sun, moon, and earth are three; and the man was originally the child of the sun, the woman of the earth, and the man-woman of the moon, which is made up of sun and earth. . . .
>
> Terrible was their might and strength, and the thoughts of their hearts were great, and they made an attack upon the gods . . . dared to scale heaven, and would have laid hands upon the gods.[5]

Fearing that they had created humans as too powerful, the gods debated annihilating them until Zeus proposed a plan to "humble their pride and improve their manners." Thus, Zeus declared, "men shall continue to exist, but I will cut them in two and then they will be diminished in strength and increased in numbers; this will have the advantage of making them more profitable to us." So Zeus divided the spherical creatures in half and "turned the parts of generation round to the front, for this had not been always their position . . . and after the transposition the male generated in the female in order that by the mutual embraces of man and woman they might breed, and the race might continue; or if man came to man they might be satisfied, and rest, and go their ways to the business of life: so ancient is the desire of one another which is implanted in us, reuniting our original nature, making one of two, and healing the state of man."[6]

Heterosexual coupling was thus explained on the basis of the reuniting of originally androgynous humans. Gay and lesbian coupling was the reunit-

5. Plato, *Symposium* 1.14, translated by Benjamin Jowett, http://www.ellopos.net/elpenor/greek-texts/ancient-greece/plato-concept.asp; or following the Stephanus reference numbers, this dialogue can be found in *Symposium* 189d-193b, in *Plato: Complete Works,* 473-76.

6. Plato, *Symposium* 1.15.

ing of the two parts of the original male or the original female, each of which had two sets of male genitals or two sets of female genitals, respectively. Each was reunited with the "true other half" of itself.

Even though he assigned males the place of honor as creatures of the sun, while women were creatures of the earth and androgynes creatures of the moon, Plato did not always emphasize the differences between the sexes.[7] At one point in the *Republic* he concedes, "But if it appears that they differ only in this respect that the female bears and the male begets, we shall say that no proof has yet been produced that the woman differs from the man for our purposes, but we shall continue to think that our guardians and their wives ought to follow the same pursuits."[8] Such pursuits were those that benefited the common life of the republic (e.g., "equal participation in governance, gymnastic exercises, and even war"), and it was Plato's emphasis on the communal nature of child rearing that allowed him to underplay reproductive differences.[9] Thomas Laqueur explains Plato's logic: "If something characteristic of men or women can be found which fits one or the other for particular arts and crafts, by all means assign them accordingly. But no such distinction exists, he maintains, and what Aristotle would take to be the critical difference between bearing and begetting counts for nothing."[10]

It may be possible to account for Plato's ambivalence about sex differences by looking to his emphasis on the soul as the seat of human personhood. For the soul existed without the body. Stronger, more rational, more virtuous souls were given male bodies. Weaker, less rational, less virtuous

7. Plato presents the pairing of male with male as the pairing of the best with the best. *Symposium* 1.16.

8. Thomas Laqueur, *Making Sex: The Body and Gender from the Greeks to Freud* (Cambridge: Harvard University Press, 1990), 54, citing Plato, *Republic* 454e, in *The Collected Dialogues,* ed. Edith Hamilton and Huntington Cairns (Princeton: Princeton University Press, 1963), 693. His note here is helpful: "Plato of course does not maintain this view of sexual equality in other contexts, as in the *Laws* or the myth of the origin of women in the *Timaeus.*" I have profited greatly in understanding the context of Plato's arguments on this subject from Monique Canto, "The Politics of Women's Bodies: Reflections on Plato," in *The Female Body in Western Culture,* ed. Susan Rubin Suleiman (Cambridge: Harvard University Press, 1986), 339-53. Whereas my reading emphasizes Plato's rejection of the biology of reproduction as a relevant political difference, Canto makes the positive case that Plato is arguing for a "communal" account of procreation that neutralizes the effects of difference; raising children communally, as is proposed elsewhere in the *Republic,* is a continuation of this political strategy. The highly contextual quality of Plato's view of women generally is made clear in Gregory Vlastos, "Was Plato a Feminist?" *Times Literary Supplement,* March 17-23, 1989, 276, 288-89.

9. Laqueur, *Making Sex,* 54.

10. Laqueur, *Making Sex,* 54.

souls were reincarnated as women. Still, the goal of all souls was to leave the body, with its sex, behind. While Plato believed this to be more difficult for women than for men, he argued that women should nevertheless be given similar opportunities to reunite themselves (i.e., their souls) with the forms.[11]

Summing up the significance of Plato's cosmology for Western philosophy and theology, Rosemary Radford Ruether writes, "The soul is seen as sharing the same life principle of the cosmos, itself derivative in part from the eternal or divine substance of the Ideas. Later Greek philosophy will identify the eternal Ideas of Plato with the governing divine Mind of Aristotle's *Metaphysics* and the cosmic *Logos* of Stoicism. So the life principle of the soul becomes more explicitly a sharing in the life principle of God."[12]

Aristotle's Metaphysics Aristotle reasoned from the ground up; from the diversity of the material, temporal world to the immaterial, the eternal, the One. Because he posited an eternal universe, his "One," his "god," was not a creator but the goal toward which all material, temporal things aspire.[13]

For Aristotle the soul was not a separate rational substance but the life, the actualization of the potentialities of particular bodies.[14] Nevertheless, it is the *nous,* the mind, the rational part of the soul, that is separable from the body, eternal, immortal, and like Ultimate Reality. This mind knows no personal existence. When separated from the body, it can have no personal knowledge.[15] Thus, even while Aristotle attempts to distance himself from Plato's formulation of substance dualism (body vs. soul), he falls into a dualism of his own (body/soul vs. mind).

Aristotle's God is pure mind, contemplating its own thoughts. It is loved but does not love. It is self-sufficient, while all else is driven by love and imitation of it. Therefore, he insisted that to be rational (and to be rational is to be virtuous) is good because it leads to happiness, which is what God experiences all the time.[16]

11. Chris Matthews, "Plato on Women," *Philosophical Misadventures* (2007-2009), 1, http://www.philosophicalmisadventures.com/?p=30.

12. Rosemary Radford Ruether, "*Imago Dei:* Christian Tradition and Feminist Hermeneutics," in *Image of God and Gender Models in Judaeo-Christian Tradition,* ed. Kari Elisabeth Børresen (Oslo: Solum Forlag, 1991), 273.

13. Norman Melchert, *The Great Conversation: A Historical Introduction to Philosophy,* 2nd ed. (Mountain View, Calif., London, and Toronto: Mayfield Publishing Co., 1995), 166.

14. Melchert, *The Great Conversation,* 171.

15. Melchert, *The Great Conversation,* 172.

16. Melchert, *The Great Conversation,* 182-83.

But Christians found this rational but impersonal god difficult to reconcile with the personal God of the Bible. Additionally, Christians' hope of a conscious, personal existence after death encouraged them to align with Plato in their attempts to prove the reasonability of the resurrection. Plato's substance dualism followed as part of the package. Still, Aristotle's theories would continue to influence philosophy, science, and medical theories well into the early modern period.

Aristotle and Galen: Biological Implications of Greek Cosmologies Aristotle's account of the closer relationship of soul and body may explain the greater emphasis he placed on sex distinctions. Rather than challenging souls to work toward reunion with the forms, Aristotle believed that the soul is the form of the body. While Plato philosophized "from above" in the *Timaeus,* asserting that less rational souls were reincarnated as women, Aristotle spent most of his time reasoning "from below," from particulars to universals. The weakness of women's bodies was taken as evidence of the weakness of women's souls. And since the soul is the form of the body and the seat of reason, women's lesser bodily strength was assumed to correspond with lesser strength of soul or mind. Thus, Aristotle surmised that by virtue of their physical and rational powers, men were suited to rule over women (and children, foreigners, and slaves). In fact, Aristotle was so concerned about rule and roles that some have concluded that gender roles were more important to him than the physical data of biological sex. Laqueur notes that "Aristotle, who was immensely concerned about the sex of free men and women, recognized no sex among slaves. . . . [I]n other words, slaves are without sex because their gender does not matter politically."[17]

Rather than an account of the cosmological origins of the sexes, Aristotle's account is biological. Women are born when something goes wrong

17. Laqueur, *Making Sex,* 54. "But within the same tradition of the one sex, and in widely varying contexts, such differences could matter a great deal and were duly regulated. Sperma, for Aristotle, makes the man *and* serves as synecdoche for citizen. In a society where physical labor was the sign of inferiority, sperma eschews physical contact with the catemenia and does its work by intellection. The *kurios,* the strength of the sperma in generating new life, is the microscopic corporeal aspects of the citizen's deliberative strength, of his superior rational power, and of his right to govern. . . . Conversely, Aristotle used the adjective *akuros* to describe both a lack of political authority, or legitimacy, and a lack of biological capacity, an incapacity that for him defined woman. She is politically, just as she is biologically, like a boy, an impotent version of the man, an *arren agonos.*" Laqueur, 54-55.

with the pregnancy. They are "misbegotten" or "mutilated" males.[18] Androgynous persons are given a similar explanation; they are misbegotten twins. Aristotle believed that the father's sperm provides the soul, which then guides the formation of matter (the contribution of the mother). In the case of androgynes or hermaphrodites,[19] the mother provides too much matter for the growth of one child and not enough for twins. The excess matter creates excess genitalia.[20] In this scheme, a hermaphrodite, rather than hearkening back to one of the original three human sexes, was a malformed twin who "really" belonged to one of two sexes, not a third.

Unlike modern physicians, Aristotle did not look to genitals or gonads to determine true sex; rather, he followed Hippocrates' theory of temperature, believing the "heat of the heart" revealed the difference. Men were warm. Women were cool.

Galen, the renowned physician of the first century C.E., whose medical influence lasted well into the modern period, built upon but also challenged Aristotle's biological account. Galen continued Aristotle's emphasis on heat while rejecting his formula that the male produced seed (containing the soul/form) while the woman contributed only matter.[21] Galen believed that both the male and the female contributed seed, and that these seeds engaged in a power struggle in utero to determine which would prevail. He combined the theory of male heat and dominance on the right side of the uterus with female coolness and passivity on the left side. If the hot male seed prevailed, the seed would settle on the right side of the uterus, the strong side. If the cool female seed prevailed, the seed would settle on the left, the weak side.

18. Aristotle, *On the Generation of Animals* 2.3, http://evans-experientialism.freewebspace.com/aristotle_genanimals02.htm.

19. While Piotr Scholz argues for a difference between androgyny ("a mystical manifestation of the existence of God") and hermaphroditism ("nothing more than the fantasy of a perverted sexuality," i.e., bisexuality), I follow the majority of scholars who employ "androgyne" and "hermaphrodite" synonymously. Scholz, *Eunuchs and Castrati: A Cultural History*, trans. John A. Broadwin and Shelley L. Frisch (Princeton: Markus Weiner Publishers, 2001), 13.

20. Anne Fausto-Sterling, *Sexing the Body: Gender Politics and the Construction of Sexuality* (New York: Basic Books, 2000), 33.

21. "The physical part, the body, comes from the female, and the Soul comes from the male, since the Soul is the essence of a particular body." Aristotle, *On the Generation of Animals* 2.4.185. "We should look upon the female state as being as it were a deformity, though one which occurs in the ordinary course of nature" (4.6.461). From Janice Delaney, Mary Jane Lupton, and Emily Toth, *The Curse: A Cultural History of Menstruation*, revised and expanded ed. (Champaign: University of Illinois Press, 1988), 45-46.

Masculine women were conceived left of center; effeminate males, right of center. Hermaphrodites came into the world when the seeds of male and female combined in the middle, neither prevailing over the other.[22] Galen's horizontal sex spectrum (from weak left to strong right) corresponded with the vertical sex/gender hierarchy that existed on the societal level.

Sex Hierarchy in the Classical Period In the classical world, sex and gender were understood as a ladder of ascent toward perfection. At the top were manly men — understood as the pinnacle not only of male perfection but also of human perfection. At the bottom were women and children. Unmanly men, hermaphrodites, and eunuchs occupied the middle. Male children could ascend the ladder as their bodies naturally matured and as they carefully crafted their bodies and behaviors according to standards of male perfection. Peter Brown's explanation, cited in the foregoing chapter, is worth repeating:

> It was never enough to be male: a man had to strive to become "virile." He had to learn to exclude from his character and from the poise and temper of his body all telltale traces of "softness" that might betray, in him, the half-formed state of a woman . . . [how he walked,] the rhythms of his speech . . . the telltale resonance of his voice. Any of these might betray the ominous loss of a hot, high-spirited momentum, a flagging of the clear-cut self-restraint, and a relaxing of the taut elegance of voice and gesture that made a man a man, the unruffled master of a subject world.[23]

Women, too, could move up the ladder toward manly perfection, but only so far. Saintly, virtuous women were thus venerated in manly terms. Melania the Younger was celebrated as one "who performed 'manly deeds' and was received by the Fathers of Nitria 'like a man': since 'she had sur-

22. Sharon Preves details how Galen's theory of bodily heat and gender influenced medical theory as late as the seventeenth century. The seventeenth-century surgeon Ambroise Paré explained the development of male secondary sex characteristics in pubescent girls (perhaps a sign of late-onset congenital adrenal hyperplasia?) as the result of excessive heat brought about by physical exertion in girls. Girls who jumped or played roughly raised their body temperature enough to "push out" their inverted female organs so that they became masculine. Preves, *Intersex and Identity: The Contested Self* (New Brunswick, N.J.: Rutgers University Press, 2003), 34. See also Fausto-Sterling, *Sexing the Body,* 33-34.

23. Peter Brown, *The Body and Society: Men, Women, and Sexual Renunciation in Early Christianity* (New York: Columbia University Press, 1988), 11.

passed the limits of her sex and taken on a mentality that was manly, or rather angelic.' "[24]

Eunuchs were caught in a virtual arrested development, preserving the beauty and sexual allure of prepubescent boys but unable to attain full masculine perfection of body, mind, or virtue. This hierarchical structure of the sexes was seen as corresponding to the structure of the universe, especially as it was developed in what some have called the "last great system of Greek speculative philosophy":[25] the cosmology of Plotinus.

Plotinus's Cosmology Though less familiar to most than Plato and Aristotle, Plotinus may have been more influential than Plato and Aristotle on the Western Church, at least until Aquinas's rediscovery of Aristotle in the thirteenth century. Plotinus's name is often lost under the general category of Neoplatonism, the reformation of Plato's thought by later writers. Plotinus himself lived in the third century C.E., from 204 to 270. He was a philosophical mystic who used ascetic practices and philosophical contemplation to dispose himself to the ecstatic — God's self-manifestation that leads to union with the divine. Like Plato and Aristotle, he wondered at the nature of the world, its mixture of physical and spiritual, eternal and temporal, and attempted to reconcile these opposites through his cosmology.[26]

Plotinus proposed that God is not separate from creation, but the pinnacle of Being, from which all that exists emanates in lesser degrees. God is One, but the Many emanate from the One in a great chain of being. This hierarchical understanding provided the philosophical and theological defense of the caste system of the medieval period as well as the "hierarchical ordering of husband, wife, children, and servants."[27]

24. Gillian Cloke, quoting the *Life of Melania the Younger,* prologue and 39, in *"This Female Man of God": Women and Spiritual Power in the Patristic Age,* AD *350-450* (New York: Routledge, 1995), 214.

25. "The Philosophy of Plotinus," Center for Applied Philosophy: The Radical Academy, 1998-99, 2001-2003, http://www.radicalacademy.com/philplotinus.htm.

26. "The Philosophy of Plotinus."

27. Alan D. Myatt, "On the Compatibility of Ontological Equality, Hierarchy and Functional Distinctions," in *The Deception of Eve and the Ontology of Women, Priscilla Papers,* special ed. (2010): 26. "In the Middle Ages this concept translated into the division of society into 'Three Estates,' each stratified according to the Chain of Being. The first estate consisted of clerics, church officials beginning with the Pope, Archbishops, Bishops, and Priests. The second estate included ruling classes of kings, nobility and knights, while the peasants and merchants made up the lower estate. Any violation of the established authority within each state was seen as a threat to the creation order and subversive to the state and to the stability

Substance Dualism and a Single Sex

Given this hierarchical understanding of human nature (and all reality), Thomas Laqueur has argued that there was only one sex recognized in the ancient world, the male, and a true male was a rare specimen. Most people existed as more or less perfect males, in other words, more or less perfect humans. Aristotle's famous dictum that a woman was a "misbegotten" or "mutilated" male supports such an argument, as do classical anatomical texts. Laqueur shows how medical texts from the ancient world all the way up through the Renaissance maintained that female reproductive organs were simply the inversion of male organs in the way they diagrammed and named female reproductive structures.[28] Women were men, turned inward, physically but also socially. Hermaphrodites were imperfect men and imperfect inverted men.

The male existed as the only true sex, the only true human. Women, eunuchs, and hermaphrodites had lesser bodies and, consequently, lesser souls. Their souls were defective in reason and virtue, for virtue was believed to be derived from *vir* (the male). Nevertheless, despite their status as lesser humans, women, eunuchs, and hermaphrodites were usually[29] granted human status and were believed to at least possess some measure of (rational)

---

of Christian culture. Any attempt to leave one's place in the chain was therefore an act of rebellion. It is critical to note that in the family there was a hierarchical ordering of husband, wife, children and servants. Each was subordinate to the previous due to their immutable places on the Chain of Being."

28. After reproducing picture after picture of female anatomy drawn as versions of the male in Renaissance medical textbooks, Laqueur concludes: "The absence of precise anatomical nomenclature for the female genitals, and for the reproductive system generally, is the linguistic equivalent of the propensity to *see* the female body *as* a version of the male. Both testify not to the blindness, inattention, or muddleheadedness of Renaissance anatomists, but to the absence of an imperative to create incommensurable categories of biological male and female through images or words. Language constrained the seeing of opposites and sustained the male body as the canonical human form. And, conversely, the fact that one saw only one sex made even words for the female parts ultimately refer to male organs. There was in an important sense no female reproductive anatomy, and hence modern terms that refer to it — vagina, uterus, vulva, labia, Fallopian tubes, clitoris — cannot quite find their Renaissance equivalents." Laqueur, *Making Sex,* 96.

29. Notwithstanding the regular exposure of hermaphroditic babies before the time of Pliny, as well as the regular exposure of infant girls. Of course, slaves — male, female, eunuchs, or hermaphrodites — were also on shaky ground when considering their status as fully human. See Julia Epstein, "Either/Or — Neither/Both: Sexual Ambiguity and the Ideology of Gender," *Genders* 7 (Spring 1990): 107, 133-34.

soul, no matter how deficient. Therefore, if they pursued virtue and reason, they could hope to progress through various stages of reincarnations to release from the body and its sex, finally participating in the sexless realm of the forms.

Substance dualism provided ambivalent results for the sexes. The possession of a soul did not protect women, eunuchs, and hermaphrodites from the status of "lesser men," because their inferior bodies were interpreted as evidence of inferior souls. Nevertheless, the possession of a soul did secure them some measure of humanity and suggested the possibility of release from the prison of the sexed body at some future date.

The One-Sex Model and Early Christian Theology

Although substance dualism is familiar to most students of Western theology, the idea of one sex sounds foreign to modern ears and distant from the biblical record. But this distance, I will argue, appears for the contemporary reader because the one-sex model was significantly altered in the course of Western history. The early Church Fathers, schooled in Greco-Roman philosophy, perceived no such distance.

The second creation account, found in Genesis 2, can be read as supporting the idea that the male is the perfect human while the female is something secondary or other.[30] This account identifies the male as *ha adam* (the human). Even after the woman is brought to the man and one finds for the first time the gendered words *ishshah* for the woman and *ish* for the male, the male in the narrative continues to be referred to as *ha adam* (the human), who has an *ishshah* (a woman or wife), rather than an *ish* who has an *ishshah.*

The early Christian Fathers certainly recognized this and found it very easy to accept the pagan beliefs, circulating in Greece and Rome, that the male is the perfect human while women, eunuchs, and hermaphrodites are imperfect, mutilated, misbegotten, or inverted humans. We find Aristotle's famous dictum: that a woman is a "misbegotten male" repeated 1,600 years later in Thomas Aquinas (thirteenth century C.E.) as he wrestled with the nature of woman. Aquinas agrees with Aristotle that women's bodies are defective.

30. Janet Martin Soskice, *The Kindness of God: Metaphor, Gender, and Religious Language* (Oxford: Oxford University Press, 2007), 42.

> As regards the individual nature, woman is defective and misbegotten, for the active force in the male seed tends to the production of a perfect likeness in the masculine sex; while the production of woman comes from defect in the active force or from some material indisposition, or even from some external influence; such as that of a south wind, which is moist, as the Philosopher observes (*De Gener. Animal.* iv, 2). On the other hand, as regards human nature in general, woman is not misbegotten, but is included in nature's intention as directed to the work of generation.[31]

Joseph Magee attempts to defend Aquinas by explaining that the Latin for "defective and misbegotten" is *deficiens et occasionatus,* "which can mean 'unfinished and caused accidentally.'" He notes that "[s]ome have argued that, because of this alternate reading, Aquinas is free of the negative connotations which attach to some translations of his works." Magee also highlights Aquinas's concession that Aristotle considered woman "misbegotten," but, Magee says, only "as an individual and only with respect to the body or matter, and not the soul."[32] For Aquinas, as for many of the Fathers who preceded him, the soul maintained the common humanity shared by the sexes and was identified as the proper location of the image of God in humans.

Early Christians reasoned that because God does not have a body, whatever likeness exists between humans and the divine cannot be located in the body. Therefore, they turned to concepts of the soul to tease out the meaning of the *imago Dei.*[33] Following Plato and Aristotle, early Christians identified reason and virtue with the soul. God as "all-wise" and "all-good" was imaged in the rationality and virtue of humans.

Irenaeus divided reason and virtue, identifying reason with "image" and virtue with "likeness." Thus, he argued that after the Fall humans retained a marred image (i.e., distorted rationality) but lost their likeness to God (i.e., they were no longer naturally virtuous). Colin Gunton assesses the significance of this theological move. "In his famous distinction between image and likeness there began the process of making reason both a chief ontological characteristic and criterion of difference between human and nonhuman. By the time of Aquinas the tendency had hardened into a dogma. Perhaps most revealing is his citation of John of Damascus: 'being after God's

31. *Summa Theologiae* Ia q.92, a.1, reply to obj.1. Joseph M. Magee, "Thomistic Philosophy Page," August 28, 1999, http://www.aquinasonline.com/Questions/women.html.

32. Magee, "Thomistic Philosophy Page."

33. Augustine, *De Trinitate* 7.7.12.

image signifies his capacity for understanding, and for making free decisions and his mastery of himself.' "[34]

Thus earlier Christian theologians defined the image of God in almost identical terms to Greek philosophers' definitions of the soul: reason, freedom, and the ability to rule. The challenge for our discussion of the sexes, of course, is that women, eunuchs, and some hermaphrodites were believed to possess these characteristics in lesser measures than men, if at all. Their lesser souls seemed to indicate that they were lesser images of God, if in fact they were images of God at all.

The Fathers debated whether women could really be considered images of God. Frederick McLeod, in his investigation *The Image of God in the Antiochene Tradition,* describes the Fathers as "ambivalent" on this point.[35]

> In our investigation of "image," the Antiochenes were found to have divided into two camps on how to interpret the scriptural statement about "man" having been created in God's image and likeness. Diodore, Chrysostom, and Theodoret looked upon image as applying to men *qua* males. They believed that God has entrusted males with total power to rule over the material universe as God's viceroys. While women share in this power, they were regarded as subordinate to men. Diodore, Chrysostom, and Theodoret frequently liked to cite Paul's statement that man *qua* male "is the image and glory of God but woman is the glory of man" (I Cor 11:7). The most they would say is that women are "images of the image." Yet, while following the same literal, rational hermeneutical principles of exegesis, Theodore, and perhaps, Nestorius, understood image as referring to how human nature — in a general sense — plays a unitive, revelatory, and cultic role within creation. It is not clear, however, what they thought about women as images of God and, if so, how they regarded women as functioning as such.[36]

There are several important items to note in the above. First is the connection between the image and participation in God's rule. Greek philosophers "knew" that women were not suited to rule. Christian theologians

34. Colin Gunton, "Trinity, Ontology and Anthropology: Towards a Renewal of the Doctrine of the *Imago Dei,*" in *Persons, Divine and Human,* ed. Christoph Schwöbel and Colin E. Gunton (Edinburgh: T. & T. Clark, 1991), 48.

35. Frederick G. McLeod, S.J., *The Image of God in the Antiochene Tradition* (Washington, D.C.: Catholic University of America Press, 1999), 192.

36. McLeod, *The Image of God,* 191.

looked to Genesis 3:16 to substantiate their cultural inheritance that women were not designed to rule. In this passage, after the sin of Eve and Adam, God says to the woman,

> "I will greatly increase your pains in childbearing;
> with pain you will give birth to children.
> Your desire will be for your husband,
> and he will rule over you." (NIV)

Early theologians believed that God, as the supreme Ruler, could not be properly imaged in one over whom another ruled.

But the subjugation of women was justified not simply on exegetical grounds, nor always as a result of sin. Many early Christian theologians believed that women were unsuited to rule by nature (i.e., ontologically inferior). According to Cyril of Alexandria, "the female sex is ever weak in mind and body."[37]

Some argued that this defectiveness was part of women's created nature, while others explained women's weakness as a result of the Fall. Still, it is important to recognize the unequal effects of the Fall upon the sexes. Following Romans 5:12-20, the Fathers taught that the whole human race fell into sin on account of Adam's transgression, resulting in the mortality of all, men and women. But women experience additional results of the Fall on account of the sin of Eve. Reading Genesis through the lens of 1 Timothy 2:11-15, Chrysostom wrote,

> A woman once taught and overturned everything. For this reason, he said: "Let her not teach." What then about the women coming after her, if she incurred this? By all means [it applies to them]! For their sex is weak and given to levity. For it is said here of the whole nature. For he did not say that "Eve" was deceived, but "the woman," which is a term for her sex

37. McLeod quotes Walter Burghardt's summary of Cyril's opinion of women's inferiority to men: "The inferiority is not purely a question of physical size or physical strength. What is more momentous, woman falls short of man in 'natural ability.' She has not the strength to achieve the virtue of which the male is capable. She is of imperfect intelligence. Unlike her male complement, she is dull-witted, slow to learn, unprepared to grasp the difficult and the supernatural; for her mind is a soft, weak, delicate thing. Briefly, 'the female sex is ever weak in mind and body.'" McLeod, *The Image of God,* 197, quoting Walter Burghardt, *The Image of God in Man according to Cyril of Alexandria* (Washington, D.C.: Catholic University of America Press, 1957), 128-29.

> in general, rather than a term for her. What then? Did the whole female nature come to be in [a state of] deviation through her? For just as he said of Adam, "In the pattern of the transgression of Adam who is a type of him who is to come," so also here the female sex has transgressed, not the male's. What therefore? Does she not have salvation? Most certainly, he said. And how is that? Through that of [having] children. Thus he was not speaking [here only] of Eve.[38]

While the sin of Adam affects men and women, the sin of Eve affects only women. Women are thus "doubly fallen," a theological position that has undergirded the perpetual subordination of women in Christianity.

One should note the substance metaphysics (i.e., ontology) undergirding the theological interpretation above. Chrysostom appears to posit a human nature (represented by Adam) as well as women's nature (represented by Eve), but he says nothing of the fall of Adam as a representative of men *qua* male. Nevertheless, thanks to Chrysostom's belief in Platonic substance dualism, women are not fallen beyond redemption. Women remain accountable to the demands of holiness despite their doubly-fallen nature.

> In external contests, which involve corporeal labors, only men are accepted as suitable. But as the entire contest here is one of the soul, the race-course is open to each of the sexes, and the spectators sit [in judgment] of each. But it is not only men who are to strip [for this kind of contest], lest women raise a specious argument [for not doing this] by appealing to their weakly nature. Nor do women alone show themselves as brave, lest mankind be steeped in shame. But there are many from both sides who have been proclaimed by the herald and crowned as victors, so that from their labors you may learn that "in Christ Jesus there is not male nor female." For neither nature nor bodily weakness, nor age nor anything else can incapacitate those running in the race of piety.[39]

Commenting on Galatians 3:28, "For there is neither Jew nor Greek, neither slave nor free man, neither male nor female; for you are all one in Christ,"

38. Chrysostom, Patrologia graeca, 62:545, quoted in McLeod, *The Image of God,* 203.

39. Chrysostom, Patrologia graeca, 61:656, cited in McLeod, *The Image of God,* 208. McLeod makes an interesting comment on Chrysostom's exegesis, noting that "Paul has used the masculine article for 'one' in the quotation cited from Galatians. Its antecedent is not 'form' which is feminine, nor a 'unique being' which is neuter, but 'we are all one in Christ.' Literally, it means that we are all 'one man' in Christ" (208 n. 39).

he asks, "Do you see that the soul is common? For by saying that we have become sons of God through faith, he is not content with this but seeks to find something more: the ability to submit more clearly to a closer unity to Christ. And when he says, 'You have been clothed with him,' he is not satisfied with this statement. But in interpreting it, he moves to a closer [explanation] of such a connection. He says that 'You are all one in Christ,' that is, you all have the same form, a unique being, that of Christ."[40]

Chrysostom appeals to substance dualism in order to preserve the possibility of women being conformed to the image of Christ. Because "the soul is common," it is the soul that enables both women and men to be clothed with Christ, being united with the "form . . . of Christ." Whether Chrysostom believed that women become male in their conformity to Christ is not clear from his commentary. What is clear is that the common humanity that allows for both men and women to be conformed to the image of Christ is located not in the body but in the soul — a soul that is "neither Jew nor Greek, neither slave nor free man, neither male nor female."

Rosemary Radford Ruether notes that in the Eastern tradition, especially in the work of Gregory of Nyssa, "the image of God was identified with the soul, which was seen as spiritual and asexual."[41] According to Nyssa, "In the original creation there was no subordination but also no gender, sex, or reproduction. Gendered bodies arose as a result of the Fall, which resulted in both sin and death and the necessity of sex and reproduction."[42]

Like his Eastern brothers, Augustine emphasizes the soul as the seat of the person,[43] but unlike Gregory of Nyssa, he does not look to the sexlessness of the soul as an indication of equality in Eden. He declares both substances, soul and body, "good" because they are created by God; and yet, in order to secure the continuation of the person after death, he gives priority to the soul. "[W]e must regard the human being as the combination of both substances, at least prior to death."[44] It is the death of the body that reveals the priority of the soul. In a similar way, Augustine emphasizes the goodness of both sexes while, at the same time, noting a hierarchy of essence

40. Chrysostom, Patrologia graeca, 61:656, cited in McLeod, *The Image of God,* 208.

41. Rosemary Radford Ruether, "Christian Anthropology and Gender," in *The Future of Theology: Essays in Honor of Jürgen Moltmann,* ed. Miroslav Volf, Carmen Krieg, and Thomas Kucharz (Grand Rapids: Eerdmans, 1996), 243.

42. Ruether, citing Gregory of Nyssa, *De opificio hominis* 16.

43. Shults, *Reforming Theological Anthropology,* 167. Shults quotes Augustine's *On the Doctrines of the Church* (1.27), where he identifies the self as the soul: "I, that is, my soul."

44. Shults, *Reforming Theological Anthropology,* 168; Augustine, *City of God* 19.3.

and function. Men rule and women obey, just as the soul rules and the body obeys. Contrary to Nyssa, Augustine does not see this subordination as a result of sin; rather, he believes the subordination of women is a part of original creation.

Augustine locates the hierarchy of the sexes in the natural propensities, ordinary attentions of the mind. In *On the Trinity* 7.7.10 he argues that a woman is not the image when spoken of as a woman, as a "help-meet," but only when united to her husband, who can be said to be the image even when not united to his wife. He qualifies this distinction in 7.7.12 when he locates the renewing of the image in the renewing of the mind following Ephesians 4:23-24 and Colossians 3:9-10. "If, then, we are renewed in the spirit of our mind, . . . no one can doubt, that man was made after the image of Him that created him, not according to the body, *nor indiscriminately according to any part of the mind, but according to the rational mind,* wherein the knowledge of God can exist" (7.7.12, italics mine).

This passage reveals Augustine dividing the mind into different parts. The rational mind is that which is directed to the knowledge of God. And it is the renewal of this part of the mind, or the giving of this mind, that is the image of God in men as well as in women.

> And it is according to this renewal, also, that we are made sons of God by the baptism of Christ; and putting on the new man, certainly put on Christ through faith. Who is there, then, who will hold women to be alien from this fellowship, whereas they are fellow-heirs of grace with us; and whereas in another place the same apostle says, "For ye are all the children of God by faith in Christ Jesus; for as many as have been baptized into Christ have put on Christ: there is neither Jew nor Greek, there is neither bond nor free, there is neither male nor female; for ye are all one in Christ Jesus"? (7.7.12; cf. Gal. 3:26-28)

Finally, Augustine asks, "Pray, have faithful women then lost their bodily sex?" He answers that the renewal of the mind in the image of God represents "no sex." But lest he be misunderstood, he explains that certain differences remain and are worthy of emphasis. "Because she differs from the man in bodily sex, *it was possible* rightly to represent under her bodily covering *that part of the reason which is diverted to the government of temporal things;* so that the image of God may remain on that side of the mind of man on which it cleaves to the beholding or the consulting of the eternal reasons of things; and this, it is clear, not men only, but also women have" (7.7.12, italics mine).

Augustine appears to be trying to make sense of what he understands to be conflicting messages in the Scriptures. He recognizes that Genesis 1:27 includes women in the image of God, and yet 1 Corinthians 11:10 speaks of males in the image of God (who therefore do not cover their heads) while women are the glory of men (as male), and thus cover their heads. But this doctor of the church is even more nuanced. He divides the mind into multiple parts so as to be able to include women in the renewing of their minds, a renewing of the image of God in women, while at the same time arguing that women's minds are not naturally directed to things above. He argues that women cover their heads because their minds are directed to earthly things, for example, the governance of their households. This interpretation of the veiling of women helps explain the practice of some consecrated virgins removing the veil — a symbol of their subordination to men (in marriage) and also a symbol of the direction of their minds (toward earthly rather than heavenly things).

Augustine is in significant agreement with the substance metaphysics bequeathed to him by Plato and Plotinus. Women are lesser men in body and in mind. Nevertheless, there is a part of their minds that can be renewed in the sexless image of God. And in the life to come, though bodily differences will remain, the inequality of sexes that exists in this life will finally give way to equality when body and soul are reunited in the resurrection and women and men relate to one another not according to hierarchically ordered marital relations but as equals, sharing a common humanity.[45]

Augustine's Platonic emphasis on the rational soul (or, the rational portion of the mind) was given succinct formulation by Boethius (480-524), whose definition of the human person as "an individual substance of a rational nature" became the standard for Western theological anthropology.[46] Boethius teaches that the human person is rational, but women are less rational; thus, women are less than human persons. While Thomas Aquinas's rediscovery of Aristotle's "psychosomatic unity of soul and body" attempted to offer a more holistic account of the person, he continued to teach the priority of the soul and the inferiority of women, based on an inferiority of mind.[47]

45. Augustine, *Sermon on the Mount* 1.15.40-41, trans. William Findlay, revised and annotated by D. S. Schaff, Christian Classics Ethereal Library, http://www.ccel.org/ccel/schaff/npnf106.v.ii.xv.html?scrBook=Matt&scrCh=22&scrV=30#v.ii.xv-p7.1.

46. Shults, *Reforming Theological Anthropology*, 168.

47. Shults, *Reforming Theological Anthropology*, 168. Aquinas, *Summa Theologiae* 1.29.1 and 1.75.6. Aquinas, *Summa Theologiae*, 1.92.1. "Subjection is twofold. One is servile, by virtue of which a superior makes use of a subject for his own benefit; and this kind of sub-

Both Plato and Aristotle bequeathed to Christian theology a hierarchy of substances that paralleled a hierarchy of sex.[48] It is important to recognize the progression from Greek ontology to Christian anthropology. The true human, the true image of God, must be the male whose rational soul governs his body and whose strong body corroborates his masculine, virtuous, rational soul. Women were misbegotten bodies with defective souls, lesser humans; thus, lesser images of God. These assumptions carried into christological reflection such that theologians concluded that the Messiah, if he was to represent true humanity, must necessarily have been incarnated as a male human — the perfect restoration of the original human.

In the classical period, hierarchically ordered substance dualism undergirded a hierarchy of sex in home, church, and society. Substance dualism did not result in sex dualism because both men and women were believed to have bodies and souls, even if the male was more often associated with the soul/mind while the female was more often associated with the body, and eunuchs and hermaphrodites displayed a mixed nature. Rather, the ancients held a view of a single sex, one true human form, the male, against which all other lesser, inverted, misbegotten males were measured. A true sex dualism was yet to come.

The Modern Period: Substance and Sex Dualism

Historical Changes: Sixteenth Century to Nineteenth Century

The Protestant Reformation, Sixteenth Century The classical identification of the true human, true image of God, as the male lasted well into the Middle Ages, with Thomas Aquinas recovering Aristotle's ancient phrase

---

jection began after sin. There is another kind of subjection which is called economic or civil, whereby the superior makes use of his subjects for their own benefit and good; and this kind of subjection existed even before sin. For good order would have been wanting in the human family if some were not governed by others wiser than themselves. So by such a kind of subjection woman is naturally subject to man, because in man the discretion of reason predominates."

48. Plato and Plotinus also handed down a disdain for the material world that can be found in so much of the writing of the early Christians. It is also important to recognize that the world of *matter* was more closely associated with the *mater* (Latin), *Mutter* (German), i.e., the mother.

identifying women as "misbegotten" males.[49] And while the Protestant reformers shared many of the sexist assumptions of their predecessors, they made several theological changes that laid the groundwork for a revolution in theological constructions of human sex.

Luther argued against the Greek and medieval assumption that women were morally inferior and lesser images of God than men were. Still, he maintained, "there is a great difference between the sexes. The male is like the sun in heaven, the female like the moon . . . therefore, let us note from this passage [Gen. 1:27] that it was written that this sex may not be excluded from any glory of the human creature, although it is inferior to the male sex."[50]

Luther had a fairly high view of female education, possibly due to his marriage to an educated nun. Calvin, on the other hand, believed that "oral instruction in the catechism was enough for women" and that female teaching was out of the question.[51] "[Woman] by nature (that is, by the ordinary law of God) is formed to obey; for . . . (the government of women) has always been regarded by all wise persons as a monstrous thing; and therefore, so to speak, it will be a mingling of heaven and earth, if women usurp the right to teach. Accordingly, he [Paul] bids them be 'quiet,' that is, keep within their own rank."[52] Similarly, in his commentary on 1 Corinthians, he avers: "He (Paul) establishes by *two* arguments the pre-eminence, which he had assigned to men above women. The *first* is, that as the woman derives her origin from the man, she is therefore inferior in rank. The *second* is, that as the woman was created for the sake of the man, she is therefore subject to him, as the work ultimately produced is to its cause. That the man is the beginning of the woman and the end for which she was made, is evident from the law."[53]

Rather than seeing Eve's creation from Adam as evidence that the two

49. Aquinas, *Summa Theologiae* 1.92.1.

50. Luther, "Lectures in Genesis," commenting on Gen. 1:27, quoted in Kristen E. Kvam, Linda S. Schearing, and Valarie H. Ziegler, eds., *Eve and Adam: Jewish, Christian, and Muslim Readings on Genesis and Gender* (Bloomington and Indianapolis: Indiana University Press, 1999), 268.

51. Mary Stewart Van Leeuwen, *Gender and Grace* (Downers Grove, Ill.: InterVarsity, 1990), 198.

52. John Calvin, *Commentaries on the Epistles to Timothy, Titus, and Philemon,* in *Calvin's Commentaries,* vol. 21, trans. William Pringle (Grand Rapids: Baker, 2003), 68; 1 Tim. 2:12.

53. John Calvin, *Commentary on the Epistles of Paul to the Corinthians,* vol. 1, trans. William Pringle (Grand Rapids: Baker, 2003), 357-58; 1 Cor. 11:8.

are equal in rank, because they were made from the same material ("flesh of my flesh, bone of my bone"), Calvin interprets the sequence of creation through the lens of the Neoplatonic chain of being.[54] Women are lower down on the chain; therefore, it is "natural" that they serve those of the rank above them.

While the Reformers emphasized the religious value of marriage, child rearing, and secular vocations (a shift that brought new dignity to the menial labor of married women and men), they continued to maintain a low view of women, even within that sphere. Luther wrote: "Women ought to stay at home. The way they were created indicates this, for they have broad hips and a wide fundament to sit upon, keep house, and bear and raise children."[55] Luther held the typical German view of women, which indicated that if one takes a woman from her housewifery, she is good for nothing.[56] Elsewhere he is said to have quipped, "If women get tired and die of childbearing, there is no harm in that; let them die as long as they bear; they are made for that."[57] The Anabaptist Reformer Menno Simons shared Luther's opinions and argued that married women should remain as cloistered as nuns within their houses.[58]

Even though the Reformers raised the status of women's work, giving it religious value, they also eliminated religious orders, the only way available for women to give themselves fully to the work of God and acquire a religious education. The elimination of monastic orders also removed a safe haven for eunuchs — a cultural and religious space where eunuchs could serve God apart from familial responsibilities.

By eliminating the monasteries and arguing for the normativity of marriage, the Reformers effectively kept all women at home under the rule of

54. Myatt, "On the Compatibility," 26.

55. Martin Luther, *The Table Talk,* trans. and ed. T. G. Tappert, in *Luther's Works,* vol. 54 (Philadelphia: Fortress, 1967), 8.

56. Will Durant, *The Reformation: A History of European Civilization from Wycliffe to Calvin, 1300-1564* (New York: Simon and Schuster, 1957), 416.

57. Jacques Maritain, *Three Reformers: Luther — Descartes — Rousseau* (London: Sheed and Ward, 1950), 184, citing *Luthers Werke,* X-2, 301.

58. "Remain within your houses and gates unless you have something of importance to regulate, such as to make purchases, to provide in temporal needs, to hear the Word of the Lord, or to receive the holy sacraments, etc. Attend faithfully to your charge, to your children, house, and family." Joyce L. Irwin, *Womanhood in Radical Protestantism: 1525-1675* (Lewiston, N.Y.: Edwin Mellen Press, 1987), 55, 63, citing Menno Simons, *The True Christian Faith* (ca. 1541), from *The Complete Writings of Menno Simons (c. 1496-1561),* trans. Leonard Verduin, ed. John Christian Wenger (Scottdale, Pa.: Herald, 1956), 376-83.

husbands with a strict division of labor, and eroded the safe spaces created by and for eunuchs during the Middle Ages. This theological and political move laid the groundwork for the hardening of sex differentiation, the elimination of a third sex, and the doctrine of separate spheres that would come to full flower in the Victorian era, but not before it passed through the philosophical revolution of the Enlightenment.

Descartes, the Seventeenth Century, and the Beginning of Modern Philosophy The Reformers had broken open the possibility of questioning the authority of the past, opening the door for the methodological questioning that would reach its iconic form in the philosophical work of René Descartes (1596-1650). Descartes inherited the Platonic and Aristotelian emphasis of the priority of the rational soul or mind; but, despite his indebtedness to the philosophers of the past, he was frustrated that the more he learned, the less certain he felt about his knowledge. His quest for certitude led him to question everything in order to discover, beneath it all, his certainty that he himself was doubting and, therefore, that he must exist. From this foundation, "I think, therefore I am," he began to reconstruct knowledge — not on the basis of received tradition but on the basis of his own thoughts and his own individual experiences of the world. Thus began the project of the modern Enlightenment, elevating individual human reason above all else.[59] Gunton observes that the classical identification of the person with the reasonable soul finds its logical conclusion in Descartes and the Enlightenment enthronement of human reason.[60]

Nevertheless, Descartes was not without his opponents, particularly those found in the empiricist and Romantic traditions, who insisted on the significance of the body, of sense experience, and of the passions. Though Descartes was willing to admit that the mind was not immune from influences from the body, he continued the Platonic, Aristotelian, and Augustinian emphasis on the mind as the rational ruler of the body and its passions.[61] The mind, for Descartes, was godlike, in its total freedom from external constraints.[62] As had the Platonic dualism of old, Descartes's dualism could be interpreted positively and negatively for those who were not male. One can either argue that women, eunuchs, and "effeminate" men have lesser minds

59. Melchert, *The Great Conversation*, 292.
60. Gunton, "Trinity, Ontology and Anthropology," 48.
61. Shults, *Reforming Theological Anthropology*, 174.
62. Melchert, *The Great Conversation*, 333.

and therefore are less godlike, or one can argue that the mind is sexless and the basis for women's equality.[63] Romantic philosopher Jean-Jacques Rousseau would follow the first argument while the pragmatists, the forerunners of liberalism, John Stuart Mill and Mary Wollstonecraft would follow the second.

Romanticism and Revolutionary Liberalism — Eighteenth Century to Nineteenth Century Calvin's language of woman being created from and for the man (rather than by and for God) found its logical conclusion in the writings of Jean-Jacques Rousseau, the Romantic philosopher, who wrote of the education of women in his treatise *Émile* in 1762. Where Calvin argued that women were created to be subject to men and legally bound by divine law to remain such, Rousseau advocated education as the means to preserve this "natural" arrangement.

> Woman and man were made for each other, but their mutual dependence is not the same. The men depend on the women only on account of their desires; the women on the men both on account of their desires and their necessities. . . .
>
> For this reason the education of women should be always relative to the men. To please, to be useful to us, to make us love and esteem them, to educate us when young, and take care of us when grown up, to advise, to console us, to render our lives easy and agreeable — these are the duties of women at all times, and what they should be taught in their infancy.[64]

How is such a disposition to be taught? Rousseau explains:

> Girls . . . should also be early subjected to restraint. This misfortune, if it really is one, is inseparable from their sex; nor do they ever throw it off but to suffer more cruel evils . . . that they may more readily submit to the will of others. . . .
>
> . . . [F]ormed to obey a being so imperfect as man, often full of vices, and always full of faults, she ought to learn betimes even to suffer injustice,

63. Laqueur argues that the new Cartesian science held that the mind is the seat of the soul and that the mind is immaterial, therefore the mind is not sexed. Thus, women's minds could theoretically be equal to men's. This debate would rage over the next few centuries, and continues even today. Laqueur, *Making Sex,* 155-56.

64. Rousseau, *Émile,* as quoted in Mary Wollstonecraft, *A Vindication of the Rights of Women* (1792), quoted in Melchert, *The Great Conversation,* 480-81.

> and to bear the insults of a husband without complaint; it is not for his sake but for her own that she should be of a mild disposition. . . .
>
> Woman has everything against her, as well as our faults as her own timidity and weakness; she has nothing in her favour, but her subtility [*sic*] and her beauty. Is it not very reasonable, therefore, she should cultivate both? . . .
>
> A man speaks of what he knows, a woman of what pleases her; the one requires knowledge, the other taste; the principal object of a man's discourse should be what is useful, that of a woman's what is agreeable. There ought to be nothing in common between their different conversation but truth.[65]

These citations of Rousseau come from Mary Wollstonecraft's 1792 publication, *A Vindication of the Rights of Women,* in which she argues that women and men are both disadvantaged by the suppression of the humanity of women. While Wollstonecraft cites Rousseau in order to show the disastrous consequences of his project, they agree on at least one point — that women cannot be faulted overmuch for excessive attention to their looks and cultivating cunning, since they have nothing else that brings them any power in the world. Rather than seeing Rousseau's educational program as the answer, Wollstonecraft identifies it as the problem. "I have not attempted to extenuate their faults; but to prove that they are the natural consequence of their education and station in society. If so, it is reasonable to suppose that they will change their character, and correct their vices and follies, when they are allowed to be free in a physical, moral, and civil sense."[66]

John Stuart Mill, writing some seventy years after Wollstonecraft, made similar arguments in his own treatise, *The Subjection of Women* (1869).

> All women are brought up from the very earliest years in the belief that their ideal character is the very opposite to that of men; not self-will, and government by self-control, but submission, and yielding to the control of others. All the moralities tell them that it is the duty of women, and all the current sentimentalities that it is their nature, to live for others; to make complete abnegation of themselves, and to have no life but in their affections. And by their affections are meant only the ones they are

65. Rousseau, *Émile,* as quoted in Wollstonecraft, *Vindication,* as quoted in Melchert, *The Great Conversation,* 480-81.

66. Wollstonecraft, *Vindication,* quoted in Melchert, *The Great Conversation,* 484.

> allowed to have — those to the men with whom they are connected, or to the children who constitute an additional and indefeasible tie between them and a man.[67]

According to Mill, it is this "tie between them and a man" that is the cause of women's "subjection." Women's subjection "never was the result of deliberation, or forethought, or any social ideal, or any notion whatever of what conduced to the benefit or humanity or the good order of society. It arose simply from the fact that from the very earliest twilight of human society, every woman (owing to the value attached to her by men, combined with her inferiority in muscular strength) was found in a state of bondage to some man."[68]

Mill argues that it is impossible to know whether women have rational capacities equal to that of men, given their perpetual subjection. Thus, he recommends with Wollstonecraft that they be given equal educational opportunities in order to discover what capabilities and differences may truly exist.[69] Their optimism rested on the belief that bodily differences, particularly differences related to size and strength, were not indicative of differences of soul/mind. Their revolutionary political ideas would soon converge with radical changes to the structures of work and family in the Industrial Revolution, bringing about a drastic shift in the construction of gender.

The Industrial Revolution — Eighteenth Century to Nineteenth Century Despite Luther's belief that women were suited to housework due to their large "fundaments" and men to moving around on account of their smaller backsides, in the daily realities of his own age most men and women shared the tasks of providing for the needs of the family and the care of children. Men and women worked in the fields and the shops, and children worked alongside them. Except for the minority in the upper class, both worked, both looked after the children, and both were at home. All this changed during the Industrial Revolution when jobs moved away from homes and into factories. No longer were men able to share in the training of their children and participate in all family meals. Factories kept them away from their families for long eight-to-twelve-hour days.

67. John Stuart Mill, *The Subjection of Women* (1869), quoted in Melchert, *The Great Conversation,* 482.

68. Mill, *The Subjection of Women,* quoted in Melchert, *The Great Conversation,* 479.

69. Melchert, *The Great Conversation,* 484.

In this period economics and politics had great influence on theological constructions of sex and gender. Only after the Industrial Revolution did Christians begin to redefine their concepts of the differences of the sexes. Once men were removed from the home, the home was left devoid of their governance, their moral influence, their modeling of perfect humanity. They were not there to supervise women and children (and servants). Women needed to do the supervising. But according to the classical Greek model and medieval and Reformation theology, women were not capable of ruling. Their minds, bodies, and moral sensitivities were weak. Women were irrational and unspiritual. How could they be left alone to raise children, instructing them in such important matters as right doctrine? How would women be able to rule the servants and manage the house without their husbands? The Victorian/Romantic reconfiguration of gender would provide the answers.

Victorian/Romantic Gender Revolution — Nineteenth Century The Industrial Revolution brought about the Romantic/Victorian reconstruction of gender ideology. It is during this period that we find the association of morality and spirituality with the home, the private life, the feminine. Rather than associating mothers with matter (that which is opposed to the soul/the spiritual/the divine), Victorians held up women as "angels in the home" who maintained a private sphere of virtue, a "haven" apart from the hostile, secular world of men.[70]

This is a far cry from women being less spiritual and more bodily. But the new economy demanded a change, and Christian thinkers obliged. Rather than identifying virtue only with the *vir* (the male), Victorian thinkers divided up the virtues among the sexes. Men were given certain virtues: courage, fortitude, shrewdness. Women were given others: piety, peacemaking, gentleness.

In some ways this was an improvement for women. At least now women were seen as having virtue as *women*. They no longer needed to become men to be considered virtuous or holy. Still, this was nothing like equality, and in some ways it excluded women from certain areas of influence that they had previously. Women's particular virtues were interpreted as making them suitable *only* for the private sphere, caring for children and working in the church (though not in any sort of leadership capacity). This historical change has also been labeled the "feminization of the church" — because if spiritu-

70. Christopher Lasch, "The Family as a Haven in a Heartless World," *Salmagundi*, no. 35 (Fall 1976): 42. See also Margaret A. Farley, *Just Love: A Framework for Christian Sexual Ethics* (New York: Continuum, 2006), 251, 259.

ality is a female quality, then men's masculinity is threatened when men are religious. This was one of the results of the Victorian gender revolution.[71]

On the other hand, this division of the sexes also opened the door to another interpretation. Women gained courage in their new status as "moral standard-bearers" and argued that if they really were responsible to uphold Christian virtue, then men needed them, not just in the home but also in the public sphere to make the wider world more Christian. Thus, the feminist movement of the nineteenth century, headed by evangelical women, drew upon this new ideology of gender. Here we find women becoming involved in suffrage and the abolition of slavery on the basis of their unique "feminine virtues."

Another result of the Victorian revolution (noted in chap. 1) was the virtual elimination of a third gender option. Public debates over the natures of the sexes — the assumptions that women and men have their own particular virtues associated with their separate spheres — added political pressure to clearly categorize anyone who blurred these important distinctions. Natural eunuchs and hermaphrodites had to be classified as either male or female; thus doctors coined a new term, "pseudohermaphrodite," to acknowledge bodily difference while maintaining social order (even if "order" required people who appeared female [e.g., persons with complete androgen insensitivity syndrome] to forgo all "homosexual" alliances with men).[72]

Rather than being seen as defective, misbegotten humans, valuable only for their contribution in generation (Aquinas), women begin to be seen as having human qualities and virtues that contribute to family (and society) in particular, unique ways, resulting in a complementary, binary anthropology, what Ruether has called "romantic dualism."[73]

71. James B. Nelson, "Male Sexuality and the Fragile Planet: A Theological Reflection," in *Redeeming Men: Religion and Masculinities,* ed. Stephen B. Boyd, W. Merle Longwood, and Mark W. Muesse (Louisville: Westminster John Knox, 1996), 273.

72. Alice Domurat Dreger, "A History of Intersex: From the Age of Gonads to the Age of Consent," in *Intersex in the Age of Ethics,* ed. Alice Domurat Dreger (Hagerstown, Md.: University Publishing Group, 1999), 9.

73. Ruether explains that there were two competing visions of humanity in this period, Romantic dualism and androgyny. The problem she identifies with androgyny — a focus on a human essence that is neither male nor female — is that it too often slipped into androcentrism — the male as the standard to which women are compared. Ruether, "Christian Anthropology and Gender," 249-50.

Ontological and Theological Shifts

As noted in our study of classical anthropology — that is, that there was a connection between ontology (human nature identified with the soul) and gender ideology — one can also see a connection between the gender revolution of the nineteenth century and ontological and theological assumptions. Romantic philosophers of the nineteenth century began to take the body more seriously and continued to challenge "the Enlightenment delight in the power of human reason to control nature and everything bodily."[74] LeRon Shults finds this shift occurring in theological reflections. "We can see the impact of this new emphasis in Schleiermacher's desire to derive his dogmatic reflections from the pious self-consciousness, which is a modification not of knowing or doing, but of 'feeling.' . . . By the end of the nineteenth century, we find the empirically oriented William James making the viscera primary, reversing the traditional view so that now the bodily manifestations of emotions drive the mind's noetic and volitional activities, rather than vice versa."[75] Whereas in the classical period reason (associated with the soul and the male) had been seen as superior to emotion (associated with the body and the female), in the Victorian period, emotions were recovered as valid media for theological engagement.

Schleiermacher retains the idea that men display a certain type of calculating rationality, but rather than presenting women as less rational or as irrational, he grants them an alternative type of rationality. In his lectures on biblical interpretation, Schleiermacher speaks of different types of knowledge in gendered categories, both of which are needed for proper interpretation of biblical texts:

> From the moment it begins, technical interpretation involves two methods: a divinatory and a comparative. Since each method refers back to the other, the two should never be separated. By leading the interpreter to transform himself, so to speak, into the author, the divinatory method seeks to gain an immediate comprehension of the author as an individual.

74. Shults, *Reforming Theological Anthropology,* 174.

75. Shults, *Reforming Theological Anthropology,* 174. He continues, "Twentieth-century behaviorism, with its reduction of all human acting (including knowing) to bodily mechanisms, was dialectically defined by its negation of the 'soul' side of Cartesian dualism. The problems with dualism have been the subject of extensive analysis and debate, but most contemporary philosophical and scientific discussions have moved beyond the focus on substances and abstract faculties to explore more holistic and dynamic models of human nature."

> The comparative method proceeds by subsuming the author under a general type. It then tries to find his distinctive traits by comparing him with the others of the same general type. Divinatory knowledge is the feminine strength in knowing people; comparative knowledge, the masculine.[76]

The binary gender model reproduced offspring for theological hermeneutics.

From One Sex to Two

Gendered politics and the practicalities of separate spheres required by the Industrial Revolution contributed to the creation of two opposite sexes. Thomas Laqueur summarizes the shift and illustrates how this new ontology transformed scientific inquiry into the body itself.

> Sometime in the eighteenth century, sex as we know it was invented. The reproductive organs went from being paradigmatic sites for displaying hierarchy, resonant throughout the cosmos, to being the foundation of incommensurable difference. . . . Here was not only an explicit repudiation of the old isomorphisms but also, and more important, a rejection of the idea that nuanced differences between organs, fluids, and physiological processes mirrored a transcendental order of perfection. Aristotle and Galen were simply mistaken in holding that female organs are a lesser form of the male's and by implication that woman is a lesser man. A woman is a woman, proclaimed the "moral anthropologist" Moreau in one of the many new efforts to derive culture from the body, everywhere and in all things, moral and physical, not just in one set of organs.[77]

Laqueur gives two reasons for the shift from one sex to two: one epistemological and the other political. He identifies two parts of the epistemological shift. The first is the Enlightenment banishment of "superstitions": "lactating monks, women who never ate and exuded sweet fragrance, sex changes at the whim of the imagination, bodies in paradise without sexual difference, monstrous births [under which label hermaphrodites were categorized],

76. Friedrich D. E. Schleiermacher, *Compendium of 1819,* with marginal notes from 1828, in *The Hermeneutics Reader,* ed. Kurt Mueller-Vollmer (New York: Continuum, 1985), 96.

77. Laqueur, *Making Sex,* 149. Page numbers inserted in the following text refer to Laqueur's work.

women who bore rabbits, and so on, were the stuff of fanaticism and superstition even if they were not so far beyond the bounds of reason as to be unimaginable" (151). The second part of the epistemological shift was the priority of the physical over the cosmological (151). "There were no books written before the late seventeenth century . . . that argued so explicitly for the biological foundations of the moral order. There were hundreds if not thousands of such works . . . in the centuries that followed" (153).

Language changed from the cosmological and theological to the biological. "Indeed the term 'generation' itself, which suggested the quotidian repetition of God's act of creation with all its attendant heat and light, gave way to the term 'reproduction,' which had less miraculous, more mechanistic connotations even if it did not quite capture the virtuosity of nature" (155). The shift from one sex to two in the modern period did enable physicians to see (possibly for the first time) women's organs *as* women's organs. Nevertheless, Laqueur cautions readers from taking these discoveries as "objective science." "Distinct sexual anatomy was adduced to support or deny all manner of claims in a variety of specific social, economic, political, cultural, or erotic contexts. . . . But no one account of sexual difference triumphed" (152). Differences between the sexes, emphasized so powerfully in the modern period, were "largely unconstrained by what was actually known about this or that bit of anatomy, 'this or that physiological process.'" Rather, they arose "from the rhetorical exigencies of the moment" (243).[78] Emphasizing the dubious nature of the shift from one sex to two, Laqueur is careful to emphasize the significance of the shift. "While the one flesh did not die — it lives today in many guises — two fleshes, two new distinct opposite sexes, would increasingly be read into the body. No longer would those who think about such matters regard woman as a lesser version of man along a vertical axis of infinite gradations, but rather as an altogether different creature along a horizontal axis whose middle ground was largely empty" (148).

The middle ground had been emptied of the ambiguous cases that once occupied it: hermaphrodites, natural eunuchs, castrated eunuchs, effeminate men, and virile women. Thus, the modern period bequeathed a legacy of two opposite and incommensurable sexes, unified by the belief in the possession of a sexless soul in the Christian tradition or a sexless mind in the tradition of Enlightenment liberalism. Substance dualism remained the unifying factor

78. "Despite the new epistemological status of nature as the bedrock of distinctions, and despite the accumulation of facts about sex, sexual difference in the centuries after the scientific revolution was no more stable than it had been before." Laqueur, *Making Sex,* 153.

undergirding a belief in the common humanity of the sexes regardless of difference, but this common denominator would come into question in the postmodern period (155-56).

Rather than understanding the image of God as the male, corporate head of a family, the modern period shifted attention to individuals, male and female, yet secured in a common humanity by the sexless soul, made in the image of a sexless God.[79] All these beliefs were to come under attack in the postmodern period when the power politics of the naming of sex, which Laqueur has illustrated, began to come to light.

Postmodern Shifts: From Substance and Sex Dualism to Relational Ontology and the Multiplication of the Sexes

The Enlightenment quest has floundered on the shoals of postmodernity. The modern pursuit of unified, universal, objective knowledge — knowledge that renders power over all that is "physical" and all that is "other" — has been abandoned. Descartes's mind was godlike, unconstrained by the body, much less by cultural, social, and historical factors. The postmodern mind is only too aware of the limits of human finitude, the situatedness of all knowing, and the impossibility of objectivity. We are not gods, and we know it.

Ironically, despite the failure of his project, Descartes's methodological skepticism finds its logical conclusion in postmodern deconstructive theory. Even the language we use to try to formulate ideas has become subject to critique. Language is now believed not only to describe the world but also to create worlds, enabling us to see some things and not others, to think some things and not others. The history of the sexes, especially the history of intersex, illustrates this very point.

In the ancient world, when there was language for eunuchs, hermaphrodites, and androgynes, people were able to see them, laws governed them, and places in society were carved out where they could live and contribute to the life of the community. Such is no longer the case. As we saw in chapter 1,

79. "Patriarchal anthropology was based on the assumption that the (free, ruling class) male was not just an individual, but a corporate person who exercises 'headship' over a 'body' of persons: women, children, servants. Women were credited with legal autonomy only through dissolving this concept of the family as the base of rights for an individualism in which each adult is autonomous. Liberal individualism abstracts men and women from their social context as isolated atoms, each motivated by self-interest." Ruether, "Christian Anthropology and Gender," 252.

during the Victorian era, at the very time physicians were documenting larger numbers of intersexed bodies, by redefining their terms, creating the new language of "pseudohermaphroditism," they were able to remake the world, virtually eliminating hermaphroditism (at least from public record) through a few strokes of the pen.

But postmodern thinkers are not only deconstructive. By recognizing the power of language to create worlds, many postmodern thinkers, both Christian and non-Christian, are using it to re-create a world that is more attentive to difference than what was allowed in the modern period. James Olthuis, a postmodern Christian theologian, explains.

> In its heart, postmodernism is a spiritual movement that resists the totalizing power of reason. It is that resistance, and the concomitant celebration of difference and diversity, that marks a wide array of disparate discourses as postmodern. Ethically, postmodern discourses share an alertness to plurality and a vigilance on behalf of the other. Modernist rational ethics, in its Enlightenment dream of a world increasingly controlled by a pure rationality, has shown itself not only blind and indifferent to those who are other and different, those who fall outside the dominant discourse, but violent and oppressive to them.[80]

Olthuis maintains that while modern thinkers attempted to take "others" seriously, even the "other" sex (i.e., women), they failed to do so because their attempts were wholly self-serving. Their versions of "others" were little more than reflections of their own desires and projections of their fears — threats to the self that had to be overcome.[81] In such a world,

> One either dominates or is dominated — as Freud, Hegel, and Sartre in particular emphasize. . . . Thus, Paul Tillich defines power as "the possibility a being has to actualize itself against the resistance of other beings." To be a self is to have enemies. Implicitly, if not explicitly, one is always at

80. James H. Olthuis, "Face-to-Face: Ethical Asymmetry or the Symmetry of Mutuality?" (1996), in *The Hermeneutics of Charity: Interpretation, Selfhood, and Postmodern Faith; Studies in Honor of James H. Olthuis,* ed. James K. A. Smith and Henry Isaac Venema (Grand Rapids: Brazos, 2004), 135.

81. "[R]eason [is] the instrument by which an ego or society of egos overpowers and totalizes, appropriates and disempowers anything that is 'other' or different." James H. Olthuis, "Crossing the Threshold: Sojourning Together in the Wild Spaces of Love" (1993), in *The Hermeneutics of Charity,* 26.

war. This apotheosis of the self is seen to crest in the idealism of Hegel in which everything becomes itself in and through its own other. In the end, since the "other" has a utilitarian function in relation to the self, relationship to the other is, finally, self-relationship. When an "other" resists this role, failing to mirror the self, when it resists being used and consumed, it must be invaded and dominated.[82]

In the postmodern period, many "others" are finding voices to resist such domination. Women are pushing back against the dominating language of the "other" sex, being compared always and everywhere to a standard that is male and required to do all the tasks men consider objectionable. They are continuing the work begun in the late modern period of resisting the language of "other" by calling for the "rights of men" to be extended to them — the right to vote; to own property; to make legal and financial decisions without the authority of a husband, father, or male guardian; and equal pay for equal work.[83] As Dorothy Sayers argued almost seventy years ago, women are not asking to be other, nor opposite, but simply to be recognized as human.[84]

In the postmodern period, men too are finding voices to resist the hegemonic accounts of masculinity that have oppressed not only women, eunuchs, hermaphrodites, and intersex, but any man failing to measure up to the standard of "masculine perfection." Thus in the postmodern period we find linguistic shifts from masculinity, or hegemonic masculinity, to masculinities in the plural.[85]

82. Olthuis "Crossing the Threshold," 23.

83. Ruether, *"Imago Dei,"* 279.

84. "[A] woman is just as much an ordinary human being as a man, with the same individual preferences, and with just as much right to the tastes and preferences of an individual. What is repugnant to every human being is to be reckoned always as a member of class and not as an individual person." Dorothy L. Sayers, *Are Women Human?* (1938; reprint, Grand Rapids: Eerdmans, 1971), 19. "They are 'the opposite sex' — (though why 'opposite' I do not know; what is the 'neighbouring sex'?). But the fundamental thing is that women are more like men than anything else in the world. They are human beings." Sayers, "The Human-Not-Quite-Human," in *Are Women Human?* 37.

85. "Hegemonic masculinity" is "a technical term designating the dominant construction of masculinity in our culture. Specifically, hegemonic masculinity denotes the ideals considered appropriate for Euro-American, educated, middle- and upper-class, heterosexual, culturally Christian males — that group of men who have held the lion's share of public power in this country. Hegemonic masculinity is implicitly contrasted with non-hegemonic masculinities — the construction of appropriate male behavior for those outside this group, including poor and lower-class men, Native American, African American, Asian American, Hispanic, and Jewish men; and gay men. . . . [T]he hegemonic masculine ideals have a

It is in this context that the intersexed are also finding voices to resist the domination of language that has erased their existence from public society. They are crying out with similar language, not to be known as another "other" but to be recognized as human. As one woman with androgen insensitivity syndrome put it, "The world has tried to make us feel like freaks. We have felt like freaks. I felt like a freak most of my life, but look at me. I'm just a human being just like everybody else. . . . I really have a place in the world. I really am a human being, a very valid human being."[86]

But what is a human being? How does one define human being in the postmodern age? Is a definition of human being even possible today? Postmodern deconstructionist Jacques Derrida insisted that it is not.[87] In the early eighteenth century, when Americans confronted intersex babies, the question of their humanity was decided on the assertion that "'tho [*sic*] their outward Shape may be deformed and monstrous; [they] have notwithstanding a reasonable Soul, and consequently their Bodies are capable of a Resurrection.'"[88] The "reasonable soul," the divine substance passed down from Plato to Augustine to Descartes, was the security of human personhood, but this very substance has come under considerable attack in the postmodern present.

Ontological Shifts

Rejection of Substance Dualism The shift from cosmology to biology, which began in the late modern period, reaches its logical conclusion in

---

significant effect on males both inside and outside the hegemonic group." The distinction of masculinities is "an extension of the effort to study men as a specific gendered group. Just as it is important to recognize that men's experience is not identical with human experience, so it is also important to appreciate that the experiences of all men are not the same. At different times, in different places and cultures, in different social and economic classes within the same culture, men have experienced their lives differently and have lived under different norms of appropriate behavior." Stephen B. Boyd, W. Merle Longwood, and Mark W. Muesse, "Men, Masculinity, and the Study of Religion," in *Redeeming Men*, xv.

86. Sharon E. Preves, "For the Sake of the Children: Destigmatizing Intersexuality," in *Intersex in the Age of Ethics*, 62, 61.

87. Kevin Vanhoozer, "Human Being, Individual and Social," in *Cambridge Companion to Christian Doctrine*, ed. Colin Gunton (Cambridge: Cambridge University Press, 1997), 170.

88. Elizabeth Reis, *Bodies in Doubt: An American History of Intersex* (Baltimore: Johns Hopkins University Press, 2009), 7-8. Reis is quoting *Aristotle's Masterpiece*, a popular seventeenth-century medical manual.

the postmodern abandonment of substance dualism. Advances in scientific understandings of the brain and its functions, along with philosophical challenges to the subject-object dualism of the modern project, have led to a thoroughgoing reconfiguration of what it means to be human. Some Christian scholars are arguing that these scientific and philosophical shifts amount to nothing less than a Copernican revolution in theological anthropology.[89]

Theologian LeRon Shults explains how even some conservative theologians have been willing to move away from the idea that humans are made of both body and soul. "The activities once ascribed to the 'soul' and its 'faculties' are now accounted for by consciousness as an emergence of patterns of neuronal functioning in the human brain, which in turn are connected to chemical interactions throughout the body. These give rise to 'feeling,' which cannot be separated from 'thinking.' Conversely, how we think affects how we feel and act."[90] Nancey Murphy, a theologian and philosopher of science at Fuller Theological Seminary, has shown how the faculties of the soul enumerated by Thomas Aquinas have brain responses that can be located for each. "Even in the most intense religious experience of contemplatives, imaging techniques have shown that during deep meditation very particular patterns of neural functioning are operative."[91]

Rather than seeing these discoveries as proofs of the impossibility of the supernatural or of communion with God, a number of biblical scholars and theologians are arguing that a rejection of substance dualism is not a rejection of Christianity but of Platonic metaphysics — non-Christian philosophical notions they believe have distorted past interpretations of the Scriptures. They insist that the Bible does not present the soul as a metaphysical substance opposed to the body. Rather, like Aristotle, they show how the term "soul" in its Hebrew and Greek variations is used to speak of the life of the person in holistic fashion — a task Joel B. Green takes on at length in *Body, Soul, and Human Life: The Nature of Humanity in the Bible.*[92] The

89. Joel B. Green, "Body and Soul? Questions at the Interface of Science and Christian Faith," in *What about the Soul? Neuroscience and Christian Anthropology,* ed. Joel B. Green (Nashville: Abingdon, 2004), 6.

90. Shults, *Reforming Theological Anthropology,* 179.

91. Shults, *Reforming Theological Anthropology,* 180. Nancey Murphy, "Darwin, Social Theory and the Sociology of Scientific Knowledge," *Zygon* 34, no. 4 (1999): 596. See also the constructive proposals of James B. Ashbrook and Carol Rausch Albright, *The Humanizing Brain* (Cleveland: Pilgrim Press, 1997).

92. Joel B. Green, *Body, Soul, and Human Life: The Nature of Humanity in the Bible* (Grand Rapids: Baker, 2008). See also Green's essay "'Bodies — That Is, Human Lives':

new challenge for theologians is not the existence of the soul and its relation to the body, but the mind/brain, body/consciousness connection and the possibility of talking about human selves at all.[93]

How does one talk about the self after abandoning the concept of the soul? Augustine spoke of these as one and the same, when he wrote, "I, that is, my soul."[94] We remember Plato and Descartes and even Wollstonecraft and Sayers, who appealed to the shared faculty of reason (which Sayers called "that great and sole true Androgyne") as the basis for the cohumanity of the sexes.[95] But the reduction of the soul to the brain disallows such a conclusion. Scientists tell us that even the brain is sexed through pre- and postnatal hormones as well as through shifting brain structures that develop through restructuring that occurs on account of experiences of living in a sexed body and a gendered society.[96] While "brain sex" is the least understood of all the categories of the science of sex differentiation, it nevertheless complicates the possibility of speaking of a "sexless" human nature — something shared by male, female, and intersex alike.

How does one secure the humanity of anyone — male, female, or intersex — without the "reasonable soul" and without even the concept of a human self? Despite Derrida's objections, postmodern thinkers continue to proffer alternative proposals.

Bodies, Relations, and the Multiplication of the Sexes Building on the assumption that humans are mere bodies, most secular, postmodern thinkers fall into one of two philosophical camps as biological determinists or social constructionists. Neither is unproblematic.

Evangelical theologian Kevin Vanhoozer summarizes the consensus: "In the twentieth century, socio-biologists have suggested that every aspect of our social lives is but a sub-plot in a broader evolutionary drama scripted

---

A Re-examination of Human Nature in the Bible," in *Whatever Happened to the Soul? Scientific and Theological Portraits of Human Nature,* ed. Warren S. Brown, Nancey Murphy, and H. Newton Malony (Minneapolis: Fortress, 1998), 149-73. See also Green, *What about the Soul?*

93. Shults, *Reforming Theological Anthropology,* 181-83.

94. Shults, *Reforming Theological Anthropology,* 167, citing Augustine's *On the Doctrines of the Church* 1.27.

95. Sayers, "The Human-Not-Quite-Human," 44.

96. I. A. Hughes et al., "Consensus Statement on Management of Intersex Disorders," *Archives of Disease in Childhood* 2 (May 4, 2006): 2. See also Melissa Hines, *Brain Gender* (Oxford: Oxford University Press, 2004), and Fausto-Sterling, *Sexing the Body.*

by human DNA. The true story of the self is about human genes that seek to survive long enough to reproduce." Given this outlook, he asks, "Is it possible to save human freedom and dignity, to preserve the person, and if so, on what grounds?"[97]

Other postmodern theologians have suggested that with the fall of modern metanarratives, humans are able to recognize the socially constructed nature of societies. While some might conclude from the discovery of the power of culture that humans are nothing but cogs in the cultural machine, without the ability for self-determination, most do not abandon all ground for human self-determination. Rather, they argue that if culture is a human creation, it can be re-created, reconstructed, at least in modest degrees. Clifford Geertz concluded, "man is an animal suspended in webs of significance he himself has spun."[98] These webs consist of the cultural constructions into which we are born and in which we participate either by cooperation or resistance, as well as our personal narratives — the stories we write to make sense of ourselves, to create our selves in the world. According to theologian Elaine Storkey, this theme of self-creation, rather than self-mastery, is central to the postmodern spirit.

> Once we recognize that the self is in the process of being constructed, it is only a short step to the notion of self-creation. . . . There is no aspect of our identity therefore which we cannot create. . . . Our sexuality is also our creation, so to take one example, there is nothing "given" about heterosexuality. It too is a product of the power concepts of modernity. There is nothing fixed about monogamy, either, and plurality of couplings fits much more comfortably into a postmodernist culture.[99]

Given the conclusion that humans are nothing but bodies, highly diverse, with no grand narrative to tell us who or what we are, or how we are to act, it is perfectly understandable that some sociologists of gender are arguing for a deconstruction of the sex/gender system. Gilbert Herdt's call for a third sex, Fausto-Sterling's identification of five sexes, David Hester's recognition of hundreds of sexes, and Kessler and McKenna's insistence on the elimination of sex and gender categories remain perfectly reasonable

97. Vanhoozer, "Human Being," 169.

98. Quoted in Vanhoozer, "Human Being," 161.

99. Elaine Storkey, "Modernity and Anthropology," in *Faith and Modernity,* ed. Philip Sampson, Vinay Samuel, and Chris Sugden (Oxford: Regnum Books, 1994), 144-45.

suggestions in the postmodern context. If bodies are all that we are, if the cultures into which we are born can be reshaped and there is no objective vantage point for better and worse constructions, then the best we can hope for are less oppressive, more peaceful relations between bodies. But even here we have no absolute vantage point from which to argue for such ethical treatment of "others."

The ancient Greeks recognized only one sex, the male. Many have found this to be oppressive to women, so it is rejected. The binary sex model of the modern period was an improvement, but this also proved to be oppressive to women — who are always constructed as the "other" sex — as well as oppressive to intersexed persons who no longer had a place on the chart. Both systems are oppressive. Neither leads to peaceful relations between persons. Both can and must be rejected. The ontological shifts allow for the multiplication of the sexes or their abandonment. Either option is open for those who would choose this path.

Theological Turn to Relationality

Given their vocation, theologians are considerably more interested in questions of ontology than are nonreligious thinkers. They are not satisfied to speak of the human as wholly biologically determined, nor as a being with the power of self-creation, no matter how circumscribed that power. Nevertheless, many acknowledge the validity of the postmodern critique of the modern self and are working to rethink theological anthropology in its wake. LeRon Shults identifies the most significant shift as the "philosophical turn to relationality":[100]

> Today most philosophers no longer describe human nature with the categories of substance ontology, as in ancient philosophy, nor in terms of autonomous subjectivity, as in early modern philosophy. In both of these models, the "self" is dualistically separated from its "knowing." The human subject is defined prior to and over against the objects of knowledge. In late modernity, however, we find a new emphasis on the self as always and already immersed in the dynamic process of knowing and

100. Shults, *Reforming Theological Anthropology: After the Philosophical Turn to Relationality.*

> being known in community. The hard dichotomy between subject and object is rejected.[101]

Even though many postmodern thinkers have concluded from these reflections that there can be no self, a number of postmodern theologians refuse to join in the lament.

James Olthuis employs the language of psychology to explain that the postmodern "'death of the self' was not a real death but . . . the death of a 'false self' which is no real loss but the beginning of healing."[102] He insists that "There is still room for an agent self that is not absolute, with no claims to self-authorization and full presence," and he returns to Christian theology to begin theological anthropology again.[103]

Likewise, Shults is hopeful that the death of the modern self, tied to a non-Christian ontology, will open up the possibility of finding more accurate descriptions of the self, complete with a revisioning of ontological categories.

> To conclude from this, as some radical deconstructionists do, that no substantial "self" exists at all follows only if we completely divorce relation from substance. If being is essentially relational, however, we may still speak of the "self" as substantial and real — precisely because of the intensity of its self-relationality. As Calvin Schrag points out, the rejection of old anthropological models does not mean a jettisoning of every sense of self. One may argue instead for a "praxis-oriented self, defined by its communicative practices, oriented toward an understanding of itself in its discourse, its action, its being with others, and its experience of transcendence."[104]

Kevin Vanhoozer agrees that "personhood, not substance, comes first in the order of being. . . . [P]ersons are not autonomous individuals. . . . [P]ersons are what they are by virtue of their relations to others."[105] Nevertheless, even while he critiques the modernist version of individuality, Vanhoozer

101. Shults, *Reforming Theological Anthropology,* 181.

102. Olthuis, "Crossing the Threshold," 27.

103. Olthuis, "Crossing the Threshold," 27. Cf. James Olthuis, "Be(com)ing: Humankind as Gift and Call," *Philosophia Reformata* 58 (1993): 153-72.

104. Shults, *Reforming Theological Anthropology,* 181, quoting Calvin O. Schrag, *The Self after Postmodernity* (New Haven: Yale University Press, 1997), 9.

105. Vanhoozer, "Human Being," 174.

insists that personhood is not lost, "assimilated into some collectivity. . . . [R]ather a particular person . . . achieves a concrete identity in relation to others."[106] Similarly, Jürgen Moltmann attempts to navigate the shoals between individuality and collectivism, which both threaten human being.

> An individual, like an atom, is literally that ultimate element of indivisibility. An ultimate element of indivisibility, however, has no relationships, and also cannot communicate. . . . If an individual has no relationships, then he also has no characteristics and no name. He is unrecognizable, and does not even know himself. By contrast, a person is the individual human being in the resonance field of the relationships of I-you-we, I-myself, I-it. Within this network of relationships, the person becomes the subject of giving and taking, hearing and doing, experiencing and touching, perceiving and responding.[107]

Theological Reconstruction

Trinitarian Relationality and the Social *Imago* These postmodern theologians have moved a long way from Boethius's definition of the human person as an "individual substance of a rational nature," focused as it was on the individual apart from society and on reason in opposition to the body. Postmodern theologians want to affirm the body as a fundamental element in human personhood even as they avoid grounding rationality in substance metaphysics. On the other hand, many of these same theologians are eager to speak of relationality in ontological categories. It is this latter shift that has led to a renewed interest in the Trinitarian nature of God.

Plato's soul and Aristotle's mind, their centers of human identity, were both grounded in their conceptions of a monistic God. Thus, their anthropology reflected their attempts to escape the body (and its sex) and become united with the divine soul/mind. Christian thinkers who built upon their ontological speculations found themselves at odds with their own unique

106. Vanhoozer, "Human Being," 174-75.

107. Jürgen Moltmann, "Christianity and the Values of Modernity and the Western World" (lecture presented at Fuller Theological Seminary, April 1996), quoted by Warren Brown, "Reconciling Scientific and Biblical Portraits of Human Nature," in *Whatever Happened to the Soul?* 225.

Christian heritage — belief in the goodness of the body, creation, and resurrection — as well as their belief in a God who is three-in-one.

As we noted in the introduction to this project, the renewal of Trinitarian studies and their significance for theological anthropology is usually traced to Karl Barth (1886-1968), who pulled together the contributions of Martin Buber, Wilhelm Vischer, Dietrich Bonhoeffer, Emil Brunner, Charlotte von Kirschbaum, and Friedrich Schleiermacher to argue that the way in which humans image God is in their existence as relational beings.[108] Barth concluded, "the analogy between God and man, is simply the existence of the I and the Thou in confrontation. This is first constitutive for God, and then for man created by God. To remove it is tantamount to removing the divine from God as well as the human from man."[109] Relationality is constitutive of divinity and humanity in God's image.

Jesus stands as the consummate image of God in his relationality. According to Barth, "Jesus is a man for His fellows, and therefore the image of God, in a way which others cannot even approach, just as they cannot be for God in the sense that He is."[110] And yet, insomuch as there is a proper location of the image of God in humans, following after the pattern of Jesus, Barth locates this in the relationality of male and female. "Could anything be more obvious than to conclude from this clear indication that the image and likeness of being created by God signifies existence in confrontation, i.e., in this confrontation, in the juxtaposition and conjunction of man which is that of male and female . . . ?"[111] Barth concludes that humankind is fundamentally relational, made in the image of the relational God. This "relational" or "social view" of the *imago Dei* is changing theological anthropology.[112] Vanhoozer

108. Barth, *Church Dogmatics* (hereafter *CD*) III/2 (Edinburgh: T. & T. Clark, 1960), 195, cited in Stanely J. Grenz, *The Social God and the Relational Self: A Trinitarian Theology of the* Imago Dei (Louisville: Westminster John Knox, 2001), 271. Cf. Shults, *Reforming Theological Anthropology,* 124. Ruether summarizes the contributions of Buber, Bonhoeffer, and Brunner, in *"Imago Dei."* Von Kirschbaum's contributions are neglected by Ruether and Shults, but her influence upon Barth's reflections on this subject were essential to his work. See Suzanne Selinger, *Charlotte von Kirschbaum and Karl Barth: A Study in Biography and the History of Theology* (University Park: Pennsylvania State University Press, 1998). Janet Soskice suggests that Barth, Bonhoeffer, and Buber may have all been indebted to Schleiermacher for their emphasis on the I-Thou of reciprocity. Soskice, *The Kindness of God,* 50.

109. Barth, *CD* III/1 (Edinburgh: T. & T. Clark, 1958), ¶ 41.2, p. 185.

110. Barth, *CD* III/2, ¶ 45.2, p. 222.

111. Barth, *CD* III/1, ¶ 41.2, p. 195.

112. This view carries various names: social, relational, special community, etc. I have chosen "social" to more clearly reflect the connection between social Trinity and social *imago.*

summarizes Barth's contribution to theological anthropology. "Sexuality, and the male-female duality in particular, becomes an image for the difference-in-relatedness that characterizes human, and divine, being in general. It is therefore impossible to speak about humanity apart from 'cohumanity': the human person is both irreducibly individual and constitutionally interrelated."[113]

The Trinity and Sex, Gender, and Sexuality Barth was the first to connect the image of God, not to an extrabodily, sexless, divine substance, but to human being *as* sexually differentiated. For Barth sex/gender differentiation represents the "center of humanity" and is inherently connected to sexuality. And while sexuality is not sinful per se, it has been deeply affected by sin since the Fall. Thus, "that awful genius of sin is nowhere more plainly revealed than in the fact that it shames man at the center of his humanity, his masculinity and femininity, before God and man, and every attempt to escape this shame, every self-justification, or concretely every denial and suppression of sexuality can only confirm and increase the shame. . . . This is the climax of this text and therefore of the whole biblical history of creation."[114]

Barth's reconfiguration moves conversations about the *imago Dei* away from disembodied attributes (e.g., rationality), substance metaphysics (e.g., the soul), and functions (e.g., dominion) and toward the relationality found between the first man and the first woman. Upon first blush, his proposal is good news for women. Women were no longer excluded from full participation in the image of God, due to a supposed inferior rationality or unnatural dominion, and one could not begin to speak about the image of God without speaking about men and women in relation to one another and to God.

Even where Barth's proposal has been roundly critiqued, it is impossible to overestimate the significance of his reflections for subsequent theological work. Theologians now regularly assume a binary model of human sex differentiation based on the creation narratives found in Genesis (not the one-sex model of the classical period), and most read equality and mutuality into sex relations, rather than hierarchy (a trend many feminists find ironic).[115] As the remaining chapters will show, recent work in theological anthropology continues to ground theological concepts such as the *imago Dei*, human personhood, and human relationality on the creation of humans as male

113. Vanhoozer, "Human Being," 172.

114. Barth, *CD* III/2, ¶45.3, p. 292.

115. See comments of Kari Elisabeth Børresen and Rosemary Radford Ruether in *The Image of God: Gender Models in Judaeo-Christian Tradition*, 3-4, 269-70, 284, 288.

and female in sexual relation with analogies to Trinitarian relationality and difference-in-relation.[116]

Postmodern Theological Anthropologies and Intersex

Even while many postmodern theologians have welcomed the turn from substance ontology to relational ontology, most Christian thinkers continue to uphold the binary sex model of the modern period, emphasizing the significance of sex differentiation (as male and female) and heterosexual relationality for *imago Dei,* human personhood, and human relationality. Their constructions continue to neglect the presence of intersexed persons within the human community and problematize not only the humanity of intersex persons but also their legitimacy as images of God.

But this binary model remains subject to the postmodern critique of the way "otherness" has been defined and employed. Even Olthuis, who defends postmodernism as a "spiritual movement . . . [alert] to plurality and vigilan[t] on behalf of the other,"[117] continues to employ the binary sex model in his revision of theological anthropology.[118] A few postmodern theologians are extending this vigilance on behalf of those who diverge from heterosexual practice,[119] but almost no one pays any attention to the theological presence of intersex.[120]

Conservative theologians are first among those who have failed to take seriously the significance of intersex for theological anthropology. Ignorance of intersex may account for some of this neglect, but not for all of it. A number of conservative theologians have worked to hide, downplay,

116. Stanley Grenz sums up the current state of Trinitarian studies, heralding the "triumph of relationality." He explains, "Although contemporary theologians vary enormously in the degree to which they are willing to renounce their allegiance to a metaphysics of substance, they seem to agree that more stress should be placed on the claim that God is *relational.*" Stanley J. Grenz, *Rediscovering the Triune God: The Trinity in Contemporary Theology* (Minneapolis: Fortress, 2004), 117.

117. Olthuis, "Face-to-Face," 135.

118. Olthuis, "Be(com)ing," 161-64.

119. Elisabeth Stuart, ed., *Religion Is a Queer Thing: A Guide to the Christian Faith for Lesbian, Gay, Bisexual, and Transgendered People* (London and Washington, D.C.: Cassell, 1997).

120. Susannah Cornwall is a noteworthy exception. See her "The Kenosis of Unambiguous Sex in the Body of Christ: Intersex, Theology, and Existing 'for the Other,'" *Theology and Sexuality* 14, no. 2 (January 2008): 182.

or dismiss intersex while others advocate medical "correction" in order to bolster their understandings of sex and gender complementarity for heterosexual monogamy. In the American context, some of the strongest resistance is coming from Roman Catholics and evangelicals (as well as conservative Anglicans of the Anglo-Catholic or evangelical variety). But after listening to the voices of the intersexed, it should now be clear that marginalization and compulsory medical "correction" are inadequate and unethical solutions. Conservative theologians must not only reconsider the binary sex model but also consider the theological edifices that have been built upon it. We must find better ways to value sex difference, to welcome the intersexed, and to craft a sexual ethic that continues to foster personal and communal wholeness and holiness through marriage and celibacy. These are the tasks of the chapters that follow.

PART II

Critique and Construction: Theological Anthropology in the Postmodern Period

In Part I we learned of the phenomenon of intersex, persons whose bodies do not fit neatly into the category of either male or female. These persons constitute a surprisingly high number despite lack of public recognition in contemporary society. We also learned that the ancients were not unfamiliar with intersex. Indeed, Jesus himself discussed those who are born eunuchs — an ancient term under which some intersex conditions would have been classified. Notwithstanding the checkered history of the treatment of eunuchs in the early Christian period, eunuchs and hermaphrodites were publicly recognized by early Christian societies — both East and West — and their bodily ambiguity prompted theological reflection on the significance of sex, gender, and sexuality for theological anthropology.

We then traced the history of the human self in the West from Plato's disembodied, sexless soul through the Enlightenment elevation of reason over sense perception on to the postmodern recovery of the body, its senses, and its sex. Along the way we also discovered parallel development in theological reflection on the image of God, from the centrality of the reasonable rule of the (masculine) soul over the (feminine) body — a presupposition that undermined the affirmation that women are also made according to the image of God — to the postmodern insistence that the image of God cannot be reflected apart from male and female in community, a social view of the *imago Dei.*

This postmodern theological account of the image of God reflects both a return to the body and the philosophical turn to relationality, and for many theologians, sexuality guides the reading of both. The return to the body is a return to the sexed body — male and female — and this turn has been construed in sexual terms by more than a handful of theologians. Chapters 5 and

6 will investigate these twin themes: image of God as sexed body and image of God as sexual community. Exploring the challenges and contributions that intersex and a more careful reading of Jesus' teaching on eunuchs bring to current theological anthropologies built upon the social *imago,* I argue in chapter 4 that the binary sex model needs to be expanded to include the intersexed while not being emptied of all notions of difference. In chapter 5, I contend that the social *imago* must remain social, resisting contemporary reinterpretation into sexual communion. Finally, in chapter 6, I follow the theological trajectories laid out in chapters 4 and 5 to ask how the eschatological goal of human identity — the identification and union of the ecclesial community with Christ — addresses the place of sex, gender, and sexuality for men, women, and intersex persons made in the image of God.

CHAPTER 4

Sex, Gender, and the Image of God: From Other to Others

Many theologians today hail the male-female difference as paradigmatic of the other. As we saw in chapter 3, Karl Barth and the theologians who have followed him in the social view of the *imago Dei* as "male-and-female-in-community" have taken up the postmodern turn to relationality and the postmodern turn to the body while holding on to a modern conception of sex/gender difference. Furthermore, this simplistic model has led a number of conservatives to overemphasize sex difference while at the same time ignoring, denying, or suppressing the existence of other others.

We must do better. Postmodern vigilance on behalf of others and the Christian command to love our neighbors as ourselves call us to more careful attention to persons as they are found in the real world rather than in the ideal world of philosophical and theological systems.[1] There is hope. By attending to "real" men, women, and intersexed persons, in all their particularities, diversity, and similarities, and by returning to the Scriptures with new eyes, we can find ways to move forward in our theological understand-

1. "In its heart, postmodernism is a spiritual movement that resists the totalizing power of reason. It is that resistance, and the concomitant celebration of difference and diversity, that marks a wide array of disparate discourses as postmodern. Ethically, postmodern discourses share an alertness to plurality and a vigilance on behalf of the other. Modernist rational ethics, in its Enlightenment dream of a world increasingly controlled by a pure rationality, has shown itself not only blind and indifferent to those who are other and different, those who fall outside the dominant discourse, but violent and oppressive to them." James H. Olthuis, "Face-to-Face: Ethical Asymmetry or the Symmetry of Mutuality?" (1996), in *The Hermeneutics of Charity: Interpretation, Selfhood, and Postmodern Faith; Studies in Honor of James H. Olthuis,* ed. James K. A. Smith and Henry Isaac Venema (Grand Rapids: Brazos, 2004), 135.

ing of sex and gender differences and their place in theological discussions of identity and *imago Dei.*

In the American context, some of the most vocal defenders of the binary ideal are conservative Roman Catholics and evangelicals (as well as conservative Anglicans — usually of the Anglo-Catholic or evangelical variety). Because of this, I will focus on the ways in which Roman Catholics and evangelicals construe sex difference. On the Roman Catholic side one must contend with the legacy of the late pope John Paul II (1920-2005), in what has come to be known as the *Theology of the Body* (a collection of homilies the late pontiff delivered from September 1979 to November 1984). It is impossible to identify a similarly representative voice for American evangelicalism. Given the diversity of evangelicalism, any such choice is suspect; nevertheless, I will risk putting forward Stanley J. Grenz (1950-2005), whose work on theological anthropology and human sexuality has been widely received within the evangelical academy.[2]

I will begin by presenting a brief overview of the ways in which the binary sex model has been construed in Roman Catholic and evangelical theology. After showing the strong consensus between these two traditions, I will examine how both are being extended in ways that continue to problematize intersex persons, as well as many nonintersexed persons, by overstating the significance of sex and gender difference. I will then suggest better ways to continue the good within these traditions in order to build more balanced, nuanced, and inclusive visions of the relations between sex, gender, and the image of God.

The Common Witness of Roman Catholic and Evangelical Theologies of the Body

There are striking similarities between Roman Catholic and evangelical theologies of the body. In part I of his *Theology of the Body,* Pope John Paul II argues that human bodies have a "nuptial meaning." In other words, sex

2. Evangelical theologian Richard Lints attests to the influence of Stanley Grenz on contemporary evangelical theological anthropology in Lints, "Introduction: Theological Anthropology in Context," in *Personal Identity in Theological Perspective,* ed. Richard Lints, Michael S. Horton, and Mark R. Talbot (Grand Rapids: Eerdmans, 2006), 7. Hollinger depends heavily on Grenz, employing Grenz's definitions of sexuality as foundational for his own work; Dennis P. Hollinger, *The Meaning of Sex: Christian Ethics and the Moral Life* (Grand Rapids: Baker Academic, 2009), 15-16.

difference points toward marriage and marriage is the foundation for sexual ethics.[3] Though he couches this in different language, Stanley Grenz identifies the same features of human sexuality in his texts *Sexual Ethics: An Evangelical Perspective* and *The Social God and the Relational Self.* Combining language from both traditions, I have labeled these meanings "personal," "sacramental," "unitive," and "procreative."[4]

Personal

According to John Paul II, the sexed body participates in the meaning of personhood. Sexual distinction is not a mere attribute of the body but fundamental, "constitutive" of the person.[5] Grenz agrees and calls sexual distinction "essential" to personhood. It is connected to but mysteriously deeper than chromosomes, hormones, genitalia, and social (affective gender) expression.[6] Both theologians assume a correspondence between biological sex and gender (what Grenz labels "affective sexuality") — a gendered sense of self, a gendered outlook on life, including emotional, psychological, and behavioral aspects of personhood.[7]

3. John Paul II, *Man and Woman He Created Them: A Theology of the Body,* trans. and ed. Michael Waldstein (Boston: Pauline Books and Media, 2006).

4. While in Roman Catholic literature the "unitive and procreative" elements often stand for the full meaning of sex, including its sacramental meaning under the unitive, I believe it is important to maintain the distinction between the two. Grenz utilizes this distinction when he argues against the acceptance of homosexual marriages. He contends that while homosexuals may be able to give themselves to one another in love and mutual submission — thus fulfilling one of the meanings of sex in marriage — their unions will never represent the "unity in difference" that the male/female union symbolizes as a prefiguring of the eschatological union between God and church. The nuance in Grenz's argument should not be missed, especially considering that it can be argued that homosexual unions can image (in a sacramental way) the Trinitarian union of persons just as well if not better than heterosexual unions — given the fact that God is beyond sex/gender distinctions (suggesting their irrelevance or limited value to the argument of union in difference), or is symbolically portrayed as a union of same sex/gender persons (Father and Son). For Grenz's position to function, the eschatological union between God and humanity must be maintained as the meaning of unity in difference and the basis for the argument. Of course, Rosemary Radford Ruether and other feminists have wisely warned of the dangers of a symbolic universe that identifies God with the male and humanity with the female. Their arguments on the limits of analogical language and the dangers of unnecessary applications of such symbolism must be heeded.

5. John Paul II, *Man and Woman,* 166-69; homily 10.

6. Stanley J. Grenz, *Sexual Ethics: An Evangelical Perspective* (Louisville: Westminster John Knox, 1990), 22-30.

7. Grenz, *Sexual Ethics,* 17. John Paul II is virtually silent on the distinction between

Sacramental

Both theologians view sexual union-in-difference as sacramental. Sexual union symbolizes and participates in the image of God as relational Trinity and the union of Christ/God and church/creation. According to the late pope, the image of God, although present in an individual human, is more fully revealed in the communion of persons, the union of the first man and the first woman.[8] Their union is specifically related to the "conjugal act."[9] Grenz believes that sexual distinction is the basis for "bonding" — that which leads us to union with others. The male/female union is the most basic form of the human community and the primitive form of the *imago Dei,* which is more fully revealed in Christ (the true image), the communion of the church, and the eschatological nuptial union between Christ and his church. Sexual union-in-difference images the Trinity and symbolizes the union of God and creation.[10]

Unitive Love as Gift of Self

The spousal meaning of the body relates to the ability of the spouses to express love through the gift of self. This gift of self "fulfills the very meaning of [human] being and existence."[11] The gift of self is the paradigm of

---

sex and gender. For him, masculinity and femininity find themselves in gendered visions of parenthood: "masculinity contains in a hidden way the meaning of fatherhood and femininity that of motherhood." *Man and Woman,* 217; homily 22:6.

8. "[M]an became the image of God not only through his own humanity, but also through the communion of persons, which man and woman form from the very beginning. . . . Man becomes an image of God not so much in the moment of solitude as in the moment of communion. He is, in fact, 'from the beginning' not only an image in which the solitude of one Person, who rules the world, mirrors itself, but also and essentially the image of an inscrutable divine communion of Persons." John Paul II, *Man and Woman,* 163; homily 9:3.

9. John Paul II, *Man and Woman,* 167; homily 10:2.

10. Stanley J. Grenz, *The Social God and the Relational Self: A Trinitarian Theology of the* Imago Dei (Louisville: Westminster John Knox, 2001); summarized by Grenz in "The Social God and the Relational Self: Toward a Trinitarian Theology of the *Imago Dei,*" in *Trinitarian Soundings in Systematic Theology,* ed. Paul Louis Metzger (London and New York: T. & T. Clark, 2005), 87-100.

11. John Paul II, *Man and Woman,* 185-86; homily 15:1. The full passage follows: "The human body, with its sex — its masculinity and femininity — seen in the very mystery of creation, is not only a source of fruitfulness and of procreation, as in the whole natural order, but contains 'from the beginning' the 'spousal' attribute, that is *the power to express love: precisely that love in which the human person becomes a gift* and — through this gift — fulfills the very meaning of his being and existence."

Christian love. Grounded in the Trinitarian nature of God,[12] it is the model of God's love for the world in Christ.[13] It is the model for marriage and the celibate religious vocation.[14] Grenz concurs and employs the language of the Catholic tradition when he argues that the sex act is an expression of mutual submission and a "gift of self."[15]

Procreative

The former pope believed the human body also carried a parental meaning. Masculinity and femininity reveal themselves more fully in paternity and maternity,[16] and paternity mirrors divine Fatherhood.[17] Grenz saw the sex act as an expression of openness beyond the couple to others — particularly children. "Sexual intercourse, through its link to procreation, constitutes an apt human analogy to the expansive love of God, which likewise creates the other as its product."[18]

The significance of the overlap in these two visions of sex, gender, sexuality, marriage, and theology should not be missed. Many find the

12. This can be clearly seen from the quote above from *Man and Woman,* 163; homily 9:3. Editor Michael Waldstein also emphasizes the centrality of Trinitarian thought in his introduction to *Man and Woman* where he quotes from John Paul II's earlier work, *Sources of Renewal.* There Wojtyla wrote: "Man's resemblance to God finds its basis, as it were, in the mystery of the most holy Trinity. Man resembles God not only because of the spiritual nature of his immortal soul but also by reason of his social nature, if by this we understand the fact that he 'cannot fully realize himself except in an act of pure self-giving' [*Gaudium et Spes,* 24:3]." Waldstein, 89, citing *Sources of Renewal: The Implementation of the Second Vatican Council* (San Francisco: Harper and Row, 1980), 61.

13. John Paul II, *Man and Woman,* 509; homily 97:4.

14. "[L]ove [is] the readiness to make the exclusive gift of self for the 'kingdom of God.'" John Paul II, *Man and Woman,* 435-36; homily 79:8.

15. Grenz, *Sexual Ethics,* 88-89.

16. "*[T]he mystery of femininity manifests and reveals itself in its full depth through motherhood. . . .* In this way, what also reveals itself is the mystery of the man's masculinity, that is, the generative and 'paternal' meaning of his body." John Paul II, *Man and Woman,* 210-11; homily 20:2.

17. "Fatherhood is one of the most prominent aspects of humanity in Sacred Scripture. The text of Genesis 5:3, 'Adam . . . begot a son *in his image, in his likeness,*' is explicitly connected with the account of the creation of man (Gen 1:27; 5:1) and seems to attribute to the earthly father the participation in the divine work of transmitting life." John Paul II, *Man and Woman,* 211 n. 33. Page 17 of the introduction indicates that the footnotes are original to John Paul II and "an integral part of the text."

18. Grenz, *Sexual Ethics,* 90-91.

common witness of these major players in conservative American Christianity compelling. At the same time, broad agreement between two major theologians does not indicate agreement among the members of these traditions. There is much to be affirmed, and yet there is room for critique so that what remains can be strengthened and can move beyond current limitations to a more comprehensive theology of human persons made in the image of God.

Sex Difference in Roman Catholic and Evangelical Theological Anthropologies

The Binary Sex Model in John Paul II's Theology of the Body

John Paul II begins his homilies in *Theology of the Body* with the same text we have been exploring at length: Matthew 19:1-12. He begins with Jesus' words in verses 1-8 but interrupts a complete analysis of the passage by jumping back to Genesis. He then inserts Jesus' statements on the indissolubility of marriage (Matt. 19:8; Mark 10:6-9), on lust (Matt. 5:28), and on the resurrection of the body (Matt. 22:30; Mark 12:25; Luke 20:35-36), followed by Paul's teaching on the resurrection in 1 Corinthians 15, before returning to the last verses of the pericope, Matthew 19:9-12. After reading "eunuchs for the sake of the kingdom" through the lens of 1 Corinthians 7, the late pope concludes with a long exposition on the sacrament of marriage (Eph. 5:21-33) and its implications for the continuing authority of *Humanae Vitae* — the prohibition of artificial contraceptives penned by Pope Paul VI in 1969. This is the shape of his theology of the body as he describes it.[19]

Given his admission of the purposes of his work, it is not surprising that *Theology of the Body* considers only certain types of bodies — those that fall into the binary pattern of Adam and Eve — excluding others. The pope does not consider what the bodies of eunuchs, intersex bodies, have to say for any theology of the body. Rather, following the pattern of many Church Fathers, he briefly acknowledges the physical nature of eunuchism but defines it as "the physical defects that make the procreative power of marriage impossible."[20] Unfortunately, this ambiguous definition could include everything from impotence to infertility. Avoiding the gender ambiguity of eunuchs

19. John Paul II, *Man and Woman,* 659-63; homily 133.
20. John Paul II, *Man and Woman,* 416; homily 74:1.

altogether, he reads the eunuch through the lens of continence or virginity translated into spiritual marriage.[21]

John Paul II's *Theology of the Body* is built upon heterosexual complementarity — which guides not only sexual ethics but is developed to ground the meaning of human existence and even Christian spirituality. He writes, "The human body, with its sex — its masculinity and femininity — seen in the very mystery of creation, is not only a source of fruitfulness and of procreation, as in the whole natural order, but contains 'from the beginning' the 'spousal' attribute, that is *the power to express love: precisely that love in which the human person becomes a gift* and — through this gift — fulfills the very meaning of his being and existence."[22] His proposal takes Jesus' statement in Matthew 19:4-5 very seriously: "Have you not read that the one who made them at the beginning 'made them male and female,' and said, 'For this reason a man shall leave his father and mother and be joined to his wife, and the two shall become one flesh'?" (NRSV). The nuptial meaning of the body insists that masculinity and femininity exist "for this reason," that is, to direct women and men to marriage. And marriage, according to John Paul II, exists as the primary metaphor for Christian love in the Scriptures. (The question of whether or not marriage *should* be seen as the primary metaphor for Christian love is the subject of the next chapter. For now, we focus our attention on his construal of masculinity and femininity.)

According to John Paul II, masculinity and femininity are relational terms. Neither can be understood apart from the other. "Thus, as Gen 2:23 already shows, femininity in some way finds itself before masculinity, while masculinity confirms itself through femininity. Precisely the function of sex [that is, being male and female], which in some way is 'constitutive for the person' (not only 'an attribute of the person'), shows how deeply man, with all his spiritual solitude, with the uniqueness and unrepeatability proper to the person, is constituted by the body as 'he' or 'she.'"[23] Unfortunately, the late pope does not unpack what he means by sex as "constitutive" of the person rather than a mere "attribute." This is regrettable, given the weight he places upon it. What he does unpack is the connection between femininity and motherhood and masculinity and fatherhood.

21. John Paul II reads "eunuch for the sake of the kingdom" through 1 Cor. 7; Rev. 14:4; Matt. 22:30; Mark 12:25; Luke 20:35-36; see *Man and Woman,* 414-62; homilies 73-86.

22. John Paul II, *Man and Woman,* 185-86; homily 15:1.

23. John Paul II, *Man and Woman,* 166, homily 10:1. Gen. 2:23 reads: "The man said, 'This is now bone of my bones and flesh of my flesh; she shall be called "woman," for she was taken out of man'" (NIV).

According to his *Theology of the Body,* masculinity and femininity are ordered toward fatherhood and motherhood. "*[T]he mystery of femininity manifests and reveals itself in its full depth through motherhood.* . . . In this way, what also reveals itself is the mystery of the man's masculinity, that is, the generative and 'paternal' meaning of his body."[24] But while woman's maternal femininity is read off of her body,[25] the connection between masculinity and fatherhood can be understood as more "hidden."[26] Rather than looking to men's bodies in order to understand fatherhood, the late pope directs his hearers to the presentation of fatherhood in the Scriptures — especially the Fatherhood of God.[27] Thus, femininity and masculinity direct women and men to marriage. Marriage is the paradigmatic form of the "gift of self" (which is the ultimate form of love — human and divine). This love is made visible in the conjugal union of husband and wife that leads naturally to motherhood and fatherhood. Marriage points to the sacramental, loving union between Christ and the church, and fatherhood points to God the Father.

Even though there are numerous problems with such an account (not least is the obvious imbalance between fatherhood and motherhood in their connection to the person and work of God),[28] there is also much to com-

24. John Paul II, *Man and Woman,* 210-11; homily 20:2.

25. "The whole exterior constitution of woman's body, its particular look, the qualities that stand, with the power of perennial attraction, at the beginning of the 'knowledge' about which Genesis 4:1-2 speaks ('Adam united himself with Eve'), *are in strict union with motherhood.* With the simplicity characteristic of it, the Bible (and the liturgy following it) honors and praises throughout the centuries 'the womb that bore you and the breasts from which you sucked milk' (Lk 11:27). These words are a eulogy of motherhood, of femininity, of the feminine body in its typical expression of creative love." John Paul II, *Man and Woman,* 212; homily 21:5.

26. "[M]asculinity contains in a hidden way the meaning of fatherhood and femininity that of motherhood." John Paul II, *Man and Woman,* 217; homily 22:6.

27. See n. 17 above.

28. While motherhood is read off of the female body, fatherhood is read off of the work of God in creation, so that fatherhood is presented as participating in the divine work in a way that motherhood is not. Note how the following quotation falls short of acknowledging woman's participation in God's work of creation: "The first woman to give birth *has full awareness of the mystery of creation, which renews itself in human generation.* She also has full awareness of the creative participation God has in human generation, his work and that of her husband, because she says, 'I acquired a man from the Lord.'" John Paul II, *Man and Woman,* 213; homily 21:6. The woman "has full awareness" of God's participation, of God's work and that of her husband. Her own work is not acknowledged as participating in this same work. Similarly in the following, "In this new man — born from the woman-parent

mend in it. First, John Paul II affirms the goodness of the body, sex differentiation, sexual desire, and marriage in the face of a long tradition of the devaluation of each. Additionally, although the sacramental image of the union of Christ and the church has historically led to a belief in the absolute authority of the husband over the wife, John Paul II insists upon a mutuality in marriage that is unprecedented in the Roman Catholic tradition up to his time.[29] The mutuality he sees in marriage is also integrated into his understanding of the relationship of masculinity and femininity as one of "reciprocal enrichment,"[30] although the details of this enrichment are not spelled out in this series of homilies.

The obvious omission from our perspective is that John Paul II does not take the time to develop a theology of the body of the eunuch. He assumes that the eunuch is one who cannot marry because "he" cannot father children, but he fails to take seriously the liminal status of the eunuch as one who is neither (fully) male/masculine nor female/feminine. Such recognition would call into question the very foundation of his project, because, according to Jesus, there are those whose bodies do not carry a nuptial meaning — they naturally do not marry. And there are still others who consider the "nuptial meaning of the body" to be of lesser importance than the priority of the kingdom.[31] While John Paul II acknowledges the broad nature of the renunciations involved in the choice of making oneself a eunuch for the sake of the kingdom, he does not recognize the challenge of the eunuch to his binary sex/gender complementary model.[32]

---

through the work of the man-parent — the same 'image of God' is reproduced every time, the image of that God who constituted the humanity of the first man" (Gen. 1:27). *Man and Woman,* 213. Here again we find that man's contribution is spoken of as work — representing the work of God in creation — while the child is simply "from the woman."

29. He interprets the submission of the wife in Eph. 5:22 in light of 5:21, the command for mutual submission of all believers (*Man and Woman,* 473; homily 89:3). In homily 30:6 (p. 252) he argues that the domination of Gen. 3:16 ("he will rule over you") is a result of the Fall. Nevertheless, he sees it as the man's responsibility to be "the guardian of the reciprocity of the gift and its true balance . . . as if it depended more on him whether the balance is kept or violated or even — if it has already been violated — reestablished" (261; homily 33:2). Cf. Lisa Sowle Cahill, "The Feminist Pope," in *Does Christianity Teach Male Headship? The Equal-Regard Marriage and Its Critics,* ed. David Blankenhorn, Don Browning, and Mary Stewart Van Leeuwen (Grand Rapids: Eerdmans, 2004), 40-48.

30. John Paul II, *Man and Woman,* 165; homily 9:5.

31. Whether this choice should be seen primarily through the lens of spiritual marriage is the question of the next chapter.

32. "Continence means *a conscious and voluntary renunciation* of this union and all that is connected with it in the full dimension of human life and the sharing of life. The one who

The Binary Model in Stanley Grenz's Evangelical Theology

In his earlier work, *Sexual Ethics,* Stanley Grenz's theological reflection on the nature of human sexuality is similar to John Paul II's in that its scope is limited by his attention to heterosexual ethics, thus assuming the male/female binary model. In his later work, *The Social God and the Relational Self,* as well as his summary essay, "The Social God and the Relational Self: Toward a Trinitarian Theology of the *Imago Dei*" (published the year of his untimely death), wherein he had the opportunity to look beyond the sexual, he does not. Rather, he expands the heterosexual model to argue that sexuality (i.e., the heterosexual drive toward marital bonding) provides the basis for all human relationality, including human relation to God (spirituality), and the bonded ecclesial community. This latter emphasis, on the place of sexuality, will be explored in the next chapter. In this chapter we must focus on his construal of male and female, rather than the nature of their bond.

For Grenz, heterosexual (marital) bonding is not the final form of the *imago Dei.* It is the foundational form. Grenz reads the development of the *imago Dei* in three canonical moves: (1) From a creation-centered anthropology beginning with Adam and Eve, who are made "in [God's] image and according to [God's] likeness" (Gen. 1:26 NRSV); (2) to a christocentric anthropology identifying Jesus Christ as the "image of the invisible God" (Col. 1:15 NRSV) and "the exact representation of [God's] being" (Heb. 1:3 NIV). But he does not stop there. (3) From here Grenz argues that the Scriptures teach us that "God's intention is that those who are in Christ participate in his destiny and thereby replicate his glorious image."[33] "For those God foreknew he also predestined to be conformed to the likeness of his Son, that he might be the firstborn among many brothers" (Rom. 8:29 NIV). Commenting on this verse, Grenz writes,

---

renounces marriage also renounces generation as the foundation of the community of the family composed of parents and children. The words of Christ to which we refer indicate undoubtedly this whole sphere of renunciation, although they do not dwell on particulars." John Paul II, *Man and Woman,* 427; homily 77:3.

33. Grenz, "The Social God," 90. "Paul's Adam-Christ typology, therefore, indicates that the creation of Adam did not mark the fulfillment of God's intention for humankind as the *imago Dei.* Instead, this divinely given destiny comes only with the advent of the new humanity, consisting of those who participate in the *pneumatikon soma* by means of their connection to the last Adam. In this manner, Paul paints Christ as the true image of God who imparts his supernatural characteristics to his spiritual progeny in a manner similar to Adam passing on his natural traits to his physical offspring." Grenz, 90.

> The climax of the verse comes in the subordinate clause that follows, "that he might be the firstborn," which expresses the Christological intent of God's foreordination, namely, the pre-eminence of Christ among those who participate in the eschatological resurrection. . . . Consequently, humankind created in the *imago Dei* is none other than the new humanity conformed to the *imago Christi,* and the *telos* toward which the Old Testament creation narrative points is the eschatological community of glorified saints.[34]

Given his larger vision of the *imago Dei* as the eschatological body of Christ, it might appear pedantic to focus on his construal of masculinity and femininity. Nevertheless, I believe that the way in which Grenz extends heterosexuality as the basis for all human relations, even eschatological relations of the bonded, ecclesial community, justifies a more careful look at the basis of his project.

In chapter 1 of his *Sexual Ethics: An Evangelical Perspective,* he argues that sexuality (i.e., sex differentiation with its [assumed] corresponding gender distinctions) is essential to the human person. Where John Paul II used the term "constitutive," Grenz uses "essential," but both argue that sex, gender, and sexuality are not mere attributes.[35]

Grenz rejects what he labels the "medieval anthropology," which located a common humanity in the sexless/rational soul, and more modern theological proposals of androgyny coming from Jungian depth psychology.[36] Rather, he insists that "men and women are different in ways that are more fundamental than simply their roles in the reproductive process. The differences lie even in the basic ways in which we view ourselves and the world. Men and women think differently; they approach the world differently."[37]

It should not go unnoticed that Grenz cites the work of John Money, the medical psychologist of Johns Hopkins University who became famous for his work on intersex and his insistence that intersex could be "fixed" through medical intervention — the very work that now comes under considerable criticism, as we recounted in chapter 1.[38] This is significant because it shows that Grenz was at least aware of the phenomena of intersex but failed to

34. Grenz, "The Social God," 91.
35. Grenz, *Sexual Ethics,* 22-30.
36. Grenz, *Sexual Ethics,* 23-24.
37. Grenz, *Sexual Ethics,* 253.
38. Grenz, *Sexual Ethics,* 24.

attend to those whose bodies do not naturally fit the categories he believes are "essential."[39]

Overextending the Work of Stanley Grenz and John Paul II

Evangelical ethicist Dennis Hollinger is indebted to Grenz in his own work, *The Meaning of Sex: Christian Ethics and the Moral Life.* Hollinger does better than Grenz in that he at least acknowledges the reality of intersex persons and their potential challenge to a heterosexual ethical program. Unfortunately, he fails to reflect theologically on intersexed bodies — beyond dismissing them as products of the Fall and suggesting that their bodies can be "rectified" (i.e., corrected through medical technology) "in the direction of divine givens."[40] Hollinger reads Matthew 19:4 as Jesus' affirmation of "creation givens" ("Have you not read that the one who made them at the beginning 'made them male and female'?" [NRSV]). He then explains these givens in ontological terms. "Jesus affirms that a basic given of reality is human maleness and femaleness. He does not define specific functions of this dual way of being; he simply posits this ontological reality as the paradigm for guiding humans in marriage and sex."[41]

There are several dangers latent in the above proposal. First, the focus on upholding heterosexual ethics has led to a dismissal of the theological significance of intersexed bodies. Second, an emphasis on the "constitutive" or "essential" nature of masculinity or femininity for human personhood, identity, and *imago Dei,* found in the work of John Paul II and Stanley Grenz, naturally leads to Hollinger's conclusion that intersex persons should seek medical help to "rectify" their bodies by conforming to creational norms or divine givens, that is, bodies that are "naturally" male or female. Third, by emphasizing sex differentiation for (hetero)sexual ethics, Hollinger illustrates how evangelical and Roman Catholic theologians are tempted to push the pendulum too far, overemphasizing sex differentiation to the point of speaking of sex difference as "ontological difference." Thus Hollinger writes of "this dual way of being . . . this ontological reality"[42] and

39. Grenz cites John Money's article "Human Hermaphroditism," in *Human Sexuality in Four Perspectives,* ed. Frank A. Beach (Baltimore: Johns Hopkins University Press, 1976). Grenz, *Sexual Ethics,* 262 n. 25.

40. Hollinger, *The Meaning of Sex,* 84.

41. Hollinger, *The Meaning of Sex,* 77.

42. Hollinger, *The Meaning of Sex,* 77.

"the male-female ontological distinction" as the foundation for marriage and sexual activity.[43]

Evangelicals are not the only ones to speak of ontological difference between the sexes. In 2004, the Vatican, under the leadership of Pope John Paul II, issued a letter to Roman Catholic bishops entitled "On the Collaboration of Men and Women in the Church and in the World." The letter was penned by Joseph Cardinal Ratzinger, head of the Offices of the Congregation for the Doctrine of the Faith, before his enthronement as Pope Benedict XVI. This letter illustrates the same tendency as found in evangelical theology. By emphasizing sex difference for heterosexual ethics and by calling for the "collaboration of men and women" on account of essentialist gender differences, Roman Catholic theologians are also overemphasizing sex differentiation to the point of risking ontological difference. The letter describes sex differentiation as "belonging ontologically to creation."[44] This is an obscure phrase that suggests giving more detailed attention to other portions of the letter.

In paragraph 8, we find an affirmation of the full dignity of men and women as persons made in the image of God, followed by an emphasis on difference.

> Above all, the fact that human beings are persons needs to be underscored: "Man is a person, man and woman equally so, since both were created in the image and likeness of the personal God." Their equal dignity as persons is realized as *physical, psychological and ontological complementarity,* giving rise to a harmonious relationship of "uni-duality," which only sin and "the structures of sin" inscribed in culture render potentially conflictual. The biblical vision of the human person suggests that problems related to sexual difference, whether on the public or private level, should be addressed by a relational approach and not by competition or retaliation.[45]

This physical, psychological, and ontological complementarity is extended into the spiritual realm later in the same paragraph.

43. Hollinger, *The Meaning of Sex,* 60.

44. "Letter to the Bishops of the Catholic Church on the Collaboration of Men and Women in the Church and in the World," May 31, 2004. http://www.vatican.va/roman_curia/congregations/cfaith/documents/rc_con_cfaith_doc_20040731_collaboration_en.html.

45. "On the Collaboration," 8, italics mine. The interior quotation is from John Paul II, Apostolic Letter *Mulieris Dignitatem* (August 15, 1988), 7.

> Furthermore, the importance and the meaning of sexual difference, as a reality deeply inscribed in man and woman, needs to be noted. "Sexuality characterizes man and woman *not only on the physical level, but also on the psychological and spiritual,* making its mark on each of their expressions." It cannot be reduced to a pure and insignificant biological fact, but rather "is a fundamental component of personality, one of its modes of being, of manifestation, of communicating with others, of feeling, of expressing and of living human love." This capacity to love — reflection and image of God who is Love — is disclosed in the spousal character of the body, in which the masculinity or femininity of the person is expressed.[46]

Grenz and Hollinger make similar statements in their own works. Hollinger actually quotes Grenz in his introduction.

> To put it another way, our sexuality is the form of our bodily or physical being within the world. It certainly encompasses our *emotional, social, and spiritual selves,* but it is related to the very way in which we as embodied beings exist in relationships to others. As Stanley Grenz puts it, "Sexuality comprises all aspects of the human person that are related to existence as male and female. Our sexuality, therefore, is a powerful, deep, and mysterious aspect of our being. It constitutes a fundamental distinction between the two ways of being human (i.e., as male or female)."[47]

Hollinger also follows Grenz in reversing the normal definitions of sex and sexuality, saying that "sex" is "particular acts of physical intimacy" while "sexuality [refers] to our maleness and femaleness as human beings."[48] Unfortunately, both use "sexuality" so broadly that it sometimes includes sex differentiation, culturally formed gendered behavior/role/identities, and (genital and social)[49] sexual expression. Again Grenz illustrates this overlap: "We give expression to the fundamental sexual dimension of our being in many ways. The most obvious, of course, is through sexual attraction and sexually determined acts. Such acts include the way we speak and touch others especially those to whom we are sexually attracted, and ultimately in

46. "On the Collaboration," 8, italics mine. The interior quotations are from Congregation for Catholic Education, *Educational Guidance in Human Love* (November 1, 1983), 4.

47. Hollinger, *The Meaning of Sex,* 16, italics mine.

48. Hollinger, *The Meaning of Sex,* 15.

49. For an explanation of the difference between social and genital sexuality, see chap. 5.

genital sexual relations. But there are other ways of expressing our sexuality. They may range from the seemingly mundane — how we dress, comb our hair, etc. — to the more sublime — the appreciation of beauty, as well as cultural and artistic preferences and activities."[50]

Grenz finds support for this view in a similar statement by the American Lutheran Church, which insisted, "Human sexuality includes all that we are as human beings. Sexuality at the very least is biological, psychological, cultural, social, and spiritual. It is as much of the mind as of the body, of the community as of the person. To be a person is to be a sexual being."[51]

Whereas Grenz followed John Money as one of his primary sources for the scientific study of sex differences, Hollinger refers to more recent "brain-imaging technologies" that "show difference in the responses of women and men to external stimulations of all sorts, even though brain responses upon gender lines frequently do not seem to represent gender differences in behavior."[52] What both fail to attend to is the fact that brain-imaging technologies have also shown that "few, if any, individuals correspond to the modal male pattern or the modal female pattern. Variation within each sex is great, with both males and females near the top and bottom of the distributions for every characteristic. . . . In fact, although most of us appear to be either clearly male or clearly female, we are each complex mosaics of male and female characteristics."[53]

Both evangelicals and Roman Catholics are committed to gender essentialist complementarity (i.e., the belief that all men think and behave in a particular way and that all women think and behave in a different but complementary way) and base their theological anthropology on this foundation. Both use this to argue that men and women should work together in the home, church, and world.[54] But for each, complementarity is a simplistic

50. Grenz, *Sexual Ethics,* 21-22.

51. Grenz, *Sexual Ethics,* 21, citing "Human Sexuality and Sexual Behavior," a statement adopted by the Tenth General Convention of the American Lutheran Church.

52. Hollinger, *The Meaning of Sex,* 74.

53. Melissa Hines, *Brain Gender* (Oxford: Oxford University Press, 2004), 18-19.

54. "The fundamentally different outlooks toward others, life, and the world that characterize males and females mean that the two sexes are supplementary. Each sex needs the supplemental approach to reality offered by the other in all the various dimensions of human life together." Grenz, *Sexual Ethics,* 253. "In this perspective, one understands the irreplaceable role of women in all aspects of family and social life involving human relationships and caring for others. . . . It implies first of all that women be significantly and actively present in the family. . . . It means also that women should be present in the world of work and in the organization of society, and that women should have access to positions of responsibility

binary model. There are only two ways of being in the world — an ideal masculinity and an ideal femininity.

And yet, none of these authors are able to define masculinity and femininity concretely. John Paul II links masculinity and femininity to the paternal and maternal. Grenz and Hollinger do not even attempt a description. The 2004 letter to the bishops, "On the Collaboration of Men and Women in the Church and in the World," comes closest to a definition of femininity by describing it as "a capacity for the other" — a definition that arises out of physical maternity but is expanded into other relations and to the spiritual. While the document does insist that "the feminine values mentioned here are above all human values [because] the human condition of man and woman created in the image of God is one and indivisible," it qualifies this by saying that "women are more immediately attuned to these values [; thus] . . . they are the reminder and the privileged sign of such values. But, in the final analysis, every human being, man or woman, is destined to be 'for the other.' "[55] Unfortunately, the letter does not define masculinity at all. It warns that "Whenever these fundamental experiences are lacking [i.e., concern for the other nourished by women's care for children in the home], society as a whole suffers violence and becomes in turn the progenitor of more violence."[56] This statement could be construed as defining masculinity only in negative terms (i.e., violence), but the text is not explicit.

It does seem strange, given the theological weight evangelicals and Roman Catholics place on gender complementarity, that they are unable to define either pole of the equation. While in past centuries theologians have argued *against* greater female participation in church and society on the basis of sex/gender differences, most contemporary evangelicals and Catholics are arguing *for* greater female participation in these areas — barring ordination to the priesthood by Roman Catholics and more conservative evangelicals.[57] This greater measure of participation and valuing of the "woman's perspective" may be heralded as an improvement; nevertheless, this complementary model inadvertently introduces other dangers.

---

which allow them to inspire the policies of nations and to promote innovative solutions to economic and social problems." "On the Collaboration," 13:4.

55. "On the Collaboration," 14.

56. "On the Collaboration," 13:4.

57. John Paul II upholds the restriction of women from ordained priesthood on the basis of his model, while Grenz argues that these essential differences do not prohibit women's ordination to senior pastoral offices. See Stanley J. Grenz and Denise Muir Kjesbo, *Women in the Church: A Biblical Theology of Women in Ministry* (Downers Grove, Ill.: InterVarsity, 1995).

Some Problems in Evangelical and Roman Catholic Theologies of the Body

By overemphasizing sex and gender difference, and its essential or constitutive relation to human personhood, both evangelicals and Roman Catholics are running headlong into theological trouble. Their emphasis on the radical (ontological) difference between men and women threatens to undermine the value of the incarnation for women.

Dennis Hollinger presents Jesus as "not an asexual being, but a male with the same physiological and hormonal makeup of all males, yet without sin (Heb. 4:15)." He quotes evangelical ethicist and theologian Lewis Smedes as follows: "Christian piety does not have to be nervous about the sexuality of Jesus. He was a male, and his masculinity shaped his human life from his hormones to his soul."[58] Such statements present two dangers: they give the mistaken impression that all men have the same physiological and hormonal makeup; and they drive a wedge between Christian women and the Savior in whose image they are created and into whose likeness they are being transformed day by day (2 Cor. 3:18). Both problems must be addressed.

First, it is inaccurate to state that all men have the same physiological and hormonal makeup. This should be obvious to the common observer who notices the great diversity among men in society. But when such common-sense arguments fail to convince those already committed to sex/gender essentialism, scientific study can assist in proving the point. The director of the Behavioral Neuroendocrinology Research Unit at City University in London explains that there are differences in hormone levels among men and that these differences should be seen as advantageous for the human species:

> One advantage of having sexual development controlled by gonadal hormones, rather than directly by genetic information, is that it allows for great variability both within and between individuals. Not only are several hormones involved, but the action of these hormones depends on a number of processes, including the amounts of each hormone produced, their conversion to other active products, and the numbers or sensitivity of receptors at each target site. As a result, individual men and women are each complicated mosaics of different sex-related traits, rather than replicas of the modal man or modal woman. In addition . . . environmental sources of hormones and other factors that modify the actions of hormones can

58. Smedes, quoted by Hollinger, *The Meaning of Sex,* 85.

> modify sexual differentiation, at least in theory. This provides more potential for flexibility than if sexual development depended directly on genetic information. Thus, the use of this secondary mechanism (i.e., hormones) allows for greater diversity in the species as well as potentially greater responsiveness to environmental changes.[59]

What physicians have documented at the neuroendocrinological level, sociologists, psychologists, and cross-cultural anthropologists have also documented in their own fields.[60] One simply cannot speak of masculinity as if it were a single unified perspective on self and world — or insist that this single perspective is the one that Jesus shared. Although some theologians are beginning to bring such studies into their accounts, speaking about masculinities in the plural, or of hegemonic masculinity in the singular, evangelicals and Roman Catholics have been slow to incorporate such insights into their theological anthropologies.[61]

It is simply inaccurate to present Jesus as a male "like every other male," as if all males were alike. Such statements may sound comforting to some Christian men, but it is imperative that we recognize the danger they present, not only to men who do not fit the mold but also to women who

59. Hines, *Brain Gender,* 35.

60. "There is certainly convincing evidence for the power of socialization to shape our perceptions of the world and even to shape the physical structures of the world. For example, the shape, strength, and specific skills of females and males are not merely a function of biological differences but are also heavily influenced by systematic differences in experience within a cultural context (Hubbard, 1990; Lorber, 1993). If these differences were indeed biologically innate, then the well-documented steady and rapid 'closing of the gap' between women and men in competitive sports and in technological competence could not occur (Lorber, 1993). Other researchers have shown that when gender differences in a trait are examined, we consistently find enormous variation within the gender 'categories,' and enormous overlap between the categories, to the extent that we must question whether these categories truly 'carve up nature at the joints' (Maccoby & Jacklin, 1974; Van Leeuwen, 1990). Furthermore, the meaning of being female or male has been shown to vary across cultures, and over time. Womanhood and manhood in the sixteenth century were experienced very differently from the late twentieth century, and they are very different for people in their teens than for those in their sixties. In one culture, males are emotional, social and talkative; in another, the reverse is true (Stephens, 1963; Tarvis & Wade, 1984)." Heather Looy, "Male and Female God Created Them: The Challenge of Intersexuality," *Journal of Psychology and Christianity* 21 (2002): 13. See also Heather Looy, "Sex Differences: Evolved, Constructed and Designed," *Journal of Psychology and Theology* 29, no. 4 (Winter 2001): 301-13.

61. Stephen B. Boyd, W. Merle Longwood, and Mark W. Muesse, eds., *Redeeming Men: Religion and Masculinities* (Louisville: Westminster John Knox, 1996), xiv-xv.

cannot and to the intersex who can only approximate likeness to Jesus in certain respects — depending on the specifics of their intersex condition. Presenting not only Jesus' body but also his soul as radically, ontologically different from the bodies and souls of women puts Jesus' humanity beyond the reach of over half of the human race. Elizabeth Johnson notes the wisdom of the Nicene and Constantinopolitan Fathers, who declared the power of the incarnation through the inclusive terms *anthropos* (Greek) and *homo* (Latin): "For us and for our salvation . . . he became incarnate from the Virgin Mary, and was made [hu]man" *(et homo factus est)*. At the same time, she reminds us of their concomitant belief that salvation comes about through the assumption of human nature by the Word. Johnson warns us not to underestimate the significance of these twin theses. "If maleness is constitutive for the incarnation and redemption, female humanity is not assumed and therefore not saved."[62] Johnson is not questioning the historicity of Jesus as a male human but the problems created by a theological emphasis on the masculinity of Jesus, combined with an insistence on essential sex/gender differences, and exacerbated by a distorted presentation of the radical nature of those differences.

We find similar problems in Roman Catholic accounts. The 2004 letter to Roman Catholic bishops does not address the masculinity or maleness of Jesus; nevertheless, it places Jesus' humanity and spirituality beyond the reach of his female followers when it emphasizes physical, psychological, and spiritual differences between men and women.[63] Roman Catholic theologian Janet Martin Soskice takes comfort in the fact that when the letter speaks of sexual difference as "belonging ontologically to creation," it "fortunately falls short of saying that there is an 'ontological difference' between men and women." Still, she is concerned that the language of ontological difference is philosophically and theologically problematic. Soskice finds it "odd" to speak of ontological difference between men and women, "for one can see an ontological difference between a stone and a tiger, between a planet and a lamb, but it would be an odd stretch to see an *ontological* difference between a man and a woman, unless one went the whole way and said there was an ontological difference between any two individuals, between George

62. Elizabeth A. Johnson, *She Who Is: The Mystery of God in Feminist Theological Discourse* (New York: Crossroad, 2003), 153. This and subsequent quotations from this volume (copyright © 1992 by Elizabeth A. Johnson) are used with permission.

63. "On the Collaboration," 8.

Bush and Nelson Mandela, for instance. That would vacate the phrase of philosophical meaning."[64]

She insists that the language of "ontological difference" is "too strong," because "it would put the 2004 letter at odds, not only with *Gaudium et Spes,* but with Scripture itself were it to suggest it is impossible for a woman to say that, in all significant senses, Christ is like me in every sense except sin."[65] Thus she concludes:

> We find ourselves to this very day teetering between two positions that are both compelling but at the same time incompatible. We must say that, Christologically speaking, women and men cannot be different for "all will bear the image of the man from heaven." But we must also say that sexual difference is not, or should not be, a matter of theological indifference. Sexual difference has something to tell us, not just about God, but also about the human being made in the image of God.
>
> The unresolved question then is — where, why and how does sexual difference make a difference?[66]

Like Grenz, Soskice looks to the triune nature of God to ground unity-in-difference, but she also falls into the same trap as Grenz and John Paul II when she assumes that there are only two categories of difference. "[T]he fullness of divine life and creativity is reflected by humankind which is male and female, which encompasses if not an ontological, then a primal difference. And this difference is not for pragmatic reasons but by divine plan."[67] Thus, her helpful critique of Roman Catholic theological anthropology also needs to be expanded by a theological reflection upon intersexed bodies. It is to that task that we now turn.

64. Janet Martin Soskice, *"Imago Dei,"* in *The Other Journal: An Intersection of Theology and Culture* 7 (April 2, 2006).

65. Soskice, *"Imago Dei." Gaudium et Spes* is a Vatican II document, "The Pastoral Constitution on the Church in the Modern World" (December 7, 1965).

66. Soskice, *"Imago Dei."*

67. Soskice, *"Imago Dei."*

A Theology of Intersex Bodies: Ontological Sameness and Real Difference

Intersex as Illustration of Ontological Sameness

Theological reflection on intersexed bodies must extend beyond their dismissal as products of the Fall.[68] As I argued in chapter 2, Jesus in his words about eunuchs, even in the context of his affirmation of the creation account of male and female, does not dismiss physical intersex conditions as a product of the Fall to be overcome. Rather, he teaches his disciples that they can learn from eunuchs. Even more, he instructs them that those who can should model their lives on those who do not fit neatly into the category of either male or female.

Reflecting on intersex bodies is helpful because it can also grant insight into the thorny question of sameness and difference among the sexes. In particular, it provides us with substantial support for arguing against the construal of sex difference as ontological difference. Intersexed bodies show, once again, how males and females are made of the same "stuff." It is not impossible for a "male" fetus (XY chromosomes and testes) to develop into a female — complete with labia, clitoris, a short vagina, breasts, feminine musculoskeletal structure, and female gender identity. This is the common pattern for intersexed persons with androgen insensitivity syndrome, one of the more common intersex conditions. Similarly, it is not impossible for a "female" fetus (XX chromosomes and ovaries) to develop into a male — complete with a phallus capable of vaginal penetration, male pattern hair growth, voice descent, masculine musculoskeletal development, and male gender identity — as is possible in more severe cases of congenital adrenal hyperplasia. To call androgens and estrogens "male hormones" and "female hormones" respectively is misleading, given that both androgens and estrogens course through the veins of men, women, and intersexed persons (albeit at different levels) and affect much more than reproductive and secondary sex characteristics.[69] Even gonadal tissue is undifferentiated in the early weeks of gestation.[70] Males, females, and intersexed persons are made of the same "stuff." We belong to the same order of being. John Paul II calls

68. Hollinger, *The Meaning of Sex,* 84, and Charles Colson, "Blurred Biology: How Many Sexes Are There?" *BreakPoint,* October 16, 1996.

69. Anne Fausto-Sterling, *Sexing the Body: Gender Politics and the Construction of Sexuality* (New York: Basic Books, 2000), 182-94.

70. Hines, *Brain Gender,* 22-23.

this "somatic homogeneity," which exists prior to sex differentiation.[71] Sexed humans are not *ontologically* different from one another. This is not to deny that there are real differences between the categories but to say that such differences do not belong to the realm of ontology.

Intersex as an Illustration of Real Difference

At the same time, to say that there is no ontological difference between male, female, and intersex does not mean that there are no differences between them. One could not even speak about intersex if there were not two categories of sex able to be "inter"-mixed in various ways. In this way, John Money's critique of Anne Fausto-Sterling's "five sexes" is valid. Intersex is "not a third sex" but "a mixed sex or an in-between sex."[72] Scientific studies on males, females, and intersexed persons illustrate similarities and differences.

Hines's work as director of the Behavioral Neuroendocrinology Research Unit at City University in London shows how it is possible to speak about sex/gender differences in a more nuanced fashion. She argues that when trying to discuss behavioral differences between males and females, it is helpful to compare them to differences in height. We often observe that men are generally taller than women, and yet, we all know exceptions to this "rule," particularly as we move from one ethnic group to another.

Comparing the average heights of males and females shows how it is possible to identify a typical male pattern as well as a typical female pattern while at the same time recognizing the significant overlap between the two norms. Hines explains that differences in behavior are much less noticeable than differences in height. Thus, when comparing typical male and female behavior in a number of categories, she shows how there is considerably more overlap.[73] It is helpful to quote her summary once more: "[F]ew, if any, individuals correspond to the modal male pattern or the modal female

71. John Paul II, *Man and Woman,* 161; homily 8:4.

72. John Money, *Sex Errors of the Body and Related Syndromes: A Guide to Counseling Children, Adolescents, and Their Families,* 2nd ed. (Baltimore: Paul H. Brookes Publishing Co., 1994), 6.

73. Hines shows that sex differences in height (standard deviation of 2) are much greater than sex differences in other behaviors, that is, 3-D rotations (.9), math problems (.3), math concepts (.1), verbal fluency (-.4), physical aggression (.4), toy preferences (.8), rough and tumble play (.4). Hines, *Brain Gender,* 10-11.

pattern. Variation within each sex is great, with males and females near the top and bottom of the distributions for every characteristic. . . . In fact, although most of us appear to be either clearly male or clearly female, we are each complex mosaics of male and female characteristics."[74]

Hines's work shows that there are real differences between the sexes — physical, psychological, social, and behavioral. But not all these differences can be neatly lumped into two (or three) sex/gender categories. While there are typical male patterns, they do not apply to every male or to males exclusively. Although there are typical female patterns, these do not apply to every female or to females exclusively. Such studies show that there are greater sameness and more differences between and among the sexes. Given this complexity, how ought Roman Catholics and evangelicals to respond? How can we take into account a more nuanced vision of sex and gender similarities and differences in a way that makes sense of the biblical data? To begin, it requires returning to Genesis with new eyes.

From Other to Others: Properly Extending the Evangelical and Roman Catholic Traditions

Interpreting the Significance of Adam and Eve

The biggest theological challenge keeping evangelicals and Roman Catholics from embracing a more nuanced version of sex/gender complementarity may be the creation accounts. It is here that John Paul II, Stanley Grenz, and others ground their accounts of the image of God as male-and-female-in-community as a reflection of the Trinitarian communion of persons. It is here that woman is presented as the necessary "other" who calls the man outside of himself and into relationality. It is here that we find only two, a male and a female, in binary complementarity. But this is an incomplete reading of the text. It neglects the fact that, within the canonical narrative, Adam and Eve are only the beginning.[75]

74. Hines, *Brain Gender,* 18-19.

75. I speak here of theological interpretation of the creation accounts, leaving the question of the historicity of Adam and Eve to the expertise of others. Evangelical scholar Peter Enns makes strong arguments against a historical reading of Adam and Eve in *The Evolution of Adam: What the Bible Does and Doesn't Say about Human Origins* (Grand Rapids: Brazos, 2001). Grenz writes, "For Christian faith, however, more important than the actual historical-scientific question concerning whether or not Adam was the first human is the

John Paul II looks upon Adam and Eve as prototypes for all human interaction. According to his *Theology of the Body,* their heterosexual union reveals the meaning of human existence as it teaches us the spousal meaning of the body, which is the gift of self, the paradigm of human and divine love.[76]

Similarly, the 2004 letter "On the Collaboration of Men and Women in the Church and in the World" presents the creation of Adam and Eve as paradigmatic of otherness.[77] The language of "uni-duality" once again construes female-male complementarity as paradigmatic of unity-in-diversity.

Grenz's account of the *imago Dei* entails more components than John Paul II's in that he sees canonical language about the image developing from Adam and Eve to Christ and culminating in the diverse eschatological community of the redeemed that is united to Christ as his body. He does well to emphasize that while the marriage of Adam and Eve "marks the climax of the second creation story . . . it does not constitute the end of the account of the origins of human community." These two bear children, begin a family, and "as the generations multiply, the primal human community expands, resulting in the building of cities (Gen. 4:17) and the advent of societies characterized by a division of labor (4:21-22)."[78] To interpret the significance of the first chapters of Genesis for theological anthropology, it is helpful to learn from Grenz's attention to the narrative and canonical development of the *imago.*

Adam and Eve: From Form to Fountainhead, Prototype to Parent Grenz does well to point out that other differences come from the union of male and female at the beginning — differences that are ultimately taken up into the eschatological body of Christ. On the other hand, he undermines the significance of those differences when he says that sex difference is essential to the person in a way that other differences, such as age and race, are not.[79]

---

theological significance of 'Adam' as marking the beginning of humankind." *Theology for the Community of God,* 2nd ed. (Grand Rapids: Eerdmans, 2000), 148.

76. John Paul II, *Man and Woman,* 185-86; homily 15:1.

77. "On the Collaboration," 8.

78. Grenz, *The Social God,* 279.

79. "Although undeniably important, racial differences and other factors do not loom as foundational in personal and social identity as do those distinctions which arise out of the fact that we are sexual beings. The first aspect noticed at birth is not race, but sex. And we carry with us throughout our lives the tendency to see our maleness and femaleness as the fundamental demarcation among ourselves. . . . Racial distinction is not presented in

He does not acknowledge how differences of race, language, culture, and age can provide other differences — also essential to the identity of the person — that can significantly alter the way bodily maleness, femaleness, and intersex are interpreted. (Returning to our commonsense analysis of height differences, we know that men are typically taller than women within a particular ethnic group, but cross-cultural analysis of height shows the relativity of these values. Swedish women are often taller than Italian men.) Because Grenz views sex difference as more essential to human personhood than other differences, he continues to view Adam and Eve as the paradigmatic forms of difference, rather than the fountainheads of even greater differences that are then incorporated in his progressive model.

That the Genesis accounts do not provide us with a comprehensive list of creational diversity should not go unnoticed. Biblical scholar Roy Ciampa has observed that Genesis 1 offers us broad categories of difference: dry land and seas (v. 10); "vegetation: seed-bearing plants and trees on the land that bear fruit with seed in it" (v. 11 NIV); sun, moon, and stars (v. 16); creatures that live in the waters and in the air (vv. 20-21) and others that live on the ground (vv. 24-27). This chapter does not list other forms or mixed forms regularly seen in creation: rivers, asteroids, planets, amphibians, dusk, dawn, etc. Few would argue that these "others" or "hybrids" are a result of the Fall, or that they stray from God's creational intent. Genesis simply does not give us a comprehensive list of all the good things God has made.[80] It is the beginning of the story, painting in broad brush strokes, with so much more to come.

Rather than interpreting creational differences as prototypes or ideal forms, Soskice sees in these distinctions the basis for the Roman Catholic emphasis on fecundity. In her account of the *imago Dei,* she notes how "fecundity . . . comes from difference, the difference of light and dark, of sea and dry land. Fecundity is the interval."[81] It is literal fecundity, coming from the sexual union of male and female, that continues to ground the commitment of many evangelicals and Roman Catholics to heterosexual marriage. At the same time, affirming the goodness of fecundity in heterosexual marriage does not necessarily lead to the belief that all persons must be fully, ideally, male/masculine or female/feminine — reproductively, so-

Genesis as arising from creation itself, as is the case with sex distinctions. Rather, the races first emerge after the Flood." Grenz, *Sexual Ethics,* 29.

80. Roy E. Ciampa, personal correspondence via Facebook comment (November 30, 2013).

81. Soskice, *"Imago Dei."*

cially, psychologically, etc. Understanding Adam and Eve as prototypes for all men and all women misreads the scope and intention of the creation narratives and overlooks the place of these two characters in the story of revelation and redemption.

Theologians may debate whether the statement "Be fruitful and multiply" should be interpreted as a command or a blessing when applied to modern-day couples, but all should recognize the importance of literal fecundity within the creation narrative. Within Genesis, literal fruitfulness was necessary to the divine project. The differences between the bodies of Adam and Eve enabled them to be literally, physically fruitful/fecund. But this was only the beginning. Male and female need not be held up as the epitome of otherness — from which comes metaphorical fecundity. Rather than identifying male and female as the paradigmatic forms of otherness, they can be interpreted as the fountainhead of others who may become more "other" than their parents could have ever conceived.

Reading the Genesis account this way allows us to hold several truths in tension. The first is the value of literal fecundity in marriage. The sexual union of male and female in marriage can be fruitful, and this fecundity is good. At the same time, the affirmation of difference arising from common, ontological sameness is also important because it protects us from the other extreme of focusing so much on difference — sex, gender, culture, language, class, race, age — that we endanger the common humanity of men, women, and intersex. Indeed, James Brownson has argued, persuasively, that the emphasis in Genesis is on sameness rather than difference — the shared humanity of Adam and Eve in contrast to the difference between Adam and the animals. "The primary movement in the text is not from unity to differentiation, but from the isolation of an individual to the deep blessing of shared kinship and community."[82] If we follow the trajectory from prototype to parent and from kinship to community, we will find a pedagogical paradigm embedded in the structure of both family and Scripture.

Adam and Eve: From Prototype to Parent to Pedagogue Building on the notion of difference and fecundity, many have noted the lessons made available to us if we are willing to learn. Many find in marriage and parenting a divinely ordained object lesson on the value of similarity and diversity —

82. James V. Brownson, *Bible, Gender, Sexuality: Reframing the Church's Debate on Same-Sex Relationships* (Grand Rapids: Eerdmans, 2013), 30.

a pedagogy of love for others. Marital love, while built upon love for one who is different from us in many ways, is taken to a new level when spouses become parents. We begin to learn to love our spouse in the spouse's similarity and otherness, and then, as children come (through natural processes or adoption), we are challenged to learn to love those who are even more different — those unable to communicate, to share our worldview, to see the reasonableness of our requests. Many of us have found that our children, because of their age difference and experiences, have perspectives on themselves, on their sex, gender, and sexuality, and on the world that are far different from our own and even from our spouse's even though they may share our biological sex. Learning to love our children, who are like us and yet different, stretches our love for others to new levels.

One finds a similar pattern in the biblical narrative. In the Old Testament there is a focus on family, kin, clan, and nation, but in the New Testament this love for family is extended to the "family" of believers. Similarly in Matthew 5:43-48, Jesus compares the old covenant to the new, saying, "You have heard that it was said, 'Love your neighbor and hate your enemy.' But I tell you: Love your enemies and pray for those who persecute you, that you may be sons of your Father in heaven. He causes his sun to rise on the evil and the good, and sends rain on the righteous and the unrighteous. If you love those who love you, what reward will you get? Are not even the tax collectors doing that? And if you greet only your brothers, what are you doing more than others? Do not even pagans do that? Be perfect, therefore, as your heavenly Father is perfect" (NIV).

Love for family is extended beyond kin. Love for neighbor is extended even to enemies. The love between two is expanded. Love grows. The binary-sex other multiplies to include ever more others. Ronald Rolheiser, a Roman Catholic writer on Christian spirituality, notes a similar pattern, arguing that sexual desire, when tied to faithfulness in marriage and openness to children, naturally matures and sanctifies the individual by expanding his or her world and desires.[83] Rolheiser focuses on the progressive nature of sexual desire, but I believe it is more helpful to focus on the nature of otherness (for reasons that will be explored further in the next chapter). Reading the Genesis account in light of the larger biblical narrative, we are able to affirm the goodness of sex difference as the fountainhead of human

83. Ronald Rolheiser, *The Holy Longing: A Search for a Christian Spirituality* (New York: Doubleday, 1999), 201.

difference without requiring the male-female pattern to become the paradigmatic form of the other.

Beyond the Binary

This revision of the "other" will sound familiar to those versed in feminist literature. As early as 1938, Dorothy Sayers was working for a larger vision of difference, arguing that differences of age, nationality, and class can be just as fundamental, if not more fundamental, than differences of sex. She quipped, "There is a fundamental difference between men and women, but it is not the only fundamental difference in the world."[84]

Roman Catholic feminist theologian Elizabeth Johnson develops this idea in her own work, *She Who Is: The Mystery of God in Feminist Theological Discourse,* and her analysis is worth quoting at length.

> On the one hand, feminist thought resists an unrelieved binary way of thinking, a notion of human nature polarized on the basis of sex, which inevitably leads to a dominant/subordinate pattern. On the other hand, reduction to an equality of sameness by ignoring sexual difference is also unacceptable. . . .
>
> A way beyond the impasse of these options is emerging: one human nature celebrated in an interdependence of multiple differences. Not a binary view of two forever predetermined male and female natures, nor abbreviation into a single ideal, but a diversity of ways of being human: a multipolar set of combinations of essential human elements, of which sexuality is but one. . . . If maleness and femaleness can be envisioned in a more wholistic context, their relationship to each other can be more rightly conceived.
>
> All persons are constituted by a number of anthropological constants, essential elements that are intrinsic to their identity. These include bodiliness and hence sex and race; relation to the earth, other persons and social groupings; economic, political, and cultural location, and the like. The constants mutually condition one another. . . . Significantly change any one of them, and a different person results.
>
> It is shortsighted to single out sexuality as always and everywhere

84. Dorothy L. Sayers, *Are Women Human?* (1938; reprint, Grand Rapids: Eerdmans, 1971), 33-34.

> more fundamental to concrete historical existence than any of the other constants. Age, race, period in history, bodily handicap, social location, and other essential aspects of concrete historical existence are at least as important in determining one's identity as sex. . . . In a multipolar model, sexuality is integrated into a holistic vision of human persons instead of being made the touchstone of personal identity and thus distorted.
>
> . . . The goal is to reorder the two-term and one-term systems into a multiple-term schema, one which allows connection in difference rather than constantly guaranteeing identity through opposition and uniformity. Respect can thus be extended to all persons in their endless combinations of anthropological constants, boundlessly concrete. And difference itself, rather than a regrettable obstacle to community, can function as a creative community-shaping force.[85]

Although Johnson does not argue for such a model on the basis of intersex, her insistence on a multipolar model creates theological space for intersex persons in addition to other others. It gives us room to reconsider the meanings of sex difference as well as other differences — not in order to dissolve differences into some melting pot of sameness but to properly value shared humanity, real differences, and the common goal of conformity to the image of Christ; to cultivate virtues that transcend sex differences even while they may be worked out in various ways depending not only on biological differences but also on cultural and historical location. We will return to these urgent practicalities in the last chapter. Meanwhile, one must lament that the nuances Johnson supplies have yet to seriously alter mainstream evangelical and Roman Catholic theological anthropologies. Nevertheless, the seedbed for such ideas has already been laid by both traditions in a shared emphasis on eschatology.

From Eden to Eschaton: The Priority of the Future

One of the similarities between the evangelical anthropology of Stanley Grenz and the Roman Catholic vision of Janet Martin Soskice is the emphasis each places on the eschaton as the final form of the human. They insist that as helpful as the creation accounts may be, they are not to be understood

85. Johnson, *She Who Is*, 155-56.

as the paradigm or final form for humanity. Rather, true humanity is a future toward which we are moving.[86]

This priority on the future fits well with an expansive notion of otherness. While the primal or primitive form of the *imago* as a community of diverse persons may be found in the creation of Adam and Eve, these do not need to remain the paradigmatic form of otherness. Other others are born from these parents: other ages, other languages, other cultures, and even others whose sex does not match either parent.

In chapter 2 we learned how, in the ancient world, it was not only women but also eunuchs who stood as the paradigmatic other. Eunuchs were legally other, morally other, sexually other, socially other, religiously other, ethnically other — "exiles from the society of the human race."[87] And yet it was to these exiles that the Lord, through the prophet Isaiah, promised a place in the kingdom of God:

> "To them I will give within my temple and its walls
> a memorial and a name
> better than sons and daughters;
> I will give them an everlasting name
> that will not be cut off. . . .
> Their burnt offerings and sacrifices
> will be accepted on my altar;
> for my house will be called
> a house of prayer for all nations." (Isa. 56:5-7 NIV)

Isaiah predicted the future inclusion of these others. Foreigners and even eunuchs would be included in the temple of God. Even this temple did not provide the final form but pointed forward to the eschatological temple, the body of Christ, the temple of the Holy Spirit, the eschatological community.

In the fourth century, when Jerome wanted to argue for the essential

86. Janet Martin Soskice, "The Ends of Man and the Future of God," in *The Blackwell Companion to Postmodern Theology*, ed. Graham Ward (Oxford: Blackwell, 2001), 77. The eschatological trajectory is less evident in John Paul II's work. When he does speak of the eschatological *imago* as *"communio personarum,"* he does not present this as an additional meaning but as the original vision presented in the Garden. John Paul II, *Man and Woman*, 400-401; homily 69:6-7.

87. Matthew Kuefler, *The Manly Eunuch: Masculinity, Gender Ambiguity, and Christian Ideology in Late Antiquity* (Chicago: University of Chicago Press, 2001), 36.

nature of sex differences, he employed the logic of the resurrection. He insisted, against Origen (his former theological mentor), that sex difference would remain at the resurrection.[88] Similarly, Augustine insisted that sex difference would remain, although it would no longer impair relations between the sexes.[89] The Scriptures speak also of differences of race and culture, nation and tribe in the eschatological community. Revelation 7:9 describes "a great multitude that no one could count, from every nation, tribe, people and language, standing before the throne and in front of the Lamb" (NIV). It can be argued that the differences enumerated in Revelation 7:9 are recognized as essential to the personal identity of individual Christians, even if they are also transformed in such a way that they no longer divide the people of God.

Following a similar logic, Susannah Cornwall has argued that there is no need for us to believe that intersexed bodies will be "healed" or "corrected" at the resurrection, that is, transformed into an ideal male or female body. She insists that new creation brings about not only the healing of individuals and their bodies, but also the healing of communities to the point that identities of difference that now divide and impair communal life will no longer be divisive or limiting.[90]

Cornwall finds helpful resources in the works of disability theologians, particularly those of John M. Hull and Nancy Eiesland. In her work *The Disabled God: Toward a Liberation Theology of Disability,* Eiesland suggests that bodily differences, which are now perceived as impairments, may persist even at the resurrection. She bases this belief on the fact that "Christ himself is portrayed in the New Testament as having a wounded body even after his resurrection."[91] Cornwall goes on to suggest,

> It is conceivable that other instances of physical impairment, and physical atypicality, will also persist in the human bodies of the general resurrection. . . . The resurrected Jesus, with his impaired hands and feet, is God's

88. Jerome, *To Pammachius against John of Jerusalem* 31, trans. W. H. Fremantle, Christian Classics Ethereal Library, http://www.ccel.org/ccel/schaff/npnf206.vi.viii.html.

89. Augustine, *Sermon on the Mount* 1.15.40, trans. William Findlay, revised and annotated by D. S. Schaff, Christian Classics Ethereal Library, http://www.ccel.org/ccel/schaff/npnf106.v.ii.xv.html?scrBook=Matt&scrCh=22&scrV=30#v.ii.xv-p7.1.

90. Susannah Cornwall, "The Kenosis of Unambiguous Sex in the Body of Christ: Intersex, Theology, and Existing 'for the Other,'" *Theology and Sexuality* 14, no. 2 (January 2008): 196.

91. Cornwall, "Kenosis," 195, quoting Nancy Eiesland, *The Disabled God: Toward a Liberation Theology of Disability* (Nashville: Abingdon, 1994), 99-100.

revelation of a new humanity — "underscoring the reality that full personhood is fully compatible with the experience of disability." The wounds of the impaired Jesus are not to be vilified, nor to be pitied; they are marks of life experience, and signposts to a new kind of life too.[92]

Conclusion

John Paul II may be correct to state that biological sex is constitutive of the human person. Stanley Grenz may be correct in insisting on the essential nature of sex for personal identity. But their proposals must be expanded through a reading of the larger scriptural narrative of which Genesis is only the beginning. Sex identity as male or female may be essential to personal identity. But there are more essentials than these two. Stanley Grenz's progressive account of the social *imago* lays the groundwork for including other essential differences in the eschatological community of God that is the fullness of the image. "Consequently, humankind created in the *imago Dei* is none other than the new humanity conformed to the *imago Christi,* and the *telos* toward which the Old Testament creation narrative points is the eschatological community of glorified saints."[93]

This eschatological community is comprised of more than males and females. It is "a great multitude that no one could count, from every nation, tribe, people and language" (Rev. 7:9 NIV). It includes eunuchs who have held fast to the covenant and foreigners who have bound themselves to the Lord (Isa. 56:3-7). It includes the intersexed who may be resurrected as intersexed and know, possibly more than females or males, the truth of Galatians 3:26-29: "You are all [male, female, and intersex] sons of God through faith in Christ Jesus, for all of you who were baptized into Christ have clothed yourselves with Christ. There is neither Jew nor Greek, slave nor free, male and female, for you are all one in Christ Jesus. If you belong to Christ, then you are Abraham's seed, and heirs according to the promise" (NIV).

Being "in Christ" does not make all believers male "sons" any more than the declaration of being "Abraham's seed" makes all believers Jewish — thus eliminating ethnic, cultural, and racial distinctions upheld in Revelation 7:9. Rather, all these distinctions, which now divide, are taken up into Christ, who is revealed as the true image of God, the seal of our shared humanity,

92. Cornwall, "Kenosis," 195.

93. Grenz, "The Social God," 91.

and the promise of its perfection. We will return to explore the connection between the *imago,* Christology, and eschatology in chapter 6, but first we must attend to the connections being made between sexuality and the image of God.

CHAPTER 5

Sexuality and the Image of God: The Relational Turn

The postmodern theological account of the social *imago* reflects both a return to the body and the philosophical turn to relationality. In the wake of Barth, many theologians insist that in order to speak of the human at all, one must speak of male and female in relation. Just as God exists as a community of divine love, so humans image God through the community of love. This social view of the image of God has been widely received because of the way in which it requires the full incorporation of women into theological constructions of the image. In the last chapter, I showed how this tradition could be improved so that the social *imago* creates space not only for women but also for intersex persons.

This chapter will explore the connections that have been made between the social view of the image of God and human sexuality. Both John Paul II and Stanley Grenz build upon the social *imago* in their discussions of human sexuality, but they emphasize the place of sexuality and heterosexual marriage to such an extent that they risk transforming the social *imago* into the spousal/sexual *imago*. Their proposals introduce a number of dangers. By sexualizing all human relations as well as the relationality between the members of the Trinity, they are inadvertently weakening the very sexual ethic they are working so hard to defend, undermining the goodness of celibacy and problematizing the sexuality of married persons. This Roman Catholic theologian and this evangelical theologian risk marginalizing not only intersexed persons but also anyone unable to enter into heterosexual marriage and married sexuality. Thankfully, many of these dangers can be avoided.

In this chapter I will lay out the ways Grenz and John Paul II shift the social view of the *imago* to the sexual/spousal *imago*. I will illuminate the dangers in their proposals and suggest ways in which these traditions can continue to uphold the goodness of sexuality and marriage without making these the primary lenses through which we read the social *imago*. I will argue that the social *imago* is the right place to begin speaking about the significance of human relationality and communities of love, provided these relations are not sexualized.

The Image of God and Spousal Sexuality in Stanley J. Grenz and John Paul II

Stanley Grenz: Social Imago *Becomes Sexual* Imago

Stanley Grenz acknowledges his debt to Karl Barth, upon whom he builds his vision of the social *imago,* but Grenz differs from Barth in his insistence that it is not simply relationships that constitute human personhood but *sexual* relations. Grenz fears that Barth's construal of the relationality between Adam and Eve as the primal I-Thou leads, however inadvertently, to a devaluation and final abandonment of human embodiment and sexuality.[1] This will not do. Grenz argues that the biblical narrative does not allow us to leave sexuality behind. According to Grenz, God did not simply make two humans to be in relationship, but a male and a female to be in sexual relationship. Rather than seeing the sexual dimension of the relationship of Adam and Eve as a feature of their marital relationship, Grenz sees even more significance in sexuality than that which draws humans into marriage. He returns to Genesis for an explanation. "Adam's cry of delight as the presence of the woman rescues him from his debilitating solitude . . . suggests . . . an even deeper aspect of human sexuality," that is, deeper than procreation.[2]

1. "[Barth] exchanges the dynamic of sexuality, understood as the sense of incompleteness that gives rise to the drive toward bonding, for the paradigm of I-Thou relationality. In spite of his concern to draw deeply from the creation of humankind as male and female, in the end Barth leaves human sexuality behind." Stanley J. Grenz, "The Social God and the Relational Self: Toward a Theology of the *Imago Dei* in the Postmodern Context," in *Personal Identity in Theological Perspective,* ed. Richard Lints, Michael S. Horton, and Mark R. Talbot (Grand Rapids: Eerdmans, 2006), 88. See also Grenz, *The Social God and the Relational Self: A Trinitarian Theology of the* Imago Dei (Louisville: Westminster John Knox, 2001), 300-301.

2. He states in a previous paragraph: "The account of the creation of man from the earth and the subsequent fashioning of the woman from the man indicates that sexuality cannot be limited to the roles of male and female in reproduction. Rather it goes to the core of human personhood. . . . Sexuality, therefore, includes the various dimensions of being in the world

> The narrative indicates that individual existence as an embodied creature entails a fundamental incompleteness or, stated positively, an innate yearning for completeness. This sensed incompleteness is symbolized by biological sex — that is, by existence as a particular person who is male or female. The incompleteness is related to existence as a sexual creature and therefore to human sexuality. Sexuality, in turn, is linked not only to the incompleteness each person senses as an embodied, sexual creature but also to the potential for wholeness in relationship to others that parallels this fundamental incompleteness. . . . Hence, sexuality is the dynamic that forms the basis of the uniquely human drive toward bonding.[3]

Two pages later he summarizes his position, saying: "The ultimate goal of sexuality, and hence of the impulse toward bonding, is participation in the fullness of community — namely, life together as the new humanity [the believing community, the bride of Christ] . . . in relationship with God and all creation. . . . Viewed in this light, sexuality, understood as the sense of incompleteness and the corresponding drive for wholeness, forms the dynamic that not only seeks human relationships but also motivates the quest for God."[4]

According to Grenz, it is sexuality that illustrates or symbolizes our "sense of incompleteness and the corresponding drive for wholeness." It is sexuality that leads humans out of isolation into community. It is sexuality that motivates bonding. It is the sense of sexual incompleteness that motivates the quest for God.

Rather than regarding the sexual relation of Adam and Eve as the first fruitful foundation for other kinds of relations, Grenz redefines sexuality as the basis for all relationality. "[S]exuality is the drive toward bonding in all its forms, even in the bonding that characterizes singleness." In other words, bonding in church community and in close friendships is also predicated upon a sexual sense of incompleteness.[5] Elsewhere in his *Sexual Ethics,* he insists, "the drive toward bonding . . . is always based on our existence as sexual beings — on our fundamental incompleteness, our inner restlessness, our desire for love and intimacy."[6]

---

and relating to it as persons embodied as male or female, together with the various internalized understandings of the meaning of maleness and femaleness." Grenz, *The Social God,* 277.

3. Grenz, *The Social God,* 277-78.

4. Grenz, *The Social God,* 280.

5. Stanley J. Grenz, *Sexual Ethics: An Evangelical Perspective* (Louisville: Westminster John Knox, 1990), 190, 191-92.

6. Grenz, *Sexual Ethics,* 193.

Despite his many helpful insights on the nature of human relationality, this is where Grenz's theological anthropology runs awry. Instead of defining incompleteness as a natural factor of human finitude, Grenz comes close to defining finitude as sexual. For Grenz, sexual incompleteness has become the symbol of any incompleteness. Whereas sexual need could have been presented as one of the many, varied ways in which humans need others, Grenz presents sexuality as the paradigm for all need, even human need for God. Thus, the fulfillment of that need — the love of friends, neighbors, spouse, children, community, church, and God — is viewed through the lens of the sexual.

The dangers of this misstep are not far behind. But, lest we suppose that this is simply one influential evangelical who has imbibed too much of the Freudian spirit of the age, let us consider the similarities we find in Pope John Paul II's *Theology of the Body.*

John Paul II: Social Imago *Becomes Spousal* Imago

In his *Theology of the Body,* John Paul II shows his affinity for the social view of the image of God drawing on a social view of the Trinity. "Man [the human] became the image of God not only through his own humanity, but also through the communion of persons, which man and woman form from the very beginning. . . . Man becomes an image of God not so much in the moment of solitude as in the moment of communion. He is, in fact, 'from the beginning' not only an image in which the solitude of one Person, who rules the world, mirrors itself, but also and essentially the image of an inscrutable divine communion of Persons."[7] According to John Paul II, "the authentic development of the image and likeness of God, in its trinitarian meaning, [is] its meaning precisely 'of communion.' "[8]

Similarly, in *The Trinity's Embrace,* he proclaimed,

> Today it is more necessary than ever to present the biblical anthropology of relationality, which helps us genuinely understand the human being's identity in his relationship to others, especially between man and woman. In the human person considered in his "relationality," we find a vestige of God's own mystery revealed in Christ as a substantial unity in

7. John Paul II, *Man and Woman He Created Them: A Theology of the Body,* trans. and ed. Michael Waldstein (Boston: Pauline Books and Media, 2006), 163; homily 9:3.

8. John Paul II, *Man and Woman,* 427, 77:2.

> the communion of three divine Persons. In light of this mystery it is easy to understand the statement of *Gaudium et Spes* that the human being, "who is the only creature on earth which God willed for itself, cannot fully find himself except through a sincere gift of himself (cf. Luke 17:33)." Interpersonal communion and meditation on the dignity and vocation of woman strengthens the concept of the human being based on communion (cf. *Mulieris Dignitatem*, 7).[9]

According to the late pope, humans image God as individuals but even more fully in community, and God has written our need for community on our very bodies — by creating humans as male or female. Masculinity and femininity lead us to marriage, which teaches us love and enables us to participate in a union with another that corresponds to the union of the three persons of the Trinity. This marital union, according to John Paul II, is specifically related to the sexual act. "The unity about which Gen. 2:24 speaks ('and the two will become one flesh') is without doubt the unity that is expressed and realized in the conjugal act. . . . The fact that they become 'one flesh' is a powerful bond established by the Creator through which they discover their own humanity, both in its original unity and in the duality of a mysterious reciprocal attraction."[10]

It is sexual union that realizes and expresses marital union, and sexual union enables the couple to "discover their own humanity." Elsewhere, the pope makes an even bolder statement, saying that sexual union in marriage fulfills the very meaning of human being and existence: "The human body, with its sex — its masculinity and femininity — . . . contains 'from the beginning' the 'spousal' attribute, that is *the power to express love: precisely that love in which the human person becomes a gift* and — through this gift — fulfills the very meaning of his being and existence."[11]

What is the meaning of human existence that masculinity and femininity teach? According to this pope, it is love. This is nothing new. Christians have always maintained that the center of the gospel is love; however, it is the nature of Christian love that is now being reconsidered. According to John Paul II, the nature of Christian love is "spousal," by which he means

9. John Paul II, "Commitment to Promoting Women's Dignity" (general audience, November 24, 1999), in *The Trinity's Embrace: God's Saving Plan, a Catechesis on Salvation History* (Boston: Pauline Books and Media, 2002), 289. Luke 17:33 reads "Whoever tries to keep his life will lose it, and whoever loses his life will preserve it" (NIV).

10. John Paul II, *Man and Woman*, 167; homily 10:2.

11. John Paul II, *Man and Woman*, 185-86; homily 15:1.

the giving of one's whole self, body and soul, to another, for the well-being of the other. Just as the Father gives himself to the Son and the Son to the Father in the eternal union of the Trinity, so spouses give themselves to one another in marriage, becoming "one flesh."

In his emphasis on the nature of spousal love as self-gift, John Paul II is developing the teaching of Saint John of the Cross (1542-1591), on whom the pope, then Karol Wojtyla, wrote his theological dissertation. Saint John of the Cross was a sixteenth-century mystic who meditated on the mysterious analogy between husband/wife and Christ/church found in Ephesians 5:21-32 and transposed the analogy from the church as bride, to the bride as individual soul. The saint remains famous for his *Spiritual Canticle,* a poetic meditation, paraphrase, and commentary on the Song of Songs in Spanish, in which the individual soul is the bride and Christ is the Bridegroom. In his writings, one finds spousal longings viewed through a spiritual lens and vice versa. According to Michael Waldstein, one of his English translators and editors, it is from Saint John of the Cross that John Paul II learned the "spousal theology of self-gift"[12] and developed the saint's "characteristic triangle of theses: love is a gift of self; spousal love between man and woman is the paradigmatic case of the gift of self; the origin and exemplar of the gift of self lies in the Trinity."[13] Waldstein is careful to point out that the pope never used spousal language of the Trinity. Nevertheless, his central text, John 17:10, is transposed from God the Father and God the Son onto marriage: "All that is mine is yours and yours is mine, and I am glorified in them."[14]

One of the difficulties in interpreting John Paul II is identifying what he means when he speaks of conjugal love. Whereas he uses the word "sex" (in the English translation) to speak of masculinity and femininity, he rarely uses the explicit language of sexuality or intercourse. Rather, he talks of "the conjugal act," "uniting so as to become one flesh," "reciprocal attraction," and "nuptial" or "spousal" love as ways to express sexual desire and action between husband and wife.[15] Unfortunately, one is left to decipher if sexual love is the focus of his intention or if he is speaking of a more general marital love in which sexuality is but one facet. It is not always clear from his writings if the image of God as *communio personarum* is related to marriage in general or married sexuality more specifically.

12. Waldstein, introduction to *Man and Woman,* 79.
13. Waldstein, introduction to *Man and Woman,* 78.
14. John Paul II, *Man and Woman,* 33.
15. John Paul II, *Man and Woman,* 167, homily 10:2; 185-86, homily 15:1.

William E. May, professor of moral theology at the John Paul II Institute for Studies on Marriage and Family at the Catholic University of America, has tried to untangle John Paul II's legacy on this point. He argues that marriage is established by "the act of irrevocable personal consent." The leaving of "father and mother" and cleaving to the spouse are acts of personal consent. According to May's interpretation of John Paul II, "[t]he act of matrimonial consent is an act of self-giving love." "A man and a woman become husband and wife when they 'give' themselves to one another in and through the act of irrevocable personal consent that makes them to be spouses. And in consenting to marriage, to being husband and wife, they consent to all that marriage implies and therefore they consent implicitly to the conjugal act, the act 'proper and exclusive to spouses.' In and through the conjugal act husband and wife literally become 'one flesh,' 'one body.' "[16]

May distinguishes between matrimonial consent and the conjugal act. The former creates marriage while the latter creates union. One finds a similar distinction in John of the Cross, who differentiated between marital consent and the conjugal act in his own writings when he separated "spiritual betrothal" (the act of promise) from "spiritual marriage" (the act of union).[17] According to John of the Cross,

> spiritual marriage is incomparably greater than the spiritual betrothal, for it is a total transformation in the Beloved, in which each surrenders the entire possession of self to the other with a certain consummation of the union of love. The soul thereby becomes divine, God through participation, insofar as is possible in this life. . . . Just as in the consummation of carnal marriage there are two in one flesh, as Sacred Scripture points out (Gen 2:24), so also when the spiritual marriage between God and the soul is consummated, there are two natures in one spirit and love.[18]

16. William E. May, "The Communion of Persons in Marriage and the Conjugal Act" (September 21, 2003), http://www.christendom-awake.org/pages/may/communionofpersons.htm.

17. Saint John of the Cross describes the nature of "spiritual betrothal" in his *Spiritual Canticle:* "There he gave me his breast / There he taught me a sweet and living knowledge / And I gave myself to him / keeping nothing back / there I promised to be his bride" (St. John of the Cross, *Spiritual Canticle,* stanza B27, quoted by Waldstein, introduction to *Man and Woman,* 29).

18. Saint John of the Cross, *Spiritual Canticle,* commentary on stanza 22, par. 3, quoted by Waldstein, introduction to *Man and Woman,* 31.

In John of the Cross's spiritual analogy, there is certainly a progression in which marital sexual union is valued above marital promise. It is difficult to know whether John Paul II reflects the same hierarchy. The language he uses could certainly be read as indicating this same elevation of sexual union, given that he speaks of the sexual union of spouses as "the conjugal act" rather than naming personal consent as the "conjugal act," that is, the act that creates marriage. But his avoidance of the common language of sexuality is better understood as an attempt to differentiate what he would consider base sexual activity from the ideal he proposes in his *Theology of the Body* — sexual activity that is attentive to the irreplaceable personal identity of the spouse, loving, self-giving, and open to the creation of life (i.e., unhindered by artificial contraception). The unloving use of the spouse's body for personal sexual satisfaction may be a sexual act, but it is not "the conjugal act." He also wants to distinguish married sexual union from unmarried sexual union. Thus, spouses may engage in sexual acts, but these can only be labeled "conjugal acts" if they meet the criteria defined above.[19]

In May's own account, when he takes the time to unpack the ways in which heterosexual marriage images God, he focuses on the sexual act — not the interpersonal dynamics of emotional union, joy, or common labor, but the ways in which male and female reproductive processes image the divine.

19. "The conjugal act can be considered merely in what St. Thomas called its 'natural' species, i.e., according to its natural, physical structure as a genital act between a man and a woman who simply 'happen' to be married. But as a *human, moral* act it is an act 'proper and exclusive to spouses,' one made possible by their marital union. As a moral, human act it is 'specified,' not by its physical structure, but by its 'object,' that is, precisely what the spouses are choosing to do in giving themselves to one another and receiving one another *as spouses*. The conjugal act, as a human, moral act, is an act that participates in the *communion of the persons who are husband and wife*, open to the 'goods' or 'blessings' of marriage. Non-married people can engage in *genital* sex because they have genital organs, but they are not capable of engaging in the conjugal act precisely because they are not married. The unmarried male cannot 'give himself in a receiving way' to the woman nor can she 'receive him in a giving way' precisely because they have failed to 'give' and 'receive' each other in and through an act of marital consent, an act of irrevocably giving and receiving each other. Their act of genital union does not and cannot, therefore, unite two irreplaceable and nonsubstitutable persons; it merely *joins* two *individuals* who are in principle replaceable, substitutable, disposable. Their act, which 'mimics' the conjugal act, is, as Pope John Paul II has correctly said, 'a lie.'" May, "The Communion of Persons in Marriage and the Conjugal Act," citing Pope John Paul II, Apostolic Exhortation on the Role of the Christian Family in the Modern World *(Familiaris Consortio)* (November 22, 1981), no. 11.

> [Male sperm] symbolizes the superabundance and differentiation of being, . . . whereas the woman in her way symbolizes the unity of being insofar as ordinarily she produces only one ovum; she symbolizes what can be called the interiority and sameness of being.
>
> . . . As we have seen, man and woman are two different and complementary ways of being the image of God. He is both the superabundant Giver of good gifts and the One who is always with us and for us, and who greatly longs to welcome us and to give our hearts refreshment and peace.
>
> . . . [T]he man, in imaging God, is called above all to bear witness to his transcendence and superabundant goodness, his Glory as the "Well-spring of the Joy of Living," while the woman, in her imaging of God, is called upon to bear witness to his immanence, his "interiority" or with-inness, his Glory as the "Ocean Depth of Happy Rest."[20]

We see in the above that it is spousal sexuality, "the conjugal act," that images God in the world in discrete masculine and feminine forms. Thus does the Roman Catholic tradition insist that only marital sexuality that is open to new life can aptly be described as "conjugal," and that the conjugal act "expresses and actualizes in a fitting way the *communion of persons*" that is the image of God.[21]

Roman Catholic theologian David Matzko McCarthy believes that May is interpreting John Paul II's legacy accurately and worries about the implications of this shift in the tradition. He fears that this way of understanding human personhood and the image of God is too influenced by "modern trends [which highlight] sex and sexual desire as ideal expressions of love." In this new Catholic theology, "Sex is considered representative of conjugal love, and conjugal intercourse is considered a good and sacramental experience. Through a sexual relationship, we discover our humanity in intimate communion with each other as 'Other,' and, in the process, encounter God's grace."[22]

McCarthy believes these theologians are trying to make up for lost time, swinging the pendulum back to correct older Roman Catholic views on marriage that saw little to no value in marital sexuality beyond procreation. "In the mid-twentieth century, theological personalism emerged, in Catholic

20. May, "The Communion of Persons in Marriage and the Conjugal Act."

21. May, "The Communion of Persons in Marriage and the Conjugal Act."

22. David Matzko McCarthy, *Sex and Love in the Home: A Theology of the Household*, 2nd ed. (London: SCM, 2004), 24.

circles, as a challenge to instrumental and juridical understandings of marriage. Personalism offered a challenge to the idea that marriage is not good in itself but produces only external goods like children and social stability."[23] The corrective impulse is needed, but the new personalist account elevates sexuality to such an extent that sexual love is now seen as the paradigm for all Christian love.

Both evangelical and Roman Catholic traditions are connecting the image of God to married sexuality — male and female in heterosexual union. For both traditions heterosexual marital unions reflect Trinitarian love. To be fair, there is much in these proposals we should affirm. The assertion that the meaning of human existence is love and that this love is grounded in God who is a community of love is central to the Christian faith. The problem comes when human love, and the divine love after which it has become an image, is labeled sexual. But this is exactly what John Paul II and Stanley Grenz have done. John Paul II has made spousal/sexual love the paradigmatic form of Christian love while Grenz has presented sexuality as the basis for all relationality. The social *imago* is shifting to become the spousal/sexual *imago*. These shifts have serious consequences.

Uncovering Hidden Dangers

One of the first dangers inherent in these shifts is the sexualization of Trinitarian love, which can lead to other intended and unintended theological consequences. It weakens arguments for monogamy, undermines the goodness of celibacy, and adds the weight of spiritual failure to sexual difficulties.

Sexualizing Trinitarian Love

Whereas John Paul II is careful not to speak of divine love as sexual or spousal, his successor, Pope Benedict XVI, comes closer to the mark when he describes divine love not only as *agape* but also as *eros*. Students of philosophy are well versed in these distinct forms of love, and some will be quick to note that *eros* can transcend bodily, sexual love, rising to the Platonic love of eternal goods, as Diotima taught Socrates so long ago.[24] At the same time,

23. McCarthy, *Sex and Love*, 4-5.

24. Plato, *Symposium* 201c-212a.

theologians know that *eros* and *agape* have been pitted against one another in the history of Christianity.[25] In *Deus Caritas Est,* Benedict XVI defended the claim that while God's love is "totally *agape,*" it is not inappropriate to speak of God's love as *eros.*[26] Fully aware that the biblical authors (and Septuagint translators) never speak of love as *eros,* Benedict defends it on the basis of Pseudo-Dionysius[27] and prophetic imagery. "The Prophets, particularly Hosea and Ezekiel, described God's passion for his people using boldly erotic images. God's relationship with Israel is described using the metaphors of betrothal and marriage; idolatry is thus adultery and prostitution."[28] *Eros* is thus connected to the erotic passions of marriage and sexual infidelity.

The pope seems concerned that divine love without the passion associated with *eros* will not be recognized as love. "God is the absolute and ultimate source of all being; but this universal principle of creation — the *Logos,* primordial reason — is at the same time a lover with all the passion of a true love. *Eros* is thus supremely ennobled, yet at the same time it is so purified as to become one with *agape.*"[29] Grenz also worries that without "the dimensions of love expressed in *philia* [friendship], *storgē* [familial affection/compassion], and to some extent even *eros,* our conception of God who is *agapē* can easily degenerate into a distant, austere, 'Stoic,' deity."[30] Like Benedict XVI, he sees marital metaphors as justification for speaking of God's love through the lens of *eros* — God's marriage to the ancient Israelites and Christ's marriage to the church.[31] And, like Benedict XVI, Grenz wants to defend divine passion.

As I noted above, the relationship of *eros* to sexuality is a difficult one. Depending on their concerns, authors employ varying definitions of *eros* to suit their needs. Benedict XVI emphasizes *eros* as passion but includes the

25. *Eros* has been understood as "ascending" love while *agape* is presented as "descending" love. Early in *Deus Caritas Est,* Benedict XVI's first encyclical, the pope differentiates between various presentations of *eros,* insisting that *eros,* when not debased, rises "in ecstasy" toward the Divine, leading us beyond ourselves. Benedict XVI, *Deus Caritas Est,* 1.5; 1.7. See also the classic contrast in Anders Nygren, *Agape and Eros,* trans. A. G. Hebert (London: SPCK, 1932).

26. Benedict XVI, *Deus Caritas Est,* 1.9; also 1.10.

27. Benedict XVI, *Deus Caritas Est,* 1.7 n. 7.

28. Benedict XVI, *Deus Caritas Est,* 1.9.

29. Benedict XVI, *Deus Caritas Est,* 1.10.

30. Stanley J. Grenz, *The Moral Quest: Foundations of Christian Ethics* (Downers Grove, Ill.: InterVarsity, 1997), 290.

31. Grenz, *The Social God,* 319.

"erotic" imagery of the Prophets. Grenz narrows the definition further, arguing that *eros* within the Godhead should be understood as "desire for communion with the beloved."[32] When he considers human relations, Grenz, like others, draws a distinction between *venus* — "the drive to propagate the species through procreation" — and *eros* — "the communion which the sex act nurtures between sex partners, which sets humans above the world of nature."[33]

> "Sexual desire" refers to the need we all have to experience wholeness and intimacy through relationships with others. It relates to the dimension often called *eros,* the human longing to possess and be possessed by the object of one's desire. Understood in this way, *eros* ought not be limited to genital sexual acts, but encompasses a broad range of human actions and desires, and it participates even in the religious dimension of life in the form of the desire to know and be known by God. For many people, the desire for sex, the longing to express one's sexuality through genital acts *(venus),* is psychologically inseparable from sexual desire. Nevertheless, for the development of true sexual maturity, a person must come to terms with the difference between these two dimensions and learn to separate them both in one's own psychological state and in overt action.[34]

Given these distinctions, Grenz is willing to include *eros* as present within the immanent Trinity and does not shy away from calling God "sexual." According to Grenz, God is sexual but not because God engages in genital sexual relations with Godself or with humans — these were ways in which the Hebrew God was distinguished from other gods of the ancient Near East. Nevertheless, Grenz is willing to speak of God as sexual for two reasons: (1) because God as Trinity is relational, and (2) because God has employed gendered language (both masculine and feminine) to reveal Godself in the Scriptures.[35]

Just as John Paul II's work is difficult to interpret because he avoids using the explicit language of sexuality, Grenz's work poses difficulties for the opposite reason. Grenz conflates the categories of sex differentiation,

32. Grenz, *The Social God,* 320.

33. Grenz, *Sexual Ethics,* 19.

34. Grenz, *Sexual Ethics,* 20-21.

35. Stanley J. Grenz, "Is God Sexual? Human Embodiment and the Christian Conception of God," in *This Is My Name Forever: The Trinity and Gender Language for God,* ed. Alvin F. Kimel Jr. (Downers Grove, Ill.: InterVarsity, 2001), 190-212.

gender, and sexual desire/acts by speaking of them all as "sexuality." He insists that sexuality pervades every human relationship because every human relationship happens between persons who have sexed bodies — either male or female. Thus, all human relations are sexual. Although God does not have a body, Grenz still insists that God is sexual because God is relational and willing to employ gendered language.

Despite his conflation of the language of sexuality with relationality, bonding, sex, gender, and the erotic, Grenz does draw a distinction by differentiating between genital sexuality and what he has called "social sexuality." He uses the term "social sexuality" to describe any relationship between humans because it recognizes that all relationships are between persons with embodied biological sex, gendered perspectives, and gendered behaviors. All human relations are sexual; some are genitally-sexual while others are merely socially-sexual. Thus, within his system of thought, a nursing mother's relationship to her child is "sexual" because it is a relationship rooted in the sexed body and a form of intimate bonding.[36]

Grenz teaches that genital sexuality is to be reserved for marriage while social sexuality extends to all human interactions in this life and the life to come. Commenting on Jesus' teaching in Matthew 22:30 ("At the resurrection people will neither marry nor be given in marriage; they will be like the angels in heaven" [NIV]), Grenz writes,

> Although genital sexual activity has no place in the eschatological reign of God, sexuality will be present in various forms.
>
> Sensuality, for example, will remain . . . a heightened appreciation for sensual joy as is indicated by the use of sensuous imagery in the biblical vision of the reign of God. Sexuality is present in the form of the aesthetic sense, as is evidenced by the biblical vision of the beauty of the place of God's eschatological reign. But of highest importance, sexuality remains present in the form of mutuality. According to the biblical vision, the eschatological community is a bonded society. . . . It is a society of transformed yet embodied human beings, the perfect community of male and female, in which all experience the fullness of interpersonal relationships.[37]

36. Lisa Graham McMinn, whose work builds on Grenz's foundation and is endorsed by Grenz himself, draws out the "sexuality" of pregnancy, childbirth, breast-feeding, and parenting. Lisa Graham McMinn, *Sexuality and Holy Longing: Embracing Intimacy in a Broken World* (San Francisco: Jossey-Bass, 2004).

37. Grenz, *Sexual Ethics,* 250-51.

For Grenz, sensuality, aesthetics, and mutuality are all aspects of sexuality. Sexuality is the broad category under which sensuality, relations, and aesthetics fall as subsets.

Grenz's conflation of sex, gender, and sexuality, and his insistence that relationality arises from sexuality, leaves him no choice but to conclude that God is sexual, even if he wants to limit the discussion to social rather than genital sexuality — an *eros* that does not arise from bodily need or incompleteness within God but from a desire for communion with the beloved.[38] Nevertheless, despite his attempt to draw careful boundaries, this language opens the door to conclusions to which Grenz would object.

Changing Christian Sexual Ethics

While Grenz wants to ground heterosexual marriage in the Trinity and limits genital sexuality to this side of the eschaton,[39] other theologians do not see the need for such limitations. Certain theologians are expanding the vision of sexuality in the eschaton, and others are bringing this new heaven to earth.

38. "Any attempt to link God with *eros* must avoid implying some kind of divine desire for creation borne from a supposed insufficiency within God. Yet Christian thinkers readily admit the role of 'desire' not just in human sexual relations but even in religious devotion. . . . Furthermore, . . . one of the most powerful theological motifs within the biblical narrative draws metaphorically from marital love. The Old Testament prophets illuminated God's relationship to Israel through a drama depicting the betrothal of Israel to Yahweh (Jer. 2:2; Isa. 62:5), Israel's subsequent adultery (Jer. 3:8; cf. Hos. 2:2, 4-5), and God's steadfast faithfulness with its promise of a future restoration (e.g., Hos. 2:23). New Testament writers such as Paul (Rom 9:25) and Peter (1 Pet. 2:9-10) applied this dramatic motif of marital love to Christ's relationship to the church. Through his self-sacrificial life and death, Christ, the loving bridegroom (Mark 2:19; John 3:29; Rev. 21:9), demonstrated his love for the church (Eph. 5:32)." Grenz, *The Social God,* 319.

39. "Sexuality, however, simply cannot be left behind. Marriage and genital sexual expression are limited to this penultimate age, of course. But sexuality is not. To leave sexuality behind is to undercut the significance of the resurrection. This central Christian doctrine indicates that sexuality is not eradicated en route to eternity. Instead, after the manner of the risen Jesus, humans participate in the transforming event of resurrection as the embodied persons — male or female — they are. Above all, however, *to relegate sexuality to the temporal is to undermine the basis for community in eternity.* Even though genital sexual expression is left behind, the dynamic of bonding continues to be operative beyond the eschatological culmination, for this dynamic is at work in constituting humans as the community of the new humanity within the new creation in relationship with the triune God." Grenz, "The Social God," 95.

Thomas Breidenthal, an Episcopal bishop, writes, "I have no doubt that in heaven we will enjoy a measure of delight and fulfillment in every other praiser of God which we should not shrink from calling sexual delight and sexual fulfillment."[40] Whereas Breidenthal does not explain exactly how sexuality will continue in heaven, Roman Catholic priest Ronald Rolheiser is more specific. Commenting on Jesus' statement in Matthew 22:30 (that there would be no marriage in heaven), Rolheiser insists that this does not mean there will be no genital sexuality. "What Jesus is saying is not that we will be celibate in heaven, but rather that, in heaven, all will be married to all. In heaven, unlike life here on earth where that is not possible, our sexuality will finally be able to embrace everyone. In heaven, everyone will make love to everyone else and, already now, we hunger for that within every cell of our being. Sexually our hungers are very wide. We are built to ultimately embrace the universe and everything in it."[41] Rolheiser anticipates communal genital sexuality in heaven while attempting to uphold monogamous heterosexual ethics this side of the eschaton. Other theologians see the need for no such distinctions.

Marilyn McCord Adams, Episcopal priest and philosopher, argues that Trinitarian relations give us the theological foundation not only for heterosexual marriage but also for a human *ménage à trois,* for incest, and for homosexual unions. She writes, "Whether or not, in which personal dimensions and to what extent, human *ménage à trois* can be an icon of godly love, depends in part on our varying assessments of human capacity for intimacy and functional household organization."[42] She notes the endurance of polygamy among African households even after their conversion to Christianity and identifies Jacob, Leah, and Rachel as a possible biblical example of holy marriage of three.[43] Adams explores incest and concludes that the problem with incest in human relations is inequality — the imposition on a minor who is unable to grant consent. But, given the equality and coeternality of Father and Son, incest in the Trinity does not suffer from the same weakness.[44] Like

40. Thomas Breidenthal, "Sanctifying Nearness," in *Theology and Sexuality: Classic and Contemporary Readings,* ed. Eugene F. Rogers Jr. (London: Blackwell, 2002), 352.

41. Ronald Rolheiser, *The Holy Longing: A Search for a Christian Spirituality* (New York: Doubleday, 1999), 206.

42. Marilyn McCord Adams, "Trinitarian Friendship: Same-Gender Models of Godly Love in Richard of St. Victor and Aelred of Rievaulx," in *Theology and Sexuality,* 335.

43. Adams, "Trinitarian Friendship," 335. More attention to the actual marriage of Jacob to Rachel and Leah should provide ample arguments against (rather than for) polygamy.

44. Adams, "Trinitarian Friendship," 335.

many other theologians, she makes the connection between Trinitarian love and homosexual love following the traditional gendered names for the first and second person of the Trinity.

Kathy Rudy takes the argument even further when she finds parallels between Christian communion and the communal sex that takes place in some gay bars.

> Each sexual encounter after that [in a bathroom or bar] shores up his membership in the community he finds there; and his participation and contribution subsequently makes the community he finds stronger for others. His identity begins to be defined by the people he meets in those spaces. Although he may not know the names of each of his sex partners, each encounter resignifies his belonging. And although no two members of the community make steadfast promises to any one person in the community, each in his own way promises himself as part of this world. Intimacy and faithfulness in sex are played out on the community rather than individual level.[45]

Stretching the conservative theology of Hans Urs von Balthasar, who depicts each person of the Trinity as both active (masculine) and receptive (feminine) in relation to the others,[46] queer theologians extend the logic. Gavin D'Costa thus argues that "metaphorically speaking, queer relationships are at the ontological heart of the Trinity."[47] Patrick Cheng interprets:

45. Kathy Rudy, "Where Two or More Are Gathered: Using Gay Communities as a Model for Christian Sexual Ethics," *Theology and Sexuality* 2 (March 1996): 89-90, cited in Elizabeth Stuart et al., *Religion Is a Queer Thing: A Guide to the Christian Faith for Lesbian, Gay, Bisexual, and Transgendered People* (London and Washington, D.C.: Cassell, 1997), 49.

46. "In Trinitarian terms, of course, the Father, who begets him, who is without origin appears primarily as (super-) masculine; the Son, in consenting, appears as (super-) feminine, but in the act (together with the Father) of breathing forth the Spirit, he is (super-) masculine. As for the Spirit, he is (super-) feminine. There is even something (super-) feminine about the Father too, since, as we have shown, in the action of begetting and breathing forth he allows himself to be determined by the Persons who thus proceed from him; however, this does not affect his primacy in the order of the Trinity." Hans Urs von Balthasar, *Theodramatik,* 4:91, quoted in Robert A. Pesarchick, *The Trinitarian Foundation of Human Sexuality as Revealed by Christ according to Hans Urs Von Balthasar: The Revelatory Significance of the Male Christ and the Male Ministerial Priesthood* (Rome: Editrice Pontificia Universita Gregoriana, 2000), 176.

47. Patrick S. Cheng, *Radical Love: An Introduction to Queer Theology* (New York: Seabury Books, 2011), 57, citing Gavin D'Costa, "Queer Trinity," in *Queer Theology: Rethinking the Western Body,* ed. Gerard Loughlin (Malden, Mass.: Blackwell, 2007), 272-79.

"D'Costa's view of the Trinity has some very radical implications. First, both transgender and 'switch' (that is, 'versatile' or both 'top' and 'bottom') relationships are at the very heart of the Trinity. That is, each person in the divine three-way is both male and female as well as top and bottom. Thus, queer relationships are divinely sanctioned as long as such relationships also represent an overflowing love to the wider community."[48]

Cheng notes other queer theologians who have compared the Trinity to "an orgy" and describes how Marcella Althaus-Reid is dissatisfied even with "restricted polyfidelity," upon which some have based a polyamorous ethic. According to Althaus-Reid, "each person of the Trinity has her/her [*sic*] own closet of lovers and 'forbidden desires' (for example, Jesus' relationships with Mary Magdalene and Lazarus), which in turn results in the death of the 'illusion of limited relationships.'"[49]

A number of contemporary theologians, both conservative and liberal, have concluded that if the ground of all being is Trinitarian love and if Trinitarian love can be understood as sexual, then genital sexual activity gives humans privileged experience of God. While conservative theologians limit such divine experience to monogamous heterosexual couples,[50] others argue that this access to the divine is possible apart from Christian marriage, regardless of who may be the lovers. Carter Heyward summarizes the conclusions of many when she writes, "The erotic is our most fully embodied experience of the love of God. As such, it is the source of our capacity for transcendence, the 'crossing over' among ourselves, making connections between ourselves in relation. The erotic is the divine Spirit's yearning, through our bodyselves, toward mutually empowering relation, which is our most fully embodied experience of God as love. Regardless of who may be the lovers, the root of the love is sacred movement between and among us."[51] James Nelson and Sandra Longfellow draw a similar conclusion: "To

48. Cheng, *Radical Love,* 56.

49. Cheng, *Radical Love,* 58-59, citing Marcella Althaus-Reid, *The Queer God* (London: Routledge, 2004), 57-59.

50. Gary Thomas, *Sacred Marriage: What If God Designed Marriage to Make Us Holy More Than to Make Us Happy* (Grand Rapids: Zondervan, 2000), 206, cited in Christine A. Colón and Bonnie E. Field, *Singled Out: Why Celibacy Must Be Reinvented in Today's Church* (Grand Rapids: Brazos, 2009), 128.

51. Stuart et al., *Religion Is a Queer Thing,* 49, quoting Carter Heyward, *Touching Our Strength: The Erotic as Power and the Love of God* (New York: Harper and Row, 1989). In Carter's (pseudonymous) conversation with her coauthors of *God's Fierce Whimsy,* we find similar assertions: "Sexual pleasure, or orgasm, is really about *ecstasy* — at least that's what it is for me. And ecstasy is a central religious theme, even a mark of revelation. It's led me to

the degree that it is free from the distortions of unjust and abusive power relations, we experience our sexuality as the basic eros of our humanness that urges, invites, and lures us out of our loneliness into intimate communication and communion with God and the world. . . . Sexuality, in sum, is the physiological and emotional grounding of our capacities to love."[52]

The work of Nelson and Longfellow has influenced some of Grenz's own theology of sexuality. He employs their definition of sexuality as he works toward his own. "As James Nelson and Sandra Longfellow declare, 'The word "sexuality" itself comes from the Latin *sexus,* probably akin to the Latin *secare,* meaning to cut or divide — suggesting incompleteness seeking wholeness and connection that reaches through and beyond our differences and divisions.' Hence, sexuality is the dynamic that forms the basis of the uniquely human drive toward bonding."[53]

Although Grenz disagrees with Nelson, Longfellow, Heyward, and others over how genital sexuality may be expressed, their theological foundation remains the same. When the social becomes the sexual, when sexuality is seen as the basis for all relations — the basic form of bonding, the ground of all human loves — it becomes quite difficult to argue for the restriction of sexual activity to marriage. When God's relationality is sexualized, it can be used as justification for sexualities of many stripes.

Undermining the Goodness of Celibacy: Reconsidering Matthew 19:12

Another danger lurking in the connection between Trinitarian love and human sexuality (and one that returns us to theological reflection on intersex) is the risk of undermining the goodness of celibacy — whether willed celibacy as a religious vocation, or unwilled celibacy as a disappointment and lifelong struggle for virtue outside the bonds of marriage, or because

---

suspect that controlling women's sexuality is also about controlling alternative sources of religious knowledge. . . . I am convinced that, to the extent that we are afraid of our sexual being, we're afraid of God, because what is God if not the wellspring of our creativity, our relationality, our ecstasy, our capacity to touch and be touched at the core of our being?" Katie G. Cannon et al., *God's Fierce Whimsy: Christian Feminism and Theological Education* (New York: Pilgrim Press, 1985), 194-95.

52. James B. Nelson and Sandra P. Longfellow, eds., *Sexuality and the Sacred: Sources for Theological Reflection* (Louisville: Westminster John Knox, 1994), xiv.

53. Grenz, *The Social God,* 278, citing Nelson and Longfellow, *Sexuality and the Sacred,* xiv.

of the death of a spouse or the sexual unavailability of a spouse. If sexuality (married or unmarried) is presented as the truest way in which humans image divine love, if sexual union gives humans a privileged experience of Trinitarian union, then it becomes difficult to insist on celibacy as an equally valuable Christian lifestyle.[54]

John Paul II tries to argue against the above conclusion by insisting that the celibate life is not a rejection of the "spousal meaning of the body" but its consummation. Still, the late pope sees only two paths for human fulfillment thus defined: heterosexual marriage (the total gift of self to another human) or spiritual marriage (religious celibacy, the gift of self "totally to Christ").[55] Both paths are viewed through the spousal/sexual lens, a lens the late pope attempts to ground in his interpretation of Matthew 19:11-12, Jesus' words about eunuchs.[56]

According to John Paul II, "This term [eunuch] refers to the physical defects that make the procreative power of marriage impossible."[57] Thus, he argues that the third type of eunuch symbolizes those who reject marriage

54. Colón and Field, *Singled Out,* 126-32.

55. "[M]an is able to choose the personal gift of self to another person in the conjugal covenant, in which they become 'one flesh,' and he is also able to renounce freely such a gift of self to another person, in order that by choosing continence 'for the kingdom of heaven' he may give himself totally to Christ." John Paul II, *Man and Woman,* 439; homily 80:6. Unfortunately, John Paul II neglects the many Christians who do not fall into the camps of married and celibate religious. His neglect of this third category only adds theological insult to personal frustration — the frustration many unmarried lay Christians experience at being treated like "second-class citizens" in the church. Colón and Field want to add another type of celibacy to that typically recognized by Christian theologians, a celibacy that bridges those actively waiting for a spouse and those committed to a lifetime of Christian singleness for service to God. This celibacy is "being called by God to live chaste lives as strong, single Christians for as long as he desires us to fulfill this role." Colón and Field, *Singled Out,* 206, 209.

56. "But [Jesus] said to them, 'Not all men can accept this statement, but only those to whom it has been given. For there are eunuchs who were born that way from their mother's womb; and there are eunuchs who were made eunuchs by men; and there are also eunuchs who made themselves eunuchs for the sake of the kingdom of heaven. He who is able to accept this, let him accept it' " (NASB). John Paul II comments on this passage, saying: "Christ's words (Mt. 19:11-12) begin with the whole realism of man's situation and with the same realism they *lead* him out, toward the call in which, in a new way, though he remains by his nature a 'dual' being (that is, directed as a man toward woman, and as a woman toward man), he is able to discover in this solitude of his, which never ceases to be a personal dimension of everyone's dual nature, a new and even *fuller form of intersubjective communion with others.*" John Paul II, *Man and Woman,* 426-27; homily 77:2.

57. John Paul II, *Man and Woman,* 416; homily 74:1.

in favor of celibacy for the kingdom. At the same time, he insists that the choice of continence arises from the awareness of the spousal meaning of the body as masculine or feminine.[58] Yet, given our exploration of eunuchs in the ancient world and our current knowledge of intersex, it seems that these phenomena may actually turn the late pope's argument on its head. He does not consider the possibility that some eunuchs from birth may be quite capable of coitus and procreation but may not be able to identify as either masculine or feminine.[59]

At the beginning of this passage (Matt. 19:4-5), Jesus does indeed connect male and female with marriage. He responds to the Pharisees' question about divorce by asking them, "Have you not read that the one who made them at the beginning 'made them male and female,' and said, 'For this reason a man shall leave his father and mother and be joined to his wife, and the two shall become one flesh'?" (NRSV). Jesus does appear to affirm the spousal meaning of masculinity and femininity — that humans enter into marriage because of their differentiation as male and female. On the other hand, Jesus speaks of eunuchs to affirm another way of life. When his disciples suggest that it is better not to marry than to be denied the possibility of divorce, Jesus responds by saying, "Not everyone can accept this teaching, but only those to whom it is given. For there are eunuchs who have been so from birth, and there are eunuchs who have been made eunuchs by others, and there are eunuchs who have made themselves eunuchs for the sake of the kingdom of heaven. Let anyone accept this who can" (Matt. 19:11-12 NRSV).

It is imperative to note that Jesus does not base the choice of religious celibacy on the "spousal meaning of the body" as masculine or feminine. Rather, he lists several reasons for not marrying. First, one may turn away from marriage because of a physical condition that would make marriage difficult or impossible. This condition may be natural, "from birth," or a result of violence accomplished by another. On the other hand, one may choose to renounce marriage by making oneself a eunuch — literally (through cas-

58. "In light of the words of Christ, we must admit that this second kind of choice, namely, continence for the kingdom of God, is made also in relation to the masculinity and femininity proper to the person who makes this choice; it is made on the basis of the full consciousness of the spousal meaning, which masculinity and femininity contain in themselves." John Paul II, *Man and Woman,* 440; homily 80:7.

59. Recall from chapter 1 the testimony of D. Cameron: Klinefelter's syndrome caused him to feel "caught between the sexes." In Alice Domurat Dreger, ed., *Intersex in the Age of Ethics* (Hagerstown, Md.: University Publishing Group, 1999), 90-96.

tration) or metaphorically (through the rejection of marriage and gendered expectations) — for "the sake of the kingdom of heaven."

Employing John Paul II's theological lenses and a renewed appreciation of the realities of eunuchs in the ancient world suggests that Matthew 19:12 may teach the very opposite of what the late pope asserted — that some bodies do *not* carry a spousal meaning. If Jesus does read sexed bodies the way John Paul II suggests, then his teaching indicates that the bodies of naturally born and castrated eunuchs may actually point away from marriage toward celibacy.[60]

Even so, does this interpretation necessarily lead to an insistence that every eunuch must remain unmarried while every noneunuch must marry? I do not believe so. Following the logic of the passage, one could argue that each can learn from the other. Jesus states that women and men can learn from eunuchs. Men (and presumably women) may choose to "cut off" their masculinity (or femininity) in order to make themselves "eunuchs for the kingdom of heaven." Some early Christian men literally castrated themselves, and others transgressed gendered hairstyles, dress, or comportment, because they recognized that the language of the eunuch suggested more than a simple renunciation of marriage; it included a renunciation of gender identity and privilege in the ancient world. The choice not to marry was a choice not to fulfill the requirements of manhood in ancient Jewish and Greco-Roman culture or to lay claim to the privileges of masculinity in a patriarchal culture. Similarly, some early Christian women rejected not only marriage but also feminine identity. They removed their veils, the symbol of their femininity in its shame and subordination to all things masculine. They saw themselves as relinquishing their feminine identity for a new identity "in Christ."[61]

60. The context of Matt. 19:1-12 seems to indicate that Jesus viewed the eunuch as one who would not marry even though we have records of non-Jewish eunuchs marrying (e.g., Nero's marriage to Sporus). Questions remain as to the modern-day application of the passage. Certainly most Protestant churches would not prohibit a castrated male (or one who had a vasectomy — another condition that would have fallen under the title of eunuch in the ancient world) from marrying a woman. Roman Catholic canon law allows infertile persons to marry, but not those with "antecedent and perpetual impotence" (*Code of Canon Law* [1983], Can. 1084, 1; cited in Todd A. Salzman and Michael G. Lawler, *The Sexual Person: Toward a Renewed Catholic Anthropology* [Washington, D.C.: Georgetown University Press, 2008], 141-42. Lawler and Salzman critique this privileging of "heterogenital complementarity" at the expense of other marital complementarities [138-61]). Within the Roman Catholic scheme, various intersex conditions would fall inside or outside of these categories such that each would need to be evaluated in turn.

61. See chap. 2.

Applying a similar hermeneutic, one could argue that just as men and women can follow Jesus' teachings by making themselves eunuchs so as not to marry, it is possible that eunuchs, or intersex persons, could make themselves like men or women in order to enter into marriage. Thus an intersex man could choose to identify as a male while an intersex woman could choose to identify as a female. Medical intervention would not be necessary but up to the choice of the individual. Such were the laws regarding the marriage of hermaphrodites in the early modern period in many parts of Europe before the medicalization of intersex.[62]

At the same time, it should be obvious by now that intersex illustrates one of the difficulties facing religious ethicists, denominational governing bodies, and marriage tribunals. It also demonstrates the challenge of applying legislation such as the recently repealed Defense of Marriage Act (DOMA) — permitting marriage only between a man and a woman — in the public sector. While for most people identification as male or female is fairly uncomplicated, intersex shows that in a number of cases determining the sex of an individual is not a straightforward process. Julie Greenberg has explored these challenges at length[63] and summarizes the difficulty of reading intersex through current marital legislation. Greenberg explains that the law is "a system of regulations which depends upon precise definitions; [the law] is obliged to classify its material into exclusive categories; it is, therefore, a binary system designed to produce conclusions of the *yes* or *no* type. Biological phenomena, however, cannot be reduced to exclusive categories so that medicine often cannot give Yes or No answers. . . . [P]eople are not either tall or short, they are taller or shorter or about average. This fundamental conflict lies at the root of all relations between medicine and law."[64]

Intersex persons who fall along a spectrum of more masculine or more feminine do not fit neatly into this binary framework. Greenberg argues that such persons should have the right to identify themselves as male, female, or intersex and marry according to the sex/gender identity they believe best

62. Anne Fausto-Sterling, *Sexing the Body: Gender Politics and the Construction of Sexuality* (New York: Basic Books, 2000), 36.

63. Julie A. Greenberg, "Defining Male and Female: Intersexuality and the Collision between Law and Biology," *Arizona Law Review* 41, no. 2 (1999): 265-328; and more recently, *Intersexuality and the Law: Why Sex Matters* (New York: New York University Press, 2012).

64. Greenberg, "Defining Male and Female," 293, citing the Hon. Sir Roger Ormrod, the judge who decided *Corbett v. Corbett*, 2 All E.R. 33 (1970), the case cited most often for defining male and female for the purposes of marriage.

fits their sense of self.[65] The challenge of course comes when one requires an individual to marry someone of the "opposite sex." What is the "other sex" for an intersex woman with XY chromosomes and testes? Given that most persons with complete androgen insensitivity syndrome identify as women, one could argue that marriage to someone of the opposite gender should be permitted, but many conservatives fear such a move because it opens the door not only to the intersexed but also to transgendered persons asking for the right to marry based on gender identity (rather than biological sex) and to discussions of sexual identities that do not match heteronormative assumptions.[66] Alternatively, some intersex advocates worry that "so-called same sex marriage excludes intersex people just as much as opposite sex marriage excludes intersex."[67] While debates continue to rage over the etiology of LGBTQ desire/identity, intersex is often employed as proof that the binary framework and heterosexual marital ethics built upon it must be reconsidered.

In light of these complexities, some Roman Catholic theologians are beginning this process of reconsideration. They are working to construct a more nuanced vision of sexual complementarity that takes into account not only a theology of certain bodily parts but also a theology that considers bodily desires and self-identification.[68] Some believe that the shift from biological (classical) anthropologies to personalist anthropologies opens the door to this kind of consideration. Todd Salzman and Michael Lawler are two such theologians.[69] They write,

> Contemporary Catholic natural law discourse reflects a fundamental shift from "human nature" to "human person." That is to say, the biological and physicalist understanding of traditional natural law and human "na-

65. Greenberg, "Defining Male and Female," 325-26.

66. Cf. Evangelical Alliance Policy Commission, *Transsexuality* (London: Evangelical Alliance, 2000); Susannah Cornwall, "'State of Mind' versus 'Concrete Set of Facts': The Contrasting of Transgender and Intersex in Church Documents on Sexuality," *Theology and Sexuality* 15, no. 1 (2009): 7-28.

67. Organisation Internationale des Intersexués (OII), "Please Support Intersex Australians Gaining the Right to Marriage via Submissions to Two Federal Enquiries," http://oiiinternational.com/blog/1832/support-intersex-australians-gaining-marriage-submissions-federal-enquiries/ (March 16, 2012).

68. Cf. Patricia Beattie Jung, with Joseph Andrew Coray, eds., *Sexual Diversity and Catholicism: Toward the Development of Moral Theology* (Collegeville, Minn.: Liturgical Press, 2001).

69. Salzman and Lawler, *The Sexual Person,* 66-67.

ture" is in the process of being transformed into a contemporary personalist, relational understanding. The former defines the morality of acts based on the physical, biological structure of those acts; the latter defines the morality of acts based on the meaning of those acts for persons and relationships.[70]

Salzman and Lawler contend that a holistic model of human complementarity must include not only bodily parts but also the affective dimension of psychological complementarity and spiritual complementarity as factors that accrue "under the umbrella of a person's sexual orientation."[71]

> Reproductive complementarity will not be a possibility in the case of homosexual couples, but genital complementarity — understood in an orientation, personal, and integrated sense, and not just in a biological, physical sense — will be. This personalist interpretation of genital complementarity, which sees the physical genitals as organs of the whole person, including his or her sexual orientation, allows us to expand the definition of a natural, reasonable, and therefore moral sexual act to include both homosexual and heterosexual nonreproductive sexual acts.[72]

David Matzko McCarthy makes a similar move when he applies the nuptial hermeneutics of the theology of the body to homosexual orientation.[73] McCarthy argues that a more careful evaluation of homosexual orientation allows us to see a parallel meaning, rather than an opposing meaning, between heterosexual marriage and same-sex unions.[74] He counters recent magisterial accounts of homosexual orientation as disordered desires and sinful acts[75] by insisting that such an approach is too narrowly focused on sexual desire. It does not recognize the way in which sexual orientation af-

70. Salzman and Lawler, *The Sexual Person,* 57.

71. Salzman and Lawler, *The Sexual Person,* 151.

72. Salzman and Lawler, *The Sexual Person,* 67.

73. McCarthy begins by quoting the first address of John Paul II's *Theology of the Body.* Summarizing the pope's argument, McCarthy writes, "As the self is known to itself, it is known as embodied, as male or female; therefore, self-discovery (rather than natural determination) comes through relationship to the other. The other, in community with us, gives us knowledge of ourselves. . . . This signification is called the nuptial meaning of the body." David Matzko McCarthy, "The Relationship of Bodies: A Nuptial Hermeneutics of Same-Sex Unions," in *Theology and Sexuality,* 208.

74. McCarthy, "The Relationship of Bodies," 213.

75. Salzman and Lawler, *The Sexual Person,* 89.

fects human relations well beyond the sexual. "Orientation is not simply a matter of attraction or tendency toward a particular object of desire. Orientation names the discursive mechanisms through which a person comes into identity and embodiment through the other. It names a confluence of physical, psychological and social movements that bring an individual into being as a person. It names a structure of interpersonal possibilities. Orientation signifies the particular form through which embodied agency communicates common life."[76] Thus he concludes that "a homosexual orientation, properly understood, is this: gay men and lesbians are persons who encounter the other (and thus discover themselves) in relation to persons of the same sex. This same-sex orientation is a given of their coming to be, that is, the nuptial meaning of human life emerges for a gay man in relation to other men, and in a woman when face to face with other women. The homosexual orientation may be anomalous, but the conceptual structure of the nuptial hermeneutics does not necessarily leave same-sex unions on the outside."[77] All three of these theologians agree that marriage should be understood as the centerpiece of Roman Catholic moral theology.[78] McCarthy argues more explicitly that heterosexual marriage remains "normative in the biblical witness and the church's theological tradition" even while folding gay couples into this framework.[79]

On the conservative Protestant side, James Brownson of the Reformed Church of America agrees, arguing that "the central category" for human sexuality as expressed in the Bible is

> the exclusive one-flesh kinship bond . . . expressed in a delight in the other; a deep desire for gratification and union; the attendant call to honor and serve the other in committed bonds of loving mutuality; and a fruitful vision of committed love that overflows in many ways — in procreation, adoption, service to the community, and hospitality to others. This central meaning of our sexuality is hedged and bounded by warnings against excessive and self-centered desire and against behaviors that shame or degrade the other.[80]

76. McCarthy, "The Relationship of Bodies," 212.

77. McCarthy, "The Relationship of Bodies," 212-13.

78. "[T]raditional Catholic sexual morality is essentially *marital* morality." Salzman and Lawler, *The Sexual Person,* 46.

79. McCarthy, "The Relationship of Bodies," 202.

80. James V. Brownson, *Bible, Gender, Sexuality: Reframing the Church's Debate on Same-Sex Relationships* (Grand Rapids: Eerdmans, 2013), 278-79.

A growing minority of Catholic and theologically conservative Protestants see the possibility of opening up space within the marital model for same-sex unions based on the prioritization of sexual identity. Unfortunately, their discussions fall short of addressing bisexuality and sexual fluidity.[81]

Some will applaud the expansive vision of McCarthy, Lawler, Salzman, and Brownson, while others will be troubled. Conservatives who feel obliged by the biblical witness to retain heteronormativity will not be satisfied.[82] Then again, neither will those working to make space for those who identify as bisexual or queer. The model proposed by Lawler, McCarthy, Salzman, and Brownson while pushing the boundaries of conservative theological ethics, falls short of the goals of many queer theologians who complain that marriage is still the model, even marriage with children.[83]

Many queer theologians look to eunuchs as "our queer antecedents" — those who may or may not have married but were not always celibate. Elizabeth Stuart and her coauthors argue that current discussions of homosexuality in the church are really discussions of how far heterosexuality can be stretched. They challenge this model, stating that whatever Matthew 19:12 means "is unclear but it evidently has something to do with people who do not follow the paths of marriage and family life. . . . Jesus seems to have sought to bring in the reign of god by calling people out of the hierarchically-based structures of marriage and family into a new type of kinship based on friendship which is inclusive of all."[84] The question remains as to whether these friendships included or should include sexual relations. I believe it is one that is difficult to answer in the affirmative considering consistent canonical concern for sexual boundaries.

The application of Matthew 19:12 to current marriage debates is fraught with difficulty. There is not enough data in this short verse to answer all the

81. Some scholars find more fluidity in female sexuality than in male sexuality. Cf. Richard A. Lippa, Travis M. Patterson, and William D. Marelich, "Looking At and Longing For Male and Female 'Swimsuit Models': Men Are Much More Category Specific," *Social Psychological and Personality Science* 1, no. 3 (2010): 238; Lisa M. Diamond, *Sexual Fluidity: Understanding Women's Love and Desire* (Cambridge: Harvard University Press, 2009). Others argue that sexual development is too complicated and personal to be able to identify such patterns at the present time; cf. Fausto-Sterling, *Sexing the Body*.

82. Richard B. Hays, *The Moral Vision of the New Testament: A Contemporary Introduction to New Testament Ethics* (New York: T. & T. Clark/Continuum, 1997, 2004), 379-406.

83. Stuart et al., *Religion Is a Queer Thing*, 2.

84. Stuart et al., *Religion Is a Queer Thing*, 44-45.

questions surrounding sexual ethics and marital norms. And yet, this passage and these phenomena should inform contemporary debates as we continue to work to find ways to uphold the human rights of all persons in secular, pluralist societies while granting religious organizations the freedom to continue the process of evaluating sexual and marital norms within their traditions.

What should be clear from Matthew 19 is that the unmarried life, even the life of celibacy, is introduced by Jesus as a valid and good path to human fulfillment — a path too often ignored by both conservatives and liberals in contemporary debates over sexual ethics. Given what we have reviewed so far, it seems that both sides are privileging sexuality for human identity to the point that celibates can only find their worth, fulfill their humanity, by reading their spirituality in sexual terms — an ironic twist of Christian history.

Returning to John Paul II's reading of Matthew 19, we note that just as Jesus does not base religious celibacy on the body as feminine or masculine, neither does he present celibacy as "spiritual marriage" or the avenue through which unmarried persons are to channel their sexuality. In other words, those who are unable to experience the so-called analogous union of the Trinity in marital sexual relations are not then given sexuality with God as a consolation prize. The metaphor of marriage found in Ephesians 5 is not presented to celibate religious individuals but to the whole church — married and unmarried, a collective whole.

John Paul II's account of the spousal meaning of the body fails to take account of the bodies of eunuchs and intersex persons. His proposal, which bases Christian love on the spousal meaning of the body, places the intersexed outside of the possibility of love. For if, as the late pope suggests, humans come to know love on the basis of the spousal meaning of the body (i.e., its masculinity and femininity), those bodies without a spousal meaning, without a clear masculinity or femininity, would at best know only a distorted view of love and at worst be placed outside the possibility of love.[85] This could not have been Jesus' intention when he elevated the eunuch from a symbol of shame to an icon of radical discipleship. The love for God that leads one to become a "eunuch for the sake of the kingdom" must be a love that is distinct from that love that arises from knowledge of the body as either masculine or feminine.

John Paul II's account of spousal love risks marginalizing not only the intersexed but also anyone unable to enter into heterosexual marriage and married sexuality. His proposal actually undermines, rather than upholds,

85. John Paul II, *Man and Woman*, 185-86; homily 15:1.

the goodness of celibacy — especially nonreligious celibacy (i.e., celibacy that is not read through a "spousal" lens of marriage to Christ). The result is that, for those who would like to be married, spiritual second-class citizenship is added to the burden of the virtuous life.[86] The spiritualization of spousal sexuality can undermine the goodness of celibacy, and it can also present problems for the married.

Spiritualizing Sexuality: Sexual Dysfunction Becomes Spiritual Dysfunction

Sexual/spousal spirituality creates problems not just for the unmarried, but also for the married. John Paul II illuminates an ideal that can feel far removed from the sexual experiences of many married persons. Eugene Rogers Jr. cites the frustration that some have expressed as a result of the spiritualization of sexuality.

> Worried about the sort of idolatry that comes from too high a view of sex and marriage, a friend has complained that "all married couples need is to have a theologian telling them that they should not only expect great sex but *spiritually significant* sex, God help us." A contrary view is that of the celibate Sebastian Moore: "The most dramatic, indeed comic, instance of cross-purposes between the Vatican and the married, is that the Vatican sees the problem as one of curbing desire, whereas the married know that the problem is to keep desire going, which means to keep it growing, which means deepening." Both remarks are true.[87]

Both remarks arise from the knowledge that sexuality, even sexuality within Christian marriage, even married sexuality that satisfies the late pope's standards for "the conjugal act" (i.e., self-giving, conscious of the irreplaceable identity of the spouse, and open to procreation), can feel at times more like a burden than an icon of Trinitarian union. Stanley Hauerwas shares concern over the spiritualization of sex, complaining that "Such a view makes us far too 'sexual.' A seminarian at Notre Dame once told me,

86. Colón and Field, *Singled Out,* 127.

87. Eugene F. Rogers Jr., "Sanctification, Homosexuality, and God's Triune Life," in *Theology and Sexuality,* 223, citing Sebastian Moore, "The Crisis of an Ethic without Desire," in *Jesus the Liberator of Desire* (New York: Crossroad, 1989), 104; reprinted in *Theology and Sexuality,* 17.

'We celibates can be happily sexually adjusted.' I told him I was married, had my share of sex, but I was sure I would never be happily sexually adjusted. What a terrible burden is put on sex: requiring it always to be fulfilling because it has no other purpose."[88] Spiritualizing the goodness of married sexuality can add spiritual frustration to sexual frustration — adding to the burdens of married Christians.

Christine Colón and Bonnie Field have documented how the spiritualization of sexuality has infiltrated evangelical teaching as well. They cite Gary Thomas, a regular contributor to *Christianity Today* and Focus on the Family, who "goes so far as to equate sex and orgasm with experiencing God's presence through the shekinah glory."[89] Colón and Field add, "Then there is the added pressure to have children, for 'creating a family is the closest we get to sharing the image of God.' Many married couples without children will attest that they, like single adults, often feel excluded from many of the messages coming from the evangelical church, and Thomas's assertion clearly demonstrates why."[90]

For those 43 percent of women and 31 percent of men whose bodies make sexual intimacy difficult, painful, or impossible at times, spiritual disappointment can be added to physical frustration.[91] Not only must these

88. Stanley Hauerwas, "Gay Friendship: A Thought Experiment in Catholic Moral Theology," in *Theology and Sexuality,* 300.

89. "The ancient Jewish text *The Holy Letter* (written by Nahmanides in the thirteenth century) sees sex as a mystical experience of meeting with God: 'Through [the act of intercourse] they become partners with God in the act of creation. This is the mystery of what the sages said, 'When a man unites with his wife in holiness, the Shekinah is between them in the mystery of man and woman.' The breadth of this statement is sobering when you consider that this *shekinah* glory is the same presence experienced by Moses when God met him face-to-face (see Exodus 24:15-18)." Thomas, *Sacred Marriage,* 206, cited in Colón and Field, *Singled Out,* 128.

90. Colón and Field, *Singled Out,* 128-29, quoting Thomas, *Sacred Marriage,* 226, 241.

91. Laumann et al. report that 43 percent (or 25-64 percent) of women and 31 percent (or 10-52 percent) of men report sexual dysfunction. Dysfunction was defined as "(1) lacking desire for sex; (2) arousal difficulties (i.e., erection problems in men, lubrication difficulties in women); (3) inability achieving climax or ejaculation; (4) anxiety about sexual performance; (5) climaxing or ejaculating too rapidly; (6) physical pain during intercourse; and (7) not finding sex pleasurable." E. O. Laumann, A. Paik, and R. C. Rosen, "Sexual Dysfunction in the United States: Prevalence and Predictors," *Journal of the American Medical Association* 281, no. 6 (February 10, 1999): 537-44. Hypoactive sexual desire disorder or low libido is reported by 33.4 percent of women; 14.4 percent report pain during intercourse. Tracee Cornforth, "Female Sexual Dysfunction: Common Sexual Disorders and Causes of Decreased Libido," *About.com,* December 10, 2009, http://womenshealth.about.com/cs/

persons struggle with unresponsive bodies or spouses, but they also fail to experience the mystical union sexuality is supposed to grant. For married couples with unequal sexual desire, spiritual guilt can be added to personal guilt and frustration. For infertile couples, spiritual failing is added to personal and familial disappointment in their inability to image God through procreation. For those 10-40 percent of girls and 5-13 percent of boys who have been sexually abused, and for the subgroup who are psychologically or physically prevented from entering into healthy sexual relations because of the trauma they have suffered, spiritual disappointment is added to disappointment with God for what feels like a failure to be protected when they were most vulnerable.[92]

To his credit, Grenz acknowledges some of these difficulties (specifically "debilitating physical problems . . . due to illness, accident, or the aging process" that interrupt sexual relations in marriage). He cautions against overvaluing the sexual act within marriage and insists that "sexual intercourse is not the 'end all' of marriage." And yet, the overall value that he places on sexuality as the basis for human relationality and Christian spirituality and his description of sex as "the most intimate and meaningful act embodying the deep union of husband and wife that lies at the basis of marriage" tend to obscure his cautionary statements.[93]

Sexuality is a good gift of the Creator. Marriage is a good gift of God. But the connection of marriage and sexuality to the image of God risks sexualizing Trinitarian relationality, weakens monogamous sexual ethics,

---

sexualdysfunction/a/femalesexdysfun.htm. "In fact, as many as one third to two thirds of women experience some type of sexual problem at some time in their lives." Elizabeth G. Stewart and Paula Spencer, *The V Book: A Doctor's Guide to Complete Vulvovaginal Health* (New York: Bantam Books, 2002), 329.

92. The World Health Organization reports that 10-25 percent of girls are victims of child sexual abuse and cites studies conducted mostly in developed countries wherein 5-10 percent of men report being sexually abused as children. The Kinsey Institute, "Frequently Asked Sexuality Questions: Sexual Violence," December 6, 2010, http://www.iub.edu/~kinsey/resources/FAQ.html#who2004; citing the World Health Organization, "Sexual Health — a New Focus for WHO," *Progress in Sexual and Reproductive Health Research* (2004): 67. Steven Tracy cites even higher figures, listing female sexual abuse between 24 percent and 32 percent, and some as high as 42 percent, in "Where Is God in the Midst of the Suffering of Abuse?" *Africanus Journal* 2, no. 2 (November 2010): 48, citing R. M. Bolen and M. Scannapieco, "Prevalence of Child Sexual Abuse: A Corrective Meta-analysis," *Social Science Review* 73 (1999): 281-313; and J. Briere and D. M. Elliott, "Prevalence and Psychological Sequelae of Self-Reported Childhood Physical and Sexual Abuse in a General Population Sample of Men and Women," *Child Abuse and Neglect* 27 (2003): 1205-22.

93. Grenz, *Sexual Ethics*, 92.

undermines the goodness of celibacy, and risks adding spiritual failings to sexual frustrations.

These dangers are avoidable. It is possible to hold to the goodness of the social *imago* without allowing it to slide into the sexual or spousal image. This can be done first by clarifying several unnecessary conflations in evangelical and Roman Catholic traditions, reconsidering the usefulness of the marriage analogy, and returning to the social Trinity as the paradigm for the social *imago.*

Clarifying Conflations

The Social Is Not the Sexual

Stanley Grenz conflates the social with the sexual in his construction of the image of God by reading all human relationality through the language of sexuality. He justifies this interpretation on his reading of Genesis, but his is not the only interpretation possible.

In the previous chapter I suggested that rather than reading the characters of Adam and Eve as divinely given prototypes of human sex differentiation, one could interpret them as progenitors of difference instead. In a similar way, it is possible to affirm with Grenz the sexual nature of the relationship between Adam and Eve while at the same time arguing that their sexual relationality not be read as paradigmatic of all human relationality. Adam and Eve can be interpreted as the progenitors rather than the paradigm of other kinds of relations. Sexual differentiation, sexual need, and sexual desire may have been what led Adam and Eve to bond with one another, but the filling of the earth brought other relations — parents to children, siblings, cousins, uncles, grandparents, friends, strangers, and even enemies.[94] Within the creation narratives, sexual differentiation and sexual desire provide the fruitful foundation for human relationality, not its paradigmatic form.

94. Susan A. Ross argues similarly "that the nuptial model hardly accounts for all the possibilities of human relationships: parent-child, sibling-sibling, friend-friend, etc. A broader familial model . . . that takes into account the diverse relationships that human beings engage in during their lives, would offer greater possibilities for conceiving of just and fulfilling personal relationships within a Christian context." Ross, "The Bridegroom and the Bride: The Theological Anthropology of John Paul II and Its Relation to the Bible and Homosexuality," in *Sexual Diversity and Catholicism,* 52-53.

A second way to correct this reading of Genesis is to recognize that male/female partnership is narrowed and distorted when viewed exclusively or primarily as sexual. Women and men cooperate in the world in many complementary ways far beyond the sexual. The partnership of men and women is needed not only in marriage and parenting but also in the church and at every level of society. Labeling these relations "social sexuality" as Grenz has done actually undermines the ability of men and women to build healthy relationships that are holy and life-giving precisely because they are nonsexual.[95]

Sex, gender, and sexuality must be differentiated. With Grenz we must affirm that all human relations take place between persons with embodied sex and culturally influenced gendered identities; nevertheless, not all these relations are sexual, that is, they do not arise from sexual need, desire, or action. A mother's relationship with her child is influenced by her biological sex as well as her culturally influenced and experientially formed gender identity, but it is not, nor should it be, sexual, that is, based on erotic desire, need, or activity.[96] It is only when we separate these categories that we are able to name some sexual relations as sin.

Grenz's definition of sexuality requires a second correction. He posits the primary meaning of sexuality as "the sense of incompleteness and the corresponding drive for wholeness, [forming] the dynamic that not only seeks human relationships but also motivates the quest for God."[97] According to Grenz, sexuality symbolizes and teaches our need for others, thus leading us out of isolation and into community.

> To be sexual — to be male or female — means to be incomplete as an isolated individual. For as isolated individuals we are unable to reflect the fullness of humanity and thus the fullness of the divine image. We see the other who is sexually different from us, and as this occurs we are reminded of our own incompleteness.
>
> The fullness of humanness, therefore, is reflected only in community.

95. Christine A. Colón and Bonnie E. Field document the difficulties faced especially by single women who are marginalized and neglected (in one example a man refused to offer a woman in his church a ride home when her car had broken down) due to the inability of others to see them as anything other than sexual temptresses, in *Singled Out,* 100-109.

96. Lisa Graham McMinn follows Grenz and Rolheiser in speaking about a mother's relationship to her child as sexual in *Sexuality and Holy Longing,* 101. See also Rolheiser, *The Holy Longing,* 198.

97. Grenz, *The Social God,* 280.

> As a result, *our existence as sexual beings gives rise to the desire to enter into community,* and thereby to actualize our design as human individuals. Sexuality, then, is an expression of our nature as social beings. We are not isolated entities existing to ourselves; nor are we the source of our fulfillment. On the contrary, we derive fulfillment beyond ourselves. This need to find fulfillment beyond ourselves is the dynamic that leads to the desire to develop relationships with others and ultimately with God.[98]

Grenz should be praised for his communitarian reworking of the *imago Dei,* for the ways in which it challenges the modernist illusion of an independent, self-sufficient self. Nevertheless, the paragraph above reveals how much Grenz is still battling the residual hold of modernist individualism. Rather than beginning with the presupposition that all humans (after Adam and Eve) come into this world already bonded by particular relations, already embedded within communities, Grenz begins with the modernist (Western, upper-class, masculine) illusion of the individual. Elsewhere, he wrote, "our fundamental sexuality gives rise to the desire *to come out of our isolation* and enter into relationship with others."[99] Who is this individual living in so-called isolation? Such a description calls to mind the Lone Ranger who only discovers his need for community through his sexuality. It is an adolescent sexuality, illustrated by a teenager who quipped: "Now that it's easy to get sex outside of relationships, guys don't need relationships."[100] The stereotype remains: men do not need relationships, or do not realize they need relationships, unless their sexuality tells them otherwise.

Wendell Berry blames such an attitude on Western attempts to escape from the body, from physical labor, from the earth.[101] He insists, "There is, in practice, no such thing as autonomy. Practically, there is only a distinction between responsible and irresponsible dependence."[102] That some Western

98. Grenz, *Sexual Ethics,* 193, italics mine.

99. Stanley J. Grenz, "Theological Foundations for Male-Female Relationships," *Journal of the Evangelical Theological Society* 41, no. 4 (1998): 621, italics mine.

100. Benoit Denizet-Lewis, "Friends, Friends without Benefits, and the Benefits of the Local Mall," *New York Times Magazine,* May 30, 2004, 34, quoted by Dennis P. Hollinger, *The Meaning of Sex: Christian Ethics and the Moral Life* (Grand Rapids: Baker Academic, 2009), 23, and Margaret A. Farley, *Just Love: A Framework for Christian Sexual Ethics* (New York: Continuum, 2006), 233.

101. Wendell Berry, "The Body and the Earth," in *The Art of the Commonplace: The Agrarian Essays of Wendell Berry,* ed. Norman Wirzba (Berkeley: Counterpoint, 2002), 93-134.

102. Berry, "The Body and the Earth," 107.

theologians can posit the possibility of existing in isolation, outside of communities of dependence until sexuality reminds them of their need for others, only shows how much they have been deluded by the partial success of the Industrial Revolution, becoming forgetful of all the relations that enabled their existence prior to their discovery of their sexed body and sexual needs.[103]

Berry insists that, historically, marriage was based on a number of needs that went well beyond the sexual. Marriage was a covenant providing for economic and physical security that extended the network of mutually dependent relations based on need, cooperation, and provision. However, after the disintegration of the household as an economic unit, the reasons for marriage became too thin to sustain the conjugal relation.

> Without the household — not just as a unifying ideal, but as a practical circumstance of mutual dependence and obligation, requiring skill, moral discipline, and work — husband and wife find it less and less possible to imagine and enact their marriage. Without much in particular that they can *do* for each other, they have a scarcity of practical reasons to be together. They may "like each other's company," but that is a reason for friendship, not for marriage. Aside from affection for any children they may have and their abstract legal and economic obligations to each other, their union has to be empowered by sexual energy alone.[104]

This, Berry believes, should not be misunderstood as the distillation of marriage, revealing its lowest common denominator; rather, the reduction of marriage to sexuality is marriage's undoing. When sexuality is "valued only for its own sake [it becomes] frivolous, . . . destructive — even of itself."[105]

Grenz's vision of sexuality as that which forms the basis of human bond-

103. In his defense, Grenz does well to note that the help that Eve brings to Adam is not the relief of (genital) sexual need. He quotes Old Testament scholar Claus Westermann "The words 'a helper fit for him' refers [*sic*] neither to the sexual nature of woman (so Augustine) nor to the help which she could offer to the farmer. Any such limitation destroys the meaning of the passage. What is meant is the personal community of man and woman in the broadest sense — bodily and spiritual community, mutual help and understanding, joy and contentment in each other" (Grenz, *The Social God,* 278-79, quoting Claus Westermann, *Genesis 1–11* [Minneapolis: Augsburg, 1984], 232). Nevertheless, by defining the "personal community of man and woman in the broadest sense" as (social) sexuality, and suggesting that sexuality is what draws all humans (not just Adam and Eve) out of isolation into community, he risks deforming the very community he is working so hard to recover.

104. Berry, "The Body and the Earth," 112.

105. Berry, "The Body and the Earth," 112.

ing — the bonding of marriage and every other bonding that employs marriage as an analogy — provides theological justification for a warped vision of sexuality and marriage that has arisen in the modern age. Envisioning sexuality as that which enables bonding is not a remedy for a society that knows much of sexuality and very little of bonded faithful relationships of any stripe. While sexuality may motivate some people to make promises of fidelity, the fulfillment of those promises has little to do with sexuality or *eros* and everything to do with *agape*. As C. S. Lewis so wisely quipped, "Eros is driven to promise what Eros of himself cannot perform."[106]

Grenz may be right to insist that incompleteness is the dynamic that grounds community, but his analysis misses the mark when he identifies incompleteness as sexual. Even when his proposal is nuanced so that Adam and Eve are properly understood as the primal form of the image of God, with Christ and the church as the telos, the eschatological *imago,* his insistence that Christ's relationship to the Father can be understood as sexual, and that sexuality provides the basis for the eschatological community, shows that his progressive-canonical vision of the *imago* never outstrips his initial definition of sexuality.[107]

In contrast, even with the use of the marital lens for the relation of Christ and church in Ephesians 5, no biblical passages suggest that the bonding of individual Christians into the collective body of the church should be viewed through the lens of the sexual. The primary analogy used for ecclesial bonding is sibling relations. The church is to learn from familial love, but not only or primarily the love of spouses. "Brotherly" love characterizes the relationality of the church through *apage, philia,* and *philostorgia,* not *eros.*[108]

106. C. S. Lewis, *The Four Loves* (Orlando: Harcourt, Brace and Co., 1960, 1988), 114.

107. Grenz, *The Social God,* 280.

108. In 1 Cor. 1:10-11, the apostle calls on the believers to eschew dissension on the basis of their status as brothers (and sisters). Rom. 12 employs the metaphor of one body, but the language is of parts held together, not by *eros* but by brotherly love *(philadelphia).* Rom. 12:10: "Love *(philadelphia)* one another with mutual affection *(philostorgos);* outdo one another in showing honor" (NRSV). Similarly, when the various parts of the body are described in 1 Cor. 12, this is followed by the "love chapter," where *agape* is unpacked as "patient" and "not jealous" — the opposite of *eros.* "Love *(agape)* must be sincere. Hate what is evil; cling to what is good. Be devoted to one another in brotherly love *(philadelphia).* Honor one another above yourselves" (Rom. 12:9-10 NIV). "Now about brotherly love *(philadelphia)* we do not need to write to you, for you yourselves have been taught by God to love *(agapan)* each other" (1 Thess. 4:9 NIV). "Thus he has given us, through these things, his precious and very great promises, so that through them you may escape from the corruption that is in the world because of lust, and may become participants of the

The analogy of sibling relations should protect against the sexualization of ecclesial love and keep us from concluding with Rolheiser that in heaven all will be married to all, enjoying sexual relations with "brothers and sisters" in Christ.[109] Reading ecclesial bonding through the lens of the sexual is counterproductive to healthy church life.

It is imperative that we untangle Grenz's conflation of the social with the sexual. Sex, gender, and sexuality are related yet distinct. To clarify, I have suggested several revisions: First, theological interpretations of the creation narratives should read Adam and Eve as the progenitors of human relations, rather than those who provide its paradigmatic form. Second, sexuality is a type of incompleteness that reveals human need for others. It is one of many needs that can build community. Finally, even when Grenz's vision of sexuality is viewed as the primal form of the *imago,* with the ecclesial community standing as the eschatological telos, Grenz's unwillingness to give up the language of sexuality undermines the promise of his proposal. Thankfully, his conflation of sex, gender, sexuality, and relationality can be corrected. In a similar way, we must nuance some of John Paul II's theological constructions in order to find a more balanced perspective.

The Spousal Is Not the Sexual

John Paul II introduced a different problem into his theological anthropology by conflating spousal with sexual. As noted above, he avoids the language of sexuality because he wants to raise the bar of what good marital sexuality must entail. Thus he speaks not of spousal sexuality but of "the conjugal act" — sexual activity in marriage that is loving, attentive to the particularity of the person, self-giving, and uninhibited by contraceptive devices. Unfortunately, by calling married sexuality "the conjugal act," he allows married sexuality to be seen as the pinnacle of marriage, the central way that love as self-gift is expressed. While it is clear that his guide, Saint John of the Cross, speaks of sexuality as a metaphor for spiritual things (the sixteenth-century saint certainly does elevate sexual union as the pinnacle of marital self-giving), John Paul II's *Theology of the Body* is less explicit on this

divine nature. For this very reason, you must make every effort to support your faith with goodness, and goodness with knowledge, and knowledge with self-control, and self-control with endurance, and endurance with godliness, and godliness with mutual affection, and mutual affection *(philadelphia)* with love *(agapēn)*" (2 Pet. 1:4-7 NRSV).

109. Rolheiser, *The Holy Longing,* 206.

point. Nevertheless, the late pope opens the door to the elevation of married sexuality as central to human identity in the image of God.

This elevation of sexuality as a good unto itself arose in reaction to earlier Roman Catholic accounts that downplayed the value of marital sexuality beyond procreation.[110] While the personalist account is an improvement in that it finds value in marital sexuality, it presents an imbalanced account by swinging the pendulum too far in the other direction. McCarthy explains:

> The chief problem in this personalist account is, not that it goes wrong, but that it says too much to be right. Every sexual act is defined as full and total, so that sex has no room to be ordinary. The act of sexual intercourse, in this theological framework, transcends its particular meaning in time, in order to reveal the complete contours of our two-in-one-flesh humanity. With this total union of body and spirit, sexual relationships are lifted out of the everyday activities of marriage. . . . Every act is understood to ritualize "a fully shared life" and the "total self-giving" of spouses. This ritual context suits a honeymoon or anniversary day consummation, but I dare to say that our everyday bodily presence is far more subtle and patient. Those who believe sex is earth shattering will put it out of marriage.[111]

In contrast to this personalist account, McCarthy wants to present sexuality in such a way as to keep it within the everyday realities of married life. "The everyday meaning of sex, in contrast, is extended through the day-to-day ebb and flow of common endeavors, joys, and struggles of love in the home. Not in an instant, but over time, we come to belong. In this regard, no sexual act represents a total self or full relationship. Rather, what we do today gains its meaning in relation to yesterday and what we will do tomorrow. For sex to have depth, it needs extended bodily communication over time."[112]

McCarthy is working to restore balance to his Roman Catholic tradition by putting the goodness of marriage and sexuality back into its proper place. He argues that the Scriptures give a different picture of marriage and sexuality than that found in John Paul II and Roman Catholic personalist accounts.

> The Christian tradition has emphasized communal love outside of the practices of marriage, particularly love within troublesome contexts, not

110. McCarthy, *Sex and Love*, 4-5.
111. McCarthy, *Sex and Love*, 43.
112. McCarthy, *Sex and Love*, 43-44.

> exotic or heavenly places, but among the poor and amid disagreements and sin. Modern romantics set the meaning of love in the face-to-face wonder of wedding vows, but the Gospels use the image of the wedding banquet as a place to deal with themes of hospitality and hope for the downtrodden. Love is characterized as a turning around for the unfortunate, as healing, generosity, and most of all, as forgiveness and reconciliation. Grace and forgiveness are basic to the theological drama of love. The stage is not the discrete context of interpersonal love but relationships of the human family and the practical matters of living well in community. The household, in this setting, is where love and sexual union are ordered to common goods and to God. Christian love, from the start, begins outside of me and you, but when contemporary theology conceives of the "Me and You" as *the* original context of love, it has difficulty bringing love and sexual desire back from the impractical and other worldly sphere of modern romance.[113]

McCarthy insists that sexuality can only find its proper place within the wider love that is marriage, and that marriage can only find its proper place within the wider love that is God's love in the community — the church. It is marriage that can mean the total gift of self, not sexuality. Within the context of marriage, sexuality can mean many things, but within the wholeness of marriage, sexuality is liberated from the daunting task of having to mean "the gift of the whole self" in every sexual encounter. Again, McCarthy explains:

> Through any given sexual act, spouses might express love, desire, generosity, frustration, fatigue, or manipulative intent, but they will do so in the semantic context of a day, week, a stage of life, and a series of specific events, and all set within the broader context of a shared life. Any particular sexual encounter need not say anything earth shattering; it need not point to the fullness or full meaning of a sexual relationship. We need not be completed by our sexual complement. Most sex within marriage is just ordinary, a minor episode in a larger story. One set of sexual expressions may need to be redeemed by another, and can be. One-night stands and passionate affairs, in contrast, need to be earthshaking and splendid because they are the whole story. They are manic attempts to overcome the fact that there is nothing else. The true superiority of sexual intercourse in marriage is that it does not have to mean very much. Expressed sexually or

113. McCarthy, *Sex and Love,* 25.

> otherwise, our "humanity" is something that accumulates quietly through small steps and comes to us as a whole only when we step back, in order to look back and to imagine the future.[114]

Marital love is distorted and diminished when it is viewed primarily through the lens of the sexual. Indeed, Ephesians 5 (the biblical passage cited so often to justify the analogy of marriage to the spiritual life) speaks of marital love in terms not of *eros* but of *agape,* giving the example of a man caring for his own body, not through erotic self-stimulation but by feeding himself.[115] This is not to say that *eros* or sexuality has no place in marital life, but that healthy marriages require more than *eros* or sexual love in order to embrace the entire person.

Differentiating Eros from Marital Love and Divine Love Both Roman Catholic and evangelical theologians are conflating *eros* with married love. Pope Benedict XVI and Stanley Grenz both suggest that biblical metaphors for marriage should be interpreted as justifying *eros* as a revelation of divine love. The question remains whether the kind of love that God displays in these actions is best illustrated by *eros* or by *agape.* These theologians insist that marriage requires *agape* as well as *eros;* nevertheless, the arguments they use to justify *eros* on the basis of marriage tend to obscure this nuance. Benedict XVI insists that *eros* without *agape* "is impoverished and even loses its own nature."[116] Grenz writes,

> Marriage as a covenantal bond brings together the two aspects of love, *agape* and *eros.* Within the context of marriage the sex act declares that the desire for the other, the physical attraction that two persons may sense toward each other (so central to *eros*), can truly be fulfilled only in the

114. McCarthy, *Sex and Love,* 8. C. S. Lewis agreed. He insisted that recent portrayals of sex as "rapt," "intense," and "swoony-devout," and the psychologists who "have so bedeviled us with the infinite importance of complete sexual adjustment and the all but impossibility of achieving it," combine to show us that what we need is a healthy dose of laughter about the whole thing. This is not to say that it is not important, nor sacramentally significant, but, he argues, eating is also important, sacramentally significant, and morally and socially ordered. Lewis, *The Four Loves,* 98-99.

115. Eph. 5:28-30: "In the same way, husbands should love *(agape)* their wives as they do their own bodies. He who loves *(agape)* his wife loves himself. For no one ever hates his own body, but he nourishes and tenderly cares for it, just as Christ does for the church, because we are members of his body" (NRSV).

116. Benedict XVI, *Deus Caritas Est,* 1.7.

> total giving of one to the other and the unconditional acceptance of the other *(agape)*. As the love of the other characterized by desire for the other *(eros)* merges with the love of the other characterized by self-giving *(agape)*, love in its highest form emerges. Sexual intercourse constitutes a visible object lesson of this reality.[117]

Grenz also writes that adultery is "the triumph of *eros* over *agape*."[118] Given the more balanced accounts of marital love the pope and Grenz offer elsewhere, it remains to be proved whether the marital love that illustrates God's faithful love of humanity is best described as *eros* or as *agape*. Following Grenz's comparison above, it seems that "the total giving of one to the other and the unconditional acceptance of the other" is best described by *agape*.[119]

When Grenz speaks of *eros* within the Trinity, he defines *eros* as "desire for communion with the beloved."[120] But desire for communion expands well beyond the sexual or marital. The father depicted in Jesus' parable of the prodigal son could also be described as desiring reunion, reconciling communion, with his son. His desire leads him not to walk but to *run* to his beloved son even while the boy is "still a long way off" (Luke 15:11-32, esp. v. 20). Similarly, two chapters earlier in Luke's Gospel, Jesus says to Jerusalem, "How often have I longed to gather your children together, as a hen gathers her chicks under her wings, but you were not willing!" (Luke 13:34 NIV). Jesus is certainly articulating desire for communion with his estranged children, his loved ones. Yet, few would label the desire expressed in these passages as *eros*, given that it occurs between Father and Son, Jesus and Jerusalem, hen and chicks, rather than between husband and wife. If *eros* means "desire for communion with the beloved," it must be unhinged from the close connection to sexuality and marriage it retains in current parlance.

C. S. Lewis rightly reminds us that "the times and places in which marriage depends on Eros are in a small minority."[121] Lewis named *eros*, along with *storge* (affection) and *philia* (friendship), natural loves that can be elevated by divine *agape* to become revelations of divine love while, nevertheless, remaining human loves. They can illustrate the love of God and create desire for the love of God, but they remain distinct. But Grenz is dissatisfied

117. Grenz, *Sexual Ethics*, 87.
118. Grenz, *Sexual Ethics*, 111.
119. Grenz, *Sexual Ethics*, 87.
120. Grenz, *The Social God*, 320.
121. Lewis, *The Four Loves*, 92.

with this answer.[122] He believes that proposals such as Lewis's "ultimately deny that the natural loves enjoy any transcendent grounding; they all lack any basis in the divine life."[123] Grenz seems worried that unless *eros* is found within God, it cannot be declared to be good. He shows the same concern when he attempts to argue that God is sexual. "God created humans to resemble in some sense their Creator. The *imago Dei* suggests that there is a connection between our essential human nature and the divine reality. As Karl Barth explains, 'in God's own sphere and being, there exists a divine and therefore self-grounded prototype to which this being can correspond.' But if God and sexuality are disjunctive, how can God be the transcendent ground for our human embodiment as sexual creatures? How can sexuality be 'good,' if it is an aspect of human existence that makes us unlike, rather than like God?"[124] Unfortunately, the logic in the last sentence falters because it suggests that nothing can be good that does not find a correspondence in God. And yet, as theists, we insist that creation is good, declared "good" by the Creator, even though distinct from and unlike God. It is possible that just as the creation is distinct from God and yet can "declare God's glory" and make visible "God's invisible qualities — his eternal power and divine nature" — so human loves can reveal divine love, even while remaining distinct (Ps. 19:1; Rom. 1:20).

The fact that biblical authors had the term *eros* at their disposal but consistently rejected it in favor of *agape* — an obscure alternative — should not go unnoticed. They knew of the association of *eros* with religious devotion, but, probably because of the rampant relationship of *eros* with sexuality and fertility religions, they avoided its use. In our present society, when sexuality is replacing the religion of many, or being confused as the high-point religious experience — even Christian religious experience — contemporary

122. Benedict XVI may also have been dissatisfied with such an answer. He writes, "Fundamentally, 'love' is a single reality, but with different dimensions; at different times, one or other dimension may emerge more clearly. Yet when the two dimensions are totally cut off from one another, the result is a caricature or at least an impoverished form of love. And we have also seen, synthetically, that biblical faith does not set up a parallel universe, or one opposed to the human phenomenon which is love, but rather accepts the whole man; it intervenes in his search for love in order to purify it and to reveal new dimensions of it" (*Deus Caritas Est,* 1.8). Still, in this passage, Benedict seems to be more concerned that human *eros* is taken up in the biblical story than he is insisting that divine love provide a transcendent archetype for human *eros.*

123. Grenz, *The Social God,* 318.

124. Grenz, "Is God Sexual?" 190-91.

theologians would do well to heed the example of the biblical authors and differentiate between *eros,* marital love, and divine love.

Reconsidering the Marriage Analogy in Saint John of the Cross Although the poetry of Saint John of the Cross provides theological fodder for envisioning spirituality through the lens of romantic sexuality, elevating marital sexuality above marital promise, the saint is also a helpful source for correcting this trend. The sixteenth-century monastic certainly bequeathed a legacy of spousal/sexual mysticism, but he also remains famous for another treatise on the nature of Christian spirituality, a spirituality that sounds less like the ecstasy of a honeymoon and more like the quotidian realities of life, including challenging seasons we have learned from him to call "dark nights of the soul."

The Dark Night is an essential counterpoint to the *Spiritual Canticle.* Both use romantic language to speak of longing, frustration at not being with God, desire for God's presence in anticipation of union with God. In this way they draw upon the experience of lovers, newly espoused, longing for their wedding day, for the day when none shall separate them. Such an analogy is fitting for the experience of the believer longing after God in this life, when the fullness of communion with God, the union so often associated with sexual union, is presented as a future reality — one hoped for but not yet experienced. This is the metaphor that ends the biblical narrative, with the Spirit and the bride saying, "Come," longing for the return of Jesus, the Bridegroom (Rev. 22:17).

The Dark Night continues the poetic theme of lovers long-estranged who now find themselves in ecstatic embrace, but the commentary the saint adds to the poem is essential for keeping readers from misunderstanding.[125] Saint John of the Cross explains:

> Before embarking on an explanation of these stanzas, we should remember that the soul recites them when it has already reached the state of perfection — that is, union with God through love — and has now passed

125. "One dark night, / fired with love's urgent longings / — ah, the sheer grace! — / I went out unseen / my house being now all stilled. . . . O guiding night! / O night more lovely than the dawn! / O night that has united / the Lover with his beloved / transforming the beloved in her Lover." John of the Cross, *Dark Night of the Soul,* in *The Collected Works of St. John of the Cross,* trans. Kieran Kavanaugh, O.C.D., and Otilio Rodriguez, O.C.D., rev. ed. (Washington, D.C.: ICS Publications, 1991), stanzas 1 and 5, http://www.ocd.or.at/ics/john/dn.html.

> through severe trials and conflicts by means of the spiritual exercise that leads one along the constricted way to eternal life, of which our Savior speaks in the Gospel *[Mt. 7:14]*. The soul must ordinarily walk this path to reach that sublime and joyous union with God. Recognizing the narrowness of the path and the fact that so very few tread it — as the Lord himself says *[Mt. 7:14]* — the soul's song in this first stanza is one of happiness in having advanced along it to this perfection of love. Appropriately, this constricted road is called a dark night, as we shall explain in later verses of this stanza.[126]

In his commentary on the poem, John of the Cross presents Christian spirituality as a journey that may begin with ecstasies able to be likened to mystical moments of union with God, but one that passes through other phases of relationship along the way.[127] In this way, his narrative is a fitting analogy to human marriage, one that begins in hope and the excitement of the wedding but becomes more difficult as the couple learns to navigate the many responsibilities of household management, financial concerns, the demands of children, aging parents, aging selves. His commentary teaches Christians not to put their trust in moments of ecstasy, nor to despair during times of doubt and difficulty, for these are all part of a Christian's relationship with God. Indeed, faithfulness in the absence of spiritual comfort is more a mark of intimacy with God than are experiences of mystical communion.[128]

126. John of the Cross, *Dark Night of the Soul,* introduction to commentary.

127. John of the Cross, *Dark Night of the Soul,* book I, chap. 1, 1-2; book I, chap. 4, 2. "After the delight and satisfaction are gone, the sensory part of the soul is naturally left vapid and zestless, just as a child is when withdrawn from the sweet breast. These souls are not at fault if they do not allow this dejection to influence them, for it is an imperfection that must be purged through the dryness and distress of the dark night." Book I, chap. 5, 1.

128. "Those who are in this situation should feel comforted; they ought to persevere patiently and not be afflicted. Let them trust in God who does not fail those who seek him with a simple and righteous heart; nor will he fail to impart what is needful for the way until getting them to the clear and pure light of love. God will give them this light by means of that other night, the night of spirit, if they merit that he place them in it. The attitude necessary in the night of sense is to pay no attention to discursive meditation since this is not the time for it. They should allow the soul to remain in rest and quietude even though it may seem obvious to them that they are doing nothing and wasting time, and even though they think this disinclination to think about anything is due to their laxity. Through patience and perseverance in prayer, they will be doing a great deal without activity on their part. All that is required of them here is freedom of soul, that they liberate themselves from the impediment and fatigue of ideas and thoughts, and care not about thinking and meditat-

When spirituality is likened to sexual desire, then lack of sexual desire can be seen as a spiritual problem. But John of the Cross speaks about times in spiritual life when Christians will lose their desire for God. He counsels them not to fear. "They must be content simply with a loving and peaceful attentiveness to God, and live without the concern, without the effort, and without the desire to taste or feel him."[129] Just as married persons go through seasons of desire and seasons of apathy and yet can remain faithfully, even lovingly, married, so Christians go through times of desire and apathy and yet can remain faithful in their love of God.

The poem speaks of the joys of ecstatic union with God, but the commentary warns the reader that these joys come after years of trials and faithfulness. In this way the analogy between sexual ecstasy and spiritual union is better likened to the joy of spouses celebrating their golden anniversary, not their honeymoon.

John of the Cross and John Paul II may be pointing us in a helpful direction when they teach that "love is a gift of self; spousal love between man and woman is the paradigmatic case of the gift of self; the origin and exemplar of the gift of self lies in the Trinity," but their analogy only holds when marital love is separated from sexual love.[130] Still, it is good to remember that when Jesus spoke of love as the gift of self, he spoke not of marriage but of martyrdom: "No one has greater love than this, to lay down one's life for one's friends" (John 15:13 NRSV).

Marriage is an important illustration of God's love and the calling God has placed upon us to live in love: "God is love, and those who abide in love abide in God, and God abides in them" (1 John 4:16 NRSV). But marital love is not entirely sexual, nor is it the only kind of love, or always the best kind of love, to use to illustrate the love of God. One must not forget all the other ways that love is revealed in the Bible, especially the Fatherly (and motherly) love of God and, ultimately, the sacrificial love shown in Jesus on the cross. While some Roman Catholic authors have tried to show how Christ's cross can be understood as "nuptials . . . the marriage bed mounted not in pleasure

---

ing. They must be content simply with a loving and peaceful attentiveness to God, and live without the concern, without the effort, and without the desire to taste or feel him. All these desires disquiet the soul and distract it from the peaceful, quiet, and sweet idleness of the contemplation that is being communicated to it." John of the Cross, *Dark Night of the Soul,* in *The Collected Works of St. John of the Cross,* trans. Kieran Kavanaugh, O.C.D., and Otilio Rodriguez, O.C.D., rev. ed. (Washington, D.C.: ICS Publications, 1991), p. 382; 1.10.3-4.

129. John of the Cross, *Dark Night of the Soul.*

130. Waldstein, introduction to *Man and Woman,* 78.

but in pain,"[131] a more careful reading of Ephesians 5:25[132] will show that marriage is redeemed through martyrdom, not martyrdom through marriage.[133]

One last observation about John of the Cross: when the saint speaks about the individual believer seeking communion with God, it is assumed that the reader is already embedded in the wider community of faith. John speaks of the community, of spiritual directors and confessors as essential coaches who encourage the believer not to give up or misinterpret spiritual dryness for lack of love. Indeed, the wider monastic community is an essential backdrop for understanding the intimate communion of the soul with God. This vision of intimacy as already embedded in wider social communities leads us to the final point of correction for the connection between sexuality and the *imago Dei.*

Restoring the Social Trinity to the Social *Imago*

Relocating Love in the Wider Community

David Matzko McCarthy, in his critique of contemporary theological accounts, argues that Roman Catholic and evangelical constructions misplace the "location" of love. Romantic and theological personalists locate love between two partners who mirror the I-Thou relation. This was the model passed down from Martin Buber to Karl Barth to Stanley Grenz and John

131. Christopher West, *The Love That Satisfies: Reflections on Eros and Agape* (West Chester, Pa.: Ascension Press, 2007), 81.

132. "Husbands, love your wives, just as Christ loved the church and gave himself up for her" (NRSV).

133. Evangelical Lisa Graham McMinn draws upon both Grenz and Rolheiser when she writes, "Men and women's willingness to give up control, to serve and nurture, to create, to give sacrificially for the sake of others, to invest in authentic relationships with others reflects a God who graciously serves, nurtures, creates, sacrifices, and invests in those whom God loves. These are acts of redemptive sexuality that maintain relationships and communities that are strong and vibrant" (*Sexuality and Holy Longing,* 176). Her statement illustrates the subtle slip that has occurred in much writing on sexuality and spirituality. McMinn calls sacrificial loving "redeemed sexuality" when it would be better to present sacrificial loving as the way to redeem sexuality. Benedict XVI comes closer to this in *Deus Caritas Est* when he argues that *eros* (self-seeking, need-love) must be purified by *agape* (love as self-gift). Nevertheless, his justification of *eros* on the basis of marital metaphors in the Scriptures shows how he, too, reduces marital love to *eros* rather than identifying *eros* as one dimension of the rich love shared between husband and wife.

Paul II. It is the model upon which the social Trinity was first constructed. But McCarthy insists that the I-Thou actually distorts the nature of love, reducing it to the romantic two abstracted from the world, from family, neighborhood, finances, and church.[134]

Instead of Me and You (I and Thou) as the location of love, McCarthy presents the home as the proper place of Christian love — not the isolated suburban nuclear home but the open home in a network of interdependent relationships within a neighborhood. "The romantic ideal of mutual absorption threatens to make friendships and other social relations appear as optional or as intrusions. John Paul II's personalism, while not quite romantic, risks the same kind of isolation. [In contrast, McCarthy suggests:] . . . Our friends [neighbors and kin] enrich our marriages and home in important and practical ways."[135] Even more than enriching, McCarthy insists that these other relations are essential for marriages to survive and thrive.

He blames this "impossible ideal" on "the idea that marriage is a complete communion," a bringing together of two halves into a complete whole — an ideal that comes from Platonic speculation, not biblical narrative.[136]

134. McCarthy, *Sex and Love,* 25.

135. McCarthy, *Sex and Love,* 123.

136. This is where I must disagree with Benedict XVI's suggestion that the creation narrative in Genesis, the creation of the woman out of the "side" or "rib" of the *adam,* should be read as similar to Plato's creation account as recorded in the *Symposium* (1.14-15). Plato recounts Zeus's division of a spherical creature with two faces, four arms, four legs, and two sets of genitalia enacted as a defense against human threat to the gods and punishment for human pride. This myth provides the narrative structure for Plato's account of love as the desire that leads one to search for one's other half — the half that will complete the self. Such a mythology supports the romantic assumption that I must find "the One" who will complete me. Benedict XVI writes, "While the biblical narrative does not speak of punishment, the idea is certainly present that man is somehow incomplete, driven by nature to seek in another the part that can make him whole, the idea that only in communion with the opposite sex can he become 'complete.' The biblical account thus concludes with a prophecy about Adam: 'Therefore a man leaves his father and his mother and cleaves to his wife and they become one flesh' (Gen 2:24)" (*Deus Caritas Est,* 1.11.1). In contrast to the pope, I would argue that there are profound differences between these creation accounts leading to alternative applications. In Gen. 2:21-22, "[God] took one from his ribs/sides . . . and the LORD God built the rib/side into a woman and brought her to the human" (translation mine). Despite the possible translation of rib as side, most Christian interpreters reject the Jewish legend of the primordial hermaphrodite. The Genesis account shows that because woman was taken out of man, they belong together. Nevertheless, it is important not to misconstrue oneness or belonging as completion (despite interpretations that support such a view, i.e., *Genesis Rabbah* 17.2; cited by Kristen E. Kvam, Linda S. Schearing, and Valarie H. Ziegler, eds., *Eve and Adam: Jewish, Christian, and*

Most spouses learn this truth soon after marriage, but many remain frustrated when they continue to measure their marriage against the myth. "It is impractical to hope that one person can be completed by another, or that one's spouse would be able to receive the 'total' personality and texture of the other. We should hope that friends and co-workers will tease out and cultivate personal qualities and make demands that our husbands and wives cannot. Even if marriage is a primary source of one's identity, it is quite a different matter to assume that we can exhaust one another's 'total' self."[137] Spousal communion is upheld and enriched by wider social, nonsexual relations. "I will discover who you really are as I come to know you in the company of others."[138]

Evangelical theologians Margaret Kim Peterson and her husband Dwight N. Peterson agree. Like McCarthy, they blame romantic interpretations of divine love for undermining the ability of Christians (especially young evangelicals) to enter into healthy relationships. They find it "profoundly ironic that the lens through which many modern Christians have come to interpret marriage, the fantasy of romance, turns out to be so splintering and isolating a phenomenon. Romance, through its exclusive focus on the one true love, ends up separating people two by two from any other substantive human relationship. And as the sociologists tell us, it is in part that very separation from supportive networks of friends and family that makes many modern marriages as brittle and prone to collapse as they are." They conclude, "It might be that what contemporary Christians need is less romance and more love."[139]

But how do Christians find "more love" to support their marriages when marital love (romantic/sexual/spousal love) is presented as the paradigmatic form of Christian love? Clearly, *eros* or sexual/spousal love is not enough, at least not as something unique or separate from other loves, as it is currently

---

Muslim Readings on Genesis and Gender [Bloomington and Indianapolis: Indiana University Press, 1999], 82-83). Marital oneness is not completion. Married persons continue to need relationships with other humans and with God. It is this romantic *mis*understanding of sexual/spousal love as "complete" that undermines the ability of spouses to sustain their love over the course of a lifetime. While there are important nuances to be developed here, such are beyond the scope of this book. James V. Brownson mounts a similar critique in *Bible, Gender, Sexuality,* 22-38.

137. McCarthy, *Sex and Love,* 123.

138. McCarthy, *Sex and Love,* 25.

139. Margaret Kim Peterson and Dwight N. Peterson, "God Does Not Want to Write Your Love Story," in *God Does Not . . . Entertain, Play "Matchmaker," Hurry, Demand Blood, Cure Every Illness,* ed. D. Brent Laytham (Grand Rapids: Brazos, 2009), 96.

conceived. But the Petersons insist that *true* spousal love is not that different from these other loves. "Intimacy is not identical with romance, and marital love is not so different from other human loves that one cannot practice on one's parents, siblings, neighbors, and friends. On the contrary: one learns to love precisely by loving and being loved."[140]

Rather than beginning with spousal love for an understanding of the nature of love as self-gift, the Petersons suggest that the Christian love upon which marriages should be built can be learned outside of marriage — as children growing up in families, in friendships, in relations in the church. It is the wider community of love that teaches and enables the particular forms of love that marriage requires/entails.

> Christian love is unitive and community forming; it weaves people together into familial and churchly networks of mutual care and dependence on one another and on God. Husbands and wives, neighbors and friends, children and grandchildren, widows and orphans, all are adopted by God into the household of the church and invited to love and care for one another in ways that certainly include the bond of marriage but also include a range of other human relationships, all of which involve real connection, real intimacy, real enjoyment of other people, a real participation in the redemptive work of God in the world.[141]

Like McCarthy, the Petersons are working to place marriage within a broader community of love. At the same time, they warn their readers, "Many of us are unaccustomed to either the demands or the rewards of the cultivation of community, but this is a fundamental Christian virtue, one that is essential to the practice of Christian marriage."[142] The Petersons and McCarthy are correct to relocate love within the wider community. Their analyses invite further theological reflection.

Relocating Love in the Social Trinity

McCarthy's critique of the theological foundations of romantic personalism points the way to the necessary correction of these traditions. "Christian

140. Peterson and Peterson, "God Does Not Want," 99.
141. Peterson and Peterson, "God Does Not Want," 96.
142. Peterson and Peterson, "God Does Not Want," 104.

love, from the start, begins outside of me and you, but when contemporary theology conceives of the 'Me and You' as *the* original context of love, it has difficulty bringing love and sexual desire back from the impractical and other worldly sphere of modern romance."[143] McCarthy highlights the Me and You, the I-Thou, as the fundamental problem. While Barth and others were right to highlight the significance of relationality for humanity made in the image of the Trinity, the I-Thou model has nevertheless come to distort the social model. Others have noted that Barth's projection of I-Thou onto the Trinity tends to "privilege Father and Son," obscuring or marginalizing the Spirit.[144]

Although Stanley Grenz leaves behind the language of I-Thou, he nevertheless employs a model of the Trinity that also privileges the relationality between the Father and the Son. Despite his willingness to use the term "social Trinity,"[145] Grenz never strays from Augustine's model that depicts the Father and the Son in loving relation and the Spirit as the bond of love that unites them.

> The narrator [of Gen. 2] presents marriage as the joining of two persons who share a fundamental sameness as "flesh of one flesh" and yet differ from each other as male and female. This human dynamic reminds us of the dynamic within the Triune God. . . . [T]he divine life entails the relationship between the first and second persons who share the same divine essence but are nevertheless differentiated from each other. The bond uniting them is the divine love, the third Trinitarian person, the Holy Spirit. As marriage incorporates its divinely-given design to be the intimate, permanent bond arising out of the interplay of sameness and difference, this human relationship reflects the exclusive relationship of love found within the Trinity, the unique relationship between the Father and the Son concretized in the Holy Spirit.[146]

143. McCarthy, *Sex and Love,* 25.

144. F. LeRon Shults, *Reforming Theological Anthropology: After the Philosophical Turn to Relationality* (Grand Rapids: Eerdmans, 2003), 131.

145. Grenz, "Theological Foundations," 617; Grenz, *The Moral Quest,* 277, 285.

146. Grenz, "Theological Foundations," 623. "Only in fellowship with others can we show forth what God is like, for God is the community of love — the eternal relationship enjoyed by the Father and the Son, which is the Holy Spirit." Stanley J. Grenz, *Theology for the Community of God,* 2nd ed. (Grand Rapids: Eerdmans, 2000), 179. Cf. Grenz, *The Social God,* 316; Grenz, *The Named God and the Question of Being: A Trinitarian Theo-Ontology* (Louisville: Westminster John Knox, 2005), 340.

While friendship *(philia)* and familial affection/compassion *(storge)* can be understood as including more than two persons, most theologians speak of *eros* as the love of two. Grenz locates *eros* in "The desire for communion [which] is especially evident in the relationship of the Son to the Father."[147]

> Moreover, the theological assertion that God is love indicates that the bonding that characterizes the divine life stands as the transcendent archetype for the dialectic of differentiation and commonality present in the dynamic of human sexuality. As was noted previously, the eternal generation of the Son constitutes the first trinitarian person as the Father of the Son and the second person as the Son of the Father, yet the two are bound together by the love they share, a bond that characterizes the divine nature as a whole but also emerges as a separate hypostasis in the third person, the Holy Spirit. In this way, the love that characterizes the relationship of the Father and the Son in the differentiation of each from the other means that they likewise share the sameness of the divine nature — that is, love.[148]

Similarly, when John Paul II compares Trinitarian love and spousal love, he highlights the relation between Father and Son, recalling Jesus' words in John 17:10, "All that is mine is yours and yours is mine, and I am glorified in them."[149] Grenz sees a similarity between his understanding of the Holy Spirit as the love (self-gift) of Father and Son, and the Trinitarian thought of John Paul II.[150] Both theologians employ Augustine's understanding of the Trinity, which identifies only the Father and the Son as persons who

147. Grenz, *The Social God,* 320. Grenz defends viewing the relation of Father and Son as *eros* with biblical references to Jesus' earthly ministry, wherein Jesus calls the Father "Abba." Aside from the obvious response that the language of "Abba" would appear to support familial love *(storge),* not *eros,* references to Jesus' earthly ministry illustrate how *eros* is apt language when understood as desire for communion with one that one does not have. Even while Jesus does nothing apart from the Father (John 8:28-29), Jesus was nevertheless separated from the Father during his earthly ministry and speaks of returning to the Father (John 14:12, 28). In his human nature he illustrates human desire for communion with God that goes beyond the "foretaste" provided by the presence of the Spirit in this penultimate age.

148. Grenz, *The Social God,* 321.

149. John Paul II, *Man and Woman,* 33.

150. "Pope John Paul II offers an especially lucid description of this eternal gifting: 'It can be said that in the Holy Spirit the intimate life of the Triune God becomes totally gift, an exchange of mutual love between the divine Persons, and that through the Holy Spirit God exists in the mode of gift. It is the Holy Spirit who is the *personal expression* of this self-giving, this being-love. He is Person-Love. He is Person-Gift.' " Grenz, *The Social God,* 328.

love while the Spirit is presented as the love or the gift exchanged/shared between these two. While neither denies the personhood of the Spirit, the emphasis placed on the first two persons within this model tends to downplay the reciprocity of the Spirit within the Trinity. As John Paul II wrote in his *Letter to Families,* "The divine 'We' is the eternal pattern of the human 'we,' formed by the man and the woman created in the divine image and likeness."[151]

The Augustinian model of the Trinity may possibly allow for the projection of *eros* onto the Godhead in a way that other presentations of the social Trinity would not.[152] More recent social models not only emphasize the relationality of the Father and the Son but also speak of the Spirit as an "I" and a "Thou," one who loves and is loved by Father and Son.[153] Reflections on divine love that begin with the relationality of three do not lead as quickly to analogies of human marriage, *eros,* or sexuality. A social model of the Trinity encourages the primacy of loves that are not restricted to a community of two. Emphasizing the difference between human marriage as a union of two and the Trinity as a union of three will highlight the difference between the type of union created by marriage and that which exists in the Godhead. Recovering the transcendent ground of love as the social Trinity places marriage and the conjugal sexual union in their proper places. They can stand as a subset, as one of the ways in which God's love can be worked out in human community, without elevating marital union to a place closer to divine union than the communion enjoyed by close friends or loving family members. Marriage is the union of two who do not complete one another

151. John Paul II, "Society Depends on Stable Families" (general audience, December 1, 1999), in *The Trinity's Embrace,* 292, citing *Letter to Families,* n. 6.

152. A thorough analysis of the relation between Trinitarian models and *eros* is beyond the scope of this paper but would be worthy of subsequent reflection.

153. Stanley Grenz identifies a shift in the development of social Trinitarianism between earlier models proposed by Barth and Rahner and the later models of Jürgen Moltmann, Wolfhart Pannenberg, and Robert Jenson whose emphasis on the priority of three laid the foundation for the work of Leonardo Boff, John Zizioulas, Catherine Mowry LaCugna, and others. Stanley J. Grenz, *Rediscovering the Triune God: The Trinity in Contemporary Theology* (Minneapolis: Fortress, 2004), 218-19. Emphasis on the three is of course not new; it can be traced especially to the Eastern formulae of Basil of Caesarea and Gregory of Nazianzus. Nevertheless, the Western tradition has tended to emphasize the oneness of God before God's existence as Trinity. Only in recent Western theological work has the priority of the three persons been rediscovered. See also J. Scott Horrell, "Toward a Biblical Model of the Social Trinity: Avoiding Equivocation of Nature and Order," *Journal of the Evangelical Theological Society* 47, no. 3 (September 2004): 399-421.

but who complement and help the other, all the while embedded in other interdependent relationships that also complement and help, enrich and uphold them. Marriage is not *the* icon of the social Trinity but *an* image of divine love. Marital love is upheld and embedded in the love of God that is higher, wider, deeper, and broader than the love marriage reflects.

Grenz's progressive account of the *imago,* which views the male-female relation as the primal image rather than the telos of the *imago Dei,* offers a way forward, but only when it is delivered from his insistence that ecclesial bonding is based upon human sexuality. While the human family grows through sexual union, the family of God grows through adoption — as humans respond out of (nonsexual) need to the redeeming love of God. The social *imago* as the ecclesial/eschatological community is the proper image of the social Trinity.

Conclusion

Gilbert Herdt, in his preface to the anthology *Third Sex, Third Gender: Beyond Sexual Dimorphism in Culture and History,* explains that he employs the category "third" not to limit the options to one more than two but to deconstruct the contrasts and comparisons that arise within a binary system.[154] A fully social Trinitarianism will take seriously the presence of a third who does not undermine duality but opens up the kinds of relations possible by moving beyond two subjects in relation. Reading divine relationality through the lens of the I-Thou or male-female leads more readily to the ontological duality of yin and yang than to the fruitful community of the Trinity. It is the Spirit who enlarges the relationship of Father and Son, beyond two and ultimately beyond three, folding the multitude of believers into the perichoretic union of the Godhead.[155] It is the Spirit who guards

154. Gilbert Herdt, preface to *Third Sex, Third Gender: Beyond Sexual Dimorphism in Culture and History,* ed. Gilbert Herdt (New York: Zone Books, 1994), 19.

155. Grenz presents the love that constitutes the ecclesial self as participation in the love Christ has for the Father: "Paul describes the mystery of the Christian life by means of the simple designation 'in Christ.' According to this metaphor, believers are constituted by their participation in Christ's own life, and their identity emerges from union with Christ. Because Jesus Christ is the eternal Son, those who are united with him share in the Son's relationship to God." Grenz, *The Social God,* 322. I would add that even though believers are grafted into Christ and enjoy his status of son, heir, brother, they nevertheless remain differentiated from Christ, even as Christ is differentiated from the Father and the Spirit.

against misreading the Trinity through an I-Thou that leaves us with little more than "the self-absorbed life of the Father and the Son, the One and the Other, exhausted in their dualism."[156]

By recovering the canonical place of Adam and Eve, theologians can affirm their position as progenitors of human relationality without holding them up as the paradigmatic form of human relationality in the image of the relational God. Relocating love from the binary model of spousal sexuality into the wider community of extended family, neighborhood, and *ecclesia* retains the social *imago* while delivering it from sexual distortions. It is the recovery of the social Trinity that can protect theologians from sexualizing Trinitarian love and from asking more of human sexuality than it can possibly bear. Such a shift should help retain the goodness of human sexuality without elevating it in such a way that monogamous sexual ethics are undermined, celibacy is devalued, and sexual dysfunction is misread as spiritual dysfunction. Such a vision makes space for the unmarried, for the nonsexually active, for eunuchs, and for intersexed persons to be recognized as fully made in the image of God — for these, too, are called into the community of faith as members of the social *imago.*

The social Trinity does provide the transcendent ground for the social *imago* — the understanding that humankind is called into being by a God who is a community of love and called to reflect that God through relations of love that restore, build, and heal community. In such a community, sex difference — male, female, and intersex — is but one difference among many and sexuality is kept in its proper place so that genuine communion can exist between male, female, and intersex persons in ways that bring wholeness to all.

This is the community John Paul II and Stanley Grenz want to ground in the social Trinity even while both understand that the fulfillment of this vision awaits the coming of God's reign. Thus, it is to the tension of the already/not yet in the postmodern present that we turn to conclude our study.

156. Janet Martin Soskice, *The Kindness of God: Metaphor, Gender, and Religious Language* (Oxford: Oxford University Press, 2007), 119.

CHAPTER 6

Jesus the True Image: Sex, Gender, and Sexuality in the Postmodern Already/Not Yet

Chapters 4 and 5 demonstrated that while evangelical and Roman Catholic theologians begin their theological anthropologies with the narratives of Adam and Eve, both traditions are looking to Jesus as the true image of God and to the eschaton for the final form of humanity conformed to the image of Christ. They insist that as helpful as the creation accounts may be, they are not to be understood as the final word. Rather, true humanity is found in Christ as a future toward which we are moving.

Jesus as the True Image: Christological and Eschatological Tensions

Jesus the Eschatological Imago *in John Paul II and Stanley Grenz*

Although he does not make this distinction in his *Theology of the Body,* in *The Trinity's Embrace* John Paul II teaches that two dimensions of life are offered to the human creature. The first is "physical and historical" and speaks to the divine image present in every human person — especially to human relationality and "the human couple's procreative capacity."[1] The second is "spiritual":

> [It] expresses our communion of love with the Father, through Christ in the power of the Holy Spirit: "The proof that you are sons is the fact that

1. John Paul II, "The Presence of the Trinity in Human Life" (general audience of June 7, 2000), in *The Trinity's Embrace: God's Saving Plan, a Catechesis on Salvation History* (Boston: Pauline Books and Media, 2002), 345-46.

> *God* has sent forth into our hearts the *Spirit* of his *Son* which cries out 'Abba!' ('Father!'). You are no longer a slave but a son! And the fact that you are a son makes you an heir by God's design" (Gal 4:6-7).
>
> Through grace this transcendent life instilled in us opens us to the future, beyond the limits of our frailty as creatures.[2]

Quoting *Evangelium Vitae (The Gospel of Life),* he concludes: "The dignity of this life is linked not only to its beginning, to the fact that it comes from God, but also to its final end, to its destiny of fellowship with God, in knowledge of love of him."[3]

Still, it is not clear in John Paul II's work whether this eschatological trajectory introduces anything new to his theological anthropology. The eschatological *imago* as *communio personarum* is presented as a return to the relationality found in the Garden.[4] Similarly, he writes that "the world itself, *restored to its original state,* facing no further obstacles, should be at the service of the just, 'sharing their glorification in the risen Jesus Christ.' "[5]

Stanley Grenz introduces his exploration of the eschatological *imago* toward the end of his theological anthropology by means of the following passage:

> [T]he claim that by means of the *imago dei* the dialectic of difference and commonality characteristic of human bonding offers an analogy to the dynamic within the eternal triune life does not mean that the true reflection of the image of God lies in the marital union of male and female. On the contrary, the New Testament reserves this place for the new humanity and, consequently, for the church as its prolepsis and sign. What John Knox concludes regarding Pauline thought, therefore, represents well the tenor of the New Testament as a whole: love "belongs essentially within the Christian community and has meaning there which it cannot have outside." In this manner, the ecclesial self becomes the self constituted by love; yet love constitutes the ecclesial self in a particular manner. Paul

2. John Paul II, "Presence of the Trinity," 347.

3. John Paul II, "Presence of the Trinity," 347, citing *Evangelium Vitae* 38.

4. John Paul II, *Man and Woman He Created Them: A Theology of the Body,* trans. and ed. Michael Waldstein (Boston: Pauline Books and Media, 2006), 400-401; homily 69:6-7.

5. John Paul II, "We Look to New Heavens and a New Earth" (general audience, January 31, 2001), in *The Trinity's Embrace,* 439-40, citing the *Catechism of the Catholic Church* (n. 1047; cf. Irenaeus, *Adversus haereses* 5.32.1), italics mine.

describes the mystery of the Christian life by means of the simple designation *"in Christ."*

According to this metaphor, *believers are constituted by their participation in Christ's own life, and their identity emerges from union with Christ.* Because Jesus Christ is the eternal Son, those who are united with him share in the Son's relationship to God. Although this is the case already in the here and now, the participation in the divine life that constitutes the ecclesial self remains ultimately future, and hence it is present in this age only in a proleptic manner. The ecclesial self, therefore, is ultimately, eschatological.[6]

As this project has shown, Grenz's progressive account of the *imago* begins with the sexual differentiation of Adam and Eve, moves from their sexual bond to Christ — the "true image" — who relates to the Father, not only through *philia* and *agape* but also through *eros* (the desire for communion with the beloved characteristic of the love between God the Son and God the Father). But the telos of the *imago* resides in the incorporation of believers into Christ, an incorporation that draws upon the metaphor of sexual bonding in marriage. Grenz believes that his project thus avoids the error he ascribed to Barth, whose use of I-Thou relations ultimately left sexuality behind.

In a similar manner, John Paul II also attempts to preserve the value of sex differentiation through his understanding of the "spousal meaning of the body," a meaning preserved in the eschaton despite the fact that marital relations are left behind. "[T]he 'spousal' meaning of the body in the resurrection to the future life will perfectly correspond both to the fact that man as male-female is a person, created in the 'image and likeness of God,' and to the fact that this image is realized in the communion of persons. That 'spousal' meaning of being a body will, therefore, be realized as a *meaning that is perfectly personal and communitarian at the same time.*"[7]

Both Grenz and John Paul II attempt to preserve the significance of sex, gender, and sexuality for human personhood by reading the relation of the believer to God and others in the ecclesial community through the lens of spousal sexuality. However, by conflating sex, gender, and sexuality they fail to recognize that sex and gender are not necessarily preserved by a

6. Stanley J. Grenz, *The Social God and the Relational Self: A Trinitarian Theology of the* Imago Dei (Louisville: Westminster John Knox, 2001), 321-22, italics mine.

7. John Paul II, *Man and Woman,* 399; homily 69:4.

vision of sexuality that can be divorced from sex and gender differentiation. If sexuality can be ascribed to God, if *eros* can properly be spoken of as one of the loves shared by Father and Son, then the preservation of sexuality, while it might preserve the differentiation of personhood, does not necessarily ensure the significance of *sex and/or gender* differentiation (given the traditional gendered names for the first and second persons of the Trinity). In addition, christological and eschatological visions of humanity as *imago Dei* can be employed to challenge the place of sex/gender differentiation for human personhood as much as they can be used to preserve them. These tensions must be addressed if we are to present a balanced vision of the place of sex, gender, and sexuality in theological anthropology in the postmodern present.

Christological and Eschatological Tensions

Jesus the Man The Vatican II document *Gaudium et Spes* lays out Roman Catholic theological anthropology as it relates to the doctrine of Christ. The authors of this document declare: "The most perfect answer to these questions [of the meaning of human existence] is found in God alone, who created women and men in his own image and redeemed them from sin; and this answer is given in the revelation in Christ his Son who became man. To follow Christ the perfect human is to become more human oneself."[8] Earlier in the document one finds a similar affirmation: "The mystery of man becomes clear only in the mystery of the incarnate Word. Adam, the first man *(primus homo),* was a type of the future, which is of Christ our Lord. Christ, the new Adam, in revealing the mystery of the Father and his love, makes man fully clear to himself, makes clear his high vocation."[9] Commenting on both of the above quotations, Janet Martin Soskice identifies "the unanswered question," that is, "does Christ make woman fully clear to herself?" She continues,

> The Latin of the instruction uses the more inclusive *homo/homine,* but the patterning is upon Adam and Christ, both male. What can it mean

8. *Gaudium et Spes,* 41, in *Vatican II: The Basic Sixteen Documents (A Completely Revised Translation in Inclusive Language),* ed. Austin Flannery (Northport, N.Y.: Costello Publishing Co., 1996), 208.

9. *Gaudium et Spes,* 22, cited in Janet Martin Soskice, *The Kindness of God: Metaphor, Gender, and Religious Language* (Oxford: Oxford University Press, 2007), 48.

> for women to say that "Whoever follows Christ, the perfect man, himself becomes more of a man" (§41: *Quicumque Christum sequitur, Hominem perfectum, et ipse magis homo fit*)? Do those aspects in which a woman is to become perfected or "more of a man" include only those aspects she shares with males, like her intellect and her life of virtue, or do they also include her mothering, her loving, her sense of her own embodiment which must be different from that of a man? Is Christ the fulfillment of female "men," as well as male "men," and if so, how?[10]

Recognizing the same problem that Soskice identifies, liberation theologian Leonardo Boff feared "that the incarnation divinized maleness explicitly but femaleness only implicitly."[11] Boff attempted to rectify the situation by suggesting that just as the Logos became incarnate in Jesus of Nazareth, so the Holy Spirit became incarnate in the female flesh of Mary. "Consequently, Boff elevates Jesus and Mary together as representing the whole of humanity as well as 'the eschatological event of the full divinization of men and women in the Kingdom of God.' "[12] Even though Boff's solution will appear unacceptable to most Protestants, and goes beyond the Mariology of the Vatican, nevertheless, he has identified one problem inherent in Roman Catholic and evangelical christological anthropologies — the problem of Jesus the man.

Some early Christians believed that redemption for women included their transformation into men, so that they could be fully conformed to the image of God, sons and heirs of God's promised redemption.[13] Certainly, as chapters 2 and 3 revealed, most ancient commentators at least presented the redemption of women as their development of *virtue* — an ideal never (fully) separated from manliness until the nineteenth and twentieth centuries. And within the one-sex model of the ancient world, the attainment of full humanity and virtue could be gained only by moving up the ladder toward masculine perfection.

Contrastively, other early Christians, along with Origen, believed that humans looked forward to a sexless existence in the eschaton. Ironically, both traditions — the tradition of masculine perfection and that of sexless

10. Soskice, *The Kindness of God,* 47-48.

11. In Stanley J. Grenz, *Rediscovering the Triune God: The Trinity in Contemporary Theology* (Minneapolis: Fortress, 2004), 128.

12. Grenz, *Rediscovering the Triune God,* 128, citing Leonardo Boff, *Trinity and Society,* trans. Paul Burns (Maryknoll, N.Y.: Orbis, 1988), 211.

13. Peter Brown, *The Body and Society: Men, Women, and Sexual Renunciation in Early Christianity* (New York: Columbia University Press, 1988), 109-11.

or androgynous humanity — draw from the same section of Paul's letter to the Galatians.

> For you are all sons of God through faith in Christ Jesus. For all of you who were baptized into Christ have clothed yourselves with Christ. There is neither Jew nor Greek, there is neither slave nor free man, there is neither male nor female; for you are all one in Christ Jesus. And if you belong to Christ, then you are Abraham's descendants, heirs according to promise. . . .
>
> But when the fullness of the time came, God sent forth His Son, born of a woman, born under the Law, so that He might redeem those who were under the Law, that we might receive the adoption as sons. And because you are sons, God has sent forth the Spirit of His Son into our hearts, crying, "Abba! Father!" Therefore you are no longer a slave, but a son; and if a son, then an heir through God. (Gal. 3:26-29; 4:4-7 NASB)

The tradition of masculine perfection follows the language of sonship. Jesus as Son brings about the redemption of every human, each becoming a son through incorporation into the Son. Jesus grants sonship to those who have clothed themselves with Christ. The tradition of sonship hearkens back to the last association of the image with Adam and Eve in the Old Testament, found in Genesis 5:1-3 ("he became the father of a son in his own likeness, according to his image, and named him Seth" [NASB]),[14] and emphasizes the similarity between Father and Son recalled in Hebrews 1:3 ("The Son is the radiance of God's glory and the exact representation of his being" [NIV]). In this tradition, the figure of a daughter would highlight dissimilarity, rather than similarity. Grenz argues that the language of sonship emphasizes love: "this is the theological meaning of the language 'Father' and 'Son,' for in ancient cultures, the son was the heir, the one upon whom the father lavishes all his wealth."[15] But his interpretation may not reflect the genuine love fathers had for daughters in the ancient world. It was not love that required the inheritance to be passed from father to son rather than from father to

14. "This is the book of the generations of Adam. In the day when God created [the *adam*], He made him [the *adam*] in the likeness of God. He created them male and female, and He blessed them and named them Man [*adam*] in the day when they were created. When Adam had lived one hundred and thirty years, he became the father of *a son* in his own likeness, according to his image, and named him Seth" (Gen. 5:1-3 NASB).

15. Stanley J. Grenz, "Belonging to God: The Quest for Communal Spirituality in the Postmodern World," *Asbury Theological Journal* 54, no. 2 (Fall 1999): 47.

daughter; it was the expectation that the son would grow up to be like the father — becoming a father himself, in need of an estate to support his own family. The emphasis on the similarity of father and son, or the preferential love of father for son, displays the challenge that emphasis on sonship introduces for women, intersex persons, eunuchs, or other "unmanly" men who did not or could not aspire to become *paterfamilias.*

1 Corinthians 11:7 and 15:47-49 were read in such a way as to support this exegetical tradition:

> For a man ought not to have his head veiled, since he is the image and reflection of God; but woman is the reflection of man. (NRSV)

> The first man *(anthropos)* was from the earth, a man of dust; the second man is from heaven. As was the man of dust, so are those who are of the dust; and as is the man of heaven, so are those who are of heaven. Just as we have borne the image of the man of dust, we will also bear the image of the man of heaven. (NRSV)

Soskice explains: "If Jesus Christ, unquestionably male, is the image of the invisible God, and we will all bear the image of the 'man of heaven,' then it seemed reasonable to some to conclude that women will be resurrected as men. Augustine to his lasting credit said 'no' to this and rejected at the same time the more orthodox view, that the resurrected body will be 'sexless.'"[16]

Although Soskice praises Augustine for rejecting such views, Augustine certainly wrestled with the tensions of these texts so that in the same section of his *De Trinitate* he can argue that women can be renewed in the image of God as they direct their minds away from "the government of temporal things" (7.7.12) *and* state that woman is not the image of God alone, but only when united to her husband (7.7.10). Augustine's argument that a woman can only be the image of God when united to her husband is not the position held by Barth, Grenz, and John Paul II (who emphasize the need for both sexes to adequately image God), for Augustine insisted that a man can be said to be the image even when not united to his wife (7.7.10).

By extension of Augustine's logic, it is only through marriage to Christ, the true husband/man/image of God, that any human (male, female, intersexed, eunuch) is renewed in the image of God. As Tyron Inbody summarizes, "Jesus himself, who is called the Christ, is unique, definitive, arche-

16. Soskice, *The Kindness of God,* 44.

typal, and normative for both the Christian understanding of the nature of God and of human beings."[17] As feminists have insisted, Jesus the God/man has transformed both God and man into male categories. These can function as emasculating all humans as they relate to the true "Man" or as a way to exclude or oppress anyone who is not a "man" — women, eunuchs, intersexed, and unmanly men.

Christ's unique place as true God, true man, true image bequeaths a complicated legacy for theological anthropology. And yet, other commentators look to this same section of Galatians, especially 3:28, as a way to counter the tradition of masculine perfection.

"In Christ There Is No Longer . . . Male and Female" As chapter 2 documented, those interpreters who emphasized the transformation of sex differentiation in the eschaton connected Galatians 3:28 with the eunuchs of Matthew 19:12 and the angels who do not marry in Matthew 22:30. Eunuchs came to be associated with angels on account of their (supposed) sexual continence, their freedom from the obligations of marriage (especially its ties to the economic structures of the day), their alternative gender, and their function as "perfect servants," loyal to their masters over natural family ties, and able to mediate divided realms (heaven/earth, male/female, sacred/secular, royalty/commoners). Eunuchs and angels represented an alternative sex, an alternative gender, and an alternative sexuality. By connecting eunuchs and angels, the Church Fathers were forced to consider the significance of sex, gender, and sexuality in the "already" and the "not yet."

Many New Testament scholars have also noted that Jesus' failure to live up to ancient ideals of masculinity, particularly his abstention from marriage and the fathering of children, may stand behind his defense of the eunuch in Matthew 19:12. Davies and Allison write, "Jesus frequently picked upon the names he was called — glutton, drunkard, blasphemer, friend of toll-collectors and sinners — to turn them around for some good end, [so] it seems possible enough that Mt 19.12 was originally an apologetical encounter, a response to the jeer that Jesus was a eunuch."[18]

Despite their willingness to suggest that Jesus was harassed as a eunuch,

17. Tyron L. Inbody, *The Many Faces of Christology* (Nashville: Abingdon, 2002), 117.

18. W. D. Davies and Dale C. Allison Jr., *A Critical and Exegetical Commentary on the Gospel according to Saint Matthew,* vol. 3 (Edinburgh: T. & T. Clark, 1988), 25. Cf. Craig S. Keener, *A Commentary on the Gospel of Matthew* (Grand Rapids: Eerdmans, 1999), 470 n. 30, and Ulrich Luz, *Matthew 8–20: A Commentary,* trans. James E. Crouch, ed. Helmut Koester (Minneapolis: Fortress, 2001), 502.

all of these commentators seem to suggest that this was only a jeer, an insult thrown at Jesus because of his unwillingness to marry. None consider whether Jesus could have accomplished salvation for the world as a literal eunuch. While many liberation feminists have argued that the Messiah may not have been recognized as such had the second person of the Trinity become incarnate as a woman — nor would a female "Christa" have been able to challenge the patriarchal order of the ancient world — none have considered what Jesus' incarnation as a eunuch, perhaps as a man with Klinefelter's syndrome, one naturally "caught between" the sexes, would mean for Christology and anthropology.[19]

Queer theologians have seized upon the declaration of Galatians 3:28 and proclaimed a queer Christ "whose own life and teaching runs against the grain of modern heterosexuality, a Jesus like us."[20] Virginia Ramey Mollenkott, in her book *Omnigender,* argues that the baptismal formula in Galatians 3:28 not only should imply "that the social and political advantages of being male in patriarchal cultures were to be shared equitably with females," but that it can and should be read literally — erasing the distinction between men and women so that others are included not only in the eschatological community but also in the present inauguration of that vision.[21] She looks for a literal fulfillment of omnigender in Jesus himself, seizing upon a scientific account of the virgin birth given by Edward L. Kessel (emeritus professor of biology at the University of San Francisco). Kessel suggested that a parthenogenetic conception (the development of an unfertilized ovum) would have rendered Jesus chromosomally female (XX, since he took his flesh entirely from Mary his mother).[22] His phenotypic presentation as male may

19. Inbody, *Many Faces of Christology,* 123.

20. Elizabeth Stuart et al., *Religion Is a Queer Thing: A Guide to the Christian Faith for Lesbian, Gay, Bisexual, and Transgendered People* (London and Washington, D.C.: Cassell, 1997), 79. "This is good news because it guarantees that eventually homophobic and heterosexist oppression will cease. It is good news because it means that God's *basileia* is being worked out in the queer community, but with that good news comes responsibility. We have to live out the vision of the *basileia* in our own lives and communities if we are to experience anything of its liberatory potential. This might mean following Jesus' example of prophetic action or transgressive practice" (83).

21. Virginia Ramey Mollenkott, *Omnigender: A Trans-religious Approach* (Cleveland: Pilgrim Press, 2001), viii.

22. Ironically, ancient embryology led to the opposite conclusion: "God as source of generation, and Logos, as seed of generation, . . . are symbolically male. In a scheme wherein only males are truly generative, then, in a sense, only males can truly give birth. The only true parent is the father, source of seed which it is the female task to nurture." Soskice, *The*

have come about through natural sex reversal.[23] While Mollenkott's recital of Kessel's proposal does not list a specific intersex condition as a possible reason for "sex reversal," I would suggest that a severe case of congenital adrenal hyperplasia in an XX fetus could have produced a substantial enough phallus for sex assignment as male and male secondary sex development. Mollenkott ponders,

> I cannot help making a connection to the Genesis depiction of a God who is imaged as both male and female and yet is literally neither one nor the other. A chromosomally female, phenotypically male Jesus would come as close as a human body could come to a perfect image of such a God. And since I do not share Kessel's view that hermaphrodites or intersexual people are necessarily pathological or defective, it seems to me that from the perspective of his findings, intersexuals come closer than anybody to a physical resemblance of Jesus.[24]

Mollenkott does not move from here to privileging intersex persons as the only adequate representatives of Jesus, as if only intersex persons should be ordained, etc. Rather, she employs this account to deconstruct the privileges conferred upon men as the only adequate representatives of a male Christ and masculine God. Her vision begins with an omnigender God, who creates humans in this image ("male and female"), who is embodied by Jesus (the parthenogenetic female-male Christ), and is ultimately consummated in the male or female, male and female, transgendered community that makes up the body of Christ, the church. "We have already seen that Jesus of Nazareth is not exclusively a male Savior after all, judging from his/her parthenogenic [*sic*] birth. Now we see that Holy Scripture depicts Christian men as his/her brides and Christian women as his/her brothers. At the very least, such biblical gender blending ought to encourage those who take scripture seriously to become less rigid about gender identities,

---

Kindness of God, 109-10. She quotes Aquinas, who defended this view. "Aquinas, in the *Contra Gentiles,* suggests that one reason why we do not speak of the First Person of the Trinity as Mother is because God begets actively, and the role of the mother in procreation is passive (IV. 11.19)" (109-10). Nevertheless, the insistence that Jesus took his flesh from his mother required her participation in more than nurturing the seed of the Father.

23. Edward L. Kessel, "A Proposed Biological Interpretation of the Virgin Birth," *Journal of the American Scientific Affiliation* (September 1983): 129-36, cited in Mollenkott, *Omnigender,* 105.

24. Mollenkott, *Omnigender,* 106.

roles, and presentations."[25] Where other scholars use the multiplicity and overlap of gendered descriptions to argue for metaphor against literality,[26] Mollenkott, and other queer theologians, argue for a literal reading of transgendered or omnigendered language in the Scriptures.

Cornwall highlights the fluidity of gendered imagery especially in medieval devotion and mysticism; she explains,

> Although it is anachronistic to project contemporary constructions of sexuality and gender identity back onto communities which understood them very differently, it is important to recognize that even Christians have not always understood maleness and femaleness, masculinity and femininity as either-or, mutually-exclusive categories in exactly the ways that one might suppose. Caroline Walker Bynum, Sarah Coakley, Michael Nausner and others have usefully reflected on unusual or even overtly "gender-bending" figurings of gender in the medieval mystics, in Gregory of Nyssa and elsewhere. . . . What this means is that "queer," transgressive and "crossing" bodies are always already present to theology in its own past, and that "atypical" intersexed or transsexual bodies therefore already map onto the mixed-up, much-inscribed Body of Christ.[27]

25. Mollenkott, *Omnigender,* 112.

26. Soskice, *The Kindness of God,* esp. 77-83, where she draws on Ricoeur (*The Conflict of Interpretations: Essays in Hermeneutics,* trans. D. Ihde [Evanston, Ill.: Northwestern University Press, 1974]) and Jürgen Moltmann ("The Motherly Father: Is Trinitarian Patripassianism Replacing Theological Patriarchalism?" in *God as Father?* ed. Metz et al. [Edinburgh: T. & T. Clark, 1981], 51). Soskice also reflects on early Syriac Christian texts that included more feminine imagery in their worship of the Trinity: "All three Persons of the Trinity can be styled in the imagery of the human masculine and of the human feminine. But better still, the play of gendered imagery keeps in place the symbols of desire, fecundity, and parental love, while destabilizing any over-literalistic reading. This seems to be the implicit strategy of the Old Testament itself, where images of God as bridegroom and father jostle against one another in a way that would make an overly literalistic reading noxious" (115).

27. Susannah Cornwall, "'State of Mind' versus 'Concrete Set of Facts': The Contrasting of Transgender and Intersex in Church Documents on Sexuality," *Theology and Sexuality* 15, no. 1 (2009): 8. Cornwall references Caroline Walker Bynum, "The Body of Christ in the Later Middle Ages: A Reply to Leo Steinberg," *Renaissance Quarterly* 39, no. 3 (Autumn 1986): 399-439; Sarah Coakley, *Powers and Submissions: Spirituality, Philosophy, and Gender* (Oxford: Blackwell, 2002); and Michael Nausner, "Toward Community beyond Gender Binaries: Gregory of Nyssa's Transgendering as Part of His Transformative Eschatology," *Theology and Sexuality* 8, no. 16 (March 2002): 55-56.

Reflecting on the same material, Janet Soskice remarks:

> A striking medieval example . . . can be found in Julian of Norwich. So much has been made of Julian's dramatic styling of Christ as mother that we almost fail to notice the splendour of Revelations of Divine Love as a piece of Trinitarian theology. . . . [I]n placing great emphasis on Christ as our Mother, she is at once provocative and altogether orthodox: Jesus was indubitably male, yet, if he is to be the perfection of our humanity, he must also be the perfection of female humanity.[28]

All these theologians are attempting to break open the maleness of Jesus, in order to open up space for women and others. Soskice looks to the gender-blending imagery of the mystics as helpful yet metaphorical ("Jesus was indubitably male"). Cornwall focuses on the ecclesial body of Christ in its plurality of human bodies — male, female, intersexed, transgendered, etc. Mollenkott looks to the gender blending of both church and Christ "him/herself."

Like Mollenkott, J. David Hester takes the sex/gender-blending of eunuchs literally, connecting the "transgressive body of the eunuch that symbolizes the kingdom" to the "baptismal formula of Gal. 3:28" in celebration of "the postgender Jesus" and "transgressive sexualities."[29] Cornwall concurs that the maleness of Jesus is "already a complicated picture," as Jesus stands for both masculinity and femininity. Jesus is the husband/head of the church/bride before whom men must become as submissive wives. But Jesus also stands as the (feminine) receiver, the other to whom God the Father relates as (masculine) initiator — the supermasculine.[30]

Given the sex/gender-blending of Jesus' person — either in his gender performance or in his very body — combined with the eschatological proclamation that in "Christ there is no longer . . . male and female," it is no wonder that intersex and transgender theologians are questioning the binary model of societal organization. The central question that frames the contemporary debate is *when: "when* the overturning of these sex-gender differences is supposed to take place."[31]

28. Soskice, *The Kindness of God,* 115.

29. J. David Hester, "Eunuchs and the Postgender Jesus: Matthew 19.12 and Transgressive Sexualities," *Journal for the Study of the New Testament* 28, no. 1 (2005): 38-39.

30. Cornwall, countering Barth's theological use of gender, in Cornwall, *Sex and Uncertainty in the Body of Christ: Intersex Conditions and Christian Theology* (London: Equinox, 2010), 79.

31. Hester, "Eunuchs," 39.

Chapter 2 illustrated that many early Christians recognized the challenge of eschatology for sex and gender distinctions; nevertheless, most relegated sexual activity to the present life — connected as it was to birth and death. The eschatological end of marriage, which Jesus declared in Matthew 22:30, was believed to indicate the end of sexual activity. After the condemnation of Origen, on account of a desire to uphold the resurrection of the body, a consensus began to form that while sex identity would remain at the resurrection, gender and sexuality would be altered in the coming kingdom. Early Christian commentators rejected the idea that sexual relations would continue after the resurrection and most envisioned a transformation of gender, particularly the transformation of female subordination brought about by the sin of Eve or the supposed natural inferiority of the female sex confirmed through the institution of marriage (which required obedience to husbands) and the hierarchical ordering of church and state.[32] Although some Church Fathers were willing to speak of a sexless soul, and the reworking of sex/gender relations in the eschaton, they continued to draw a sharp divide between this life and the next. As Matthew Kuefler observed, their theological anthropologies protected the power structures of the present age, "rendering the genderless ideal of earliest Christianity quaint but harmless."[33]

Given the renewed emphasis on the place of eschatology for theological anthropology, contemporary commentators are reconsidering that interpretive move. Some contemporary theologians believe that by putting off the reordering of sex and gender to an eschatological future, significant harm will continue to be perpetrated in the present. The power of the eschatological vision to transform injustices in this life, inaugurating the justice of the coming kingdom, has led theologians to reconsider the significance of Galatians 3:28 for life in the "already." Cornwall wrestles with these complexities, noting that the inauguration of sex/gender transformation in the "realized temporal world . . . seems too unrealistic or utopian for most theologians to take seriously." She explains,

> I am not proposing that intersexed individuals are harbingers of the Gal. 3.28-order, liminal or united firstfruits of the coming age. It would be

32. See especially Jerome, Letter 48, *To Pammachius* 14; and Augustine, *Sermon on the Mount* 1.15.40-41.

33. Matthew Kuefler, *The Manly Eunuch: Masculinity, Gender Ambiguity, and Christian Ideology in Late Antiquity* (Chicago: University of Chicago Press, 2001), 230.

> highly problematic to use them in this way. But even if it would be naïve to read Gal. 3.28 as a simple prophecy of sexual androgyny in this present realm, it must be read as questioning something about the way in which females and males relate to one another in God's economy. The Galatians text implies that there is something about participation in Christ, about *perichoresis* between Christ and the church and between humans, which means that even such apparently self-evident concepts as sexed nature are not to be taken as read in the nascent new order.[34]

In her exegesis of Galatians 3:28, Cornwall focuses on the conjunction male *and* female as opposed to the comparison found in the first two couplings (Jew *or* Greek, slave *or* free). She argues, "The assertion that there is no male *and* female in Christ does not necessarily mean that there is no male *or* female; biological reproduction in its present form is therefore still possible. However, what no longer exists in Christ is the all-encompassing cipher 'male-and-female' for humanity. Humanity does not exist in Christ only as male-and-female as they relate to each other . . . wherein humans are completed as humans only by so-called sexual complementarity."[35]

Like Mollenkott, Cornwall wants to open up space for others, envisioning "a society where sex and gender do not work as a binary but rather as a continuum or a multiplicity, and where anatomy (particularly genital anatomy) is not unproblematically used as a cipher for identity." She continues,

> If male-and-female is passing away, then it need not stand for or encompass everyone; human bodies need not be altered to "fit" it, particularly before those who live in them (like neonates with intersex/DSD conditions) can express an opinion. . . . The "no more male-and-female in Christ," then, means no more taxonomies of goodness or perfection attached to the success or otherwise of how a given body meets certain criteria for maleness or femaleness. . . . The end — the cessation — of male-and-female is the end — the *telos* — for humanity. This is the crux of reading Gal. 3.28 in a more than future sense, for a realized eschatology is rooted in the *already,* the possibility for the redemption of this present realm.[36]

34. Cornwall, *Sex and Uncertainty,* 72.
35. Cornwall, *Sex and Uncertainty,* 72-73.
36. Cornwall, *Sex and Uncertainty,* 73-74.

Inaugurating Christ's Eschatological Justice

While eschatology and Christology do provide fruitful ground for theological anthropology, their answers to the significance of sex, gender, and sexuality are ambivalent — at times raising more questions than they answer. What can be clearly observed, however, is that those who have shifted away from the "Jesus the man" paradigm to "In Christ there is no longer . . . male and female" do so on account of a concern to address injustices in the human community in light of the righteousness of God to be revealed in the coming kingdom, inaugurated already but not yet fulfilled.

Cornwall notes how eschatology can be used either as an escape from responsibility to pursue justice in the present or as motivation to work with God in inaugurating the kingdom.[37] Reflecting on the implications for the debates surrounding intersex surgery, she writes, "A belief that bodies will be 'fixed' after death sometimes makes it too easy to dismiss the struggles faced currently, but an attitude that human beings might be co-redeemers with Christ encourages endeavouring to do everything possible to eradicate enforced discommodity and promote inclusion."[38] She insists, "Healing is not simply about individuals, but about communities — overcoming fears about a subsuming of identity which then provoke a desperate clinging to arbitrary categories. It is this which then leads to an unwillingness to accept those who are 'other' — the impaired, the intersexed, the liminal — perhaps out of a fear that to speak with someone necessitates losing one's own voice."[39]

The question to be answered is how best to work toward the eschatological justice that God's kingdom is already bringing but is far from complete. Those thinking theologically about intersex have proffered three solutions: omnigender, proposed by Virginia Ramey Mollenkott; the end of gender proposal of J. David Hester; and the *kenosis* of sex identity posited by Susannah Cornwall. All three begin with an earnest desire to bring freedom to the oppressed: to intersex persons, LGBTQ persons, and anyone else oppressed by the binary gender model and the heteronormativity upon which it is based.

Omnigender Mollenkott argues that opening up the binary model to include more gender options and the blurring/queering of these categories are

37. Susannah Cornwall, "The Kenosis of Unambiguous Sex in the Body of Christ: Intersex, Theology, and Existing 'for the Other,'" *Theology and Sexuality* 14, no. 2 (January 2008): 187-88.

38. Cornwall, "Kenosis," 194-95.

39. Cornwall, "Kenosis," 196.

the ways to correct gender injustice in society. She laments, "the traditional assignment of males to the more powerful roles of the public sphere and females to the more supportive roles of the private sphere has brought with it a host of inequities. Money, prestige, influence, and honor are accorded to those who function publicly but domestic work is hardly respected as work, let alone financially rewarded. . . . [S]uch injustice renders urgent the need for a new gender pluralism, a nonhierarchical omnigender paradigm."[40] Following the recommendations of Martine Rothblatt, transwoman (male-to-female transsexual) and author of *The Apartheid of Sex,*[41] Mollenkott suggests the following changes to societal organization:

> Children would be brought up as males, or females, or simply as persons, according to the option of their parents — at least until the child is old enough to decide and express their own gender identity. . . . In such a society intersexual babies could comfortably be brought up that way until they could express their own preference about sex assignment, hormones, and surgery.
>
> There would be no sex/gender typing on governmental records such as birth, marriage or death certificates, passports, and motor vehicle licenses. . . .
>
> Bathrooms in a gender-fluid society would be unisexual. Inside they would look like women's restrooms today: no urinals, only sit-down toilets enclosed in privacy stalls. (As I write, a marine troop carrier, the USS *San Antonio,* is being built without urinals in any of the heads, as precursor of the society to come.) Children would be taught to sit down to urinate, regardless of their genitals. To discourage sexual predators, public lavatory space would be under automatic video surveillance; but simply the fact that any person of any gender, age, strength, and sexuality might enter the rest room at any time should in itself be an important deterrent to rape or other unwanted attentions.[42]

Sports and prisons would no longer be sex segregated; she believes this would make matters more equitable for all. "Since separate is never equal, athletes with vaginas would at last have equal access to sports arenas, practice times and areas, top athletic scholarships and salaries, and first-rate

40. Mollenkott, *Omnigender,* 3.
41. Martine Rothblatt, *The Apartheid of Sex* (New York: Crown, 1995).
42. Mollenkott, *Omnigender,* 167-69.

coaching. And people with atypical chromosomal makeup would no longer be humiliated by exclusion from competition."[43]

In many ways the proposal suggests a return to something like the one-sex paradigm of the classical Greco-Roman period, except that in this model the differences inhering in the one sex are not organized hierarchically. In this, Mollenkott parts ways with other transgender theorists, such as Holly Devor, who suggests that masculinity and femininity are immature stages in human development and transgender is the new model of gender perfection. Writes Mollenkott, "I hope and trust that in an omnigender culture, 'masculine' men and 'feminine' women would not necessarily be judged as immature but would be acceptable as anyone else as long as they were truly comfortable and fulfilled by that gendering. Our goal is not to produce a different gender underclass, but to do away with gender hierarchies altogether."[44]

Mollenkott should certainly be applauded for her genuine concern for equality, but her proposal overlooks the fact that justice often requires treating people differently rather than the same. Justice requires special attention to the vulnerable, and global statistics continue to show that women and children make up the largest percentage of the most vulnerable. When "[w]omen aged fifteen through forty-four are more likely to be maimed or die from male violence than from cancer, malaria, traffic accidents, and war combined," eliminating gender-segregated bathrooms and prisons hardly sounds like the most compassionate response.[45] It is true that intersex, transgendered, and queer persons are also targets of (typically male) violence. In light of this, it would seem that working toward equal safety for all might require paying more attention to difference (e.g., family, unisex, handicapped bathrooms) rather than eliding difference in the name of equality.

The End of Gender J. David Hester's scheme is slightly different. Hester is dissatisfied with proposals such as those by Kessler and McKenna that employ intersex to argue that there is no such thing as sex, that there is only gender. He reverses the constructivist's perspective by arguing that the recognition of multiple sexes eradicates the gender paradigm altogether.

43. Mollenkott, *Omnigender,* 170.

44. Mollenkott, *Omnigender,* 172.

45. Nicholas D. Kristof and Sheryl WuDunn, *Half the Sky: Turning Oppression into Opportunity for Women Worldwide* (New York: Vintage, 2009), 61.

> "Having" a sex is different than "being" a gender, because even with the fluidity of "gender" (and therefore the implicit freedom to deviate) it presumes a stable body through which gender can be performed, or upon which gender can be carved out. But while people ponder the possibility of multiplying genders, asking what does it mean to "enact" feminine/masculine/queer/straight/bi-/trans identities, very rarely do people ponder the possibility of having no clearly identifiable sex.[46]

Hester asks, "why must we have a sex? . . . The question to occupy us is no longer how do *we* shape the body, but how does the body *also* shape us?"[47]

> I am suggesting a fundamental alternative for gender theorists and gender ethicists to ponder: sex is far more important than gender. So important, in fact, that when sex does not fit, gender concepts will come and *make* a sex. The body is required to have a sex *before* subjectivity and agency can be ascribed and recognized. Indeed, I would suggest that the lesson from intersexed people is that the obligation of a body to have an identifiable sex is the most fundamental ethical obligation of our culture. It is only on this basis that medical intervention in non-emergent cases of intersexuality can be justified. It is only on this basis that legal requirements for sexed identity can be explained.[48]

Whereas social constructionists assume a passive body that is given meaning through culture, Hester argues that "intersexed bodies show just the opposite *as well:* there is no such thing as gender, it is all *sex.*"[49]

Responding to Hester's assertion that intersex brings about the end of gender, Cornwall counters by recalling that some intersexed persons are content with the two-gender model.

> ISNA [Intersex Society of North America], for example, insisted that claiming an intersexed identity does *not* necessarily entail situating oneself within a liminal or third gender (Herndon 2006), although some people with intersex/DSD conditions do identify as androgynous. What Hester's argument actually implies is that intersex/DSD bodies are post*sex,* not

46. J. David Hester, "Intersexes and the End of Gender: Corporeal Ethics and Postgender Bodies," *Journal of Gender Studies* 13, no. 3 (November 2004): 222.

47. Hester, "End of Gender," 223.

48. Hester, "End of Gender," 222.

49. Hester, "End of Gender," 220.

> postgender. ISNA's point was that it is possible to have a clear gender (which is not necessarily the same as a permanent gender) without having an "unambiguous" binary sex.[50]

Rather than arguing for omnigender or the end of gender, Cornwall suggests an alternative proposal.

Kenosis of Sex Identity Although she is willing to draw parallels between intersex and gender-queer theorists/theologians, Cornwall reminds these same authors to consider those intersex persons who are not asking for a remaking of the world of gender. She warns, "Making a person 'mean' concepts with which they may not wish to be associated — as when an intersexed individual is held up as necessarily queering heterosexual gender-mapping even if they themselves would not wish to be aligned with such a project — risks distorting and misrepresenting them. This might be interpreted as doing violence to their personhood."[51] Following Iain Morland, she suggests that concern for "weaker members" of Christ's body (1 Cor. 12) might lead to an alternative application, namely, that it is "those whose bodies are considered unremarkable in terms of a sex-gender harmony who must be prepared to relinquish the (unsolicited) power and status which currently comes with such a state of affairs."[52] Following the language of Philippians 2:7 used to describe the example of Jesus who did not cling to the privileges associated with his divinity but "emptied himself" *(ekenōsen),* Cornwall asks, How would such a *kenosis* be enacted? Cornwall suggests opting out of declaring one's sex on questionnaires where such information is not pertinent and rejecting gender stereotypes in our own language or that of others. She continues: "Within churches, it could be refusing to participate in disseminating teaching or liturgy grounded in essentialist, complementarist norms of maleness and femaleness on which masculinity and femininity are supposed unproblematically to supervene. Crucially, however, rather than eliding bodily differences (as Mollenkott's 'omnigender' society threatens to do), a multiplicity and immense range of variation should be acknowledged and celebrated."[53] Morland goes even further, suggesting that "[n]on-intersexed people who seek justice for the intersexed should refuse the identities 'male' or 'female.'"[54]

50. Cornwall, *Sex and Uncertainty,* 206.
51. Cornwall, "Kenosis," 186.
52. Cornwall, "Kenosis," 188.
53. Cornwall, *Sex and Uncertainty,* 105.
54. Iain Morland, "Narrating Intersex: On the Ethical Critique of the Medical Man-

There is arguably more fluidity for the category of gender — especially given Hester's call for the "end of gender." However, refusing to identify as male or female when the category fits does not aid in personal identification. It might be more helpful to allow other markers into the category of sex, such as intersex, male-to-female transsexual (transwoman), female-to-male transsexual (transman), etc., for identification purposes on governmental and medical records.

Still, Cornwall's more modest suggestions do merit consideration, especially as one recognizes the privilege — "the (unsolicited) power and status" — attending unambiguous bodies.[55] "Kenosis for non-intersexed people necessitates thinking ourselves into the margins — not in order to colonize experience which is not ours" but to learn from and work with the intersexed for justice and inclusion.[56] She agrees with Hester, who has argued that "one strategy for overcoming the marginalization of people with intersex/DSD conditions might be one which recognizes that 'healing' is not 'healing from,' but living comfortably and healthily with oneself as intersex."[57]

Certainly communities of care, educated about intersex and willing to learn from the experiences of others, can aid in this kind of healing, but only as they learn to overcome their own fears that intersex can raise. Cornwall highlights these fears by comparing intersex with disability. She names what Frances Young, Jean Vanier, and others have noted, that "the able bodied fear the disabled not because disability is so far away from the 'good' body but because it is so close."[58] Just as Peter Brown's study revealed that ancient eunuchs were feared because they were reminders of what men could become, so, Cornwall suggests, the nonintersexed fear the intersexed for similar reasons.[59] "There are those of us whose bodies match the current

---

agement of Intersexuality, 1985-2005" (Ph.D. diss., Royal Holloway, University of London, 2005), 131, cited in Cornwall, "Kenosis," 189.

55. Cornwall, "Kenosis," 188.

56. Cornwall, "Kenosis," 197.

57. Cornwall, "Kenosis," 183, citing J. David Hester, "Intersex(es) and Alternative Strategies of Healing: Medicine, Social Imperatives and Counter Communities of Identity" (in German), *Zeitschrift für Ethik in der Medizin* (2004); available in English at http://www.ars-rhetorica.net/J_David_Hester/Intersexes_files/AlternativeStrategies.pdf, 5.

58. Cornwall, "Kenosis," 195, citing Frances M. Young, *Face to Face: A Narrative Essay in the Theology of Suffering* (Edinburgh: T. & T. Clark, 1990), 170. See also Jean Vanier with Krista Tippett, "The Wisdom of Tenderness" ([interviewed] October 28, 2007, [aired] December 20, 2007, and December 24, 2009), http://being.publicradio.org/programs/2009/wisdom-of-tenderness.

59. Brown, *The Body and Society,* 10-11.

criteria for accepted maleness or femaleness, but this does not necessarily mean that this will be so forever. Perhaps intersexed bodies threaten nonintersexed people because, as historian and activist for intersex issues Alice Dreger says, 'The questioned body forces us to ask exactly what it is — if anything — that makes the rest of us unquestionable.' "[60] Returning to the question of eschatology, Cornwall suggests that "rather than assuming intersexed bodies will be perfected to unambiguity, we ought to ask what eschatologies of perfection suggest about our own body anxieties."[61] Working from the question of the resurrection of nonintersexed bodies to those of the intersexed, she ponders:

> Both male and female bodies have already undergone enormous changes, particularly at puberty, before reaching adulthood. The bodies of women who have borne children also appear different afterwards: is it the pre- or post-motherhood body that is more perfect and will be retained in the general resurrection? What body might we expect for someone shorn of an undersized penis and brought up as a girl, who has decided to make the best of a bad gender-assignment despite experiencing gender dysphoria? *Quite simply, it is neither possible nor desirable to specify what resurrection bodies will be like; but the one thing they will all share will be a redeemed body story rather than an unproblematically "perfected" body by human standards. . . .* Conceivably, the pain and prejudice attached to a particular physical configuration will melt away without thereby erasing either the beauty of that specific configuration, or the geneaological importance of the life lived in this body in its joy and woundedness.[62]

Cornwall believes that an eschatological vision of inclusion is a powerful motivator for Christians seeking justice for the intersexed in the present. Such communities of care not only bring healing to intersexed who have experienced exclusion and shame but can also work to heal the nonintersexed of their own bodily anxieties.

Evaluating the Contributions of Mollenkott, Hester, and Cornwall Mollenkott, Hester, and Cornwall have provided important and thoughtful

60. Cornwall, "Kenosis," 195-96, citing Alice Domurat Dreger, *Hermaphrodites and the Medical Invention of Sex* (Cambridge: Harvard University Press, 1998), 6.

61. Cornwall, "Kenosis," 184.

62. Cornwall, *Sex and Uncertainty*, 189, italics mine.

contributions to the challenges intersex raises for Christian theology and ecclesial communities. They are right to point out the injustices that have been and continue to be perpetrated in societies that privilege unambiguous bodies, one sex over another, and certain gendered behaviors over others. They raise prophetic voices, calling Christians to account for our failings in these areas, preaching repentance, and culling the Scriptures and the history of Christianity for resources to stem the tide of injustice and work for the inbreaking of God's eschatological justice. Evaluating the devastating effects of sex/gender abuse around the world, *New York Times* correspondents Nicholas Kristof and Sheryl WuDunn have surmised: "In the nineteenth century, the central moral challenge was slavery. In the twentieth century, it was the battle against totalitarianism. We believe that in this century the paramount moral challenge will be the struggle for gender equality around the world."[63] Certainly Mollenkott, Hester, and Cornwall are right that working with God to bring about Christ's eschatological justice should include not just equality for women but also justice and equality for the intersexed whose contributions and abuses have yet to be recorded in most histories. And yet, questions remain about how best to accomplish this.

Despite the careful attention of Mollenkott, Hester, and Cornwall to the voices of some intersexed persons and their insightful contributions for bringing about greater measures of justice, their proposals come with baggage likely to prejudice more conservative Christians against even their more modest contributions. The structural changes they recommend, namely, the dismantling of "heteronormativity," go well beyond opening up space for the intersexed in our communities. While they disagree in their proposed solutions, Mollenkott and Cornwall both work from the premise that intersex challenges the binary framework, and so that framework should be eliminated.[64] Cornwall writes, "[I]ntersex does not only exist as an example of something which stands between two distinct things; actually, it problematizes the model of there being two distinct things in the first place. Intersex shows that human sex is not a simple binary; and, since any exception to a dualistic model necessarily undermines the model in its entirety, this makes essentialist assumptions about what constitutes 'concrete facts' even more precarious."[65]

63. Kristof and WuDunn, *Half the Sky*, xvii.

64. Mollenkott, *Omnigender*, 51.

65. Cornwall, "State of Mind," 17.

Because they view "heteronormativity" as the central problem, they are working not only to open up space for the intersexed but also to dismantle entirely the system upon which marriage has been traditionally established. They supply no rationale for heterosexual coupling beyond procreation and no reason for marriage — the permanence of the sexual bond — beyond personal preference. Following Kathy Rudy's work, in *Sex and the Church: Gender, Homosexuality, and the Transformation of Christian Ethics,*[66] Mollenkott writes, "[T]he pertinent question is not whether we are living monogamously or in communities where loving support exists in a different pattern, but whether our acts unite us into one body and whether our contexts enable our lives to transcend meaninglessness."[67] And again, "To expand on one of Kathy Rudy's statements, 'When sex acts [or identities or even performances], whether gay or straight [or otherwise], monogamous or communal, function in a way that leads us to God, they ought to be considered moral. The family does not guarantee such moral status, and indeed sometimes prevents us from fully participating in community. . . .' "[68] How to discern which acts lead us to God is a question Mollenkott neither raises nor answers. It is true that the family does not guarantee the moral status of sexual acts — abuse within the family is of grave concern for all Christians — but it is not evident that dismantling the family is the best solution.

Cornwall's generous evaluation of proposals such as Rudy's — which presents polyamory and communal sexual activity as both moral and Christian — leads one to wonder just where she draws the line for sexual ethics. She is clear that there must be boundaries for Christian sexual behavior but says little more than that sexual practice must promote love, the well-being of the participants, and the well-being of society as a whole. She admits that these decisions are difficult and demurs from detailing one particular response to the complexities of sexual desire and practice. Still, she admits, "There might still, and always, be aspects of some behaviors held to be incompatible with certain tenets of Christianity: it would be difficult to argue that any kind of non-consensual sex, such as rape or sex with children, could be deemed just or pleasurable for everyone concerned."[69]

Like Kessler and McKenna, many queer theologians are quick to look to technological interventionsas advances that relegate procreative marriage

66. Kathy Rudy, *Sex and the Church: Gender, Homosexuality, and the Transformation of Christian Ethics* (Boston: Beacon Press, 1997).

67. Mollenkott, *Omnigender,* 162.

68. Mollenkott, *Omnigender,* 163.

69. Cornwall, *Sex and Uncertainty,* 220-21.

to the past. McKenna and Kessler write, "Some people, at some points in their lives, might wish to be identified as sperm or egg cell carriers. Except for those times, there need be no differentiation among people on *any* of the dichotomies which gender implies. Because the reproductive dichotomy would not be constituted as a lifetime dichotomy, it would not be an essential characteristic of people. Even the reproductive *dichotomy* might someday be eliminated through technology."[70] Georgia Warnke makes a similar jump from intersex to the infertility of some, and the nonreproductive choices of others, to reproductive technologies: "Finally, with the present and future birth technologies of sperm banks, artificial insemination, artificial wombs, and cloning, and with the availability of these to 'men' as well as 'women' our current identities as male or female, as well as heterosexual or homosexual, seem at the very least unnecessary."[71] While some point out the theological good of adoption, they fail to address the reality Dennis Hollinger accurately describes: "In adoption we attempt to bring care and moral goodness to an already confused and broken situation. In surrogacy [as in some other reproductive technologies] we willfully confuse family ties and bring brokenness to the procreative process and life of the child."[72] Raising children within their own loving biological family is the ideal with which we tamper only at our peril and the peril of our children. Loving adoptive families provide a necessary and salutary service in response to the breakdown of this ideal. Discarding the family unit in order to correct gender injustice may inadvertently introduce other social problems. Bringing justice to the family seems, to me, to be the wiser course of action.

"Compulsory" Heterosexuality and Binary Gender Model But what does bringing justice to the family entail? Does justice for children require the permanence of the marriage bond, for better or worse? Does procreative complementarity provide the just form for all couples? Certainly for infertile couples and persons past childbearing age, procreative complementarity is not a prerequisite for Christian marriage while gender complementarity remains (in many denominations) inviolable. And yet, if gender complementarity is based upon procreative complementarity, we begin to see the challenge.

70. Suzanne J. Kessler and Wendy McKenna, *Gender: An Ethnomethodological Approach* (Chicago: University of Chicago Press, 1978, 1985), 166.

71. Georgia Warnke, "Intersexuality and the Categories of Sex," *Hypatia* 16, no. 3 (Summer 2001): 134.

72. Hollinger, *The Meaning of Sex,* 215.

The restructuring of marriage and sexual ethics that can be seen in the works of Cornwall, Mollenkott, and Warnke is based on the real difference between procreative complementarity and gender complementarity. These scholars follow gender theorist Judith Butler, who insisted that gender identity is a "regulatory ideal" resulting from "compulsory heterosexuality."[73] Let go of heterosexual marriage, and gender complementarity loses its power. Question gender complementarity, and the foundations of heterosexual marriage begin to fracture. This is what many conservatives fear and why some would rather sweep their intersex siblings under the rug of exceptions that do not (or should not) challenge the rules.

But we cannot stick our heads in the sand. It is true that reflection on the science of sex difference and the history of gender is what has led many to reconsider the rules — rules of gender, rules of marriage. Rather than avoid the conversation, conservatives must find a way to enter into it. While Butler would prefer to discard the rules altogether, others are asking if the rules can be updated to include all God's children. This is exactly what some biblical scholars are doing — returning to the Bible and tradition to read and reconsider old passages with new eyes as they hold the experiences and lives of intersex and LGBTQ persons before them. Following the example of the Jews who, through their commentaries on Torah, made space for naturally born eunuchs, theologians and Scripture scholars are looking for ways to include, within their communities of faith, persons who do not fit the typical patterns.

Reformed New Testament scholar James Brownson has taken pains to carefully examine traditionalist biblical arguments for heteronormativity — a conviction he shared until recently. He details how the idea of gender complementarity that traditionalists derive from biological (procreative) complementarity is something contemporary scholars bring to the text. The creation accounts, when read in their own contexts, speak to the similarity of male and female, not sex or gender, differences.[74] Similarly, biblical legislation on sexual activity is supported not by the logic of complementarity but more often by patriarchal values that many traditionalists now reject.[75] He goes on to explain how a closer look at the texts traditionally believed to proscribe homosexual sex reveals that while these passages ban certain

73. Judith Butler, *Gender Trouble: Feminism and the Subversion of Identity,* 2nd ed. (New York: Routledge, 1990), 24.

74. James V. Brownson, *Bible, Gender, Sexuality: Reframing the Church's Debate on Same-Sex Relationships* (Grand Rapids: Eerdmans, 2013), 26-38.

75. Brownson, *Bible, Gender, Sexuality,* chap. 4.

sexual activities, they do not speak as universally or as clearly to the contemporary marriage debate as conservatives have believed. If Brownson is right, that the Scriptures do not base sexual ethics on gender complementarity and that they do not address the question of consensual, monogamous, egalitarian, loving same-sex relationships, then the way is opened to reconsider the moral legitimacy of these relationships, and by extension, the marriages of intersex and transgender persons.[76]

Eugene F. Rogers Jr. has provided a number of thoughtful, theological defenses of homosexual unions in his anthology, *Theology and Sexuality,* in particular his own essay, "Sanctification, Homosexuality, and God's Triune Life." Patricia Beattie Jung has done similar service in her edited volume, *Sexual Diversity and Catholicism.* Their work is also worthy of careful consideration. Both Rogers and Jung recognize that embracing nonheterosexual unions requires a hermeneutic strategy that acknowledges the limitations of the biblical witness. Jung argues simply that heteronormativity is one more facet of the Bible reflecting divine accommodation to ancient cultural perspectives — accommodation that can also be seen in geocentrism, young-earth creationism, slavery, and patriarchy.[77] Just as we have learned to move past patriarchy and slavery, so too we can move past heteronormativity.

For Rogers, recognizing the contextual nature of the Bible helps us to see movement within the text that can lay the groundwork for movement in our own day. He believes that we must grant God the freedom to do something new, something radical, analogous to the radical inclusion of the Gentiles.[78] Looking closely at the book of Romans, Rogers notes that the very phrase so often interpreted to denounce female homoeroticism as "unnatural" in Romans 1:26 *(para phusin)* is found again in Romans 11:24, where God's grafting Gentiles into the covenant is "contrary to nature."[79] Rogers argues

76. Brownson, *Bible, Gender, Sexuality,* chap. 12.

77. Patricia Beattie Jung, "Christianity and Human Sexual Polymorphism," in *Ethics and Intersex,* ed. Sharon E. Sytsma (Dordrecht: Springer, 2006), xxv; Patricia Beattie Jung, "The Promise of Postmodern Hermeneutics for the Biblical Renewal of Moral Theology," in *Sexual Diversity and Catholicism: Toward the Development of Moral Theology,* ed. Patricia Beattie Jung, with Joseph Andrew Coray (Collegeville, Minn.: Liturgical Press, 2001), 77-107.

78. This line of argument has been used by a number of theologians and exegetes. Cf. Stephen E. Fowl, *Engaging Scripture: A Model for Theological Interpretation* (London: Blackwell, 1998), 127. Quoted in Ellen F. Davis, "Critical Traditioning: Seeking an Inner Biblical Hermeneutic," in *The Art of Reading Scripture,* ed. Ellen F. Davis and Richard B. Hays (Grand Rapids: Eerdmans, 2003), 179.

79. Rom. 1:26: "For this reason God gave them over to degrading passions; for their

that God retains the freedom to graft gays into the vine of Christian marriage so that marriage can do its sanctifying work in the lives of these believers.[80] For these scholars the Bible is an important part of divine revelation, but it is not uniform, nor does it give the final word on every subject. Rather, God continues to speak and act in our day, sometimes in ways that surprise us.

The truth of the matter is that a similar shift from heteronormativity to equal marriage is surprising given the weight of the tradition. From the creation narratives to the Song of Songs to the sacramental imagery of Christ as Bridegroom and the church as bride, heterosexual imagery dominates the canon. In ancient Israel heterosexual marriage was virtually compulsory; and yet, moving from the Old Covenant to the New, we find that Jesus' statement in Matthew 19:12 not only opened up space for the alternative sex/gender identities of eunuchs but also made heterosexuality no longer compulsory for naturally born eunuchs, eunuchs made so by others, and those who made themselves eunuchs. Some scholars have attempted to connect the figure of the eunuch to homosexual, bisexual, and queer sexualities.[81] They are certainly correct that many non-Jewish eunuchs were sexually active, but their arguments suggesting that Jesus was overturning heteronormativity, in the very passage in which he cited the creation narrative to argue for the

---

women exchanged the natural function for that which is *unnatural (para phusin)*" (NASB). Rom. 11:24: "After all, if you were cut out of an olive tree that is wild by nature, and *contrary to nature (para phusin)* were grafted into a cultivated olive tree, how much more readily will these, the natural branches, be grafted into their own olive tree!" (NIV).

80. Eugene F. Rogers, "Sanctification, Homosexuality, and God's Triune Life," in *Theology and Sexuality: Classic and Contemporary Readings*, ed. Eugene F. Rogers Jr. (London: Blackwell, 2002), 225. Rogers argues, "Marriage is a sacrament because it gives desire time and space to stretch forward . . . into things that are *more* desirable. Marriage allows sex to mean *more*. 'Decisions about sexual lifestyle . . . are about how much we want our bodily selves to mean, rather than what emotional needs we're meeting or what laws we're satisfying.' 'Who devalues the body? Those for whom its gestures make no commitments, or those for whom they can make irrevocable commitments? Those who find freedom in casual nakedness, or those who reserve this most visible word for those to whom they have something extraordinary to say?' 'Marriage is a place where our waywardness begins to be healed and our fear of commitment overcome — that, and much more'" (223; interior quotations come from Rowan Williams, Robert W. Jenson, and a group of Jewish and Christian thinkers writing in *First Things* in 1994, respectively).

81. Some, in order to recommend celibacy for eunuchs, others in order to overturn heterosexual ethics: "This flouting [of heterosexual norms] is particularly evident in the part played by eunuchs in the history of salvation. Nancy Wilson from a lesbian perspective and Victoria Kolakowski from a transgendered perspective argue that eunuchs are our queer antecedents." Stuart et al., *Religion Is a Queer Thing*, 44.

indissolubility of marriage, sound a bit hollow in the face of the overarching narrative. Still, such a surprising shift is not unprecedented.

Like Rogers, evangelical biblical scholar Kenton Sparks takes up the example of the inclusion of the Gentiles at the Jerusalem Council, although he does not address the question of sexual ethics. Still, his analysis is helpful (maybe even more so) for illustrating how conservative Christians should wrestle with difficult matters of biblical interpretation. Sparks explains the surprising conclusion of the ancient council, which eventually sided with the pro-Gentile faction against circumcision, despite the stronger biblical warrant for the Judaizers.

> Circumcision is a central rite in the Hebrew canon, and the text explicitly describes it as an "eternal covenant" (Gen 17:13) to be observed by Jews and, most importantly, by any foreigner who wished to join Judaism (Gen 17:27; Exod 12:48). Nevertheless, in a decision that must have surprised and befuddled the Jewish party, the council finally decided that the Gentiles could become Christians without circumcision and without observing Jewish law. This decision was partly based on Scripture, but the deciding factor, according to Acts, was that the Gentiles had received the gift of the Holy Spirit without circumcision. So the Holy Spirit's "voice" (its supernatural activity) tilted the theological scale in the direction of the pro-Gentile party. The weaker position from Scripture supported by the Spirit, bested the stronger position opposed by the Spirit.[82]

Many Christian communities find themselves in a similar place today, wrestling to reconcile what they believe to be the stronger biblical position — which consistently describes marriage as heterosexual (even if not always monogamous), legislates against sexual practices outside of this pattern,[83] and prohibits at least some kinds of homosexual activity — with godly, Spirit-filled, gay, and transgender Christians whom they know, respect, and love.[84]

82. Kenton L. Sparks, *Sacred Word, Broken Word: Biblical Authority and the Dark Side of Scripture* (Grand Rapids: Eerdmans, 2012), 119.

83. Cf. Richard B. Hays, *The Moral Vision of the New Testament: A Contemporary Introduction to New Testament Ethics* (New York: T. & T. Clark/Continuum, 1997, 2004), 379-406.

84. Stanley Hauerwas has argued that these friendships matter in the process of moral discernment in "Gay Friendship: A Thought Experiment in Catholic Moral Theology," in *Theology and Sexuality,* 289-308.

Sparks warns that Christians ought not make analogous interpretive moves lightly. We do not "lord it over" the text. We do not "trump Scripture with a human viewpoint." Rather, we listen to "God's living voice, which includes not only Scripture but also the voices of creation, tradition, and the Spirit." If we do move "beyond the Bible," we must do so "biblically."[85] Sparks does not apply his hermeneutic to the question of sexual ethics in these texts, so it is difficult to say where he stands on the topic at hand.[86] What is clear is that the only way that conservative Christians will be able to move beyond heteronormativity is by adopting a similar hermeneutic and weighing the evidence accordingly.

Some will surmise that the evidence in this book has provided sufficient grounds for abandoning heteronormativity, but for many Christians the jury is still out. Intersex certainly does show the complexity of human sex differentiation and development, but intersex does not unlock all the mysteries of LGBTQ experiences. One of the ways we differentiate between those who identify as LGBTQ and intersex is the lack of physical or physiological markers in the former. The developing field of "brain sex" may very well connect the dots between intersex and sexual orientation and gender identity, but at present it is the least developed field of sexology and resists deterministic readings.[87] Time will tell as science advances. Evidence will continue to need to be weighed alongside biblical, experiential, and hermeneutic approaches.

In the meantime, what are theologians, pastors, educators, and lay Christians to do? How do we find our way in the complexity of sex, gender, and sexuality? Is Christine Gudorf correct that "the shift from dimorphous to polymorphous sexuality, combined with decreased conceptual clarity about

85. Kenton L. Sparks, *God's Word in Human Words: An Evangelical Appropriation of Critical Biblical Scholarship* (Grand Rapids: Baker Academic, 2008), 299.

86. In *God's Word in Human Words,* Sparks draws heavily on William Webb, whose analysis in *Slaves, Women, and Homosexuals* found biblical material to move beyond the Bible in a liberating perspective on the first two topics but not the last. Sparks does argue that Christian academics should learn from gay and lesbian theologians (287), but his conservative position that upholds the authority of the husband in marriage (while affirming women's ordination) makes it seem improbable that he would go beyond heteronormativity (354).

87. The brain is sexed through pre- and postnatal hormones as well as through shifting brain structures that develop on account of experiences of living in a sexed body and a gendered society. I. A. Hughes et al., "Consensus Statement on Management of Intersex Disorders," *Archives of Disease in Childhood* 2 (May 4, 2006): 2. See also Melissa Hines, *Brain Gender* (Oxford: Oxford University Press, 2004), and Anne Fausto-Sterling, *Sexing the Body: Gender Politics and the Construction of Sexuality* (New York: Basic Books, 2000).

sexuality, will continue to encourage a greater reliance on experience and experimentation" so that sexual ethics will become little more than a relic of a bygone era?[88]

Certainly, the complexity of human sexuality, coupled with the challenge of biblical interpretation and application, should lead to humility on the part of all who wrestle with these issues. What should be clear by now is the inadequacy of the simplistic binary model and its naïve repetition in theological anthropologies. Conservative theologians cannot continue to speak about sex difference in ways that avoid scientific studies of sex, gender, and sexuality. Recognizing this complexity, all must refrain from issuing hasty conclusions that either dismiss intersex for its supposed association with alternative sexualities or conflate intersex with LGBTQ perspectives in the hopes of justifying the latter.[89] In recognition of the complexities of sex development, theologians must cultivate humility and empathy for those who differ from them — both in their sexual desires and in their theological convictions.[90] At the same time, given the consistent concern of Scripture and tradition for sexual ethics, theologians cannot abandon the necessity of calling Christians to sexual holiness in ways that promote the health of individuals, families, and society at large.

Some fear that the harm done to the individual through sexual repression is greater than the harm done via sexual license. Others fear that sexual license has greater repercussions on the individual and society and argue in favor of sexual restraint. Some will distrust their own reason and desires, believing that "the heart is deceitful above all things / and beyond cure"(Jer. 17:9 NIV). Others read bodily desires as natural goods and look for alternative applications of the "nuptial meaning of the body."

Heterosexuality may not be compulsory (as Butler has charged), but McCarthy is right that "heterosexual marriage is normative in the biblical

88. Christine E. Gudorf, "The Erosion of Sexual Dimorphism: Challenges to Religion and Religious Ethics," *Journal of the American Academy of Religion* 69, no. 4 (December 2001): 887.

89. Chuck Colson's short essay, "Blurred Biology," labeling intersex a tool of the "homosexual lobby," serves as a prime example of an inadequate reactionary approach by conservatives. Virginia Mollenkott makes the opposite mistake when she states, "In short, intersexual people are the best biological evidence we have that the binary gender construct is totally inadequate and is causing terrific injustice and unnecessary suffering." Mollenkott, *Omnigender,* 51.

90. Caroline J. Simon, *Bringing Sex into Focus: The Quest for Sexual Integrity* (Downers Grove, Ill.: InterVarsity, 2012), 101-2.

witness and the church's theological tradition."[91] Nevertheless, he goes on to argue, with Rogers, Lawler, Salzman, Jung, and Brownson, that gay, lesbian, bisexual, transgender, and intersex persons may be grafted into the heart of the tradition — the covenantal union of marriage.[92]

Containing sexual activity within celibacy and monogamous unions — either as a pastoral accommodation (analogous to divorce and remarriage) or as an affirmation of an alternative good — may provide the kind of common ground sufficient to bring together those who differ on heteronormativity.[93] Contrastively, those who advocate polyamorous, queer, or communal sexual practices will have a harder time making sense of the normative nature of marriage in Scripture and tradition.[94]

In all cases, "Most people, whether heterosexual or homosexual [intersexual, bisexual, or other] have sexual desires that outstrip the boundaries of marriage."[95] Natural desire has never been a sufficient condition for moral sanction in the Christian tradition; self-deceit is possible for all of us, regardless of sexual orientation. This is why we must continue to wrestle with ourselves, with the Scriptures, with traditions of interpretation, and with interpretive communities as we seek ways to move forward not only in love and justice, but also in sexual holiness. Our hearts should be moved with compassion for so many with frustrated sexual desires — those who long to be married but have not found a suitable spouse; spouses in loveless marriages; spouses with sexual dysfunction; the divorced; the widowed. Sexual frustrations are burdens we all bear in various degrees, but they also provide opportunities for us to grow in holiness.

But holiness extends well beyond personal, sexual purity. Holiness also calls communities to peacemaking, reconciliation, generosity, and love. In light of these challenges, Caroline Simon asks,

91. David Matzko McCarthy, "The Relationship of Bodies: A Nuptial Hermeneutics of Same-Sex Unions," in *Theology and Sexuality,* 202.

92. McCarthy, "The Relationship of Bodies," 202.

93. Ken Wilson argues for inclusion as a pastoral accommodation in his *Letter to My Congregation: An Evangelical Pastor's Path to Embracing People Who Are Gay, Lesbian, and Transgender into the Company of Jesus* (Canton, Mich.: David Crumm Media, 2014).

94. In Elizabeth Stuart's edited volume, *Religion Is a Queer Thing,* Stuart rightly observes that debates over gay marriage are really discussions as to how far heterosexual marriage can be stretched. She laments that this fails to address bisexual persons as well as others, for example, those who advocate polyandry and communal sexuality. I must agree with her that marriage does remain the model for Christian sexual ethics, including the debate over same-sex and intersex marriage. Stuart, 2.

95. Simon, *Bringing Sex into Focus,* 112.

> Is dimness on this issue and other issues a result of the Fall? Or is this a disguised blessing? Could our divergence of perspectives become a resource for Christian discipleship? When you love those who love you, what credit is that to you? When you love those who share your views on matters you think central to the faith, what credit is that to you? You don't need grace for *that*. We do need grace and mercy and wisdom, and a life saturated with prayerful seeking, to live out our life together in light of our very real disagreements.[96]

In humility, we should be able to find ways to partner with Christians who disagree with us so long as we can locate sufficient common ground on sexual ethics and continue to work together for personal and sexual holiness.

If Judith Butler is right that gender identity is a "regulatory ideal" constructed upon "compulsory heterosexuality,"[97] and if heterosexuality should prove to not be compulsory, even for Christians, does this then lead to an abandonment of gender? Feminist philosopher Georgia Warnke dismisses the usefulness of sex categories even for medical research and care.[98] Even though some men, such as those with Klinefelter's syndrome, might need mammograms to screen for breast cancer, such recognition does not require testing all men or rejecting evidence that most women require such exams. Rather, it requires careful attention to the needs of each individual. Statistically significant differences remain useful for medicine, politics, psychology, sociology, and theology, so long as they are not employed in oppressive ways. Intersex certainly requires an alteration of the binary model. It necessitates opening up space in between the categories of male and female. Instead of two discrete categories, intersex shows how these overlap in various ways.

Intersex research adds weight to critiques of essentialist understandings of sex/gender differences without making the categories of male/masculine/masculinity or female/feminine/femininity meaningless. Dr. Melissa Hines, director of the Behavioural Neuroendocrinology Research Unit at City University in London, England, shows how discussions of sex/gender differences remain useful so long as they are understood as "two overlapping distributions for males and females, with average differences between the two groups."[99] Hines is well aware of intersex and its challenge to the

96. Simon, *Bringing Sex into Focus,* 115.

97. Butler, *Gender Trouble,* 24.

98. Warnke, "Intersexuality," 134-35.

99. Hines, *Brain Gender,* 4.

gender construct (she includes an entire chapter on intersex in her text), and yet she continues to view statistical research on sex/gender difference as valuable. Her example shows how statistical averages for physiology and behavior in men and women can be helpful for understanding humankind so long as we balance such observations with the recognition that "few, if any, individuals correspond to the modal male pattern or the modal female pattern. Variation within each sex is great, with both males and females near the top and bottom of the distributions for every characteristic. . . . In fact, although most of us appear to be either clearly male or clearly female, we are each complex mosaics of male and female characteristics."[100] Recognizing that "few, if any, individuals correspond to the modal male . . . or . . . female pattern" (the statistical average) can help liberate everyone from oppressive gender stereotypes so long as we are willing to differentiate between statistical norms and ethical or aesthetic ideals.

Statistical research on sex difference can be helpful for self-understanding or the understanding of others, provided the proverbial shoe fits. Of course, when it doesn't, but we insist that it should or it must, we become like the "ugly stepsisters" in the Brothers Grimm's original *Cinderella* — cutting off our toes and heels (or the toes and heels of others) in order to fit into the glass slipper, in our attempts to find love or friendship, get the job or the promotion. Mollenkott describes the pain:

> What I have learned in my most recent studies is that gender normality is a myth as long as it is forced to locate itself within a binary paradigm that fits very few members of the human race. I am not the only person who limited, shrank, and truncated aspects of myself in an attempt to fit that paradigm. Millions have done the same; and some have killed themselves or been murdered because of their inability to pass gender muster. Many transgender youngsters have run away from home or been evicted by their parents, have lived on the streets and been used by predatory adults, and have become HIV positive. Others have been institutionalized for no other reason than their inability to satisfy society's gender expectations.
>
> So much pain. So much waste of human potential. It cannot continue.[101]

Even while debates continue to rage over the most effective and moral means to address gender dysphoria, those conservatives have a responsibility to

100. Hines, *Brain Gender,* 18-19.
101. Mollenkott, *Omnigender,* ix-x.

address the oppressive ways in which sex/gender ideals (e.g., strong male rational-initiator-leaders, beautiful female intuitive-receiver-followers) are held up as moral or biblical imperatives.[102]

Resisting Sex/Gender Perfection I believe Cornwall raises some particularly helpful insights in questioning how visions of "perfection" (whether of unambiguously sexed bodies or gendered visions of health and beauty) can work against the healing and wholeness that all individuals require. At the same time, her acknowledgment of the fears of the nonintersexed leads me to question her model of *kenosis* of sex identity as the best possible solution for promoting equality within the church and society at large.

While an unambiguously sexed body may be the cause of some unsolicited privileges, it can nevertheless remain a source of personal insecurity. Certainly, many women have been willing to "give up" their unambiguous sex identity in favor of a masculine or androgynous ideal.[103] The intersexed are not alone in needing to come to terms with their own embodiment — the possibilities and limitations, abilities and disabilities, temptations and strengths, trials and joys vary in each individual. As Kessler noted in her study of intersex, there is a connection between the medicalization of intersex and the medicalization of beauty/perfection in contemporary American society: in everything from orthodontics to nose jobs to silicone implants.[104] There are myriad anxieties arising from human embodiment, particularly attending sex, gender, and sexuality. Calling for the *kenosis* of the privileges of the nonintersexed may begin to move us in the right direction, but more is needed for the healing of the human community.

102. For a quick entry into the debate concerning the ethics of sex reassignment surgeries for transsexuals, compare the Evangelical Alliance Policy Commission's brief text, *Transsexuality* (London: Evangelical Alliance, 2000), to Susannah Cornwall's "'State of Mind' versus 'Concrete Set of Facts.'"

103. Brown, *The Body and Society,* 81.

104. "Surgical solutions for variant genitals need to be seen in the context of a cultural tide that is shrinking rather than expanding the range of what is considered normal for all parts of the body. . . . Imperfections [are] remediable today with the early help of a skilled surgeon." Suzanne J. Kessler, *Lessons from the Intersexed* (New Brunswick, N.J.: Rutgers University Press, 1998), 157-58. She argues correctly that "[i]f we want people to respect particular bodies, they need to be taught to lose respect for ideal ones" (118). For a similar critique of medical fixes for "normal" (i.e., natural) deviations from the (statistical) norm, see Carl Elliott, *Better Than Well: American Medicine Meets the American Dream* (New York: Norton, 2003).

Christology, Identity, and *Imago*

Decentering and Reconciling Identities "in Christ"

Christology and Reconciliation in the Conflicts of Identities Evangelical theologian Miroslav Volf, in his study *Exclusion and Embrace: A Theological Exploration of Identity, Otherness, and Reconciliation,* looks to Christology to cut through the Gordian knot of conflicts surrounding personal identity in the postmodern world. He insists that while revisioning social arrangements is an important piece of working toward justice, theologians must also attend carefully to "fostering the kind of social agents capable of envisioning and creating just, truthful, and peaceful societies, and on shaping a cultural climate in which such agents will thrive."[105] His reflections stem from the battles that rage over ethnic identities, but many of his insights apply to conflicts that sex and gender identities bring to communities. He is conscious of the connection. "I will explore *what kind of selves we need to be* in order to live in harmony with others. My assumption is that selves are situated; they are female or male, Jew or Greek, rich or poor — as a rule, more than one of these things at the same time ('rich Greek female'), often having hybrid identities ('Jew-Greek' and 'male-female'), and sometimes migrating from one identity to another. The questions I will be pursuing about such situated selves are: How should they think of their identity? How should they relate to the other? How should they go about making peace with the other?"[106] I would add the query, How do we go about making peace with ourselves — with our hybrid identities or anxieties attending our sex, gender, and sexuality, whether we are intersexed or nonintersexed or other?

Volf notes how in times of peace, diverse groups have lived together, sometimes merely coexisting, sometimes helping, sometimes even mixing and marrying. But in times of conflict identities become hardened, loyalties are demanded.[107] While theological/ethical "culture wars" are not identical to ethno-religious conflicts, in contemporary battles of sex, gender, and sexuality there is little room for mediating positions.[108] Certainly intersex

105. Miroslav Volf, *Exclusion and Embrace: A Theological Exploration of Identity, Otherness, and Reconciliation* (Nashville: Abingdon, 1996), 21.

106. Volf, *Exclusion and Embrace,* 21.

107. Volf, *Exclusion and Embrace,* 14-16.

108. I experienced this personally when I was scheduled to present a lecture entitled "What We Can Learn from the Intersexed" at the annual meeting of Christians for Biblical Equality (CBE) in St. Louis in 2009. A senior scholar embroiled in battles over gay ordi-

persons have found themselves as both players and pawns, casualties and crusaders in the culture wars at hand. Reflecting on the effects of war on personal identity, Volf writes:

> I have Czech, German, and Croatian "blood" in my veins; I grew up in a city which the old Hapsburg Empire had made into a meeting place of many ethnic groups. . . . But the new Croatia, like some jealous goddess, wanted all my love and loyalty. I must be Croat through and through, or I was not a good Croat.
>
> It was easy to explain this excessive demand of loyalty. After forced assimilation under communist rule, the sense of ethnic belonging and cultural distinctness was bound to reassert itself. Moreover, the need to stand firm against a powerful and destructive enemy who had captured one-third of Croatian territory, swept it clean of its Croatian population, and almost completely destroyed some of its cities, left little room for the luxury of divided loyalties. The explanations made sense and they gave reasons to believe that *the disturbing preoccupation with the natural self was a temporary phase, a defense mechanism whose services would no longer be needed once the danger was past.* Yet the unsettling questions remained: did I not discover in oppressed Croatia's face some despised Serbian features? Might not the enemy have captured some of Croatia's soul along with a good deal of Croatia's soil?[109]

Volf's analysis illuminates the experiences of some intersex persons who claim that "intersex" as an identity category has arisen from negative experiences of medical intervention in order to address the medical establishment and promote better care. Kessler identifies a correspondence between medicalization and identity. She quotes Morgan Holmes, an intersex member of Intersex Society of North America (Canada):

> "Was I intersexed before I was medicalized?" [Holmes] compares herself to a woman friend with a three-and-a-half-inch clitoris that escaped "cor-

---

nation in his denomination attempted to have my workshop removed from the conference agenda. Without reviewing my materials, this particular scholar insisted that there is "nothing that we can learn from the intersexed" and that I must have a subversive agenda. To their credit, after reviewing a manuscript of my presentation, CBE decided to keep me in the program. Participants in the wars over sexual ethics wanted my singular allegiance and wanted to quash any discussion that appeared to threaten or problematize their arguments.

109. Volf, *Exclusion and Embrace,* 16-17, italics mine.

> rection." Holmes's friend refuses the intersex label for herself, claiming that this would be an additional burden, making her even more of an outsider than her lesbianism already does. I suspect that her rejection of the label has more to do with an identity fit. She was not diagnosed; she was not "surgicalized"; she does not feel like an intersexual. Holmes's own argument confirms this: "It is partly in the naming that bodies become intersexed."[110]

For some intersexed, the invading army represents the medical establishment or parents who consented to surgicalization and suppression of the truth. Others look to the oppression of the binary sex system or compulsory heterosexuality and those who uphold it. Whatever is the case, their experience supports recent developments in philosophical notions of identity that suggest that personal identity is not simply an essence that resides within individuals; rather, identity comes into being through relations.[111] Heeding the insight that identity formation arises in relation to others as well as Hester's and Cornwall's contentions that healing for the intersex is less about medical intervention and more about the healing of communities (i.e., small support groups of other intersex persons as well as larger communities that include the nonintersexed), we must work simultaneously on structural changes to address the injustices perpetrated upon the intersexed as well as education and reconciliation among intersexed and nonintersexed alike if we want to build just, equitable, healing communities.

Just as some intersex persons have had their personhood, identity, and even lives threatened by the binary sex system, so have some nonintersex persons — especially those comfortable with the binary sex system — felt threatened by the presence of the intersexed. Identities that were once secure feel secure no longer. Given such a situation, how is reconciliation to take place? How do we reconcile personal identities and anxieties, as well as relations between persons? Volf argues that this kind of radical reconciliation is only possible through the cross of Christ — the cross understood as providing solidarity with the oppressed, atonement for the oppressors, and the embrace embodied in Christ's outstretched arms. "[T]he most basic thought that [the metaphor of embrace] seeks to express is important: *the*

110. Kessler, *Lessons from the Intersexed,* 89, quoting Morgan Holmes, "Homophobia in Health Care: Abjection and the Treatment of Intersexuality" (paper presented at the Learned Societies CSAA meetings, Montreal, June 1995).

111. Volf, *Exclusion and Embrace,* 19.

will to give ourselves to others and 'welcome' them, to readjust our identities to make space for them, is prior to any judgment about others, except that of identifying them in their humanity. The *will to embrace* precedes any 'truth' about others and any construction of their 'justice.' This will is absolutely indiscriminate and strictly immutable; it transcends the moral mapping of the social world into 'good' and 'evil.'"[112]

Volf does not deny the need to struggle to identify good and evil, truth and justice, but he insists that the way we proceed is essential. We must follow

> the "wisdom of the cross": within social contexts, truth and justice are unavailable outside of the *will to embrace* the other. I immediately continue to argue, however, that *the embrace itself* — full reconciliation — cannot take place until the truth has been said and justice done.
>
> . . . The practice of "embrace," with its concomitant struggle against deception, injustice, and violence, is intelligible only against the backdrop of a powerful, contagious, and destructive evil I call "exclusion" . . . and is for Christians possible only if, in the name of God's crucified Messiah, we distance ourselves from ourselves and our cultures in order to create space for the other.[113]

How, then, do we distance ourselves from ourselves in order to draw near to ourselves and near to others in the embrace of healthy reconciliation? How do we distance ourselves from identities as personal and "constitutive" as sex, gender, and sexuality in order to reconcile ourselves to ourselves and others? Once again, Christology provides the way forward.

Putting to Death Identities in Christ Christology does not provide a facile answer to questions of personal identity. Nevertheless, it does offer wisdom for wrestling with them. On the one side, Christology calls for a death to self that seems to challenge any notion of personal identity. Returning again to Galatians, we find Paul declaring, "I have been crucified with Christ and I no longer live, but Christ lives in me. The life I live in the body, I live by faith in the Son of God, who loved me and gave himself for me" (Gal. 2:20 NIV). Volf recounts Jewish scholar Daniel Boyarin's concerns that a particular reading of Galatians 3:28 ("no more Jew or Greek, slave or free, male and female") can be understood as calling for the death of personal identities.

112. Volf, *Exclusion and Embrace,* 29.
113. Volf, *Exclusion and Embrace,* 29-30.

Despite granting the possibility of a positive intention, that is, an "equality at the expense of difference," Boyarin argues that this vision nevertheless "contained the seeds of an imperialist and colonizing practice; Paul's 'universalism even at its most liberal and benevolent has been a powerful force for coercive discourses of sameness, denying . . . the rights of Jews, women, and others to retain their difference.' "[114] Volf responds that the cross and life "in Christ" can be read differently. "Far from being the assertion of the one against many, the cross is the *self-giving of the one for many*. . . . From a Pauline perspective, the wall that divides is not so much 'the difference' as *enmity* (cf. Ephesians 2:14)."[115]

Belden Lane insists that in the Christian life "nothing is more important or more difficult" than discerning what to "put to death" and what to cultivate.[116] Finding one's identity in Christ may require the death of certain identities, even "good" identities, especially those that have become idols or false selves — identities in which we put our confidence when our security should rest in God alone.[117]

In her book *Men and Women in the Church,* Sarah Sumner illustrates how even a secure heterosexual/sex/gender identity can prove to be a stumbling block when it comes to transformation into the image of Christ.

> When Jim and I were first married, I wanted him to be my Superman. I didn't like it when he felt afraid. I wanted him to rescue me from my fears and not have any fears of his own. My picture of marriage called for me to be human and for him to be superhuman. For me to be vulnerable, and for him to be invulnerable. I expected our marriage to be a comforting refuge where I would be held safe in the arms of my hero and where he would be admired by me. Jim would be Zorro, and I'd be Cinderella. And we would serve Christ in our home.

114. Volf, *Exclusion and Embrace,* 46, citing Daniel Boyarin, *A Radical Jew: Paul and the Politics of Identity* (Berkeley: University of California Press, 1997), 234, 233.

115. Volf, *Exclusion and Embrace,* 47.

116. "Attentiveness and indifference are, respectively, the constructive and deconstructive poles of the spiritual life. They tell us when to pay attention and when to let go, what to concentrate on and what to ignore. . . . They stand in paradoxical relationship to each other, these two disciplines of the spirit: how to pay attention and how to not pay attention (and when to apply which of the two standards). Nothing else is more important or more difficult in one's faltering practice of a life of prayer." Belden C. Lane, *The Solace of Fierce Landscapes: Exploring Desert and Mountain Spirituality* (Oxford: Oxford University Press, 1998), 188-89.

117. Lane, *Solace of Fierce Landscapes,* 72.

> I am on a journey of repenting from my worldly view of marriage. I am letting go of my selfish expectations. I am surrendering my selfish desire to feel sorry my husband doesn't save me from my fears. I am in the process of learning to accept the full responsibility for my stuff. And through it all, I am discovering a new vision of marriage, one that's based on love instead of fantasy.
>
> . . . From the time they are boys, men are challenged to attain manhood. Their consciences are trained by society and church and also by women such as myself. Every time I long for my husband to sweep me off my feet so that I don't have to walk on the difficult path of Christlike suffering, in essence I am asking him to prove that he is a man so that I won't have to prove that I'm a Christian.[118]

Secure sex, gender, and sexual identities can be just as much a stumbling block to transformation in the image of Christ as ambiguous identities. Whatever the identity, it must be placed under the scrutiny of the Scriptures by the help of the Spirit so that we may discern what must be put to death and what must be cultivated.

Decentering and Recentering Identities in Christ Rather than insisting on the death of personal identities, Volf argues that while ethnic, racial, national, gender, sexual, and other identities remain, they must nevertheless be decentered in the life of the believer.

> What happened to the self in the process of re-centering? Has the self been simply erased? Has its own proper center been simply replaced by an alien center? . . . Not exactly. For if "Christ lives *in* me," as Paul says, then *I* must have a center that is distinct from "Christ, the center."[119]

> Re-centering entails no self-obliterating denial of the self that dissolves the self in Christ. . . . To the contrary, re-centering establishes the most proper and unassailable center that allows the self to stand over against persons and institutions which may threaten to smother it.[120]

118. Sarah Sumner, *Men and Women in the Church: Building Consensus on Christian Leadership* (Downers Grove, Ill.: InterVarsity, 2003), 89.

119. Volf, *Exclusion and Embrace,* 70.

120. Volf, *Exclusion and Embrace,* 71.

It may be that certain identities must be recovered before they can be decentered. Such was the critique Daphne Hampson lodged against the imitation of Christ's *kenosis* when she argued that asking women to empty themselves or die to themselves, when they have never been permitted to develop as genuine selves, is destructive rather than life-giving. Sarah Coakley has countered that Hampson's vision of *kenosis* is misconstrued. In contrast, Coakley insists that *kenosis* "can be an important element of holding vulnerability and personal empowerment together, precisely by creating the 'space' in which non-coercive divine power manifests itself."[121] Volf's analysis of "preoccupation" with identity as a temporal phase, no "longer needed once the danger was past," may also provide a way forward.[122]

Heeding the voices of Hampson, Volf, and Coakley, we may surmise that the affirmation and acceptance of an "intersex identity" and even the construction of an "intersexed Christ" (such as that proffered by Virginia Mollenkott) may be the first step along the path of healing and reconciliation for some Christian intersex persons. It is an affirmation of the full humanity of intersex persons, their place in society and in the community of faith. I believe that reflection on the possibility of an intersex Christ reveals a confidence that Christ stands with the intersexed, that "his" humanity does not stand over against them, that Jesus is with them in their struggles for identity, for love, for acceptance, for wholeness. The vision of an intersexed Christ (or of a black Christ or a female Christa) is useful for challenging the orthodoxy and hegemony of a male/masculine Christ to whom many cannot relate — either via similarity (as a male in the image of a male Christ) or via complementarity (as the female/feminine bride). It enables those who put too much stock in maleness and masculinity to put these idols, and the "false selves" constructed upon them, to death. At the same time, new theological constructions must also be held with care. Each must heed the warning Elaine Storkey raised against feminist Christologies — that just as Christ became incarnate to become like us, Christ is at the same time unlike any of us. She warns that feminism (and other liberation theologies by comparison) must be wary of being

> bewitched by the very anthropomorphism which [feminism] warns against. For it needs to recognize that, though Christ is God-with-us in

121. Sarah Coakley, *Powers and Submissions: Spirituality, Philosophy, and Gender* (Chichester: Wiley-Blackwell, 2002), 5.

122. Volf, *Exclusion and Embrace,* 16-17.

> our humanity, pain, new life and joy, God in Christ is not ultimately like us, any of us. There is no need to hold against the features of Christ's particularity some checklist, so that we can be assured of our inclusion in the mystery of divine love. For God does not incorporate into Godself our gender, time, language, ethnicity, religion, skin-color, lifestyle — nor confront us with any other which undermines our own. God does not need to be re-imagined in our image.[123]

Holding these poles in tension allows us to find the security of recognition that Christ stands with us in our humanity while preserving the distinction that allows Christ to stand over against us as God and Messiah — able to judge our just and unjust actions, things spoken and unspoken, done and undone. Holding these poles in tension can liberate us from old oppressions while protecting us from erecting new systems of tyranny. Holding these poles in tension creates space for a new self, with a new center, what Volf calls "a decentered center." So that "through faith and baptism the self [can be] re-made in the image of 'the Son of God who loved me and gave himself for me,' [as] Paul writes. At the center of the self lies self-giving love. No 'hegemonic centrality' closes the self off, guarding its self-same identity and driving out and away whatever threatens its purity. To the contrary, the new center opens the self up, makes it capable and willing to give itself for others and to receive others in itself."[124]

This openness of the self to others returns us to the Trinity, whose relationality is imaged in the eschatological-ecclesial self to which Grenz has been pointing. Volf describes it with different language as a "catholic personality":

> Spirit re-creates us and sets us on the road toward becoming what I like to call a "catholic personality," a personal microcosm of the eschatological new creation. . . . A catholic personality is a personality enriched by otherness, a personality which is what it is only because multiple others have been reflected in it in a particular way. The distance from my own culture that results from being born of the Spirit creates a fissure in me

123. Elaine Storkey, "Who Is the Christ? Issues in Christology and Feminist Theology," in *The Gospel and Gender: A Trinitarian Engagement with Being Male and Female in Christ*, ed. Douglas A. Campbell (London: T. & T. Clark, 2003), 122.

124. Volf, *Exclusion and Embrace*, 71.

> through which others can come in. The Spirit unlatches the doors of my heart saying: "You — are not only you; others belong to you too."[125]

Drawing again on the language of Trinitarian studies, Volf writes, "Everything in the idea of perichoresis — or 'mutual interiority,' as I prefer to put it — depends on success in resisting the slide into pure identity."[126]

While we need not put to death our sex/gender/sexual identities, all of us — male, female, and intersex — must place the privileges and pain associated with these identities under the cross of Christ — dying to pride and privilege in the *kenosis* that Cornwall has recommended, but also dying to the need for revenge, to insecurities, to self-hatred, and to despair. One Christian intersex woman describes how this process has enabled her to come to terms with herself.

> I too am intersexual. I lived in anonymity for years, sincerely committed to a scripturally conforming role, while denying my own existence. You see, I was the leader of the Baptist Women's Bible study who experienced the utter hate and repulsion shown me by those who should have drawn nearest me. God's grace alone has compelled me to step into the light, in accountability, and declare who I was, who I am, and who I am in Christ. The genetic purée of my life is simply the way God has formed the "clay pot" (Isaiah 64:8), only now with the "broken handle" removed. My heart's desire as a woman of God, a spiritual being, (not merely physical), is that the work of God might be displayed in my life. By eternal perspectives the whole jumbled genetic stew just doesn't matter.
>
> God created the eunuch (intersexual) unique. Join me to stop destroying unique lives while demanding conformity to a standard that is genetically impossible.
>
> We must conform only to Christ's Image.[127]

The cross decenters as well as recenters the self. It is a decentering and recentering available and necessary to all — male, female, and intersex — in order that we may be renewed in the image of God in Christ.

125. Volf, *Exclusion and Embrace,* 51.

126. Volf, *Exclusion and Embrace,* 128.

127. Intersex Support Group International, "Director's Page" (1999-2002), http://www.xyxo.org/ isgi/director.html.

Imago Christi: *Love, Purity, and Mystery*

Being remade into the image of Christ entails not only a death to (certain parts of or certain identities of) self, but also a decentering of personal identity, which makes space for rebirth, and the recentering of a healthy identity, an identity rooted in Christ — more specifically, an identity rooted in the love God lavishes upon Christ and those in Christ. As the apostle John wrote, "See what love the Father has given us, that we should be called children of God; and that is what we are. The reason the world does not know us is that it did not know him. Beloved, we are God's children now; what we will be has not yet been revealed. What we do know is this: when he is revealed, we will be like him, for we will see him as he is. And all who have this hope in him purify themselves, just as he is pure" (1 John 3:1-3 NRSV). John's words highlight three features of life in Christ: the centrality of love, the necessity of purity, and the continuing mystery of human identity. Although each of these deserves lengthy exploration, a few terse comments must suffice to conclude.

The love of which John speaks is the love of God for us — the love that provides the proper ground for our love of self, death to self, decentering and recentering of self, and loving (i.e., relating in mutual-interiority to) others. This is the kind of love Mollenkott, Hester, and Cornwall have also heralded, the love of God that fills our work for justice and peace in the world.

At the same time, being remade into the image of Christ — growing in the imitation of Christ — entails more than love, more than working for social justice. As John wrote, "all who have this hope in him purify themselves, just as he is pure." Being remade in the image of Christ not only entails faith in the love of God and the forgiveness offered to sinners on the basis of Christ's life, death, and resurrection, it also includes offering this love to others as well as the choice to grow in purity, in holiness. This is where my own proposal parts ways with those of Mollenkott, Hester, and Cornwall, for I believe that being remade in the image of Christ requires not only just dealings and the reordering of societal oppressions but also the cultivation of personal holiness — a life of worship,[128] prayer, humility, kindness, generosity, and other virtues, including sexual chastity — monogamous chastity

128. Richard Lints has developed a strong case for understanding the image of God as underlying the challenge of idolatry throughout the Old and New Testaments. "Both concepts carry a sense of worshipping something outside the self as well as being influenced by that object of worship. This then explains in part the continuous concern of the biblical writers with idolatry as the natural devolution of persons who chase after gods they've created in their own image. It also opens the door to a fresh examination of Jesus Christ as the

within marriage and celibate chastity outside of marriage. This kind of holiness has value for the community and the individual.

Although the Christian call to virtue is as old as the gospel, it is imperative that we recognize that, whatever its etymological root, "virtue" does not arise from *vir.*[129] Although the hierarchical scale upon which masculinity was modeled in the classical period imposed an oppressive system that devalued women, intersex, and unmanly men, the classical model did recognize an important truth about humankind: we are not as we should be. Mark R. Talbot explains that every culture — no matter its religion — operates under this assumption. It is the basis upon which child rearing and education are founded. "[H]uman beings, as we arrive in this world, are probably less what we can and indeed must become than any other creaturely being."[130] "Yet what all societies want done with their young makes clear what kind of creatures we should be. In this sense, we can say that human societies view their members as 'meant' to function in particular self-regulating ways."[131] Talbot explains that even non-Christian thinkers, such as Richard Rorty, grant that to reach our potential as human beings we must be guided by what Rorty names a "final vocabulary" — "some 'set of words which [we] employ to justify [our] actions, [our] beliefs, and [our] lives'; these are the words 'in which we formulate praise of our friends and contempt for our enemies, our long-term projects, our deepest self-doubts, our highest hopes'; these are the words 'in which we tell, sometimes prospectively and sometimes retrospectively, the story of our lives.' The fact that Christians, then, are committed to a particular 'word' on life does not distinguish them from anyone else; the need to be committed to some such word is a feature of distinctively human being that we share with everyone."[132] For Christians, this final vocabulary is found in the Word made flesh — in the person and story of Jesus Christ, in God who took up human nature in order to redeem and perfect all of us, men, women, and intersex.

It may be that virtue was conflated with *vir* in the ancient world, as one of the most powerful rhetorical devices for motivating men to change

---

perfect image." Richard Lints, introduction to *Personal Identity in Theological Perspective,* ed. Richard Lints, Michael S. Horton, and Mark R. Talbot (Grand Rapids: Eerdmans, 2006), 10.

129. *Vir* is Latin for the human male.

130. Mark R. Talbot, "Learning from the Ruined Image: Moral Anthropology after the Fall," in *Personal Identity in Theological Perspective,* 166. Talbot clarifies his "must become" in note 12 by saying that "we will not even survive if we don't develop in specific ways."

131. Talbot, "Ruined Image," 166.

132. Talbot, "Ruined Image," 175. The interior quotations come from Richard Rorty, *Contingency, Irony, and Solidarity* (Cambridge: Cambridge University Press, 1989), 73.

their behavior was shaming them with accusations of being or becoming effeminate.[133] Unfortunately, it is a rhetorical device still employed by some preachers today. Although arguably effective, the conflation of virtue with manliness replaces the gospel of holiness and maturity with a hierarchically gendered system of oppression — shaming men into virtue instead of calling men, women, and intersex adults and children to grow in holiness, being conformed to the image of God in Christ.

Christ Jesus is "the image of the invisible God" (Col. 1:15 NRSV), and all Christians — male, female, intersexed — are "being transformed into his likeness with ever-increasing glory, which comes from the Lord, who is the Spirit" (2 Cor. 3:18 NIV). Despite its potential effectiveness as a rhetorical strategy for men, growth in holiness must not be misconstrued as growth toward manhood. Holiness must be separated from any gendered understandings of virtue — masculine, feminine, intersex, or transgendered. Holiness must not be presented as pink, blue, or purple. Christ is the model for all. All Christians are to model his victory (1 Cor. 15:54-57; Eph. 6:10-17). All Christians receive his inheritance as sons (Gal. 3:26–4:7). All Christians become his bride (Eph. 5:25-27). These mixed metaphors illustrate the universal call of conformity to Christ, but they do even more than this; they also testify to the mystery that remains in any exploration of the Christian life, no less in any exploration of the image of God.

Eastern Orthodox theologian Sister Nonna Verna Harrison, in her exploration of the *imago Dei* for Christian formation, writes of the different facets of the *imago* recognizable in the Scriptures, Christian history, and contemporary thought. She explores the splendors of the following: (1) human freedom and responsibility conditioned by finitude; (2) the love of God, forgiveness of Christ, and renewal in the Spirit; (3) spiritual perception and relationship to God and others; (4) virtue cultivated over a lifetime; (5) royal dignity — a dignity that "belongs equally to all who are human . . . the intrinsic value, honor, and splendor of the children of God that lies hidden at the inmost core of every human being";[134] (6) the gift of human embodiment;

133. "The success of the Western Christian ideology of masculinity derived in no small part from the ability of the men who crafted it to maintain a cultural connection with more traditional Roman formulations of masculinity while at the same time criticizing the inability of those traditional formulations to respond adequately to the social disruptions of late antiquity and offering a new model to potential members. The ideology of Christian masculinity *did* attract male converts." Kuefler, *The Manly Eunuch,* 13.

134. Nonna Verna Harrison, *God's Many-Splendored Image: Theological Anthropology for Spiritual Formation* (Grand Rapids: Baker Academic, 2010), 188.

(7) responsibility for creation; (8) creativity and scientific advancement; and (9) human identity as fundamentally unique yet situated within wider human communities — "just as the divine Trinity is three distinct persons in one essence."[135] She agrees with Stanley Grenz and John Paul II that the image of God is ultimately found in Christ, "the origin and center of a new humankind, a new community."[136] And yet, as she closes, she reminds her readers that the *imago* will always remain a mystery — for in this, too, humans image God. "As Gregory of Nyssa says, human identity is an unfathomable depth of mystery, which is itself an image of the inexhaustible and boundless mystery of the divine being and life. This means that the divine image at the core of what we are as human remains multifaceted and is open to transformation in a future that is now unknown to us."[137]

This mystery leads us not only to humility but also to worship and to hope. "To live according to God's image and likeness . . . is to be truly alive. And we can dare to hope to become more fully alive in ways that we cannot now imagine. The human likeness to God is participation in God's life and immortality; it is abundant new life here and now and eternal life with God in the age to come."[138]

Conclusion: Male, Female, and Intersex in the Image of God: Theological Anthropology in the Already/Not Yet

This book has attempted to explore a small slice of the many-splendored image of God, particularly the social view of the image of God as it relates to human embodiment: to sex, gender, and sexuality. This study has shown that there is even more mystery with which Christians must wrestle as we delve deeper into the complexities of sex, gender, and sexuality in the postmodern period.

It can be disconcerting to have one's presuppositions challenged — par-

135. She continues, "When people live together in the likeness of the Trinity, as far as is humanly possible, they hold in balance likeness and difference, harmony and mutual respect, giving and receiving, equality and leadership; in this way justice can flourish. Then diversity strengthens community while community enables diversity to flourish." Harrison, *God's Many-Splendored Image,* 190.

136. Harrison, *God's Many-Splendored Image,* 191.

137. Harrison, *God's Many-Splendored Image,* 194. See Gregory of Nyssa, *On the Creation of Humanity* 11.2-4.

138. Harrison, *God's Many-Splendored Image,* 194.

ticularly presuppositions so closely tied to personal identity and theological orthodoxies as notions of sex, gender, and sexuality tend to be. To take up a defensive posture and resist change would be natural, reasonable reactions, and yet, other aspects of the image of God require a different response. As Sister Nonna argued, the virtues "compose the most important dimension of the divine likeness for which every human being is called. . . . Above all, we need the virtue of humility to keep us grounded and open to help and guidance from God and other people."[139] Humility and love for the other, particularly a love for intersex persons whose presence among us has been overlooked, marginalized, and outright oppressed, behoove us to make space for them and to listen to their concerns.

In this book I have done my best to heed the voices of the intersexed who are calling for recognition and inclusion in the human family as well as for better medical care — easier access to medical records, collaborative medical intervention, and a moratorium on nonconsensual surgeries (chap. 1). In light of their voices, I have worked to show that Christian theological anthropologies, even conservative evangelical and Roman Catholic theological anthropologies, do not necessarily stand in the way of these goals. On the contrary, Christian theological anthropology can aid the case of the intersexed by showing that intersex persons have been among the human family and have been recorded in the history of Christianity for millennia. They were honored by Jesus (who raised them up from symbols of shame to become icons of radical discipleship), they have participated in church leadership and public service in the church and in Christian societies, and they have provided resources for thinking theologically about the significance of sex, gender, and sexuality in this life and in the life to come — both in the early church and in the Middle Ages (chap. 2), and again in the postmodern period (chaps. 3 and 6).

Having established the validity of including the intersexed in the human family *as intersex,* I went on to explore how intersex can challenge, correct, and help us construct better theological anthropologies. I urged theologians to move beyond discussions of the woman as paradigmatic "other" to include other others — not only making space for intersex persons but also laying the groundwork for theological inquiry into the experiences of transgender persons.[140] The primary shift I recommended was a change in how

139. Harrison, *God's Many-Splendored Image,* 188.

140. I have wrestled with whether or not to extend my research into the experiences of transpersons whose lives also push us beyond the binary category of male and female.

we interpret the theological significance of Adam and Eve. I noted that the creation narratives are constructed with a focus on shared humanity, rather than emphasizing sex difference. I also argued that where sex difference is highlighted, this difference must be placed in canonical context: Adam and Eve, in their sexed difference, function as *progenitors* rather than *paradigms* of human difference-in-relation. They inaugurate the story of God's redemptive work, which begins with a biological family but presses beyond biology to include other others in the family of God (chap. 4).

In chapter 5 I tried to bring balance to discussions of sexuality, reversing the pendulum swing in conservative theological discussions from fear and sin at one extreme to sexuality as the centerpiece of human personhood and relationality. I noted the dangers of both liberal and conservative emphases on sexuality, calling for sexual desire to be valued as one kind of relational good, relational need, without becoming paradigmatic for all human relations. I then argued that discussions of the social *imago* must retain their basis in the social Trinity — inclusive of sex/gender difference as *one* important difference within community without grounding all relationality (human or divine) on sex differentiation or sexual desire/activity on the one hand and without conflating the related but discrete categories of sex, gender, and sexuality on the other.

Moving from the binary pattern of Eden to the "not male and female" of the eschaton, I worked to show how Christology and eschatology both challenge and enrich our notions of human personhood made in the image

---

Transgender is an important issue that deserves in-depth discussion in its own right, rather than being tagged onto other discussions, such as this one. That discussion would add many more pages to this text — daunting the average reader. It is also a task for which I am not yet adequately equipped. Nevertheless, I do believe my discussion of bodily sex difference lays the groundwork for conservative theologians to enter into transgender discussions with less trepidation. If Adam and Eve function as progenitors of difference, rather than paradigms, then there is space to consider these others too. Transpersons have been documented in many societies throughout history — at times welcomed and revered, at others marginalized and feared. The main difference between intersex persons and transpersons as they are currently defined is the lack of identifiable physical phenomena undergirding transgender experience, making it seem like trans- is all "in the mind" rather than the body. However, given the infancy of the science of brain sex, we may come to find that trans-, too, is located in the body, even if not clearly identifiable in gonads or genitals or in what we normally think of as secondary sex characteristics. Susannah Cornwall provides a helpful discussion of the similarities and differences of trans- and intersex in her article "'State of Mind' versus 'Concrete Set of Facts.'" Her article is a good place to begin theological discussions once the reader has become acquainted with transgender persons and their experiences.

of God. Rather than dismantling the categories of male and female, space should be opened up for the addition and inclusion of intersex, whose humanity was also taken up by Jesus Christ in the incarnation. I concluded by suggesting that while sex, gender, and sexual identities are not erased by identification "in Christ," they must nevertheless be decentered in order to promote the healing of individuals and reconciliation in the community so that male, female, and intersex can emulate and participate in the mutual dependence of the perichoretic love of the Trinity in purity (chap. 6).

Male, female, and intersex persons are all created in the image of God and all called to be conformed to the image of Jesus — the One who has brought God near and made God visible — by the power of the Spirit — the One who remains invisible and uncategorizable as male, female, or intersex.[141] Jesus stands before us not in male perfection but as the true human into

141. I have written elsewhere on the grammatical gender of the Spirit. See my chapter with John R. Franke, "Recovering the Spirit of Pentecost: Canon and Catholicity in Postcolonial Perspective," in *Evangelical Postcolonial Conversations: Global Awakenings in Theology and Praxis,* ed. L. Daniel Hawk, Kay Higuera Smith, and Jayachitra Lalitha (Downers Grove, Ill.: InterVarsity, 2014). Briefly, Hebrew grammar allows only two gendered categories — male and female. There is no neuter in Hebrew. The Hebrew word for spirit *(ruaḥ)* is both masculine and feminine — a common noun. Most often it appears in its feminine form, as in Judg. 3:10, "The Spirit of the LORD [she] came upon him" (NIV), or 1 Sam. 10:6, "The Spirit of the LORD [she] will come upon you in power" (NIV), but at other times it is masculine: "the Spirit of the LORD [he] may carry you" (1 Kings 18:12 NIV). English translations mask the complexity of the biblical witness, sometimes by accident, sometimes out of fear that "regular folk" won't be able to handle the truth. Of course, things get even more complicated when we move from Hebrew where the spirit is mostly feminine, and Aramaic (feminine), to Greek (neuter), to Latin (masculine). The Latin tradition, upon which the English builds, confesses the Spirit as "Lord, the Giver of life." Meanwhile, the Syriac (Aramaic) tradition prays, "Come, Compassionate Mother." Sebastian P. Brock, "Come, Compassionate Mother . . . Come, Holy Spirit: A Forgotten Aspect of Early Eastern Christian Imagery," *Aram* 3, no. 2 (1989): 254-55.

Most English speakers don't like this kind of ambiguity. We like to know a thing. We are children of the West — Christians of the cataphatic way — we analyze and dissect, outline and explain. We prefer Jesus to the Spirit. Jesus who makes God visible, audible, analyzable, crucifiable . . . But the Spirit returns us to the apophatic way, teaching us to confess the limits of our understanding, to expect to be baffled, awed, amazed by the majesty of mystery. Still, we expect mystery when it comes to the divine. We can imagine a God beyond our categories even if we can't find ways to speak of him/her/it. But when it comes to our neighbors, our family members, even ourselves . . . mystery, ambiguity often get in the way. How do we engage, address, welcome, and embrace the intersexed among us — those whose bodies, like the Spirit, are not easily nameable . . . those whose selves do not fit neatly into the grammar of gender? This book is written in the hopes that we can find ways to do just that.

whose image we are transformed as we grow in love, in virtue, in faith, in holiness, in hope, by the Spirit who fills us, convicts us, breathes life into us, and empowers us for the journey. In all, great mystery remains — mysteries of human nature, mysteries of God, mysteries of sex difference, mysteries of self, mysteries of others — but that just keeps things interesting!

Bibliography

Accord Alliance. http://www.accordalliance.org.

Adams, Marilyn McCord. "Trinitarian Friendship: Same-Gender Models of Godly Love in Richard of St. Victor and Aelred of Rievaulx." In *Theology and Sexuality: Classic and Contemporary Readings,* edited by Eugene F. Rogers Jr., 322-40. London: Blackwell, 2002.

Ahmed, S. F., R. Dobbie, A. R. Finlayson, J. Gilbert, et al. "Prevalence of Hypospadias and Other Genital Anomalies among Singleton Births, 1988-1997, in Scotland." *Archives of Disease in Childhood. Fetal and Neonatal Edition* 89, no. 2 (March 2004): 149-51.

American Psychiatric Association. *Diagnostic and Statistical Manual of Mental Disorders.* 4th ed. Washington, D.C.: American Psychiatric Association, 1994.

Androgen Insensitivity Syndrome Support Group (AISSG), UK. "What Is AIS? Forms of AIS (Complete and Partial)." http://www.aissg.org/21_OVERVIEW.HTM.

Anonymous. "Transsexuality in the Church: A Pastor Responds." http://www.parakaleo.co.uk/article2.html.

Aristotle. *On the Generation of Animals.* http://evans-experientialism.freewebspace.com/aristotle_genanimals02.htm.

Augustine. *De bono coniugali. De sancta uirginitate.* Edited and translated by P. G. Walsh. Oxford: Clarendon, 2001.

———. *The City of God against the Pagans.* Translated by Eva Matthews Sanford and William McAllen Green. Loeb Classical Library, vol. 5. Cambridge: Harvard University Press, 1965.

———. *Sermon on the Mount.* Translated by William Findlay. Revised and annotated by D. S. Schaff. Christian Classics Ethereal Library. http://www.ccel.org/ccel/schaff/npnf106.v.ii.xv.html?scrBook=Matt&scrCh=22&scrV=30#v.ii.xv-p7.1.

Balswick, Judith K., and Jack O. Balswick. *Authentic Human Sexuality: An Integrated Christian Approach.* Downers Grove, Ill.: InterVarsity, 2000.

Barth, Karl. *Christ and Adam: Man and Humanity in Romans 5.* Translated by T. A. Small. New York: Octagon Books, 1983.

———. *Church Dogmatics.* Edited by G. W. Bromiley and T. F. Torrance. Translated by J. W. Edwards, O. Bussey, and Harold Knight. 14 vols. Edinburgh: T. & T. Clark, 1936-1969.

Batty, David. "Mistaken Identity." *Guardian,* July 31, 2004. http://www.parakaleo.co.uk/MistakenID-Guardian31-07-2004.html.

Beh, Hazel Glenn, William S. Richardson, and Milton Diamond. "Letter to the Editor: Variations of Sex Development Instead of Disorders of Sex Development." *Archives of Disease in Childhood* 91 (July 27, 2006).

Bem, S. L. *The Lenses of Gender.* New Haven: Yale University Press, 1993.

Ben Asher, Bachya. *Torah Commentary.* Translated by Eliyahu Munk. Brooklyn, N.Y.: Oambda Publishers, 2003.

Benedict XVI. *Deus Caritas Est.* December 25, 2005. http://www.vatican.va/holy_father/benedict_xvi/encyclicals/documents/hf_ben-xvi_enc_ 20051225_deus-caritas-est_en.html.

Berry, Wendell. "The Body and the Earth." In *The Art of the Commonplace: The Agrarian Essays of Wendell Berry,* edited by Norman Wirzba. Berkeley: Counterpoint, 2002.

———. *Sex, Economy, Community, and Freedom.* New York: Pantheon Books, 1992.

Blackless, Melanie, Anthony Charusvatstra, Amanda Derryck, Anne Fausto-Sterling, Karl Lausanne, and Ellen Lee. "How Sexually Dimorphic Are We? Review and Synthesis." *American Journal of Human Biology* 12 (2000): 151-66.

Blanchard, Ray, Betty W. Steiner, and Leonard H. Clemmensen. "Gender Dysphoria, Gender Reorientation, and the Clinical Management of Transsexualism." *Journal of Consulting and Clinical Psychology* 53, no. 3 (June 1985): 295-304.

Bornstein, Kate. *Gender Outlaw: On Men, Women, and the Rest of Us.* New York: Routledge, 1994.

Børresen, Kari Elisabeth, ed. *The Image of God: Gender Models in Judaeo-Christian Tradition.* Minneapolis: Fortress, 1995.

Boswell, John. *Christianity, Social Tolerance, and Homosexuality: Gay People in Western Europe from the Beginning of the Christian Era to the Fourteenth Century.* Chicago: University of Chicago Press, 1980.

Bouma, Hessel, III. "Neither Male Nor Female, God Created Them: The Science and Ethics of Intersexuality." Lecture presented at Gordon College, Wenham, Mass., March 27, 2008.

Boyd, Gregory A., and Paul R. Eddy. *Across the Spectrum: Understanding Issues in Evangelical Theology.* Grand Rapids: Baker Academic, 2002.

Boyd, Stephen B., W. Merle Longwood, and Mark W. Muesse, eds. *Redeeming Men: Religion and Masculinities.* Louisville: Westminster John Knox, 1996.

Breidenthal, Thomas. "Sanctifying Nearness." In *Theology and Sexuality: Classic and Contemporary Readings,* edited by Eugene F. Rogers Jr. London: Blackwell, 2002.

Brower, Gary Robert. "Ambivalent Bodies: Making Christian Eunuchs." Ph.D. diss., Duke University, 1996.

Brown, Peter. *The Body and Society: Men, Women, and Sexual Renunciation in Early Christianity.* New York: Columbia University Press, 1988.

Brown, Warren S., Nancey Murphy, and H. Newton Malony, eds. *Whatever Happened to the Soul? Scientific and Theological Portraits of Human Nature.* Minneapolis: Fortress, 1998.

Brownson, James V. *Bible, Gender, Sexuality: Reframing the Church's Debate on Same-Sex Relationships.* Grand Rapids: Eerdmans, 2013.

Brueggemann, Walter. *Genesis: A Bible Commentary for Teaching and Preaching.* Atlanta: John Knox, 1982.

Buchanan, George Wesley. *The Gospel of Matthew.* Mellen Biblical Commentary: New Testament Series, vol. 1, bk. 2. Lewiston, N.Y.: Mellen Biblical Press, 2006.

Bullough, Vern, and James Brundage. *Sexual Practices and the Medieval Church.* Buffalo: Prometheus Books, 1982.

Butler, Judith. *Gender Trouble: Feminism and the Subversion of Identity.* 2nd ed. New York: Routledge, 1990.

Bynum, Caroline W. *The Resurrection of the Body in Western Christianity, 200-1336.* New York: Columbia University Press, 1995.

Cahill, Lisa Sowle. *Between the Sexes: Foundations for a Christian Ethics of Sexuality.* Philadelphia: Fortress, 1985.

———. "Christology, Ethics, and Spirituality." In *Thinking of Christ,* edited by Tatha Wiley, 193-210. New York: Continuum, 2003.

———. *Family: A Christian Social Perspective.* Minneapolis: Augsburg Fortress, 2000.

———. "The Feminist Pope." In *Does Christianity Teach Male Headship? The Equal-Regard Marriage and Its Critics,* edited by David Blankenhorn, Don Browning, and Mary Stewart Van Leeuwen, 40-48. Grand Rapids: Eerdmans, 2004.

Callahan, Gerald N. *Between XX and XY: Intersexuality and the Myth of Two Sexes.* Chicago: Chicago Review Press, 2009.

Calvin, John. *Commentaries on the Epistles to Timothy, Titus, and Philemon,* in *Calvin's Commentaries,* vol. 21. Translated by William Pringle. Grand Rapids: Baker, 2003.

———. *Commentary on the Epistles of Paul to the Corinthians,* vol. 1. Translated by William Pringle. Grand Rapids: Baker, 2003.

———. *Institutes of the Christian Religion.* Translated by Henry Beveridge. Grand Rapids: Eerdmans, 1989, 1997.

Cameron, D. "Caught Between: An Essay on Intersexuality." In *Intersex in the Age of Ethics,* edited by Alice Domurat Dreger, 90-96. Hagerstown, Md.: University Publishing Group, 1999.

Cannon, Katie G., Beverly W. Harrison, Carter Heyward, Ada Maria Isasi-Diaz, Bess B. Johnson, Mary D. Pellauer, and Nancy D. Richardson. *God's Fierce Whimsy: Christian Feminism and Theological Education.* New York: Pilgrim Press, 1985.

CARES Foundation (Congenital Adrenal Hyperplasia Research Education Support). "What Is the Prader Scale?" http://www.caresfoundation.org/productcart/pc/surgery_considerations_cah.html#prader.

Carr, Anne E. *Transforming Grace: Christian Tradition and Women's Experience.* San Francisco: Harper and Row, 1988.

Carson, D. A., R. T. France, J. A. Motyer, and G. J. Wenham, eds. *New Bible Commentary, 21st Century Edition.* Downers Grove, Ill.: InterVarsity, 1994.

Catechism of the Catholic Church. New York: Doubleday, 1994.

Cheng, Patrick S. *Radical Love: An Introduction to Queer Theology.* New York: Seabury Books, 2011.

Cloke, Gillian. *"This Female Man of God": Women and Spiritual Power in the Patristic Age, AD 350-450.* New York: Routledge, 1995.

Coakley, Sarah. *Powers and Submissions: Spirituality, Philosophy, and Gender.* Chichester: Wiley-Blackwell, 2002.

Cohen, Alfred. "*Tumtum* and Androgynous." *Journal of Halacha and Contemporary Society* 38 (1999): 62-85.

Cohen, Jeffrey Jerome, and Bonnie Wheeler. *Becoming Male in the Middle Ages.* New York: Garland, 2000.

Colapinto, John. "Gender Gap: What Were the Real Reasons behind David Reimer's Suicide?" *Slate.com* (Thursday, June 3, 2004, at 3:58 P.M. Eastern time).

Colón, Christine A., and Bonnie E. Field. *Singled Out: Why Celibacy Must Be Reinvented in Today's Church.* Grand Rapids: Brazos, 2009.

Colson, Charles. "Blurred Biology: How Many Sexes Are There?" *BreakPoint,* October 16, 1996. http://www.colsoncenter.org/commentaries/5213-blurred-biology.

Consortium on the Management of Disorders of Sex Development. *Clinical Guidelines for the Management of Disorders of Sex Development in Childhood.* Rohnert Park, Calif.: Intersex Society of North America, 2006.

———. *Handbook for Parents.* Rohnert Park, Calif.: Intersex Society of North America, 2006.

Cook, Ann Thompson. *Made in God's Image: A Resource for Dialogue about the Church and Gender Differences.* Washington, D.C.: Dumbarton United Methodist Church, 2003.

Cornforth, Tracee. "Female Sexual Dysfunction: Common Sexual Disorders and Causes of Decreased Libido." *About.com.,* December 10, 2009. http://womenshealth.about.com/cs/sexualdysfunction/a/femalesexdysfun.htm.

Cornwall, Susannah. "The Kenosis of Unambiguous Sex in the Body of Christ: Intersex, Theology, and Existing 'for the Other.'" *Theology and Sexuality* 14, no. 2 (January 2008): 181-200.

———. "No Longer Male and Female: The Challenge of Intersex Conditions for Theology." Ph.D. diss., University of Exeter, 2007.

———. "Running to Catch Up with Intersex." *Church Times* 7644 (September 18, 2009): 13.

———. *Sex and Uncertainty in the Body of Christ: Intersex Conditions and Christian Theology.* London: Equinox, 2010.

———. "'State of Mind' versus 'Concrete Set of Facts': The Contrasting of Transgender and Intersex in Church Documents on Sexuality." *Theology and Sexuality* 15, no. 1 (2009): 7-28.

Cullum, P. H., and Katherine J. Lewis, eds. *Holiness and Masculinity in the Middle Ages.* Toronto: University of Toronto Press, 2004.

Davies, W. D., and Dale C. Allison Jr. *A Critical and Exegetical Commentary on the Gospel according to Saint Matthew.* Vol. 3. Edinburgh: T. & T. Clark, 1988.

Davis, Ellen F. "Critical Traditioning: Seeking an Inner Biblical Hermeneutic." In *The*

Art of Reading Scripture, edited by Ellen F. Davis and Richard B. Hays, 163-80. Grand Rapids: Eerdmans, 2003.

Davis, Ellen F., and Richard B. Hays, eds. *The Art of Reading Scripture.* Grand Rapids: Eerdmans, 2003.

Denny, Dallas, ed. *Current Concepts in Transgender Identity.* New York: Garland, 1998.

Devor, Holly. *FTM: Female-to-Male Transsexuals in Society.* Bloomington: Indiana University Press, 1997.

Diamond, Milton. "Sex, Gender, and Identity over the Years: A Changing Perspective." *Child and Adolescent Psychiatric Clinics of North America* 13 (2004): 591-607.

Diamond, Milton, and H. Keith Sigmundson. "Management of Intersexuality: Guidelines for Dealing with Individuals with Ambiguous Genitalia." *Archives of Pediatrics and Adolescent Medicine* 151 (June 10, 1997): 1046-50.

———. "Sex Reassignment at Birth: A Long Term Review and Clinical Implications." *Archives of Pediatrics and Adolescent Medicine* 151 (March 1997): 298-304.

Dixon, Thomas. "Theology, Anti-Theology, and Atheology: From Christian Passions to Secular Emotions." *Modern Theology* 15 (1999): 297-330.

Dreger, Alice Domurat. "'Ambiguous Sex' — or Ambivalent Medicine? Ethical Issues in the Treatment of Intersexuality." *Hastings Center Report* 28, no. 3 (1998): 24-35.

———. "Doubtful Sex: The Fate of the Hermaphrodite in Victorian Medicine." *Victorian Studies* (Spring 1995): 335-70.

———. *Hermaphrodites and the Medical Invention of Sex.* Cambridge: Harvard University Press, 1998.

———. "A History of Intersex: From the Age of Gonads to the Age of Consent." In *Intersex in the Age of Ethics,* edited by Alice Domurat Dreger, 5-28. Hagerstown, Md.: University Publishing Group, 1999.

———, ed. *Intersex in the Age of Ethics.* Hagerstown, Md.: University Publishing Group, 1999.

Dreger, Alice D., Cheryl Chase, Aron Sousa, Philip A. Gruppuso, and Joel Frader. "Changing the Nomenclature/Taxonomy for Intersex: A Scientific and Clinical Rationale." *Journal of Pediatric Endocrinology and Metabolism* 18, no. 8 (2005): 729-33.

Dreger, Alice, and Ellen K. Feder. "Bad Vibrations." *Bioethics Forum,* June 16, 2010. http://www.thehastingscenter.org/Bioethicsforum/Post.aspx?id=4730&blogid=140.

Durant, Will. *The Reformation: A History of European Civilization from Wycliffe to Calvin, 1300-1564.* New York: Simon and Schuster, 1957.

Elliott, Carl. *Better Than Well: American Medicine Meets the American Dream.* New York: Norton, 2003.

Epstein, Julia. "Either/Or — Neither/Both: Sexual Ambiguity and the Ideology of Gender." *Genders* 7 (Spring 1990): 99-142.

Eugenides, Jeffrey. *Middlesex.* New York: Picador, 2002.

Evangelical Alliance Policy Commission. *Transsexuality.* London: Evangelical Alliance, 2000.

Evdokimov, Paul. *The Sacrament of Love.* Crestwood, N.Y.: St. Vladimir's Seminary Press, 1997.

Farley, Margaret A. *Just Love: A Framework for Christian Sexual Ethics.* New York: Continuum, 2006.

Fausto-Sterling, Anne. "The Five Sexes: Why Male and Female Are Not Enough." *The Sciences,* March/April 1993, 20-24; reprinted in *Sexuality and Gender,* ed. Christine L. Williams and Arlene Stein (Malden, Mass.: Blackwell, 2002), 468-73.

———. *Sexing the Body: Gender Politics and the Construction of Sexuality.* New York: Basic Books, 2000.

Ferguson, Everett. *Backgrounds of Early Christianity.* 2nd ed. Grand Rapids: Eerdmans, 1993.

Foucault, Michel. *Herculine Barbin.* New York: Pantheon Books, 1978.

———. *History of Sexuality.* New York: Pantheon Books, 1980.

France, R. T. *The Gospel of Matthew.* Grand Rapids: Eerdmans, 2007.

Franke, John R. *The Character of Theology.* Grand Rapids: Baker Academic, 2005.

Fulkerson, Mary McClintock. "The *Imago Dei* and a Reformed Logic for Feminist/Womanist Critique." In *Feminist and Womanist Essays in Reformed Dogmatics,* edited by Amy Plantinga Pauw and Serene Jones. Louisville: Westminster John Knox, 2006.

Gaillardetz, Richard R. *A Daring Promise: A Spirituality of Christian Marriage.* New York: Crossroad, 1995.

Gaudium et Spes. In *Vatican II: The Basic Sixteen Documents (A Completely Revised Translation in Inclusive Language),* edited by Austin Flannery. Northport, N.Y.: Costello Publishing Co., 1996.

Green, Joel B. "'Bodies — That Is, Human Lives': A Re-examination of Human Nature in the Bible." In *Whatever Happened to the Soul? Scientific and Theological Portraits of Human Nature,* edited by Warren S. Brown, Nancey Murphy, and H. Newton Malony. Minneapolis: Fortress, 1998.

———. *Body, Soul, and Human Life: The Nature of Humanity in the Bible.* Grand Rapids: Baker, 2008.

———, ed. *What about the Soul? Neuroscience and Christian Anthropology.* Nashville: Abingdon, 2004.

Greenberg, Julie A. "Defining Male and Female: Intersexuality and the Collision between Law and Biology." *Arizona Law Review* 41, no. 2 (1999): 265-328.

Grenz, Stanley J. "Belonging to God: The Quest for Communal Spirituality in the Postmodern World." *Asbury Theological Journal* 54, no. 2 (Fall 1999): 41-52.

———. "Is God Sexual? Human Embodiment and the Christian Conception of God." In *This Is My Name Forever: The Trinity and Gender Language for God,* edited by Alvin F. Kimel Jr., 190-212. Downers Grove, Ill.: InterVarsity, 2001.

———. "Jesus as the *Imago Dei:* Image-of-God Christology and the Non-Linear Linearity of Theology." *Journal of the Evangelical Theological Society* 47, no. 4 (December 2004): 617-28.

———. *The Moral Quest: Foundations of Christian Ethics.* Downers Grove, Ill.: InterVarsity, 1997.

———. *The Named God and the Question of Being: A Trinitarian Theo-Ontology.* Louisville: Westminster John Knox, 2005.

———. *Rediscovering the Triune God: The Trinity in Contemporary Theology.* Minneapolis: Fortress, 2004.

———. *Sexual Ethics: An Evangelical Perspective.* Louisville: Westminster John Knox, 1990.

———. *The Social God and the Relational Self: A Trinitarian Theology of the* Imago Dei. Louisville: Westminster John Knox, 2001.

———. "The Social God and the Relational Self: Toward a Theology of the *Imago Dei* in the Postmodern Context." In *Personal Identity in Theological Perspective,* edited by Richard Lints, Michael S. Horton, and Mark R. Talbot, 70-92. Grand Rapids: Eerdmans, 2006.

———. "Theological Foundations for Male-Female Relationships." *Journal of the Evangelical Theological Society* 41, no. 4 (1998): 615-30.

———. *Theology for the Community of God.* 2nd ed. Grand Rapids: Eerdmans, 2000.

———. *Welcoming but Not Affirming: An Evangelical Response to Homosexuality.* Louisville: Westminster John Knox, 1998.

Grenz, Stanley J., and Denise Muir Kjesbo. *Women in the Church: A Biblical Theology of Women in Ministry.* Downers Grove, Ill.: InterVarsity, 1995.

Griggs, Claudine. *S/he: Changing Sex and Changing Clothes.* Oxford: Berg, 1998.

Gross, Sally. "Intersexuality and Scripture." *Theology and Sexuality* 11 (1999): 65-74.

———. "The Journey from Selwyn to Sally." *The Natal Witness Features* (South Africa), February 21, 2000. http://www.intersex.org.za/publications/witness1.pdf.

———. "Shunned by the Church." *The Natal Witness Features* (South Africa), February 22, 2000. http://www.intersex.org.za/publications/witness2.pdf.

———. "The Struggle to Be Sally." *The Natal Witness Features* (South Africa), February 23, 2000. http://www.intersex.org.za/publications/witness3.pdf.

Gudorf, Christine E. "The Erosion of Sexual Dimorphism: Challenges to Religion and Religious Ethics." *Journal of the American Academy of Religion* 69, no. 4 (December 2001): 863-91.

Gundry-Volf, Judith M. "Beyond Difference? Paul's Vision of a New Humanity in Galatians 3:28." In *The Gospel and Gender: A Trinitarian Engagement with Being Male and Female in Christ,* edited by Douglas A. Campbell, 8-36. London: T. & T. Clark, 2003.

Gunton, Colin E. *The One, the Three, and the Many: God, Creation, and the Culture of Modernity.* Cambridge: Cambridge University Press, 1993.

———. "Trinity, Ontology and Anthropology: Towards a Renewal of the Doctrine of the *Imago Dei.*" In *Persons, Divine and Human,* edited by Christoph Schwöbel and Colin E. Gunton, 47-61. Edinburgh: T. & T. Clark, 1991.

———. *The Triune Creator: A Historical and Systematic Study.* Grand Rapids: Eerdmans, 1998.

Hammond, Graeme. "Suffering for the Sake of Identity." *Sunday Herald Sun,* March 28, 2004. www.sundayheraldsun.com.au.

Harrison, Nonna Verna. *God's Many-Splendored Image: Theological Anthropology for Spiritual Formation.* Grand Rapids: Baker Academic, 2010.

Hays, Richard B. *The Moral Vision of the New Testament: A Contemporary Introduction to New Testament Ethics.* New York: T. & T. Clark/Continuum, 1997, 2004.

Hefner, Philip. *Technology and Human Becoming.* Minneapolis: Fortress, 2003.

Hekma, Gert. "A Female Soul in a Male Body: Sexual Inversion as Gender Inversion in Nineteenth-Century Sexology." In *Third Sex, Third Gender: Beyond Sexual Dimorphism in Culture and History,* edited by Gilbert Herdt, 213-39. New York: Zone Books, 1994.

Herdt, Gilbert, ed. *Third Sex, Third Gender: Beyond Sexual Dimorphism in Culture and History.* New York: Zone Books, 1994.

Hester, J. David. "Eunuchs and the Postgender Jesus: Matthew 19.12 and Transgressive Sexualities." *Journal for the Study of the New Testament* 28, no. 1 (2005): 13-40.

———. "Intersex(es) and Alternative Strategies of Healing: Medicine, Social Imperatives and Counter Communities of Identity" (in German). *Zeitschrift für Ethik in der Medizin* (2004); available in English at http://www.ars-rhetorica.net/J_David_Hester/Intersexes_files/AlternativeStrategies.pdf, 5.

———. "Intersexes and the End of Gender: Corporeal Ethics and Postgender Bodies." *Journal of Gender Studies* 13, no. 3 (November 2004): 215-25.

Hillman, Thea. *Intersex (for Lack of a Better Word).* San Francisco: Manic D Press, 2008.

Hines, Melissa. *Brain Gender.* Oxford: Oxford University Press, 2004.

Hoekema, Anthony A. *Created in God's Image.* Grand Rapids: Eerdmans, 1986.

Hollinger, Dennis P. *The Meaning of Sex: Christian Ethics and the Moral Life.* Grand Rapids: Baker Academic, 2009.

Holmes, Morgan. "Homophobia in Health Care: Abjection and the Treatment of Intersexuality." Paper presented at the Learned Societies CSAA meetings, Montreal, June 1995.

———. *Intersex: A Perilous Difference.* Selinsgrove, Pa.: Susquehanna University Press, 2008.

Hopkins, Julie M. *Towards a Feminist Christology: Jesus of Nazareth, European Women, and the Christological Crisis.* Grand Rapids: Eerdmans, 1994.

Horrell, J. Scott. "Toward a Biblical Model of the Social Trinity: Avoiding Equivocation of Nature and Order." *Journal of the Evangelical Theological Society* 47, no. 3 (September 2004): 399-421.

Horton, Michael S. "Image and Office: Human Personhood and the Covenant." In *Personal Identity in Theological Perspective,* edited by Richard Lints, Michael S. Horton, and Mark R. Talbot, 178-203. Grand Rapids: Eerdmans, 2006.

———. "Post-Reformation Reformed Anthropology." In *Personal Identity in Theological Perspective,* edited by Richard Lints, Michael S. Horton, and Mark R. Talbot, 45-69. Grand Rapids: Eerdmans, 2006.

Hughes, I. A., C. Houk, S. F. Ahmed, P. A. Lee, and LWPES/ESPE [Lawson Wilkins Pediatric Endocrine Society/European Society for Paediatric Endocrinology]

Consensus Group. "Consensus Statement on Management of Intersex Disorders." *Archives of Disease in Childhood* 2 (May 4, 2006): 1-10. www.archdischild.com.
Inbody, Tyron L. *The Many Faces of Christology.* Nashville: Abingdon, 2002.
Intersex Society of North America. http://www.isna.org.
Intersex Society of South Africa. http://www.intersex.org.za/.
———. "Biographies: Sally Gross." http://www.intersex.org/za/biography.html.
Intersex Support Group International. http://www.wywo.org/isgi/index.html.
Irwin, Joyce L. *Womanhood in Radical Protestantism: 1525-1675.* Lewiston, N.Y.: Edwin Mellen Press, 1987.
Isasi-Diaz, Ada Maria. "Christ in *Mujerista* Theology." In *Thinking of Christ: Proclamation, Explanation, Meaning,* edited by Tatha Wiley, 157-76. New York: Continuum, 2003.
Issues in Human Sexuality: A Statement by the House of Bishops; General Synod of the Church of England. Harrisburg, Pa.: Morehouse, 1991.
Jardine, Murray. *The Making and Unmaking of Technological Society.* Grand Rapids: Brazos, 2004.
Jenson, Robert. "Thinking Love." In *On Thinking the Human: Resolutions of Difficult Notions.* Grand Rapids: Eerdmans, 2003.
Jerome. *The Perpetual Virginity of Blessed Mary, against Helvidius* 23. Translated by W. H. Fremantle. Christian Classics Ethereal Library. http://www.ccel.org/ccel/schaff/npnf206.vi.v.html.
Jewett, Paul K. *Man as Male and Female.* Grand Rapids: Eerdmans, 1975.
John of the Cross. *Dark Night of the Soul.* In *The Collected Works of St. John of the Cross,* translated by Kieran Kavanaugh, O.C.D., and Otilio Rodriguez, O.C.D. Rev. ed. Washington, D.C.: ICS Publications, 1991.
John Paul II. *Man and Woman He Created Them: A Theology of the Body.* Translated and edited by Michael Waldstein. Boston: Pauline Books and Media, 2006.
———. "On the Family" *(Familiaris Consortio):* Letter to Families. November 22, 1981.
———. *The Trinity's Embrace: God's Saving Plan, a Catechesis on Salvation History.* Boston: Pauline Books and Media, 2002.
Johnson, Elizabeth A. *Consider Jesus: Waves of Renewal in Christology.* New York: Crossroad, 1990.
———. *She Who Is: The Mystery of God in Feminist Theological Discourse.* New York: Crossroad, 2003.
Jones, Stanton L., and Mark A. Yarhouse. "Anthropology, Sexuality and Sexual Ethics: The Challenge of Psychology." In *Personal Identity in Theological Perspective,* edited by Richard Lints, Michael S. Horton, and Mark R. Talbot. Grand Rapids: Eerdmans, 2006.
Jung, Patricia B. "Christianity and Human Sexual Polymorphism: Are They Compatible?" In *Ethics and Intersex,* edited by Sharon E. Sytsma, 293-309. Dordrecht: Springer, 2006.
Jung, Patricia Beattie, with Joseph Andrew Coray, eds. *Sexual Diversity and Catholicism: Toward the Development of Moral Theology.* Collegeville, Minn.: Liturgical Press, 2001.

Karkazis, Katrina. *Fixing Sex: Intersex, Medical Authority, and Lived Experience.* Durham, N.C., and London: Duke University Press, 2008.

Keener, Craig S. *A Commentary on the Gospel of Matthew.* Grand Rapids: Eerdmans, 1999.

Kelsey, David H. "Personal Bodies: A Theological Anthropological Proposal." In *Personal Identity in Theological Perspective,* edited by Richard Lints, Michael S. Horton, and Mark R. Talbot, 139-58. Grand Rapids: Eerdmans, 2006.

Kessler, Suzanne J. *Lessons from the Intersexed.* New Brunswick, N.J.: Rutgers University Press, 1998.

———. Letter in response to Anne Fausto-Sterling's "The Five Sexes." *The Sciences,* July/August 1993, 3.

———. "The Medical Construction of Gender: Case Management of Intersexed Infants." *Signs: Journal of Women in Culture and Society* 16 (1990): 3-26.

Kessler, Suzanne J., and Wendy McKenna. *Gender: An Ethnomethodological Approach.* Chicago: University of Chicago Press, 1978, 1985.

Koyama, Emi, ed. *Teaching Intersex Issues: A Guide for Teachers in Women's, Gender, and Queer Studies.* 2nd ed. Portland, Ore.: Intersex Initiative Portland, 2003.

Koyama, Emi, and Lisa Weasel. "From Social Construction to Social Justice: Transforming How We Teach about Intersexuality." In *Teaching Intersex Issues: A Guide for Teachers in Women's, Gender, and Queer Studies,* edited by Emi Koyama. 2nd ed. Portland, Ore.: Intersex Initiative Portland, 2003.

Kristof, Nicholas D., and Sheryl WuDunn. *Half the Sky: Turning Oppression into Opportunity for Women Worldwide.* New York: Vintage, 2009.

Kuefler, Matthew. *The Manly Eunuch: Masculinity, Gender Ambiguity, and Christian Ideology in Late Antiquity.* Chicago: University of Chicago Press, 2001.

Kvam, Kristen E., Linda S. Schearing, and Valarie H. Ziegler, eds. *Eve and Adam: Jewish, Christian, and Muslim Readings on Genesis and Gender.* Bloomington and Indianapolis: Indiana University Press, 1999.

LaCugna, Catherine M. *God for Us: The Trinity and Christian Life.* San Francisco: HarperCollins, 1991.

Lancaster, Roger N. *The Trouble with Nature: Sex in Science and Popular Culture.* Berkeley: University of California Press, 2003.

Lane, Belden C. *The Solace of Fierce Landscapes: Exploring Desert and Mountain Spirituality.* Oxford: Oxford University Press, 1998.

Laqueur, Thomas. *Making Sex: Body and Gender from the Greeks to Freud.* Cambridge: Harvard University Press, 1990.

Lasch, Christopher. "The Family as a Haven in a Heartless World." *Salmagundi,* no. 35 (Fall 1976): 42-55.

Laumann, E. O., A. Paik, and R. C. Rosen. "Sexual Dysfunction in the United States: Prevalence and Predictors." *Journal of the American Medical Association* 281, no. 6 (February 10, 1999): 537-44.

Lebacqz, Karen. "Difference or Defect? Intersexuality and the Politics of Difference." *Annual for the Society of Christian Ethics* 17 (1997): 213-29.

Lewis, C. S. *The Four Loves.* Orlando: Harcourt, Brace and Co., 1960, 1988.

Lints, Richard. "Imaging and Idolatry: The Sociality of Personhood." In *Personal Identity in Theological Perspective,* edited by Richard Lints, Michael S. Horton, and Mark R. Talbot, 204-25. Grand Rapids: Eerdmans, 2006.

Lints, Richard, Michael S. Horton, and Mark R. Talbot, eds. *Personal Identity in Theological Perspective.* Grand Rapids: Eerdmans, 2006.

Lips, Hillary M. *Sex and Gender: An Introduction.* 2nd ed. Mountain View, Calif.: Mayfield Publishing Co., 1993.

Looy, Heather. "How *Not* to Do a Sex Change." *Books and Culture* 6, no. 5 (September/October 2000): 13.

———. "Male and Female God Created Them: The Challenge of Intersexuality." *Journal of Psychology and Christianity* 21 (2002): 10-20.

———. "Sex Differences: Evolved, Constructed and Designed." *Journal of Psychology and Theology* 29, no. 4 (Winter 2001): 301-13.

Looy, Heather, and Hessel Bouma III. "The Nature of Gender: Gender Identity in Persons Who Are Intersexed or Transgendered." *Journal of Psychology and Theology* 33, no. 3 (2005): 166-78.

Luther, Martin. *The Table Talk.* Translated and edited by T. G. Tappert. In *Luther's Works,* vol. 54. Philadelphia: Fortress, 1967.

Luz, Ulrich. *Matthew 8–20: A Commentary.* Translated by James E. Crouch. Edited by Helmut Koester. Minneapolis: Fortress, 2001.

———. *Matthew 21–28: A Commentary.* Translated by James E. Crouch. Edited by Helmut Koester. Minneapolis: Fortress, 2005.

MacKenzie, Gordene Olga. *Transgender Nation.* Bowling Green, Ohio: Bowling Green State University Popular Press, 1994.

Mackin, Theodore. *What Is Marriage?* New York: Paulist, 1982.

Maritain, Jacques. *Three Reformers: Luther — Descartes — Rousseau.* London: Sheed and Ward, 1950.

Mathews, Alice, and Gay Hubbard. *Marriage Made in Eden: A Premodern Perspective for a Post-Christian World.* Grand Rapids: Baker, 2004.

Matthews, Chris. "Plato on Women." *Philosophical Misadventures.* 2007-2009. http://www.philosophical misadventures.com/?p=30.

May, William E. "The Communion of Persons in Marriage and the Conjugal Act." September 21, 2003. http://www.christendom-awake.org/pages/may/communion ofpersons.htm.

McCarthy, David Matzko. *The Good Life: Genuine Christianity for the Middle Class.* Grand Rapids: Brazos, 2004.

———. "Homosexuality and the Practices of Marriage." *Modern Theology* 13, no. 3 (July 1997): 371-97.

———. "The Relationship of Bodies: A Nuptial Hermeneutics of Same-Sex Unions." In *Theology and Sexuality: Classic and Contemporary Readings,* edited by Eugene F. Rogers Jr., 200-216. Malden, Mass.: Blackwell, 2002.

———. Review of *Welcoming but Not Affirming: An Evangelical Response to Homosexuality,* by Stanley J. Grenz. *Christian Century* (October 1999).

———. *Sex and Love in the Home: A Theology of the Household.* 2nd ed. London: SCM, 2004.

McConville, Gordon. "Deuteronomy." In *New Bible Commentary, 21st Century Edition,* edited by D. A. Carson et al. Downers Grove, Ill.: InterVarsity, 1994.

McHugh, Paul. "Surgical Sex." *First Things* 147 (November 2004): 34-38.

McKain, T. L. "Acknowledging Mixed-Sex People." *Journal of Sex and Marital Therapy* 11 (1996): 265-79.

McKnight, Scot. *The Blue Parakeet: Rethinking How You Read the Bible.* Grand Rapids: Zondervan, 2008.

McLeod, Frederick G., S.J. *The Image of God in the Antiochene Tradition.* Washington, D.C.: Catholic University of America Press, 1999.

McMinn, Lisa Graham. *Sexuality and Holy Longing: Embracing Intimacy in a Broken World.* San Francisco: Jossey-Bass, 2004.

Melchert, Norman. *The Great Conversation: A Historical Introduction to Philosophy.* 2nd ed. Mountain View, Calif., London, and Toronto: Mayfield Publishing Co., 1995.

Meyerowitz, Joanne. *How Sex Changed: A History of Transsexuality in the United States.* Cambridge: Harvard University Press, 2002.

Mollenkott, Virginia Ramey. *Omnigender: A Trans-religious Approach.* Cleveland: Pilgrim Press, 2001.

Mollenkott, Virginia Ramey, and Richard Mouw, with Krista Tippett. "Gay Marriage: Broken or Blessed? Two Evangelical Views." On *Speaking of Faith,* August 3, 2006. http://being.publicradio.org/programs/gaymarriage/index.shtml.

Money, John. "Letter to the Editor." *The Sciences,* June/July 1993, 4.

———. *Sex Errors of the Body and Related Syndromes: A Guide to Counseling Children, Adolescents, and Their Families.* 2nd ed. Baltimore: Paul H. Brookes Publishing Co., 1994.

Money, John, and Anke A. Ehrhardt. *Man and Woman, Boy and Girl.* Baltimore: Johns Hopkins University Press, 1972.

Morris, Esther. "The Self I Will Never Know." *New Internationalist* 364 (February 2004). http://newint.org/features/2004/02/01/self/.

MRKH Support Group, UK. http://www.mrkh.org.uk/.

Mueller-Vollmer, Kurt, ed. *The Hermeneutics Reader.* New York: Continuum, 1985.

Murphy, Nancey. "Nonreductive Physicalism: Philosophical Challenges." In *Personal Identity in Theological Perspective,* edited by Richard Lints, Michael S. Horton, and Mark R. Talbot, 95-117. Grand Rapids: Eerdmans, 2006.

Myatt, Alan D. "On the Compatibility of Ontological Equality, Hierarchy and Functional Distinctions." A paper presented at the sixty-first annual meeting of the Evangelical Theological Society, New Orleans, November 20, 2009. http://www.myatts.net/papers/. Also found in *The Deception of Eve and the Ontology of Women, Priscilla Papers,* special ed. (2010): 23-26.

Myers, David G. "There's a Wideness in God's Mercy." *Perspectives: A Journal of Reformed Thought* (May 2010).

Nelson, James B. "Male Sexuality and the Fragile Planet: A Theological Reflection." In

Redeeming Men: Religion and Masculinities, edited by Stephen B. Boyd, W. Merle Longwood, and Mark W. Muesse. Louisville: Westminster John Knox, 1996.

Nelson, James B., and Sandra P. Longfellow, eds. *Sexuality and the Sacred: Sources for Theological Reflection.* Louisville: Westminster John Knox, 1994.

Nordling, Cherith Fee. "Embodied, Human, Sexual: The Only Way to Be Christian." *Perspectives: A Journal of Reformed Thought* (November 2007): 11-15.

Nygren, Anders. *Agape and Eros.* London: SPCK, 1953.

O'Donovan, Oliver. "Transsexualism and Christian Marriage." *Journal of Religious Ethics* 11 (Spring 1983): 135-62.

Olthuis, James H. "Be(com)ing: Humankind as Gift and Call." *Philosophia Reformata* 58 (1993): 153-72.

———. "Face-to-Face: Ethical Asymmetry or the Symmetry of Mutuality?" In *The Hermeneutics of Charity: Interpretation, Selfhood, and Postmodern Faith; Studies in Honor of James H. Olthuis,* edited by James K. A. Smith and Henry Isaac Venema, 135-56. Grand Rapids: Brazos, 2004. First published 1996.

———. "Crossing the Threshold: Sojourning Together in the Wild Spaces of Love." In *The Hermeneutics of Charity: Interpretation, Selfhood, and Postmodern Faith; Studies in Honor of James H. Olthuis,* edited by James K. A. Smith and Henry Isaac Venema, 23-40. Grand Rapids: Brazos, 2004. First published 1993.

Paris, Jenell Williams. "Always Sex, All the Time: A Christian Approach to the Legacy of Alfred Kinsey." *Cresset,* Advent/Christmas 2008, 52-59.

———. *Birth Control for Christians: Making Wise Choices.* Grand Rapids: Baker, 2003.

———. "Love beyond Romance: Contemporary Worship Music and the American Romantic Ideal." *Mutuality* (Winter 2006): 11-13.

———. "The Truth about Sex." *Christianity Today,* November 12, 2001. www.christianitytoday.com/ct/2001/november12/5.62.html.

Paul VI. *On the Regulation of Birth (Humanae Vitae).* July 25, 1968.

Pentz, Rebecca D. "Can Jesus Save Women?" In *Encountering Jesus: A Debate on Christology,* edited by Stephen T. Davis, with responses by Stephen T. Davis, John B. Cobb Jr., John Hick, and James M. Robinson. Atlanta: John Knox, 1988.

Peterson, Margaret Kim, and Dwight N. Peterson. "God Does Not Want to Write Your Love Story." In *God Does Not . . . Entertain, Play "Matchmaker," Hurry, Demand Blood, Cure Every Illness,* edited by D. Brent Laytham. Grand Rapids: Brazos, 2009.

Plato. *Plato: Complete Works.* Edited by John M. Cooper. Indianapolis and Cambridge: Hackett, 1997.

Potter, Kerry. "Free to Discover My Destiny." http://www.parakaleo.co.uk/kerrypotter.html.

Preves, Sharon E. "For the Sake of the Children: Destigmatizing Intersexuality." In *Intersex in the Age of Ethics,* edited by Alice Domurat Dreger, 50-65. Hagerstown, Md.: University Publishing Group, 1999.

———. *Intersex and Identity: The Contested Self.* New Brunswick, N.J.: Rutgers University Press, 2003.

Quigley, Charmian A., Alessandra De Bellis, Keith B. Marschke, Mostafa K. El-Awady,

Elizabeth M. Wilson, and Frank S. French. "Androgen Receptor Defects: Historical, Clinical and Molecular Perspectives." *Endocrine Reviews* 16, no. 3 (June 1995): 271-321.

Ranke-Heinemann, Uta. *Eunuchs for the Kingdom of Heaven: Women, Sexuality, and the Catholic Church.* Translated by Peter Heinegg. New York: Doubleday, 1990.

Rashi. *The Pentateuch and Rashi's Commentary: Genesis.* Translated by Abraham ben Isaiah, Benjamin Sharfman, et al. Brooklyn, N.Y.: S. S. and R. Publishing, 1949.

Ratzinger, Joseph Cardinal. "Letter to the Bishops of the Catholic Church on the Collaboration of Men and Women in the Church and in the World." From the Offices of the Congregation for the Doctrine of the Faith. May 31, 2004.

Reis, Elizabeth. *Bodies in Doubt: An American History of Intersex.* Baltimore: Johns Hopkins University Press, 2009.

———. "Divergence or Disorder? The Politics of Naming Intersex." *Perspectives in Biology and Medicine* 50, no. 4 (Autumn 2007): 535-43.

Richard of St. Victor. *Richard of St. Victor: The Twelve Patriarchs, The Mystical Ark, Book Three of the Trinity.* Translated by Grover A. Zinn. Classics of Western Spirituality. New York: Paulist, 1979.

Ricoeur, Paul. "Wonder, Eroticism, and Enigma." In *Sexuality and the Sacred: Sources for Theological Reflection,* edited by James B. Nelson and Sandra P. Longfellow. Louisville: Westminster John Knox, 1993.

Ringrose, Kathryn M. "Living in the Shadows: Eunuchs and Gender in Byzantium." In *Third Sex, Third Gender: Beyond Sexual Dimorphism in Culture and History,* edited by Gilbert Herdt. New York: Zone Books, 1994.

———. *The Perfect Servant: Eunuchs and the Social Construction of Gender in Byzantium.* Chicago: University of Chicago Press, 2004.

Robertson, Annabelle. "Transgender: Nature, Nurture and When It All Goes Awry." 2002. http://www.crosswalk.com/news/1278894.html?view=print.

Rogers, Eugene F., Jr. "Sanctification, Homosexuality, and God's Triune Life." In *Theology and Sexuality: Classic and Contemporary Readings,* edited by Eugene F. Rogers Jr., 217-46. London: Blackwell, 2002.

———, ed. *Theology and Sexuality: Classic and Contemporary Readings.* London: Blackwell, 2002.

Rolheiser, Ronald. *The Holy Longing: A Search for a Christian Spirituality.* New York: Doubleday, 1999.

Ross, Susan A. "The Bridegroom and the Bride: The Theological Anthropology of John Paul II and Its Relation to the Bible and Homosexuality." In *Sexual Diversity and Catholicism: Toward the Development of Moral Theology,* edited by Patricia Beattie Jung, with Joseph Andrew Coray, 39-59. Collegeville, Minn.: Liturgical Press, 2001.

Rubio, Julie Hanlon. *A Christian Theology of Marriage and Family.* New York: Paulist, 2003.

Ruether, Rosemary Radford. "Christian Anthropology and Gender." In *The Future of Theology: Essays in Honor of Jürgen Moltmann,* edited by Miroslav Volf, Carmen Krieg, and Thomas Kucharz, 241-52. Grand Rapids: Eerdmans, 1996.

———. "Christology and Patriarchy." In *Thinking of Christ: Proclamation, Explanation, Meaning,* edited by Tatha Wiley, 122-34. New York: Continuum, 2003.

———. "*Imago Dei:* Christian Tradition and Feminist Hermeneutics." In *Image of God: Gender Models in Judaeo-Christian Tradition,* edited by Kari Elisabeth Børresen. Oslo: Solum Forlag, 1991.

———. *Introducing Redemption in Christian Feminism.* Sheffield: Sheffield Academic Press, 1998.

Russell, Robert John. "Five Attitudes toward Nature and Technology from a Christian Perspective." *Theology and Science* 1, no. 2 (2003): 149-59.

Salzman, Todd A., and Michael G. Lawler. *The Sexual Person: Toward a Renewed Catholic Anthropology.* Washington, D.C.: Georgetown University Press, 2008.

Sax, Leonard. *Boys Adrift: The Five Factors Driving the Growing Epidemic of Unmotivated Boys and Underachieving Young Men.* New York: Basic Books, 2007.

———. "How Common Is Intersex? A Response to Anne Fausto-Sterling." *Journal of Sex Research* 39, no. 3 (August 2002): 174-78.

———. *Why Gender Matters: What Parents and Teachers Need to Know about the Emerging Science of Sex Differences.* New York: Doubleday, 2005.

Sayers, Dorothy L. *Are Women Human?* 1938. Reprint, Grand Rapids: Eerdmans, 1971.

Schleiermacher, Friedrich D. E. *Compendium of 1819,* with marginal notes from 1828. In *The Hermeneutics Reader,* edited by Kurt Mueller-Vollmer. New York: Continuum, 1985.

Schmidt, Thomas E. *Straight and Narrow? Compassion and Clarity in the Homosexuality Debate.* Downers Grove, Ill.: InterVarsity, 1995.

Scholz, Piotr O. *Eunuchs and Castrati: A Cultural History.* Translated by John A. Broadwin and Shelley L. Frisch. Princeton: Markus Weiner Publishers, 2001.

Schrag, Calvin O. *The Self after Postmodernity.* New Haven: Yale University Press, 1997.

Schüssler Fiorenza, Elisabeth. *Jesus: Miriam's Child, Sophia's Prophet; Critical Issues in Feminist Christology.* New York: Continuum, 1994.

Schwöbel, Christoph, and Colin Gunton, eds. *Persons: Divine and Human.* Edinburgh: T. & T. Clark, 1991.

Scola, Angelo. *The Nuptial Mystery.* Translated by Michelle K. Borras. Grand Rapids: Eerdmans, 2005.

Scroggs, Robin. *The Last Adam: A Study in Pauline Anthropology.* Philadelphia: Fortress, 1966.

Selinger, Suzanne. *Charlotte von Kirschbaum and Karl Barth: A Study in Biography and the History of Theology.* University Park: Pennsylvania State University Press, 1998.

Sexton, Jason S. "The *Imago Dei* Once Again: Stanley Grenz's Journey toward a Theological Interpretation of Genesis 1:26-27." *Journal of Theological Interpretation* 4, no. 2 (2010): 187-206.

———. "Stanley Grenz's Ecclesiology: Telic and Trinitarian." *Pacific Journal of Baptist Research* 6, no. 1 (April 2010): 21-45.

Sheriffs, R. J. A. "Eunuch." In *New Bible Dictionary,* edited by J. D. Douglas et al. 2nd ed. Downers Grove, Ill.: InterVarsity, 1993.

Shults, F. LeRon. "The 'Body of Christ' in Evangelical Theology." *Word and World* 22, no. 2 (Spring 2002): 178-85.

———. *Reforming Theological Anthropology: After the Philosophical Turn to Relationality.* Grand Rapids: Eerdmans, 2003.

———. "Sharing in the Divine Nature: Transformation, *Koinōnia* and the Doctrine of God." In *On Being Christian . . . and Human,* edited by Todd Speidell, 87-127. Eugene, Ore.: Wipf and Stock, 2002.

Simon, Caroline J. *Bringing Sex into Focus: The Quest for Sexual Integrity.* Downers Grove, Ill.: InterVarsity, 2012.

Smedes, Lewis. *Sex for Christians.* Grand Rapids: Eerdmans, 1976, 1994.

Smith, Amanda Riley. "What Child Is This? Making Room for Intersexuality." *Regeneration Quarterly* 8, no. 2 (Winter 2002): 27-30.

Smith, Christian. *The Bible Made Impossible: Why Biblicism Is Not a Truly Evangelical Reading of Scripture.* Grand Rapids: Brazos, 2011.

Smith, Richard W. "What Kind of Sex Is Natural?" In *The Frontiers of Sex Research,* edited by Vern Bullough, 103-11. Buffalo: Prometheus Books, 1979.

Soskice, Janet Martin. "The Ends of Man and the Future of God." In *The Blackwell Companion to Postmodern Theology,* edited by Graham Ward. Oxford: Blackwell, 2001.

———. *"Imago Dei." The Other Journal: An Intersection of Theology and Culture* 7 (April 2, 2006).

———. *The Kindness of God: Metaphor, Gender, and Religious Language.* Oxford: Oxford University Press, 2007.

Spalding, Clara Jane. "What Do Children Know?" http://www.obgyn.net/young-woman/young-woman.asp?page=/young-woman/articles/xyturner. Originally published at http://www.sonoworld.com/Client/Fetus/page.aspx?id=389 (August 6, 1999).

———. "Mosaic in the Mirror." http://www.xyxo.org/jane.htm. Accessed January 13, 2011.

Sparks, Kenton L. *God's Word in Human Words: An Evangelical Appropriation of Critical Biblical Scholarship.* Grand Rapids: Baker Academic, 2008.

———. *Sacred Word, Broken Word: Biblical Authority and the Dark Side of Scripture.* Grand Rapids: Eerdmans, 2012.

Speiser, Phyllis W., and Perrin C. White. "Congenital Adrenal Hyperplasia Due to 21-Hydroxylase Deficiency." *Endocrine Reviews* 21, no. 3 (2000): 245-91.

Stephenson, Lisa. "Directed, Ordered, and Related: The Male and Female Interpersonal Relation in Karl Barth's *Church Dogmatics." Scottish Journal of Theology* 61, no. 4 (2008): 435-49.

Stewart, Elizabeth G., and Paula Spencer. *The V Book: A Doctor's Guide to Complete Vulvovaginal Health.* New York: Bantam Books, 2002.

Storkey, Elaine. "Modernity and Anthropology." In *Faith and Modernity,* edited by Philip Sampson, Vinay Samuel, and Chris Sugden. Oxford: Regnum Books, 1994.

———. "Who Is the Christ? Issues in Christology and Feminist Theology." In *The Gospel and Gender: A Trinitarian Engagement with Being Male and Female in Christ,* edited by Douglas A. Campbell, 105-23. London: T. & T. Clark, 2003.

Stuart, Elizabeth, with Andy Braunston, Malcolm Edwards, John McMahon, and Tim Morrison. *Religion Is a Queer Thing: A Guide to the Christian Faith for Lesbian, Gay, Bisexual, and Transgendered People.* London and Washington, D.C.: Cassell, 1997.

Sumner, Sarah. *Men and Women in the Church: Building Consensus on Christian Leadership.* Downers Grove, Ill.: InterVarsity, 2003.

Sytsma, Sharon E., ed. *Ethics and Intersex.* Dordrecht: Springer, 2006.

Taylor, Charles. *Sources of the Self: The Making of the Modern Identity.* Cambridge: Harvard University Press, 1989.

Tertullian. *On Monogamy.* Translated by S. Thelwall. In *Fathers of the Third Century: Tertullian, Part Fourth; Minucius Felix; Commodian; Origen, Parts First and Second,* edited by Alexander Roberts and James Donaldson, and revised by A. Cleveland Coxe. American ed. Peabody, Mass.: Hendrickson, 1999.

The Third Sex. DVD. 52 min. Directed by Howard Reay. Produced by the Mission for TLC, Discovery Communications Incorporated, 1997. Princeton: Films for the Humanities and Sciences, 2004.

Thomas, Barbara. "Report on Chicago Consensus Conference October 2005." www.AISSG.org.

Tigay, Jeffrey H. *The JPS Torah Commentary: Deuteronomy.* Philadelphia: Jewish Publication Society, 1996.

Tolman, Deborah L. *Dilemmas of Desire: Teenage Girls Talk about Sexuality.* Cambridge: Harvard University Press, 2002.

Torrance, Alan J. "'Call No Man Father!': The Trinity, Patriarchy and God-Talk." In *The Gospel and Gender: A Trinitarian Engagement with Being Male and Female in Christ,* edited by Douglas A. Campbell. London: T. & T. Clark, 2003.

———. "God, Personhood and Particularity: On Whether There Is, or Should Be, a Distinctive Male Theological Perspective." In *The Gospel and Gender: A Trinitarian Engagement with Being Male and Female in Christ,* edited by Douglas A. Campbell. London: T. & T. Clark, 2003.

Tougher, Shaun F. "'The Angelic Life': Monasteries for Eunuchs." In *Byzantine Style, Religion, and Civilization,* edited by Elizabeth Jeffreys. Cambridge: Cambridge University Press, 2006.

———. "Byzantine Eunuchs: An Overview, with Special Reference to Their Creation and Origin." In *Women, Men, and Eunuchs: Gender in Byzantium,* edited by Liz James. London and New York: Routledge, 1997.

———. "Holy Eunuchs! Masculinity and Eunuch Saints in Byzantium." In *Holiness and Masculinity in the Middle Ages,* edited by P. H. Cullum and Katherine J. Lewis. Cardiff: University of Wales Press, 2004.

———. "Social Transformation, Gender Transformation? The Court Eunuchs, 300-900." In *Gender in the Early Medieval World: East and West, 300-900,* edited by Leslie Brubaker and Julia M. H. Smith. Cambridge: Cambridge University Press, 2004.

Tracy, Steven. "Where Is God in the Midst of the Suffering of Abuse?" *Africanus Journal* 2, no. 2 (November 2010): 45-52.

Traina, Christina L. H. "Papal Ideals, Marital Realities: One View from the Ground." In

Sexual Diversity in Catholicism, edited by Patricia Beattie Jung and Joseph Andrew Coray. Collegeville, Minn.: Liturgical Press, 2001.

Trumbach, Randolph. "London's Sapphists: From Three Sexes to Four Genders in the Making of Modern Culture." In *Third Sex, Third Gender: Beyond Sexual Dimorphism in Culture and History,* edited by Gilbert Herdt. New York: Zone Books, 1994.

Urology Science Research Foundation. "The Guevedoces of the Dominican Republic." http://www.usrf.org/news/010308-guevedoces.html.

Vanhoozer, Kevin. "Human Being, Individual and Social." In *Cambridge Companion to Christian Doctrine,* edited by Colin Gunton. Cambridge: Cambridge University Press, 1997.

Vanier, Jean, with Krista Tippett. "The Wisdom of Tenderness." Interview of October 28, 2007, airing December 20, 2007, and December 24, 2009. http://being.publicradio.org/programs/2009/wisdom-of-tenderness.

Van Leeuwen, Mary Stewart. *Gender and Grace.* Downers Grove, Ill.: InterVarsity, 1990.

———. *My Brother's Keeper: What the Social Sciences Do and Don't Tell Us about Masculinity.* Downers Grove, Ill.: InterVarsity, 2002.

———, ed. *After Eden: Facing the Challenge of Gender Reconciliation.* Grand Rapids: Eerdmans, 1993.

Volf, Miroslav. *After Our Likeness: The Church as the Image of the Trinity.* Grand Rapids: Eerdmans, 1998.

———. *Exclusion and Embrace: A Theological Exploration of Identity, Otherness, and Reconciliation.* Nashville: Abingdon, 1996.

Volf, Miroslav, and Michael Welker, eds. *God's Life in Trinity.* Minneapolis: Fortress, 2006.

von Rad, Gerhard. *Genesis: A Commentary.* Translated by John H. Marks. Rev. ed. Philadelphia: Westminster, 1972.

———. *Old Testament Theology.* Translated by D. M. G. Stalker. 2 vols. Louisville: Westminster John Knox, 2001.

Warnke, Georgia. "Intersexuality and the Categories of Sex." *Hypatia* 16, no. 3 (Summer 2001): 126-37.

Webb, William J. *Slaves, Women, and Homosexuals: Exploring the Hermeneutics of Cultural Analysis.* Downers Grove, Ill.: InterVarsity, 2001.

Weinrich, William C. "Homo Theologicus: Aspects of a Lutheran Doctrine of Man." In *Personal Identity in Theological Perspective,* edited by Richard Lints, Michael S. Horton, and Mark R. Talbot, 29-44. Grand Rapids: Eerdmans, 2006.

Wenham, Gordon J. *Genesis 1–15.* Word Biblical Commentary, vol. 1. Waco, Tex.: Word, 1987.

West, Christopher. *Theology of the Body for Beginners.* West Chester, Pa.: Ascension Press, 2004.

———. *The Love That Satisfies: Reflections on Eros and Agape.* West Chester, Pa.: Ascension Press, 2007.

Whitehead, Neil E. "Are Transsexuals Born That Way?" http://www.parakaleo.co.uk/article1.html.

———. "Should Transsexuality Be Freely Endorsed by Christians?" April 1999. http://www.parakaleo.co.uk/article3.html.

Wiesemann, Claudia, Susanne Ude-Koeller, Gernot H. G. Sinnecker, and Ute Thyen. "Ethical Principles and Recommendations for the Medical Management of Differences of Sex Development (DSD)/Intersex Children and Adolescents." *European Journal of Pediatrics* 169 (2010): 671-79.

Wilken, Robert Louis. "Biblical Humanism." In *Personal Identity in Theological Perspective,* edited by Richard Lints, Michael S. Horton, and Mark R. Talbot. Grand Rapids: Eerdmans, 2006.

Wilson, Ken. *A Letter to My Congregation: An Evangelical Pastor's Path to Embracing People Who Are Gay, Lesbian, and Transgender into the Company of Jesus.* Canton, Mich.: David Crumm Media, 2014.

Winner, Lauren F. "In Search of the Good Marriage." *Books and Culture,* September/October 2004.

———. *Real Sex: The Naked Truth about Chastity.* Grand Rapids: Brazos, 2005.

Woodhead, Linda. "God, Gender and Identity." In *The Gospel and Gender: A Trinitarian Engagement with Being Male and Female in Christ,* edited by Douglas A. Campbell. London: T. & T. Clark, 2003.

Wright, N. T. "Adam in Pauline Christology." In *SBL Seminar Papers,* 359-89. Chico, Calif.: Scholars Press, 1983.

Zinn, Andrew. "Turner Syndrome — the Basics, Genetic Overview." http://www.turnersyndrome.org/index.php?option=com_content&task=view&id=40&Itemid=57.

Zizioulas, John D. *Being as Communion: Studies in Personhood and the Church.* Crestwood, N.Y.: St. Vladimir's Seminary Press, 2002.

Zucker, Kenneth J. "Commentary on Diamond's Prenatal Predisposition and the Clinical Management of Some Pediatric Conditions." *Sex and Marital Treatment* 22, no. 3 (1996): 148-60.

———. "Intersexuality and Gender Identity Differentiation." In *Annual Review of Sex Research,* vol. 10, edited by Raymond C. Rosen et al., 1-69. Mt. Vernon, Iowa: Society for the Scientific Study of Sexuality, 1999.

Zuk, M. *Sexual Selections: What We Can and Can't Learn about Sex from Animals.* Berkeley: University of California Press, 2002.

Index of Subjects and Names

Adam and Eve, 1-5, 11, 17, 47, 66, 70, 95, 117, 120-21, 126, 157-58, 160, 162, 175-78, 182, 187-88, 216, 218-21, 231n136, 238, 241-42, 244, 287

Ambrose, 88-89, 91

Androgen insensitivity syndrome (AIS), complete (CAIS) and partial (PAIS), 25-29, 42n76, 45, 56, 68, 105, 133, 140, 173, 208; grades of virilization, 27-28

Androgyne. *See* Hermaphrodites

Aquinas, Thomas, 115, 117-18, 124, 125-26, 133, 140, 141, 248n22

Aristotle, 108, 124, 141, 146; hermaphrodite, 47, 112; sex difference, 47, 110-13, 116-18, 125, 135

Augustine, 91-95; eunuchs, 69, 77-78, 92; gender, 93-94; hermaphrodites, 69; image of God, 123-24, 245; sex difference, 183, 219n103, 251n32; soul, 118n33, 122-23, 140, 142; Trinity, 234-36; women, 122-24, 245

Barth, Karl, 3-4, 147-49, 153, 186, 187, 226, 230, 234, 241, 245

Basil of Caesarea, 95-96, 236n153

Benedict XVI, 165, 195-97, 224, 226n122, 230n133, 231n136

Blackless, Melanie, et al. *See* Fausto-Sterling

Boethius, 124, 146

Brain sex, 142, 267, 287n140

Brown, Peter, 72, 76, 83-90, 95n117, 114, 258

Butler, Judith, 64, 263, 268, 270

Calvin, John, 5, 126-27, 129

Cassian, John, 95

Castrati. *See* Eunuchs: castrated

Celibacy, 14, 16, 64, 65n177, 66, 72n12, 86n82, 96, 100, 102, 150, 157, 186, 195, 200, 202-7, 211-14, 216, 238, 265n81, 269, 283

Chain of being, 115-16, 127

Chase, Cheryl, 9, 54, 57

Chrysostom, John, 96-97, 98-99, 119-22

Classical testicular feminization. *See* Androgen insensitivity syndrome

Clitorectomy and clitoral reduction. *See* Medicalization of intersex

Colson, Charles, 7n14, 11-12, 67n182, 173n68, 268n89

Complete androgen insensitivity syndrome (CAIS). *See* Androgen insensitivity syndrome (AIS)

Congenital adrenal hyperplasia (CAH), 14n37, 27n13, 30-35, 173, 248; late-onset CAH, 32-33, 44, 48, 114n22

Cornwall, Susannah, 11, 57, 63n167, 102,

149n120, 183-84, 249-53, 256-61, 272, 275, 281-82, 286-87n140
Cybele, cult of, 77, 83, 92

Descartes, René, 128, 137, 140, 142
Diamond, Milton, 40, 51-53, 55-56, 59, 63, 65
Disability, 11, 183-84, 253, 258
Disorders of sex development (DSD), 5, 24, 56-57, 65, 252, 256, 258
Dreger, Alice, 10n19, 49-51, 55, 64, 66, 69, 259

Enlightenment, 128, 135-37, 151
Eunuchs: angels, 83-85, 89-90, 246; castrated, 74, 77-79, 92, 98, 102, 104-6, 206; church leaders, 97; exiles/otherness, 80, 105, 182; for the sake of the kingdom, 82-83, 104-5, 158, 161, 204-6; hagiography, 97; healing, 104, 183, 253; iconography, 83, 94; Jesus as eunuch, 86n82, 246-48; laws, 80, 98, 137, 207; marriage to, 75, 206; monasteries, 98, 127-28; naturally born, 80-81, 205; priests, 77, 92, 99; prostitutes, 77; servants/slaves, 73-74; sex slaves, 75; sexuality, 221, 265; singers, 83, 98, 101; virtue, 76-77, 99, 101-2, 115

Fausto-Sterling, Anne: cultural differences, 34, 48-50; five sexes, 29, 53-54, 57, 143, 174; frequency rates, 32, 35, 39, 41, 44-45; laws for hermaphrodites, 48-50; male/female, 23; medicalization, 34; multiple sexes/sexualities, 36, 38, 57-59, 62, 64, 65, 143
Feminized male. *See* Klinefelter's syndrome
Five-alpha reductase deficiency syndrome (5-ARDs), 42-45

Galen, 47-48, 76, 112-14, 135
Galli. *See* Eunuchs: castrated, and Eunuchs: priests
Gonadal dysgenesis, 36
Gregory of Nazianzus, 96, 100, 236n153
Gregory of Nyssa, 122, 249, 285
Gross, Selwyn/Sally, 9n17, 13-17, 64

Hermaphrodites: 5, 17, 47, 112, 136; Abraham and Sarah as, 16; Adam and Eve as, 16, 47, 231n136; beauty, 75; classified as men, 69, 117, 133, 139; exposure of infants, 116n29; human, 116, 117, 136, 140; Jesus as, 248; laws concerning, 48-49, 51, 116-17, 133, 137, 207; medical explanations for, 50, 112-13, 116; monstrous births, 48, 135; mythological, 35, 46-47, 57, 69, 108-9; sexuality, 64, 75; soul, 119. *See also* Eunuchs: naturally born; Ovo-testes
Hester, J. David, 10, 59, 104, 143, 250, 253, 255-58, 259-60, 275, 282
Hines, Melissa, 10n19, 30, 169, 174-75, 270
Hollinger, Dennis, 12, 164-67, 169, 262
Hormones, 25, 142, 155, 169-70, 173, 254
Hypospadias, 27-28, 31, 33, 41-42, 45

Industrial Revolution, 131-32, 135, 219
Intersex Society of North America (ISNA), 7n15, 19n10, 25, 32, 39, 46, 54-57, 62, 256-57, 274
Irenaeus, 118
Isaiah, 68n1, 78-79, 82, 182, 184, 199n38, 281

Jerome, 89-91, 182-83, 251n32
John/Joan. *See* Reimer, David
John of the Cross, 191-93, 221, 227-30
Johnson, Elizabeth, 171, 180-81

Kessler, Suzanne, 29, 34, 40-42, 53n128, 54-55, 60-63, 143, 255, 261-62, 272, 274-75
Klinefelter's syndrome, 38, 44, 103, 205n59, 247, 270

Laqueur, Thomas, 110, 112, 116, 129, 135-37
Laurent, Bo. *See* Chase, Cheryl

Laws, legal recognition of intersex, 47-49, 55n137, 63, 80, 140, 207
Lewis, C. S., 220, 224n114, 225-26
Luther, Martin, 126-27, 131

McCarthy, David Matzko, 194-95, 209-11, 222-24, 230-34, 268-69
McKenna, Wendy, 29, 60, 143, 255, 261-62
May, William E., 192-95
Mayer-Rokitansky-Küster-Hauser syndrome (MRKH), 39, 45
Medicalization of intersex, 8, 34, 51-61, 150, 256, 272, 274-75; dilation of vagina, 40; hormone therapy, 38; surgery, 8, 34, 41, 51-53, 55; vaginoplasty, 34, 40
Mill, John Stuart, 129, 130-31
Mollenkott, Virginia Ramey, 10-11, 60, 247-61, 268n89, 271, 279, 282
Money, John, 10n18, 33, 41, 44-45n91, 52-53, 58-59, 163, 164n39, 167, 174

Nicaea, Council of, 72, 89

Origen, 72, 86-91, 102, 182, 243, 251
Ovo-testes, 26, 35-36

Paul, Saint, 15, 88, 92, 119, 126; celibacy, 72, 84-85
Personalism, theological, 194-95, 208-9, 222, 230-34
Plato: 146, 151; hermaphrodite, 47, 109, 231; human, 108, 112, 118, 140; matter, 125n48; sex difference, 108-11, 121, 125; sexual love, 109-10, 195, 231; soul, 108, 110-12, 115, 121, 124-25, 128, 140-42, 146, 151
Plotinus, 115, 124, 125n48
Prader, Andrea: Prader Scale, 27n13, 30-31
Pseudohermaphrodite, 26, 29, 33-34, 50-51, 57, 63, 69, 133, 138
Pseudohermaphrodite, female, 50. *See also* Congenital adrenal hyperplasia
Pseudohermaphrodite, male, 26. *See also* Androgen insensitivity syndrome

Ratzinger, Joseph Cardinal. *See* Benedict XVI
Reformation, Protestant, 107, 125-28, 132
Reimer, David, 52-53
Resurrection, 14, 83, 90, 93-94, 96, 106, 112, 124, 140, 147, 158, 163, 183-84, 198-99, 241, 245, 251, 259, 282
Ringrose, Kathryn, 74, 95-97, 99-102, 106
Romanticism, 128-34
Romantic dualism, 133
Rousseau, Jean-Jacques, 129-30
Ruether, Rosemary Radford, 111, 122, 133, 137n79, 155n4

Sax, Leonard, 32-33, 35, 37-40, 44-45
Sayers, Dorothy, 139, 142, 180
Schleiermacher, Friedrich, 134-35, 147
Sex, biological: definition of typical male and female, 23-24
Sexual dysfunction, 213-16, 238, 269
Sigmundson, Keith, 40, 52-53, 55, 59, 63, 65
Soskice, Janet Martin, 117, 147n108, 171-72, 177, 181-82, 238, 242-43, 245, 247n22, 249-50
Surgery, corrective. *See* Medicalization of intersex
Swyer syndrome, 36, 42, 45, 68

Tertullian, 81n63, 85-86, 93-94, 99
True hermaphrodite, 50-51. *See also* Ovo-testes
Turner syndrome, 36-38, 44, 45, 68

Vaginal agenesis, 39-40, 44
Victorian Era/Revolution, 26, 29, 35, 49-51, 65-66, 69, 107, 128, 132-34, 138
Volf, Miroslav, 273-81

Wollstonecraft, Mary, 129-31, 142